I0308467

*"This landmark interdisciplinary volume fills a huge gap in our discussions of the theological impact of the discovery of extraterrestrial intelligence. Heretofore, the focus has been on Christianity, but for the first time we have multiple scholarly views of the potential impact on Islamic theology and the Earth's two billion Muslims. This is a substantial contribution to the new and growing field of astrotheology, and should be read by anyone interested in the future evolution of religions on Earth."*

Steven J. Dick, Former NASA Chief Historian, Former Baruch S. Blumberg NASA/Library of Congress Chair in Astrobiology

*"The Qur'ān meets exotheology. This is a most informative, comprehensive, and reflective compilation of Islamic thinking about the prospect of sharing God's cosmos with other intelligent creatures on exoplanets. Now, aliens do not seem so alien any more."*

Ted Peters, Co-Editor, *Theology and Science*

*"This is a fascinating collection – due both to the intrinsic interest of the topic and to the richness and creativity of the Islamic philosophical, theological, and literary traditions engaging with it. Out of this world."*

Stephen Bullivant, Professor of Theology and the Sociology of Religion, St Mary's University, UK, and Professorial Research Fellow in Theology and Sociology, University of Notre Dame, Australia

*"As realization grows that we are a global community across the Earth, researchers have increasingly considered the question of whether we are alone. What would the encounter with an extraterrestrial mean for our assumptions about the nature of reality, of the human, of gods, and for some of the most fundamental theological and ethical questions that follow, concerning goodness, recompense, and the life of the soul? It also reminds us of the importance of philosophical and theological questions raised by sci-fi that is also worth pursuing to make sense of Muslim futurism. This pioneering volume – and there is little doubt that it not only is the first but potentially seeks to open up a broader field of the intersection of Islamic studies and exotheology – attempts to address these by looking at the resources and possibilities within the Islamic traditions (one should*

*emphasize the plural here) in order to create positive theologies for the future. An exciting turn in the literature on religion and science."*

Sajjad Rizvi, Professor of Islamic Intellectual History and Director of the Institute of Arab and Islamic Studies, University of Exeter, UK

*"The discovery of extraterrestrial life, if made, will likely impact all cultures, societies and religions. It is important to assess such an impact as James Webb Space Telescope is searching for bio signatures in exoplanet atmospheres, there are rovers currently on Mars, and the SETI programme is actively looking for signals from technological civilizations in our Galaxy. This eclectic collection of essays fills in a crucial gap in literature and provides a glimpse into potential Islamic theological and jurisprudential responses to such a discovery."*

Salman Hameed, Charles Taylor Chair and Professor of Integrated Science and Humanities, Hampshire College, United States

"Islamic Theology and Extraterrestrial Life *takes one small, but significant, step as a pioneer work in exotheology, but potentially representing one giant leap for a forthcoming discipline."*

*"Through a series of thought-provoking chapters that span various disciplines, including Islamic theology, jurisprudence, and Christianity, this work delves into hitherto relatively uncharted scholarly territories. It explores scholarly, complex and intellectually intriguing questions, such as how the discovery of extraterrestrial life forms aligns with religious beliefs. Do these forms of life possess souls and spirituality? How do we ethically and spiritually relate to them?"*

*"This volume offers a captivating journey into unexplored realms of religion and science, inviting readers to contemplate the mysteries of the cosmos."*

Mohammed Ghaly, Professor of Islam and Biomedical Ethics, Hamad Bin Khalifa University, Qatar

# Islamic Theology and Extraterrestrial Life

# Islamic Theology and Extraterrestrial Life

## *New Frontiers in Science and Religion*

Edited by
Shoaib Ahmed Malik and Jörg Matthias Determann

I.B.TAURIS
LONDON • NEW YORK • OXFORD • NEW DELHI • SYDNEY

I.B. TAURIS
Bloomsbury Publishing Plc, 50 Bedford Square, London, WC1B 3DP, UK
Bloomsbury Publishing Inc, 1385 Broadway, New York, NY 10018, USA
Bloomsbury Publishing Ireland, 29 Earlsfort Terrace, Dublin 2, D02 AY28, Ireland

BLOOMSBURY, I.B. TAURIS and the I.B. Tauris logo are
trademarks of Bloomsbury Publishing Plc

First published in Great Britain 2024
This paperback edition published 2025



Cover design by Adriana Brioso
Cover images © Everett Collection Inc/
Alamy Stock Photo & Adobe Stock



A catalogue record for this book is available from the British Library.

Library of Congress Cataloging-in-Publication Data
Names: Determann, Jörg Matthias, editor. | Malik, Shoaib Ahmed, editor.
Title: Islamic theology and extraterrestrial life: new frontiers in science and religion / edited by Shoaib Ahmed Malik and Jörg Matthias Determann.
Description: New York: I.B Tauris, an imprint of Bloomsbury Publishing, 2024. | Includes bibliographical references and index.
Identifiers: LCCN 2023029234 (print) | LCCN 2023029235 (ebook) | ISBN 9780755650880 (hardback) | ISBN 9780755650927 (paperback) | ISBN 9780755650897 (pdf) | ISBN 9780755650903 (epub) | ISBN 9780755650910
Subjects: LCSH: Life on other planets–Religious aspects–Islam. | Extraterrestrial beings–Religious aspects–Islam.
Classification: LCC BP190.5.L45 I85 2024 (print) | LCC BP190.5.L45 (ebook) | DDC 297.2/65–dc23/eng/20230712
LC record available at https://lccn.loc.gov/2023029234
LC ebook record available at https://lccn.loc.gov/2023029235

ISBN: HB: 978-0-7556-5088-0
PB: 978-0-7556-5092-7
ePDF: 978-0-7556-5089-7
eBook: 978-0-7556-5090-3

Typeset by Deanta Global Publishing Services, Chennai, India

For product safety related questions contact productsafety@bloomsbury.com.

To find out more about our authors and books visit www.bloomsbury.com and sign up for our newsletters.

*This book is dedicated to Sarah Khalayleh, the daughter of one of our contributors, Moamer Khalayleh. Your father presented his paper for our conference while you were 'landing' on our Earth from the heavens. You are the special little alien of this project. God bless you!*

# Contents


List of Contributors x

Islamic theology on the final frontier *Shoaib Ahmed Malik and Jörg Matthias Determann* 1

1 Theological information on the existence of intelligent life outside our solar system: Metaphysics, scripture and science *Hamza Karamali* 25

2 Does the Qur'ān affirm extraterrestrial life? A hermeneutic analysis of Sūrat al-Naḥl (Q. 16:8) *Moamer Khalayleh* 43

3 Islamic sacred resources on extraterrestrials and their possible eschatological implications *Mohammad Mahdi Montasseri* 59

4 Extraterrestrials and moral accountability: Non-human moral personhood through the lens of classical Sunnī theology and law *David Solomon Jalajel* 87

5 Classical Muslim thought and the theological implications and possibility of non-human intelligence *Faisal Abdullah* 115

6 Extraterrestrial intelligent life and Islamic beliefs: Investigating six potential conflicts *Shoaib Ahmed Malik* 139

7 The alien in the lamp? The jinn and alien life in Islamic theology *Richard Playford* 159

8 A Qur'ānic ufology? Seven exotheological hypotheses of the Indonesian 'Islamic UFO' community *Ayub and Ilham Ibrahim* 175

9 Exotheology in contemporary Egyptian science fiction: A comparative appraisal *Emad El-Din Aysha* 205

Index 231

# Contributors

**Faisal Abdullah** received his PhD in Islamic studies from the Department of Near Eastern Languages and Cultures at UCLA. His dissertation was the first Western work to demonstrate explicit Muslim legal engagement with biblical law. He was the recipient of various scholarly awards including the Foreign Language and Area Studies Fellowship for the study of Arabic and Hebrew and was a visiting fellow at the King Faisal Center for Research and Islamic Studies in Riyadh. He received training in the traditional Islamic sciences in Jordan and South Africa, including the fields of ḥadīth authentication, law, legal theory and theology.

**Emad El-Din Aysha**, formerly an adjunct assistant professor at the American University in Cairo, is an academic researcher, journalist, translator, author and SF enthusiast. He is a member of both the Egyptian Society for Science Fiction (ESSF) and the Egyptian Writers' Union and has two books to his name, a sci-fi anthology (in Arabic) and a non-fiction work – *Arab and Muslim Science Fiction: Critical Essays* (2022) – which he co-authored and co-edited with the head of the ESSF. He also writes political commentary and movie and book reviews and has made presentations at conferences and universities on a wide range of SF-related topics, in addition to his academic articles on SF, Arabic culture and Islamic history and politics.

**Ayub** is a lecturer in the Department of Quranic Studies (Qur'an and Tafsīr Studies) at the Faculty of Ushuluddin and Islamic Thought, Sunan Kalijaga State Islamic University in Yogyakarta, Indonesia. He obtained his master's degree from SOAS University of London. His current research area focuses on the history of Tafsīr, particularly the intersection between Tafsīr and other disciplines of knowledge throughout history. He explores how scientific advancements, both in natural and social sciences, shape Muslim community's reception of the Qur'ān as manifested in their interpretive traditions.

**Jörg Matthias Determann** is Professor of History at Virginia Commonwealth University in Qatar. He also serves as an associate editor of the *Review of Middle*

*East Studies* and as book review editor of the *Journal of Arabian Studies*. He holds a doctorate from the School of Oriental and African Studies, University of London, and two master's degrees from the University of Vienna. He is the author of four books including *Islam, Science Fiction and Extraterrestrial Life* and *Space Science and the Arab World*.

**Ilham Ibrahim** is currently pursuing his master's studies in the Interdisciplinary Islamic Studies (IIS) program at the State Islamic University of Sunan Kalijaga Yogyakarta, Indonesia, with a concentration in Islamic educational psychology. He is a journalist in the official media of Muhammadiyah, one of the largest Islamic organizations in Southeast Asia. Currently, he is focusing on writing his master's thesis on the topic of mental health issues in the context of education within the Islamic tradition (*turath*).

**David Solomon Jalajel** is a consultant with the Prince Sultan Research Institute at King Saud University and holds a PhD in Arabic and Islamic studies from the University of the Western Cape. Formerly, he was a lecturer in Islamic theology and legal theory at the Dar al-Uloom in Cape Town, South Africa.

**Hamza Karamali** has degrees in computer engineering and the traditional Islamic sciences. He is the founder of Basira Education, where he develops courses and curricula on the intersection of modern science, Islamic theology and philosophy.

**Moamer Khalayleh** is a PhD candidate in religious and theological studies at Cardiff University. His area of research is contemporary atheism and Islamic theology. Moamer has a bachelor's degree in communications engineering and obtained a master's degree in multidisciplinary studies from the State University of New York at Buffalo. He trained traditionally in Islamic theology and Shāfiʿī law while studying in several institutions and with private teachers in Jordan. In addition to his doctoral studies, Moamer is an instructor of Islamic theology and physics at King's Academy, an international boarding school in Madaba, Jordan, and lectured on Ashʿarī theology and Shāfiʿī law at al-Maʿārij and al- Ḥawrāʾ institutes in Amman, Jordan.

**Shoaib Ahmed Malik** is a Visiting Researcher at St. Mary's University, Twickenham, UK, holding dual PhDs in Chemical Engineering and Theology. He serves on the editorial board of *Theology and Science* and is a trustee of the *International Society for Science and Religion* (ISSR). His monograph, *Islam and*

*Evolution: Al-Ghazālī and the Modern Evolutionary Paradigm*, published by Routledge, was selected as the best academic book of science and religion in 2022 by ISSR. He is currently engaged in crafting educational textbooks and micrographs on Islam and evolution under Routledge's imprint and curating several edited volumes and special issues. Notably, he is serving as the Chief Editor for Palgrave Macmillan's newly established Islam and Science book series (monographs) and encyclopaedia, both world-firsts, all of which contribute significantly to the scholarly discourse at the intersection of Islam and Science.

**Mohammad Mahdi Montasseri** has a PhD in Islamic philosophy and Kalam from the University of Tehran, Iran. He holds two master's degrees and two bachelor's degrees (in Philosophy and fiqh), all from the esteemed Razavi University of Islamic Sciences in Mashhad, Iran. In addition to their formal education, he has also studied extensively in traditional Islamic seminary settings. He serves as a university lecturer and has published numerous peer-reviewed academic papers in his area of expertise and is a reviewer in some related journals. He is a former visiting researcher at the University of Jyväskylä in Finland and currently continues his research in Islamic studies as a non-affiliated researcher, seeking to contribute to the broader understanding of the field.

**Richard Playford** is a Senior Lecturer in Philosophy, Ethics and Religion at Leeds Trinity University. Before that, until 2022, he was a Lecturer in Religious Studies at St Mary's University. He completed a PhD in philosophy at the University of Reading in 2017 where he was employed as a sessional lecturer. He has a master's degree in philosophy from the University of Birmingham and a bachelor's degree in philosophy with ancient history from the University of Exeter. He is a fellow of the Royal Society of Arts and a fellow of the Higher Education Academy. He has published numerous papers and book chapters on philosophy and ethics.

# Islamic theology on the final frontier

Shoaib Ahmed Malik and Jörg Matthias Determann

Over the last thirty years, humanity has discovered over 5,000 planets outside our solar system.[1] Each of these extrasolar planets or exoplanets represents a unique world whose composition and climate we have only begun to explore. Scientists in Muslim-majority countries have been key contributors to this exciting field of exoplanet research. In 2017, astronomers from the Oukaimeden Observatory in Morocco and the King Abdullah Centre for Crescent Observations and Astronomy in Saudi Arabia were among the co-authors of a paper in the journal *Nature* announcing the detection of seven temperate terrestrial planets around the nearby star TRAPPIST-1.[2] During the same decade, the Qatar Exoplanet Survey directed by Khalid Alsubai presented the discovery of ten massive planets, named Qatar-1, Qatar-2b, Qatar-3b, and so on, to the global scientific community.[3] Exoplanets were thus added to the long list of celestial objects associated with the Muslim world. They include some of the brightest stars carrying Arabic names (like Rigel, meaning 'foot') and Burçin's Galaxy (nicknamed after the Turkish astrophysicist Burçin Mutlu-Pakdil).[4]

Over 5,000 planets, as confirmed by 2023, are most probably only a minuscule fraction of the number of worlds out there. Young Muslim astronomers across our globe are very excited about a universe that might be teaming with life. One of them is Nour Skaf, a French scientist of Lebanese origins whose first name (*nūr*) means 'light' in Arabic. 'Let's talk numbers', she told us. 'There are between 100 to 200 billion stars in our galaxy alone.' If we assume that there are four times more planets and stars, we can expect 400 billion planets in our galaxy alone. If only 1 per cent of them were in the habitable zone of their stars, which is a careful conservative estimation, 4 billion celestial bodies might be Earth-like. Multiplying that by the number of galaxies in the universe, she said,

1 Brennan, 'Cosmic Milestone'.
2 Gillon et al., 'Seven Temperate Terrestrial Planets around the Nearby Ultracool Dwarf Star TRAPPIST-1'.
3 Alsubai et al., 'Qatar-1b'; Alsubai et al., 'Qatar Exoplanet Survey'.
4 Zakeer, 'Meet the Woman Who Discovered a Whole New Type of Galaxy'.

'it is statistically impossible that there isn't another planet that had the good conditions to develop life.' She concluded, 'It's mainly a matter of time before we find something and we're barely starting to have the technology to search for it.'[5]

After alien worlds had been mainly the purview of science fiction creators prior to the 1990s, they have since become an established research field in astronomy. It has increasingly attracted some of the brightest young minds at leading institutions. Nour Skaf said that 'finding alien life is one of the main priorities' of her discipline. 'Much effort and funding is put into answering the question "are we alone?".' Skaf herself completed a doctoral thesis on 'Self-optimization of adaptive optics and characterization of exoplanetary systems' at the Paris Observatory in 2023.[6] She previously won a L'Oréal-UNESCO prize for Women in Science.[7] Another rising star is Munazza Alam, a Muslim American whose parents hailed from Pakistan and India.[8] Her last name, in Arabic *ʿālam*, means 'world'. She earned a doctorate from Harvard University in 2021 with a dissertation on the atmospheres of giant planets.[9] Among her awards was a National Geographic Young Explorers grant. She succeeded despite discrimination based on her religious identity. 'During a visit to another institution for an in-person seminar, I was harassed for wearing a headscarf', she recounted.[10]

Although the term 'exoplanet' is a recent coinage, Muslim researchers in this field also saw themselves as part of an ancient tradition. 'Human beings have always looked up to the stars and wondered about our place in the universe and the existence of other worlds', wrote Nour Skaf in her dissertation. 'In the Golden Age of the Muslim world, several Muslim scholars endorsed the idea of cosmic pluralism, such as Muhammad al-Baqir (676–733), the theologian and scientist and Fakhr ad-Din ar-Razi (1149–1209).' The astrophysicist explained, 'They based their reasoning on one of the main verses of the Quran "All praise belongs to God, Lord of the Worlds", with worlds being plural.'[11]

As many Muslim astronomers see themselves as connected to the history of Islamic civilization, it is not surprising that they also espoused an Islamic identity. Like the South Asian American Munazza Alam, her Turkish peer Burçin Mutlu-Pakdil donned a hijab, despite hostility from some people around her.

[5] Nour Skaf, personal communication, May 2023.
[6] Skaf, 'Self-Optimization of Adaptive Optics and Characterization of Exoplanetary Systems'.
[7] Observatoire de Paris, 'Nour Skaf, lauréate du prix "L'Oréal-UNESCO pour les femmes et la science"'.
[8] Zuckerman, 'Meet Munazza Alam, the Woman Searching for Planet Earth's Twin'.
[9] Alam, 'Characterizing Distant Worlds'.
[10] Sayeed, 'Women's History Month: Dr. Munazza Alam'.
[11] Skaf, 'Self-Optimization of Adaptive Optics and Characterization of Exoplanetary Systems', 6–7.

When Mutlu-Pakdil studied at Bilkent University in Ankara in the 2000s, the prohibition on headscarves at public institutions in Turkey was still in place. 'The secular people wanted the government places (including public universities)' free from headscarves, she commented. 'But (about) 98 per cent of Turkey is Muslim, so you are basically banning Muslim women from pursuing education.' She circumvented the law by wearing a hat to cover her head. 'Education is my right', she thought.[12] She also encouraged younger Turkish girls to follow in her footsteps. 'You don't need to choose your career over your identity.'[13] By 2018, Mutlu-Pakdi had become a TED Fellow and had a whole galaxy named after her. She thus inspired people far beyond Turkey. 'I'm getting emails from all over the world, especially in Muslim countries, girls are contacting me saying . . . "You are the first covered scientist I have seen. This tells us that's okay, Muslim women can do science too."'[14]

Conscious of their religious identity, many Muslim astronomers acknowledged their debt to the Islamic as well as broader human astronomical tradition. In an article entitled 'Contemplating the Cosmos', Munazza Alam wrote: 'Before we delve into where the study of astronomy is taking us, we must begin with what that study has already given us. Various civilizations around the world have contributed to our understanding of the cosmos.' Those included the Babylonian, Indian, Egyptian, Greek, Chinese and Persian in Alam's narrative. She stated, for instance, that 'In Islamic Persia, the astronomer Azophi described the constellations and our neighbouring Andromeda Galaxy in detail in *The Book of Fixed Stars,* while Abu Mahmud Hamid ibn Khidr al-Khujandi made the first sextant to measure the axial tilt of the Earth.' Alam further wrote that 'the 15th-century Muslim astronomer, Ulugh Beg, noted that in the Holy Qur'an it says, "And among His Signs is the creation of the heavens and the earth, and of whatever living creatures He has spread forth in both."'[15]

Mediaval Muslim scholars, of course, did not have the same cosmology as their modern successors like Alam and Skaf did. 'Our understanding of the cosmos has vastly changed over the past thousand years', Alam acknowledged.[16] The cosmos in the Middle Ages, whether in the Islamic or Christian lands, was predominantly a geocentric one, in which the Sun, Moon, stars and planets all orbit Earth. It was based on a legacy of earlier Greek learning, specifically the

12 Willett, 'This UA Astrophysicist Has a Galaxy Named after Her'.
13 Lee and Sayeed, 'Women's History Month: Dr. Burçin Mutlu-Pakdil'.
14 Willett, 'This UA Astrophysicist Has a Galaxy Named after Her'.
15 Alam, 'Contemplating the Cosmos'.
16 Ibid.

work of Aristotle and Ptolemy. Astronomers working in Arabic not just adopted but also refined and repeatedly cast doubts over Ptolemy's work. Their criticism indirectly contributed to the replacement of Ptolemaic geocentrism with Copernican heliocentrism during the early modern period.[17] In this process, Earth would come to be seen as only one of many planets.

For Alam, the differences between older and more recent cosmologies should not be exaggerated, however. 'Our ancestors, looking at the same celestial bodies we do, invested them with significance and meaning', she wrote in 2020. 'And in the modern era, we look at the same sky, albeit with more refined instruments, and build the foundation of new technologies and new knowledge.' Astronomers' core goals have remained unchanged, according to the Muslim American scientist: 'to contextualize human existence within the temporal and spatial expanses of the universe. This desire is driven by human curiosity and awe. As the philosopher Plato wrote, "Astronomy compels the soul to look upwards and leads us from this world to another."'[18]

Astrobiology, the study of life in the universe, relies not only on discoveries of faraway planets like the ones studied by Nour Skaf and Munazza Alam. We have also found life even in the most extreme environments in our solar system, suggesting that they might exist in hostile environments elsewhere in the universe too. During the 1950s already, at the dawn of the Space Age, self-described astrobotanists from the Kazakhstan Academy of Sciences travelled to the cold and arid Pamir Mountains to better understand plants that might survive on Mars.[19] Although life outside of Earth has been elusive, scientists have only intensified their search efforts since. In 2018, the founder of the Astrobiology Network of Pakistan, Nozair Khawaja, contributed to reporting macromolecular organic compounds being ejected from Saturn's moon Enceladus.[20]

Whether on the surface of an exoplanet or in the oceans of one of Saturn's moons, the discovery of extraterrestrial life might thus be imminent. The encounter with other life forms, especially intelligent ones, could radically change our view of the cosmos and our place in it. Nour Skaf stated that 'life beyond our planet has historically been intrinsically linked with how one defines God'. She elaborated, 'would God create Humans in his image, and thus human

[17] Saliba, *Islamic Science and the Making of the European Renaissance*. Feldhay and Ragep, *Before Copernicus*.
[18] Alam, 'Contemplating the Cosmos'.
[19] Briot, 'The Creator of Astrobotany'.
[20] Postberg et al., 'Macromolecular Organic Compounds from the Depths of Enceladus'.

beings must be unique, and the Earth unique, or would God create the universe in his own image, immensely diverse and complex, with a multitude of worlds?'[21]

This book seeks to explain how scientific confirmation of life elsewhere in the cosmos might impact Islamic theology and thus affect its 2 billion adherents. Our volume brings together a range of experts, including Muslim theologians, scholars of comparative religion, philosophers, and social scientists. Together, we try to address some of humankind's biggest questions through an Islamic lens: Are humans alone in the cosmos? Are we unique? What makes us unique? What is the ethics of dealing with other sentient beings? And how universal is salvation?

Although our book primarily examines theology, the questions it asks are also on the minds of many Muslim scientists and other people with no advanced formal training in Islamic studies. Munazza Alam is one of them. Although she was raised as a Muslim, she attended a Catholic school, Notre Dame Academy in Staten Island, for fourteen years. 'The only thing I was absolutely certain of was my sense of otherness', she commented. Thereafter, she studied physics and astronomy at the City University of New York and Harvard University. Along the way, she gained more sense of certainty. 'College was the first time where people just knew me for me', she says. 'Faith is an important part of my life. It's a defining characteristic that makes my identity unique, and I want people to know.'[22] In 2020, she told the *Review of Religions*: 'The Holy Qur'an categorically states the existence of life in the Universe.' She added, 'Guided by the beautiful wisdom of the Holy Qur'an, I am inspired to pursue my research.'[23]

Our book discusses various facets of how the discovery of aliens could impact Islamic theology, including scriptural investigations and ethical deliberations. Our contributors seek to re-examine discussions of human uniqueness and look at the eschatological or soteriological implications. We do not claim to establish a single Islamic perspective on extraterrestrials. Rather, we provide a range of opinions and intra-Islamic (Sunnī and Shīʿī) positions, hopefully making it a reference work that is more representative of the global Muslim community. We also have chapters that compare Islamic perspectives with Christianity. Finally, the volume covers the reception of extraterrestrial life in the societies of the Arab world and Indonesia. You will find between the covers of this work a variety of different insights on the question of Islam and extraterrestrial life. Given the

21 Skaf, 'Self-Optimization of Adaptive Optics and Characterization of Exoplanetary Systems', 7.
22 Strauss, 'Finding Clarity in the Stars'.
23 Ghauri, 'Reaching for the Stars'.

accelerating advances in exoplanet research and astrobiology, we hope to have created a timely, important and necessary resource.

While we focus on one particular set of religious traditions, we hope to explore new frontiers in science and religion in general. These explorations would be of interest to Muslims and non-Muslims alike. Many Muslim astronomers share a global outlook inclusive of people of all faiths. Nour Skaf wrote that 'as human species, we have always wondered about our place in the universe to understand who we truly are, and every single culture in the world was once connected to the stars'. She further suggested: 'The discovery of exoplanets and the potential for finding other forms of life can lead to a greater understanding of our small place in this majestic universe, and inspire a sense of unity and connectedness among humanity.'[24]

## Astrobiology and extraterrestrials

Astrobiology is thus an endeavour that is universal in more than one sense of the word. It is a multidisciplinary field of science with contributors around the world. It studies the origin, evolution, distribution and future of life in the universe.[25] It seeks to understand the conditions necessary for life to exist and thrive as well as to identify and explore potentially habitable environments within our solar system and beyond. It draws on a range of scientific disciplines, including astronomy, biology, chemistry, geology and planetary science, and uses information from remote sensing, computer modelling and space exploration.

Extraterrestrial life refers to beings that exist beyond planet Earth in other planetary systems and could take various forms, ranging from simple microbial life to very advanced intelligent civilizations.[26] The actual existence of extraterrestrial life is currently unknown and remains a topic of scientific debate. However, given the vastness of the universe and the abundance of potentially habitable planets, many scientists like Nour Skaf believe that it is likely that life exists elsewhere in the universe, which has led to many attempts to discover them.

The search for extraterrestrial intelligence (SETI) has a long and fascinating history that spans several decades.[27] In the 1950s, astronomers began to consider

24 Skaf, 'Self-Optimization of Adaptive Optics and Characterization of Exoplanetary Systems', 2.
25 Also known as exobiology.
26 Basalla, *Civilized Life in the Universe.*
27 Dick, *The Biological Universe*; Dick, *Space, Time, and Aliens.*

the possibility of searching for extraterrestrial intelligence by scanning the radio waves emitted by other planets or civilizations. This idea was first proposed by Frank Drake – founder of the famous Drake equation that we will look at shortly – who conducted the first SETI experiment known as Project Ozma in 1960.[28] The project searched for signals from two nearby stars using a radio telescope, but no signals were detected.

In the decades that followed, other SETI projects were established, such as the Ohio State University Radio Observatory (OSURO) and the Arecibo Observatory in Puerto Rico. The OSURO conducted several searches in the 1970s and 1980s, but no signals were found. However, a mysterious radio signal was detected by Ohio State University's Big Ear radio telescope on 15 August 1977, humorously called the 'WOW signal'.[29] It appeared to have originated from the direction of the constellation Sagittarius and lasted for seventy-two seconds. It was named the 'WOW signal' after astronomer Jerry Ehman wrote 'WOW!' in the margin of the printout of the signal when he saw it. The signal's unusual characteristics, including its narrow frequency range and its strength, which was significantly higher than the background noise, led to speculation that it may have been an extraterrestrial signal. However, despite numerous efforts to detect the signal again, no repeat of the WOW signal has ever been detected, and there is no conclusive evidence that the WOW signal was of extraterrestrial origin. Many theories have been proposed to explain the signal, including that it was a natural phenomenon or a result of human interference. The mystery surrounding the signal continues to intrigue scientists and the public alike, and it remains one of the most famous and intriguing unexplained events in the search for extraterrestrial intelligence.[30]

In the late 1990s and early 2000s, private organizations such as the SETI Institute and the Planetary Society began to take a more significant role in SETI research.[31] The SETI Institute, established in 1984, conducted numerous SETI searches using radio telescopes and optical telescopes. The Planetary Society launched its own SETI project, known as Project Phoenix, in 1995, which used the Parkes Observatory in Australia and the Arecibo Observatory in Puerto Rico.[32] In recent years, SETI research has expanded beyond radio waves to include other methods of detecting extraterrestrial life, such as searching for biosignatures in

28 Shuch, *Searching for Extraterrestrial Intelligence*, 13–18.
29 Ibid., 47–63.
30 Caballero, 'Source of the WOW! Signal'.
31 Pierson, 'SETI Institute'; McDonough, 'Planetary Society's SETI Program'.
32 Tarter, 'Project Phoenix'.

the atmospheres of exoplanets.[33] The Breakthrough Listen project, funded by Russian billionaire Yuri Milner in 2015, is also using advanced technologies to search for signals from other civilizations.[34]

More recently, the James Webb Space Telescope (JWST) was launched into space on 25 December 2021.[35] Munazza Alam commented at the time: 'On Christmas Day 2021, the world watched as humanity set out to accomplish one of the greatest scientific and technological feats in human history.'[36] Designed for infrared astronomy and observing faint objects in the universe, the JWST is poised to enhance and expand the discoveries of its predecessor, the Hubble Space Telescope.[37] With extended wavelength coverage and superior sensitivity, the JWST aims to detect light from the earliest stars and galaxies, explore the development of galaxies, investigate the genesis of life and examine the formation of stars and planetary systems in dusty clouds. Alam herself was especially excited about the potential benefits of the instrument for the field of astrobiology. 'With JWST, we will be able to obtain data precise enough to characterize the atmospheres of smaller, Earth-like exoplanets to infer if the can host extraterrestrial lifeforms', she stated. 'Thus, modern advancements in technology will get us closer to answering a question we've been asking for hundreds of years.'[38]

The JWST holds the distinction of being the biggest and the most powerful space telescope ever assembled to date.[39] The collaboration on the instrument itself was also inspiring to Nour Skaf. The astrophysicist wrote, 'over three decades, more than 20,000 people have worked together for one of humanity's greatest achievements, despite the cultural, political, religious, and ethnic differences.' She concluded, 'This is a powerful example of the fact that peace will come from our understanding that we are actually no different from one another.'[40]

Advanced facilities like the JWST should generate further data for numerical speculations that have occupied scientists for a long time. In 1961, Frank Drake developed the Drake equation, which is still a widely recognized probabilistic tool used by scientists to estimate the number of active, communicative

[33] NASA, 'TESS Exoplanet Mission'; NASA, 'Kepler and K2'. Kreidberg, 'Exoplanet Atmosphere Measurements'.
[34] Worden et al., 'Breakthrough Listen'.
[35] Space Telescope Science Institute, 'Webb Space Telescope'.
[36] Alam, 'Seeing Deeper into Space - Launch of the James Webb Space Telescope'.
[37] NASA, 'Webb vs Hubble Telescope'.
[38] Alam, 'Contemplating the Cosmos'.
[39] NASA, 'James Webb Space Telescope'.
[40] Skaf, 'Self-Optimization of Adaptive Optics and Characterization of Exoplanetary Systems', 2.

extraterrestrial civilizations that might exist in the Milky Way galaxy. The equation is as follows:

$N = R^* \times f_p \times n_e \times f_l \times f_i \times f_c \times L$

Where:

N = the number of communicative civilizations in the Milky Way galaxy
$R^*$ = the rate of star formation in the Milky Way galaxy
$f_p$ = the fraction of stars with planets
$n_e$ = the number of planets per star that are in the habitable zone
$f_l$ = the fraction of habitable planets that develop life
$f_i$ = the fraction of planets with life that develop intelligent life
$f_c$ = the fraction of intelligent civilizations that develop communication technologies
L = the length of time that a communicative civilization exists

One of the strengths of the Drake equation is that it highlights the many variables that must be considered when contemplating the possibility of extraterrestrial life. By considering these variables, the equation provides a comprehensive approach to assessing the probability of extraterrestrial life and helps to guide research efforts in this area.[41]

However, there are several limitations to the Drake equation that should be noted.[42] First, the equation relies heavily on speculation and assumptions about the likelihood of certain variables. For example, the fraction of habitable planets that develop life is largely unknown, and estimates of this value can vary widely. This uncertainty means that any estimates of the number of communicative civilizations using the Drake equation are necessarily speculative. Another limitation of the Drake equation is that it assumes that all communicative civilizations will develop in the same way and will be detectable using current scientific methods. In reality, there may be many different ways that civilizations could develop, and some may not use the same communication methods as humans. This means that the Drake equation may not accurately reflect the actual number of communicative civilizations that could exist in the universe.

Another key idea that is usually discussed alongside the Drake equation is Fermi's Paradox. If there are billions of other planets in the universe that could potentially support intelligent life, why haven't we detected any signals or other

[41] Vakoch and Dowd, *The Drake Equation*.
[42] Ibid.

evidence of their existence? The paradox is named after Enrico Fermi, an Italian American physicist, who in 1950 posed the question 'Where is everybody?' during a discussion with colleagues about the possibility of extraterrestrial life.[43] This question has since become known as the Fermi Paradox, and it has led to numerous hypotheses and explanations, including the possibility that extraterrestrial civilizations are too far away or too different from us to detect, that they are intentionally avoiding contact or that they have already come and gone, among others. The paradox continues to be a subject of much debate and speculation in the scientific community.[44]

Notwithstanding these limitations, the Drake equation remains a valuable tool for discussing the potential number of communicative extraterrestrial civilizations in the universe and serves as a starting point for further scientific inquiry into the search for extraterrestrial life. At the very least, it provides enough theoretical fodder for theological considerations to which we shall now turn.

## Exotheology and astrotheology

Exotheology is an emerging field of study that seeks to explore the theological implications of the existence of extraterrestrial life. Sometimes also called astrotheology,[45] it is an interdisciplinary field that involves the intersection of religion, philosophy and science. It seeks to answer fundamental questions about the nature of God, the meaning of human existence and the role of religion in a cosmological landscape. To help bridge the religious discussion, it is useful to demarcate between non-intelligent extraterrestrial life (NIEL) and intelligent extraterrestrial life (IEL). The former will be of significant interest to the scientific community, as it shows that life can and does exist on planets apart from our own.[46] The latter will be of more interest to religion, particularly in cases where IEL is equal or superior to humans.[47]

43 Webb, *Where Is Everybody?*
44 Ćirković, *The Great Silence.*
45 Peters, *Astrotheology.*
46 To be sure, Islam already does acknowledge other non-human entities that possess intelligence, such as angels and jinn, and they are known to be deeply involved with the affairs of human beings. However, this is not the scope of inquiry of this book. In this volume, we are specifically talking about *intelligent biological entities* that could exist on other planetary bodies. This point will be relayed in all the chapters.
47 Peters, 'Introducing Astrotheology'.

One of the central questions that exotheology seeks to answer is whether the existence of IEL is compatible with religious beliefs. For many religions, the concept of life beyond Earth is not explicitly mentioned in their holy texts, which can make it challenging to reconcile their beliefs with the possibility of IEL. Another important question that exotheology seeks to answer is whether extraterrestrial life has a soul or can experience spirituality. Many religions believe that humans are the only beings with souls, which can make it challenging to incorporate the idea of extraterrestrial life into religious beliefs.[48] However, some theologians argue that it is possible that extraterrestrial life may have a different type of soul, or that they may be capable of experiencing spirituality in a different way than humans.[49] The discovery of extraterrestrial life also raises important philosophical and ethical questions. For example, if intelligent life exists beyond Earth, what is the relationship between these beings and God? Does God have a plan for these beings, and if so, what is it? Additionally, if humans were to make contact with extraterrestrial life, what ethical deliberations must be considered? How should we treat these beings, and what responsibilities do we have to them? In other words, the existence of IEL raises several significant issues for religious believers.

Most of the current literature on exotheology has been written and framed by Christian sensitivities.[50] Against this context, Paul Davies, a theoretical physicist and cosmologist, claims that the discovery of extraterrestrial life could lead to very negative implications for belief systems, particularly Christianity:

> The existence of extra-terrestrial intelligence would have a profound impact on religion, shattering completely the traditional perspective of God's special relationship with man. The difficulties are particularly acute for Christianity, which postulates that Jesus Christ was God incarnate whose mission was to provide salvation for man on Earth. The prospect of a host of 'alien Christs' systematically visiting every inhabited planet in the physical form of the local creatures has a rather absurd aspect. Yet how otherwise are the aliens to be saved?[51]

Some Christian theologians concur with Davies in that IEL poses significant issues for Christianity.[52] However, other theologians argue that the existence of extraterrestrial life does not necessarily contradict religious beliefs and that it is

[48] Weintraub, *Religions and Extraterrestrial Life*.
[49] Parkyn, *Exotheology*.
[50] Weintraub, *Religions and Extraterrestrial Life*; Peters, *Astrotheology*.
[51] Davies, *God and the New Physics*, 71.
[52] Peters, *Science, Theology, and Ethics*, 121–38.

possible to incorporate the idea of extraterrestrial life into religious teachings. For example, Ted Peters is a Lutheran theologian who has written extensively on the subject of exotheology.[53] He has argued that the discovery of extraterrestrial life is consistent with Christian beliefs. More recently, Joel Parkyn runs a *tour de force* in his brilliant contribution, *Exotheology: Theological Explorations of Intelligent Extraterrestrial Life*, in which he maps out the various options for Christians.[54] These writers are just a few examples of the many theologians and writers who have explored the subject of exotheology from Christian perspectives.

While Christianity has many similarities with Islam, they are still two very different religious traditions, with distinctive holy texts in dissimilar languages, varying histories and intellectual corpora. Most significantly, Muslims do not hold on to the idea of the Fall, Incarnation and Atonement. This significantly affects their outlooks on human theological anthropology, the discussion of human uniqueness and nature. Accordingly, while Christian perspectives may provide useful insights for Muslims thinking about exotheology, they can not necessarily conclude for Muslims and Islamic thought.

To date, there are only a handful of major academic publications that discuss Islamic perspectives on IEL in the English language. These are summarized in Table 0.1.[55]

The latest publication is by Haider et al., who have penned down what seems to be the first Shīʿī perspective on exotheology in 2023, which was freshly published during the write-up of this introduction. They claim that not only does Shīʿī theology affirm the existence of IEL, but it also seems to provide a framework for interactions between humans and IEL.[56] The second most recent publication is by one of the editors of this volume, Jörg Matthias Determann. By charting Arabic, Bengali, Malay, Persian, Turkish and Urdu texts and films, Determann shows how the notion of IEL has creatively induced a rich growth of science fiction along with its interaction with Islamic theology in Muslim-majority countries.[57] Third is Muzaffar Iqbal's book chapter in a volume edited by Ted Peters. In there, he provides a concise perspective on IEL, suggesting that it poses no serious challenge to Islamic thought.[58] Another publication is

53 Ibid; Peters, *Astrotheology*.

54 Parkyn, *Exotheology*.

55 In this list, we restrict ourselves to academic monographs, book chapters and journal articles. However, there are further accounts in English published on websites and in popular books. Examples include Mimouni and Guessoum, 'Islam and Extraterrestrial Life'; Ahmad, *Revelation, Rationality, Knowledge and Truth*.

56 Haider et al., 'Shīʿī Imāmī Thought on Existence, Life, and Extraterrestrials'.

57 Determann, *Islam, Science Fiction and Extraterrestrial Life*.

58 Iqbal, "Islamic Theology Meets ETI".

**Table 0.1** Summary of Detailed Investigations of Islamic Perspectives on IEL

| Author | Name | Date | Type | Publisher |
|---|---|---|---|---|
| Shahbaz Haider, Abdullah Ansar and Syed Ali Asdaq Naqvi | Shīʿī Imāmī Thought on Existence, Life and Extraterrestrials | 2023 | Journal article | Theology and Science |
| Jörg Matthias Determann | Islam, Science Fiction and Extraterrestrial Life: The Culture of Astrobiology in the Muslim World | 2021 | Monograph | I.B. Tauris |
| Muzaffar Iqbal | Islamic Theology Meets ETI | 2018 | Book chapter in an edited volume | Cascade Books |
| David A. Weintraub | Religions and Extrate-rrestrial Life: How Will We Deal with It? | 2014 | Book chapter in a monograph | Springer |

an eclectic book chapter in a monograph by David A. Weintraub. The entire monograph is a large-scale survey of how IEL might impact several traditions, with Islam being no exception. Given the clear dearth of literature available to him, he attempts to synthesize the thoughts of various Muslim thinkers, for example, Seyyed Hossein Nasr, to bring forth considerations to form an Islamic perspective.[59]

Recognizing a clear gap in the literature, particularly detailed analyses of Islamic exotheology, the editors of this volume – Shoaib Ahmed Malik and Jörg Matthias Determann – met up and organized a conference titled *Islamic Perspectives on Exotheology*.[60] In the dwindling end of the Covid-19 pandemic, this was hosted as an online event in May 2022 under the auspices of Virginia Commonwealth University in Qatar. The proceeding of that conference is this edited volume that you are reading.

## Chapters on Islamic theology's final frontier

This volume tries to provide a broad analysis of exotheology from multiple perspectives. Our book is divided into four sections. Each one contains two

[59] Weintraub, *Religions and Extraterrestrial Life*.
[60] Virginia Commonwealth University, 'Conference Co-hosted by VCUarts Qatar'.

**Table 0.2** Breakdown of the Edited Volume

| Section | Chapter Title | Contributor(s) |
|---|---|---|
| Theology and Scripture | Theological Information on the Existence of Intelligent Life Outside Our Solar System: Metaphysics, Scripture and Science | Hamza Karamali |
| | Does the Qur'ān Affirm Extraterrestrial life? | Moamer Khalayleh |
| | A Hermeneutic Analysis of Sūrat al-Naḥl (Q. 16:8) | |
| | Islamic Sacred Resources on Extraterrestrials and Their Possible Eschatological Implications | Mohammad Mahdi Montasseri |
| Jurisprudence | Extraterrestrials and Moral Accountability: Non-human Moral Personhood through the Lens of Classical Sunnī Theology and Law | David Solomon Jalajel |
| | Classical Muslim Thought and the Theological Implications and Possibility of Non-Human Intelligence | Faisal Abdullah |
| Islam and Christianity | Extraterrestrial Intelligent Life and Islamic Beliefs: Investigating Six Potential Conflicts | Shoaib Ahmed Malik |
| | The Alien in the Lamp? The Jinn and Alien Life in Islamic Theology | Richard Playford |
| Society | A Qur'ānic Ufology? Seven Exotheological Hypotheses of the Indonesian 'Islamic UFO' Community | Ayub and Ilham Ibrahim |
| | Exotheology in Contemporary Egyptian Science Fiction: A Comparative Appraisal | Emad El-Din Aysha |

chapters except for the first, which has three. The structure is summarized in Table 0.2.

## Theology and scripture

The first quarter of the book deals with some of the central concerns regarding IEL: (1) Could they exist? (2) What does scripture say about them?

Hamza Karamali takes the late Sunnī *kalām* tradition as his focal point to address these two questions. He engages these questions through a three-stage process: (1) metaphysics, (2) scripture and (3) science. He argues that it is perfectly acceptable for God to create IEL. He grounds his scriptural analysis in a well-known ḥadīth which asserts the existence of other 'earths' with prophets like our own, suggesting that not only are there IEL, but they could contain prophets therein, too. He then explains why the Sunnī ḥadīth tradition has critiqued its epistemic weight and, despite it not being epistemically robust, shows how that discussion reveals that this is the only explicit scriptural statement about the existence of IEL. Karamali then argues that, while the Qurʾān does not rule out the existence of IEL, we can infer from it that if IEL does exist, then humans will be the most superior creation (*afḍal al-khalq*).

Moamer Khalayleh's chapter analyses a particular verse of the Qurʾān:

> And livestock – He created them too. You derive warmth and other benefits from them: you get food from them; you find beauty in them when you bring them home to rest and when you drive them out to pasture. They carry your loads to lands you yourselves could not reach without great hardship – truly your Lord is kind and merciful – horses, mules, and donkeys for you to ride and use for show, and *other things you know nothing about.*[61] (italics for emphasis)

By mining ten major exegetical works in Sunnī Islam to interpret this verse, he identifies five interpretations of the statement 'other things you know nothing about'. The most widely accepted takes the verse at face value as an open declarative statement with no qualifications: that God has made creatures that human beings have no knowledge of, independent of where or when they may be created. A second opinion suggests the verse is discussing life on Earth, including land and sea creatures. The other three opinions appeal to the traditions of the Prophet Muḥammad to make more specific interpretations. The third view is the verse that refers to the creations of God in Paradise and Hellfire, while the fourth perspective suggests that the beings indicated are angels created in the heavens. Of the more extraordinary interpretations, the fifth position references a ḥadīth attributed to the Prophet Muḥammad in which he states that there exist sentient creatures a great distance away who know not that God is disobeyed, and they know not of Adam nor Iblīs (Satan). A significant conclusion of this paper, argues Khalayleh, is that of all the interpretations, none deny the possibility of the existence of IEL. According to the most dominant opinion, it may very well be possible.

Mohammad Mahdi Montasseri's chapter explores Islamic scripture to see how mention of or inferences to extraterrestrials could help us re-envisage Islamic eschatology. He analyses both Sunnī and Shīʿī sources. Certain Qurʾānic verses imply the existence of extraterrestrials, and many of the prominent

[61] Q. 16:5–8.

interpreters (*mufassirūn*) have forthrightly affirmed that those verses refer to extraterrestrials. The most explicit descriptions, however, are reported in the sayings of the Prophet Muḥammad and the Imams of Shīʿism. According to these resources, extraterrestrials live on different planets; some are not aware of others, and some are connected to each other (despite living on different planets) through 'pillars of light.' Also, the number of their colonies is innumerable. Their physical formations are not necessarily like that of humans, and they are juridically accountable (*mukallaf*). Drawing on these reports, Montasseri investigates how this body of work can help us reimagine Muslims' views of the Day of Judgement (*yawm al-qiyāma*).

## Jurisprudence

The second quarter of the book mostly focuses on the jurisprudential and ethical side of IEL. (1) How might Islamic law see the agency of IEL? (2) And would Islamic law (*Sharīʿa*) be applicable to them?

By adopting a broad Sunnī framework – Ashʿarī, Māturīdī and Salafī – supplemented by the four Sunnī legal schools – Ḥanafī, Ḥanbalī, Mālikī, Shāfiʿī – David Solomon Jalajel's chapter engages with the discussion of human uniqueness and transposes it to the question of personhood and moral accountability of IEL. He argues that it is impossible to reject the possibility that God may have created morally responsible beings in other parts of the universe based on theological, doctrinal or scriptural grounds. Hence, if we encounter another group of rational beings that demonstrate volition and discretion, we cannot deny their moral agency and treat them as non-persons without contradicting this belief, at least not with the Sunnī framework.

Faisal Abdullah's chapter explores a large number of discussions found in the Muslim scholarly tradition relevant to IEL, showing how premodern Muslim thought was not only capable of addressing the possible existence of non-human intelligent beings but also that it had *already* entertained a universe wherein this may have been a reality. He identifies Abū al-Ḥasan al-Māwardī (d. 1058) as perhaps the first Muslim to comment on the implications of human contact with intelligent beings from a different 'earth.' The chapter also draws insights from the works of Taqī al-Dīn al-Subkī (d. 1355) and Jalāl al-Dīn al-Suyūṭī (d. 1505), among others, on how and whether the Prophet Muḥammad's message extended to jinn, angels and potentially other classes of beings. Abdullah suggests that these discussions provide ample material for potential road maps should humankind encounter IEL.

## Islam and Christianity

This quarter of the book deals with the engagement between Muslims and Christians on the topic of exotheology. What can they learn from one another?

Shoaib Ahmed Malik, one of the editors of this volume, was inspired by the work of C. A. McIntosh and Tyler Dalton McNabb, who penned an article with the title, *Houston, Do We Have a Problem? Extraterrestrial Intelligent Life and Christian Belief*. They identify six potential points of conflict between Christian belief and ETI, which were appropriated as needed for Islamic considerations. They include (1) incompatibility with theism, (2) conflict with Islamic scriptures, (3) conflict with central doctrines of Islam, (4) issue with the Islamic tradition, (5) how ETIs may exacerbate the problem of evil and (6) conflict with the Islamic narrative. In resonance with the conclusions of McIntosh and McNabb, Malik argues that none of the identified problems raises any concerns about Islamic belief, except for perhaps one issue in (4). Despite the broad similarities in the conclusions of Islamic and Christian responses to these questions, Malik does not fail to highlight the underlying dissimilarities between the two religious traditions and how they impact their approaches.

Richard Playford uses the ontology of jinn in the Islamic framework to stimulate his take on IEL in Christianity. By comparing the jinn in Islam with angels and demons in Christianity, Playford demonstrates that Islam, in particular, has the intellectual resources to accommodate IEL by modifying their pre-existing belief in the existence of the jinn.

## Society

The last quarter of the book looks at the Islamic exotheology that plays out in the wider society. How have Muslims received the idea of IEL? Ayub and Ilham Ibrahim write that in Indonesia, it is rare to find a study of the Islamic perspective on the existence of extraterrestrial beings conducted by mainstream theologians. Nevertheless, discussions about extraterrestrial beings and related phenomena, such as Unidentified Flying Objects (UFOs), are quite popular among lay Muslims. One of these discussion groups is Islamic UFO, an association of UFO enthusiasts that discusses the issue of extraterrestrial beings from an Islamic perspective. Although they admit that ufology is still considered a pseudoscience by many, they still seriously discuss these themes and offer what they consider an Islamic perspective of ufology. Since its establishment in 2012, this discussion group has been actively discussing the topic of Islam and UFOs both offline and online. In their discussion, this group put forward seven hypotheses regarding the existence of extraterrestrial beings from an Islamic perspective, namely the (1) *Banī* Adam Hypothesis, (2) pre-Adamic beings Hypothesis, (3) Smart *Dābbah* Hypothesis, (4) *Man* (من) Hypothesis, (5) *Jinn* Hypothesis, (6) *Iblīs*' Trickery Hypothesis and (7) the Permanent *Ghayb* Hypothesis. It focuses on the construction of arguments for each of these hypotheses and examines their hermeneutic and metaphysical plausibility. Furthermore, this article will also compare the seven hypotheses with exotheological opinions that have developed among Muslims outside of Indonesia.

Emad El-Din Aysha discusses how Arab and Muslim science fiction is open-minded about exotheology and religious pluralism. Even conservative Muslim authors in Egypt are excited about finding IEL for religious reasons. He argues that, unlike Christianity, Islam is a non-anthropocentric and non-anthropomorphic religion, so discovering aliens does not pose the same dilemmas for Muslims. He shows how Arab-Islamic science fiction often includes jinn as champions of the faith, similar to extraterrestrials. Jinn are not mere demons in Islamic lore but sentient beings with their own kingdoms and civilizations and are held morally accountable by God, and the same holds true in many works of Arabic science fiction. Furthermore, by taking various cues from Islamic intellectual history, Emad El-Din suggests that Islamic history supports these ideas; rationalism, spiritualism, alchemy and evolutionism all make themselves felt in modern Arab-Muslim science fiction. Western science fiction, however, tends towards secularism, presuming an antagonism between scientific advance and faith narrowly conceived, and often affirms humankind's central role in the universe when supposedly challenging it. Many canonical works of Western SF presume to dethrone man in the universe, after removing God from the picture, only to have alien life forms mimicking humans in their appearance or praising the unstoppable advance of the human race.

## Outer limits

Although our contributors have tried to cover much ground, many aspects of the relationship between Islam and astrobiology are still left to be explored. We have only begun to deal with questions of Islamic theological anthropology. How do the different Muslim traditions view the human condition in relation to creation and non-human animals on Earth? How do Muslim views of extraterrestrial life relate to the climate crisis and the ongoing Anthropocene extinction event?

Answering such would require a broader engagement with feminist perspectives, environmental concerns, animal theology, race and colonialism, among other topics. Fortunately, young Muslim astronomers like Burçin Mutlu-Pakdil are equally interested in the structure of distant galaxies and in social justice here on Earth. They thus give us hope of a better world that we don't need a spaceship to get to. Mutlu-Pakdil described herself as both a 'feminist' and a 'scientist'. 'To all whose dreams are questioned because of all of the social norms, do not give up and follow your dreams!', she exclaimed. 'Anyone could be anything, regardless of any of the social identities (gender, religion, race, etc).'[62]

Even in the questions that our chapters addressed head-on, we cannot claim comprehensiveness. Source texts in different languages, such as Turkish, or theological tracts belonging to groups like the Ismailis remain underexplored in the book you are reading.[63] While we have attempted comparisons between Islam and Christianity, comparative views on other religions are still lacking.[64]

Finally, cultural productions about extraterrestrials here on Earth are too abundant to be fully addressed in a single volume. Aliens can be found in advertisements, children's literature and television shows, among other media. In the run-up to the FIFA World Cup Qatar 2022, they even became associated with the mundane area of football. In a campaign for the telecommunications company Ooredoo from the year 2000, footballer Lionel Messi is abducted by a flying saucer. Coinciding with Eid al-Fitr in 2022, the first episode of the animated series *Kawkabani* was released. It was sponsored by the Supreme Committee for Delivery & Legacy of the World Cup, the Doha Film Institute and Ooredoo's main competitor Vodafone. *Kawkabani* follows a crazy soccer fan from the planet Kepler-438b who crashes in the Qatari desert. Director Hossein Heydar explained: 'The series shows the culture, tradition and lifestyle of the Qatari community through the eyes of an Alien who asks most of the questions that revolve in the mind of any visitor. It also aims to introduce Qatar as a tourist destination.'[65]

While you can find an increasing number of studies on science fiction in the Muslim world,[66] further advances in this field are needed and expected. Many existing books, short stories and films still lack sufficient engagement from critics, and every year, new works come out. Extraterrestrials will thus remain

62 Willett, "This UA Astrophysicist Has a Galaxy Named after Her".
63 See, however, Khan, "Earthly and Celestial Beings".
64 See, however, Ahmad, "Islamic-Confucian Perspective on Extraterrestrial Life".
65 Baluyut, "Qatari Animated Web Series 'Kawkabani' Releases First Episode".
66 Campbell, *Arabic Science Fiction*; Determann, *Islam, Science Fiction and Extraterrestrial Life*.

on the frontiers not only of science and religion but also on those of cultural and literary studies more broadly. We hope you enjoy the explorations in this volume, ideally whetting your appetite for more.

## Cosmic debts

We thank all the participants at the online conference on *Islamic Perspectives on Exotheology* hosted by Virginia Commonwealth University in Qatar in May 2022. The Religion and Astrobiology in Culture and Society (RACS) Network led by Stephen Bullivant, Richard Playford and Janet Siefert was an immensely valuable partner in organizing our workshop. Mary Joseph and Layla Azmi Goushey provided valuable media coverage for this event.[67] Further support came from Safaruk Chowdhury, Ramon Harvey, Khalil Andani, David Solomon Jalajel and Nazif Muhtaroğlu. In the background, Patty Paine, Kathryn London-Penny, Nadia AbuDayeh and Mike Gallagher were indispensable.

Outside our original conference, we had the opportunity to discuss this project in a number of venues. Both of us, Shoaib and Matthias, had the honour of appearing at a livestream panel event in 2023 on *Historical Perspectives on Science and Religion in the Middle East*, which was sponsored by the International Research Network for the Study of Science and Belief in Society. One of us, Matthias, also gave a seminar at the RACS Network in 2022. He subsequently spoke at a catalyst event on *Space Temples* hosted by the UCL Centre for Outer Space Studies the following year. He further benefited from his involvement in the project *A Sign in Space* led by Daniela de Paulis in collaboration with the SETI Institute, European Space Agency, the Green Bank Observatory and the Istituto Nazionale di Astrofisica.

At I.B. Tauris, an imprint of Bloomsbury, we are deeply grateful to Sophie Rudland and Yasmin Garcha for believing in this project. Nayiri Kendir and Faiza Zakaria were similarly crucial to our editing process, while Almudena Gutierrez provided further support. We thank Emma Tranter and Mahesh Meiyazhagan for managing the production process of our book. The anonymous peer reviewers commissioned by our publisher made very helpful suggestions on both our initial proposal and the complete manuscript. In the process of producing this volume, every author had the opportunity to comment on

[67] Goushey, 'Islamic Exotheology'; Marhaba, 'Online Conference Discusses Possibility of Life Outside Earth'.

everyone else's chapter. We also depended on excellent feedback from external reviewers, such as Munazza Alam, Nour Skaf, Paul Williams, Ibrahim Hafidh and Ayisha Yahya.

Finally, we must acknowledge our debt to our families. Our spouses, Ellie and Jeanne Juliana Vaz, allowed us to spend not just precious time on this work but also sizable amounts of money on acquiring related literature. Matthias further thanks his daughter Maria for regular opportunities to read Arabic children's books about extraterrestrial life. He could enjoy such fun times, because his nanny, Marilou Magsayo Semetara, took care of many of the more onerous tasks of child-rearing. Matthias's parents, Michael and Sibylle Determann, and his parents-in-law, Peter and Sophia Vaz, inspired him through many conversations about Islam and science. His brothers, Christian Pils and Claudius Determann, first explored with him the worlds of science fiction. Shoaib still laughs about his son's questions. After getting used to his daddy talking about evolution and then moving to extraterrestrials, he kept asking about how exotheology is different from evolution.

## Bibliography

Ahmad, Mirza Tahir. *Revelation, Rationality, Knowledge and Truth*. Tilford: Islam International Publications, 1998.

Ahmad, Muhammad Aurangzeb. 'Islamic-Confucian Perspective on Extraterrestrial Life'. Presentation at the online conference Islamic Perspectives *on* Exotheology, Virginia Commonwealth University, 2022.

Alam, Munazza. 'Contemplating the Cosmos'. *The Review of Religions*, 21 September 2020. https://www.reviewofreligions.org/24405/astronomy-science-galaxies/.

Alam, Munazza. 'Seeing Deeper into Space - Launch of the James Webb Space Telescope'. *The Review of Religions*, 26 January 2022. https://www.reviewofreligions.org/36963/seeing-deeper-into-space-launch-of-the-james-webb-space-telescope/.

Alam, Munazza Khalida. 'Characterizing Distant Worlds: Atmospheric Reconnaissance of Giant Planets with Hubble'. PhD diss., Harvard University, 2021.

Alsubai, Khalid, Zlatan I. Tsvetanov, Stylianos Pyrzas, David W. Latham, Allyson Bieryla, Jason Eastman, Dimitris Mislis, et al. 'Qatar Exoplanet Survey: Qatar-8b, 9b, and 10b—A Hot Saturn and Two Hot Jupiters'. *Astronomical Journal* 157, no. 6 (2019): 224.

Alsubai, K. A., N. R. Parley, D. M. Bramich, R. G. West, P. M. Sorensen, A. Collier Cameron, D. W. Latham, et al. 'Qatar-1b: A Hot Jupiter Orbiting a Metal-Rich K Dwarf Star'. *Monthly Notices of the Royal Astronomical Society* 417, no. 1 (2011): 709–16.

Baluyut, Joelyn. 'Qatari Animated Web Series "Kawkabani" Releases First Episode'. *The Peninsula*, 3 May 2022. https://thepeninsulaqatar.com/article/03/05/2022/qatari-animated-web-series-kawkabani-releases-first-episode.

Basalla, George. *Civilized Life in the Universe: Scientists on Intelligent Extraterrestrials.* Oxford: Oxford University Press, 2006.

Brennan, Pat. 'Cosmic Milestone: NASA Confirms 5,000 Exoplanets'. National Aeronautics and Space Administration, 21 March 2022. https://exoplanets.nasa.gov/news/1702/cosmic-milestone-nasa-confirms-5000-exoplanets/.

Briot, Danielle. 'The Creator of Astrobotany, Gavriil Adrianovich Tikhov'. In *Astrobiology, History, and Society: Life beyond Earth and the Impact of Discovery*, edited by Douglas A. Vakoch, 175–85. Heidelberg: Springer, 2013.

Caballero, Alberto. 'An Approximation to Determine the Source of the WOW! Signal'. *International Journal of Astrobiology* 21, no. 3 (2022): 129–36.

Campbell, Ian. *Arabic Science Fiction.* Cham: Palgrave Macmillan, 2018.

Ćirković, Milan M. *The Great Silence: The Science and Philosophy of Fermi's Paradox.* Oxford: Oxford University Press, 2018.

Davies, Paul. *God and the New Physics*. London: Penguin Books, 1983.

Determann, Jörg Matthias. *Islam, Science Fiction and Extraterrestrial Life: The Culture of Astrobiology in the Muslim World.* New York: I.B. Tauris, 2021.

Dick, Steven J. *The Biological Universe: The Twentieth Century Extraterrestrial Life Debate and the Limits of Science*. Cambridge: Cambridge University Press, 1996.

Dick, Steven J. *Space, Time, and Aliens: Collected Works on Cosmos and Culture*. Dordrecht: Springer, 2020.

Feldhay, Rivka and F. Jamil Ragep, eds. *Before Copernicus: The Cultures and Contexts of Scientific Learning in the Fifteenth Century*. Montreal: McGill-Queen's University Press, 2017.

Ghauri, Munavara. 'Reaching for the Stars: An Interview with Astronomer Munazza Alam'. *The Review of Religions*, 2 September 2020. https://www.reviewofreligions.org/24448/interview-astronomer-munazza-alam/.

Gillon, Michaël, Amaury H. M. J. Triaud, Brice-Olivier Demory, Emmanuël Jehin, Eric Agol, Katherine M. Deck, Susan M. Lederer, et al. 'Seven Temperate Terrestrial Planets around the Nearby Ultracool Dwarf Star TRAPPIST-1'. *Nature* 542, no. 7642 (2017): 456–60.

Goushey, Layla Azmi. 'Islamic Exotheology: Viewpoints on Extraterrestrial Intelligence'. *Patheos*, 31 May 2022. https://www.patheos.com/blogs/allmuslim/2022/05/islamic-exotheology-viewpoints-on-extraterrestrial-intelligence/.

Haider, Shahbaz, Abdullah Ansar and Syed Ali Asdaq Naqvi. 'Shīʿī Imāmī Thought on Existence, Life, and Extraterrestrials'. *Theology and Science* 21, no. 2 (2023): 261–72.

Iqbal, Muzaffar. 'Islamic Theology Meets ETI'. In *Astrotheology: Science and Theology Meet Extraterrestrial Life*, edited by Ted Peters, Martinez Hewlett, Joshua M. Moritz and Robert John Russell, 216–27. Eugene: Cascade, 2018.

Khan, Mir Baiz. 'Earthly and Celestial Beings: Qurʾānic Interpretation from Classical Ismaili Literature'. Presentation at the online conference Islamic Perspectives *on* Exotheology, Virginia Commonwealth University, 2022.

Kreidberg, Laura. 'Exoplanet Atmosphere Measurements from Transmission Spectroscopy and Other Planet Star Combined Light Observations'. In *Handbook of Exoplanets*, edited by Hans J. Deeg and Juan Antonio Belmonte, 1–23. Cham: Springer, 2018.

Lee, Abigail and Maryum Sayeed. 'Women's History Month: Dr. Burçin Mutlu-Pakdil'. *Astrobites*, 10 April 2022. https://astrobites.org/2022/04/10/template-post-10/.

Marhaba. 'Online Conference Discusses Possibility of Life Outside Earth, Its Impact on Religions'. Marhaba, 26 May 2022. https://www.marhaba.qa/online-conference-discusses-possibility-of-life-outside-earth-its-impact-on-religions/.

McDonough, Thomas R. 'Review of the Planetary Society's SETI Program'. *Progress in the Search for Extraterrestrial Life* 74 (1995): 419–24.

Mimouni, Jamal and Nidhal Guessoum. 'Islam and Extraterrestrial Life'. *Islam & Science*, 16 January 2015. http://islam-science.net/islam-and-extraterrestrial-life-2908/.

NASA. 'James Webb Space Telescope'. *Solar System Exploration*. https://solarsystem.nasa.gov/missions/james-webb-space-telescope/in-depth/ (accessed 9 April 2023).

NASA. 'Kepler and K2'. National Aeronautics and Space Administration. https://www.nasa.gov/mission_pages/kepler/overview/index.html (Accessed 9 April 2023).

NASA. 'TESS Exoplanet Mission'. National Aeronautics and Space Administration. https://www.nasa.gov/tess-transiting-exoplanet-survey-satellite (Accessed 9 April 2023).

NASA. 'Webb vs Hubble Telescope'. James Webb Space Telescope. https://webb.nasa.gov/content/about/comparisonWebbVsHubble.html (Accessed 9 April 2023).

Observatoire de Paris. 'Nour Skaf, lauréate du prix "L'Oréal-UNESCO pour les femmes et la science"'. Observatoire de Paris, 12 October 2021. https://www.observatoiredeparis.psl.eu/nour-skaf-receives-the-l.html?lang=fr.

Parkyn, Joel L. *Exotheology: Theological Explorations of Intelligent Extraterrestrial Life*. Oregon: Pickwick Publications, 2021.

Peters, Ted, ed. *Astrotheology: Science and Theology Meet Extraterrestrial Life*. Eugene: Cascade, 2018.

Peters, Ted. 'Introducing Astrotheology'. In *Astrotheology: Science and Theology Meet Extraterrestrial Life*, edited by Ted Peters, Martinez Hewlett, Joshua M. Moritz and Robert John Russell, 3–26. Eugene: Cascade, 2018.

Peters, Ted. *Science, Theology, and Ethics*. Hants: Ashgate Publishing Limited, 2003.

Pierson, Thomas. 'SETI Institute: Summary of Projects in Support of SETI Research'. In *Progress in the Search for Extraterrestrial Life*, edited by G. Seth Shostak, 433–46. San Francisco: Astronomical Society of the Pacific, 1995.

Postberg, Frank, Nozair Khawaja, Bernd Abel, Gael Choblet, Christopher R. Glein, Murthy S. Gudipati, Bryana L. Henderson, et al. 'Macromolecular Organic Compounds from the Depths of Enceladus'. *Nature* 558, no. 7711 (2018): 564–8.

Saliba, George. *Islamic Science and the Making of the European Renaissance*. Cambridge, MA: MIT Press, 2007.

Sayeed, Maryum. 'Women's History Month: Dr. Munazza Alam'. *Astrobites*, 24 March 2022. https://astrobites.org/2022/03/24/munazza-alam/.

Shuch, H. Paul. *Searching for Extraterrestrial Intelligence: SETI Past, Present, and Future*. Cham: Springer, 2010.

Skaf, Nour. 'Self-Optimization of Adaptive Optics and Characterization of Exoplanetary Systems'. Thèse de doctorat, PSL Université Paris, 2023.

Space Telescope Science Institute. 'Webb Space Telescope'. NASA James Webb Space Telescope. https://webbtelescope.org/ (Accessed 9 April 2023).

Strauss, Gary. 'Finding Clarity in the Stars'. *National Geographic*, 21 October 2016. https://www.nationalgeographic.com/science/article/munazza-alam-explorer-moments-dwarf-stars.

Tarter, J. C. 'Project Phoenix: The Australian Deployment'. *Proceedings of SPIE Optical Meeting*, San Jose, California, 31 January 1996.

Vakoch, Douglas A. and Matthew F. Dowd, eds. *The Drake Equation: Estimating the Prevalence of Extraterrestrial Life through the Ages*. Cambridge: Cambridge University Press, 2015.

Virginia Commonwealth University. 'Conference Co-hosted by VCUarts Qatar Discusses the Possibility of Life Outside of Earth'. *VCUarts Qatar*, 9 April 2023. https://qatar.vcu.edu/news/conference-co-hosted-by-vcuarts-qatar-discusses-the-possibility-of-life-out.

Webb, Stephen. *If the Universe Is Teeming with Aliens . . . Where is Everybody? Seventy-Five Solutions to the Fermi Paradox and the Problem of Extraterrestrial Life*. Cham: Springer, 2015.

Weintraub, David A. *Religions and Extraterrestrial Life: How Will We Deal with It?* Dordrecht: Springer, 2014.

Willett, Johanna. 'This UA Astrophysicist Has a Galaxy Named after Her'. This is Tucson, 4 February 2018. https://thisistucson.com/tucsonlife/this-ua-astrophysicist-has-a-galaxy-named-after-her/article_fdd22e3a-02df-11e8-82c0-13b25ac97a9e.html.

Worden, S. Pete. Jamie Drew, Andrew Siemion, Dan Werthimer, David DeBoer, Steve Croft, David MacMahon, Matt Lebofsky, Howard Isaacson, Jack Hickish, Danny Price, Vishal Gajjar and Jason T. Wright. 'Breakthrough Listen – A New Search for Life in the Universe'. *Acta Astronautica* 139 (2017): 98–101.

Zakeer, Fehmida. 'Meet the Woman Who Discovered a Whole New Type of Galaxy'. *National Geographic*, 21 November 2018. https://www.nationalgeographic.com/science/article/meet-woman-discovered-new-type-galaxy-burcin-mutlu-pakdil-astrophysics.

Zuckerman, Catherine. 'Meet Munazza Alam, the Woman Searching for Planet Earth's Twin'. *National Geographic*, 8 March 2019. https://www.nationalgeographic.com/science/article/meet-the-woman-searching-for-planet-earth-s-twin.

1

# Theological information on the existence of intelligent life outside our solar system

## Metaphysics, scripture and science

Hamza Karamali

## Introduction

The great seminaries of the premodern Muslim world were part of a global academic network that engaged in scholarly debates on the margins of a common set of highly developed teaching manuals. These debates universally accepted a set of scholarly works and conclusions as authoritative starting points for the exploration of answers to new religious questions.[1] This chapter locates itself within the late tradition of that premodern scholarly discourse and explores how that premodern scholarly community (which I will henceforth refer to as the 'late Sunnī scholarly tradition') would have engaged with the question of intelligent extraterrestrial life today. I will show both (1) that the Sunnī scholarly tradition explored the question of intelligent extraterrestrial life centuries before the age of science and (2) that the late Sunnī tradition coalesced on several important conclusions that allow us to infer how it would have informed our scientific search for intelligent extraterrestrial life today. I will show that it would have concluded that theological information on intelligent extraterrestrial life leads us to conclude that:

1. it is possible for intelligent extraterrestrial life to exist, and
2. that if intelligent extraterrestrial life does exist, then it has been less honoured by God than human beings have.

[1] Karamali, *Madrasa Curriculum in Context.*

Furthermore, I will also show that it would have sought out scientific information on intelligent extraterrestrial life because:

1. it is not possible for any scientific information on intelligent extraterrestrial life to conflict with theological information on the same, and
2. scientific information on intelligent extraterrestrial life can give us insight into the meanings of some Qur'ānic verses.

As I develop the argument of this chapter, I will sometimes cite the rational and scriptural evidence that the late Sunnī scholarly tradition would have used to come to its conclusions, and sometimes, I will not cite it. That is because my goal is to build an argument on the methods and inferential starting points of that tradition to understand what that tradition would have said today. A full exploration of the correctness of their methods and inferential starting points is beyond the scope of this paper.

## Metaphysics, revelation and science

The first set of methods that the Sunnī scholarly tradition would apply to the question of intelligent extraterrestrials is found in the science of *kalām* (Islamic theology). Its relevance derives from the fact that it critically integrated the philosophical ideas of Avicenna, whose goal was to gain knowledge of all existent things.[2] Late Sunnī theologians observed that his ideas merged so thoroughly with *kalām* that the latter 'became virtually indistinguishable from *falsafā* (the Muslim engagement with Greek philosophy) were it not for its inclusion of matters related to the afterlife'.[3] This integration means that the late *kalām* tradition contains methods of reasoning that allow us to gain some knowledge regarding the actual or potential existence of everything, including (as we shall see later) the existence of intelligent extraterrestrials.

There are three methods of *kalām*-reasoning for gaining knowledge of actual or potentially existent things. The first relies on the ability of the mind to discern metaphysical contingency (*imkān*), necessity (*wujūb*) and impossibility (*istiḥāla*) – I will call this *metaphysical reasoning*. The second relies on revelation that has been proven to be genuinely from God – I will call this *revelatory reasoning*. The

[2] *Ḥāshīya* of al-Kastalī in Ramaḍān et al., *Al-Majmūʿa*, 82; Karamali, *Madrasa Curriculum in Context*, 6–11 and 19–21.

[3] Al-Taftāzānī, *Sharḥ*, 14.

**Table 1.1** *Mutakallimūn* Cited in this Article

| *Mutakallim* | Date of Death | Work |
|---|---|---|
| Al-Ījī | 1356 | *Al-Mawāqif fī 'Ilm al-Kalām* |
| Al-Taftāzānī | 1390 | *Sharḥ al-'Aqā'id al-Nasafiyya* |
| Al-Kastalī | 1495 | *Ḥāshīyat al-Kastalī alā Sharḥ al-'Aqā'id al-Nasafiyya* |
| Al-Laqānī | 1631 | *Hidāyat al-Murīd li Jawharat al-Tawḥīd* |

third relies on the sense observation of regularities in the universe – I will place modern *scientific reasoning* into this category.[4]

The *mutakallimūn* (scholars of *kalām*) would therefore investigate the existence of intelligent extraterrestrials by gathering information through each of these three kinds of reasoning. The *mutakallimūn* and their works that I will rely on are summarized in Table 1.1.

I have organized this chapter in the different modalities highlighted earlier (metaphysics, revelation and science). The first section gathers information through metaphysical reasoning, the second section gathers information through revelatory reasoning, and the third section concludes this chapter by exploring scientific reasoning in light of all previous sections.

## Metaphysical reasoning about intelligent extraterrestrials

Metaphysical reasoning is based on the intuitive metaphysical perception of the universe as *contingent* (*mumkin*). The contingency of the universe means that it is possible for everything inside it to be different from the way that it is (e.g. it is possible for it to be daytime or night-time). That means that it doesn't have to be the way that it is (if it is now night-time, then it is possible for it to be daytime, and vice versa). And that means that it needs something else to make it the way that it is (the day needs something to make it day, and the night needs something to make it night).[5]

From this contingency, the *mutakallimūn* inferred the existence of a necessary being (*wājib al-wujūd*) which, through a series of supplementary arguments, they identified with the God of Islam.[6] Recall that our goal is to discover whether or not intelligent extraterrestrials exist. Metaphysical reasoning has not yet given

4 Metaphysical reasoning corresponds to what the *mutakallimūn* call *ḥukm 'aqlī*, revelatory reasoning to *ḥukm shar'ī* and scientific reasoning to *ḥukm 'ādī*. See al-Laqānī, *Hidāyat al-Murīd*, 1: 166–71; al-Taftāzānī, *Sharḥ*, 24–41.

5 Ījī, *Al-Mawāqif*, 68 and 71–4.

6 Ibid., 90–9 and 261–96.

us any information on that, but it has proven the existence of another existent thing, namely a necessary being, on whom all contingent things utterly depend.

The *mutakallimūn* argued that while metaphysical reasoning can prove the actual existence of a necessary being, it cannot prove the actual existence or the actual non-existence of any contingent thing. The most that it can tell us about any contingent thing is that it is metaphysically possible for it to exist.[7] Another way of saying that is that it lies within the scope of God's omnipotence to make it exist should He choose to do so. (God's omnipotence relates to contingent things, which need God to make them exist, but it does not relate to something that is necessary (i.e. God Himself), because that does not need anything to make it exist.)[8]

Metaphysical reasoning, then, can tell us about the actual existence of a necessary being. Regarding contingent things, however, all it can tell us is that their existence is possible. It cannot tell us whether or not they actually exist. It can also tell us about one more thing: the actual non-existence of impossible things, such as for a physical object to be both moving and still at the same time (that would be a logical contradiction). Impossible things, too, lie outside the scope of God's omnipotence because it is metaphysically impossible for them to exist.[9]

In summary, metaphysical reasoning can tell us whether the existence of something is contingent, necessary or impossible. The question, therefore, is whether the existence of intelligent extraterrestrials is contingent, necessary or impossible.

In order to answer that question, we need to define what exactly we mean by 'intelligent extraterrestrial'. For the purposes of this chapter, I will define an intelligent extraterrestrial as someone who (1) is made of mass-energy, (2) is alive, (3) is capable of advanced rational thought and (4) exclusively inhabits a body of mass (whether a planet, moon or spaceship) outside our solar system.

This definition excludes angels and jinn. They are both non-human intelligent beings. They are frequently mentioned in the Qurʾān, and belief in them is part of the Sunnī creed. But they are not the kinds of intelligent extraterrestrials that scientists are searching for because they do not exclusively inhabit a planet, a moon or a spaceship outside our solar system, as required by (4) in the list of features mentioned in the previous paragraph. Rather, their lives are intertwined with ours, and they are part of the story of human life on this planet. And since

[7] This idea is widespread throughout the *kalām* tradition. See, for example, al-Taftāzānī, *Sharḥ*, 133.
[8] Al-Laqānī, *Hidāyat al-Murīd*, 1:424–8.
[9] Ibid., 1:166–71 and 1:427–8.

they are part of the unseen world, they cannot be studied scientifically and we are unable to confirm whether or not they are made of mass-energy, as required by the first of the four features mentioned previously.

The first part of the earlier definition stipulates that our hypothetical intelligent extraterrestrials are made of the same kind of stuff as all other physical things in the universe, that is, mass-energy. From that, we can reason as follows:

1. If intelligent extraterrestrials exist, they are made of mass-energy.
2. Everything that is made of mass-energy can change.
3. Everything that can change can be different from the way that it is.
4. Everything that can be different from the way that it is contingent.
5. Therefore, if intelligent extraterrestrials exist, they are contingent.

This leads us to our first piece of theological information:

> **Theological Information 1:** It is metaphysically possible for intelligent extraterrestrials to exist and also for them not to exist.

But this does not tell us if intelligent extraterrestrials actually exist. Nor does it tell us if they don't exist. For that, we need to turn to the other two kinds of reasoning, which are revelatory and scientific reasoning. I shall now turn to revelation reasoning.

## Revelatory reasoning about intelligent extraterrestrials

Revelatory reasoning in the Sunnī scholarly tradition builds on metaphysical reasoning. In the context of this chapter, revelatory reasoning means reasoning about the existence or non-existence of contingent things based on the Qur'ān, Sunna or scholarly consensus (I explain later why scholarly consensus is included in revelatory reasoning). Our ability to use revelation to infer the existence or non-existence of things is based on the fact that, for the *mutakallimūn*, the genuine prophethood of the Prophet Muḥammad (God bless him and give him peace) is not based on mere faith. Rather, it is a fact that is based on evidence.[10]

Once the genuine prophethood of the Prophet Muḥammad (God bless him and give him peace) is established with evidence, then the revelation that he received becomes a source of knowledge about things that exist. That is why, when reasoning about the existence of things in the afterlife, such as

[10] To prove this is one of the goals of every *kalām* manual. See, for example, Ījī, *Al-Mawāqif*, 349–58.

resurrection, judgement, Paradise and the Hellfire, the *mutakallimūn* used a famous principle: 'Every contingent thing of whose existence we are informed by genuine revelation does, in fact, exist.'[11] A straightforward entailment of this principle is that every contingent thing of whose non-existence we are informed by genuine revelation does not, in fact, exist. This means that contingent things can be divided into three categories from the perspective of what revelation tells us about them:

1. Contingent things that are mentioned in revelation and whose existence it affirms, such as the events of the afterlife (revelation enables us to discover that these things exist and that they possess the qualities that it describes);
2. Contingent things that are mentioned in revelation and whose existence it denies, such as the life, agency and power of idols (revelation enables us to discover that these things do not exist and that they do not possess the qualities that some people imagine them to); and
3. Contingent things that are not mentioned in revelation at all, such as the moons of Jupiter (revelation does not enable us to know anything about these things, and we need other sources, such as science, to discover information about them).

Our goal now is to discover which category intelligent extraterrestrials belong to.

## *The seven-earths ḥadīth*

An important revelatory statement related to the existence of extraterrestrial life is found in scholarly debates over the exegesis of the following verse of the Qurʾān:

> Allah it is Who created the seven heavens, and of earth the like thereof. The command descends between them that you may know that God has power over all things and that God encompasses all things in knowledge.[12]

The relevant part of this verse is that God has created seven heavens and 'of the earth the like thereof'. Even though there are many ways in which the Earth could resemble the heavens, the overwhelming majority of exegetes interpret this resemblance as a resemblance in number: just as there are seven heavens,

[11] This principle is universally applied in the *kalām* tradition. See, for example, al-Taftāzānī, *Sharḥ*, 113.

[12] Q. 65:12.

there are also seven earths.[13] This interpretation is confirmed by many authentic ḥadīths that explicitly mention seven earths.[14]

The following exegetical statement (which I will henceforth refer to as the 'seven-earths ḥadīth') from Ibn ʿAbbās seems to describe the seven earths as places that are inhabited by intelligent beings to whom God has sent messengers just as he sent them to human beings: 'There are seven Earths, and, on every Earth, there is a prophet like your prophet, an Adam like Adam, a Noah like Noah, an Abraham like Abraham, and a Jesus like Jesus.'[15]

The seven-earths ḥadīth is important because its narrator Ibn ʿAbbās was a companion of the Prophet (God bless him and give him peace) and one of the most important exegetes of the Qurʾān.[16] If his exegetical statement can be authentically traced back to the Prophet (God bless him and give him peace), then we have theological information about six other Earths that are inhabited by intelligent non-human beings.

The seven-earths ḥadīth is well known by the ḥadīth authorities of the Sunnī scholarly tradition as an archetypical example of an anomalous (*shādhdh*) ḥadīth, that is, a ḥadīth that an experienced ḥadīth critic is able to detect as inauthentic because (1) it is only narrated by a single narrator and (2) it has a strange and unfamiliar meaning. Together, these facts reveal to the ḥadīth critic that there has been a mistake in the transmission of the ḥadīth, even if he cannot determine exactly where the mistake is coming from.[17]

Al-Sūyūṭī cites this ḥadīth as an example of an anomalous ḥadīth. He comments, 'I continued to find it strange that Ḥākim judged it to be authentic until I saw Bayhaqī say, "Its chain of transmission is authentic, but it is completely anomalous (*shādhdh bi marra*)."'[18] This is only a partial quote. Bayhaqī's complete original statement is that the ḥadīth is 'completely anomalous and I don't know of any narrator who corroborated Abū al-Ḍuḥā's narration'[19] (i.e. of this ḥadīth

[13] See, for example, al-Bayḍāwī et al., *Anwār al-Tanzīl*, 4:138; al-Sūyūṭī et al., *Futūḥāt*, 4:362; al-Rāzī, *Al-Tafsīr al-Kabīr*, 10:566; and Ibn Kathīr, *Tafsīr*, 8:156.

[14] Ibn Kathīr, *Al-Bidāya*, 1:34–41.

[15] Bayhaqī, *Kitāb al-Asmāʾ wa-l-ṣifāt*, 389–90. This ḥadīth is also narrated with chains of transmission by Ḥākim in his well-known ḥadīth collection *al-Mustadrak ʿalā al-Ṣaḥīḥayn* and by Ṭabarī in his well-known exegesis *Jāmiʿ al-Bayān fī Tafsīr Āyi al-Qurʾān*. However, the two narrations in Bayhaqī's *Kitāb al-Asmāʾ wa al-ṣifāt* are sufficient for our ḥadīth analysis because he narrates both ḥadīths from Abū ʿAbdullah al-Ḥāfiẓ, which is the agnomen of his teacher Ḥākim, and because the narration of Ṭabarī merges with the second narration of Bayhaqī at Shuʿba, as illustrated in Figure 1.1.

[16] Al-Suyūṭī lists him as one of the ten Companions who were famous for their knowledge of Qurʾānic exegesis and narrates more praise from the Prophet and his Companions for Ibn ʿAbbās' knowledge of Qurʾānic exegesis than any of the other Companions. See al-Suyūṭī, *al-Itqān*, 2:189–90.

[17] Al-Sūyūtī, *Tadrīb*, 1:367–9.

[18] Ibid., 1:369.

[19] Al-Bayhaqī, *Kitāb al-Asmāʾ wa-l-Ṣifāt*, 390.

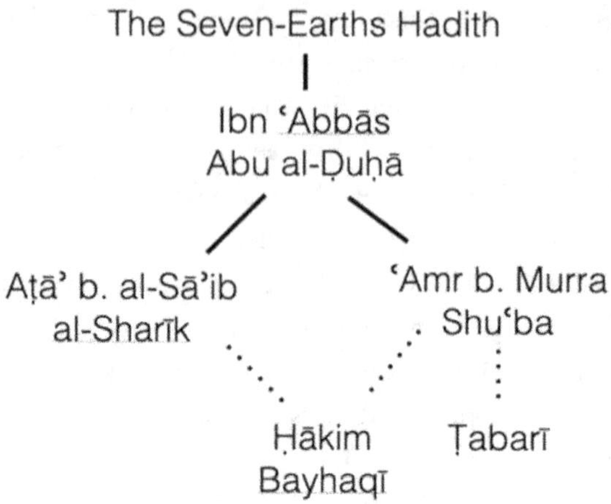


**Figure 1.1** Diagram of the chains of transmission of the seven-earths ḥadīth. The only one to narrate its strange and unfamiliar content from Ibn ʿAbbās is Abū al-Ḍuḥā. That is why Bayhaqī said it was anomalous

from Ibn ʿAbbās). In other words, Bayhaqī considers the seven-earths ḥadīth inauthentic because (1) the only one to narrate it from Ibn ʿAbbās is Abū al-Ḍuḥā and (2) the idea that there are six other Earths that are inhabited by intelligent non-human beings to whom God has sent messengers from their own species is an anomalous meaning that requires further attestation before it is can be accepted as revelatory evidence. The chains of transmission of this ḥadīth are illustrated in Figure 1.1.

Like al-Sūyūṭī, Ibn Kathīr, another prominent ḥadīth authority, confirmed Bayhaqī's judgement.[20] Ibn Ḥajar al-Haytamī, a late authority in the seminary tradition, sealed the case of its inauthenticity with the following response to a question about the meaning of the seven-earths ḥadīth:

> When it has become clear that the ḥadīth is inauthentic, that frees us from needing to figure out its meaning because subjects as religiously significant as this cannot be established with inauthentic ḥadīths.[21]

According to the Sunnī scholarly tradition, the seven-earths ḥadīth does not come from the Prophet (God bless him and give him peace), and it, therefore,

[20] He indicates his approval of Bayhaqī's judgement by relating it in his Qurʾānic exegesis without further comment, and he elaborates elsewhere that if, hypothetically, the seven-earths ḥadīth was authentically ascribed to Ibn ʿAbbās, then we would have to conclude that he learned it from Jewish and Christian sources (*isrāʾīliyyāt*) rather than from the Prophet. Ibn Kathīr, *Al-Bidāya*, 1:39; Ibn Kathīr, *Tafsīr*, 8:157.

[21] Al-Haytamī, *Al-Fatāwā al-Hadīthiyya*, 165.

cannot be used as a basis for revelatory reasoning about the existence of intelligent extraterrestrial life. And the way that the tradition reasoned to this conclusion tells us something even more. Its judgement that the ḥadīth is anomalous tells us that *there is no other revelatory statement apart from the seven-earths ḥadīth that establishes the existence of intelligent extraterrestrials.* If there were, then the ḥadīth critics would not have found the meaning of the ḥadīth to be strange and unfamiliar.

But the fact that there is no revelatory evidence for the existence of intelligent extraterrestrials does not entail that intelligent extraterrestrials don't exist. All it means is that we remain where we were when we completed our metaphysical reasoning, namely that both the existence and the non-existence of intelligent extraterrestrials are possible. As Ālūsī explains in his exegesis:

> Even though the seven-earths ḥadīth is not something that the Prophet said, if, hypothetically, it were true that non-human intelligent beings existed . . ., then [it would not conflict with metaphysical or revelatory reasoning because] neither metaphysical nor revelatory reasoning leads us to conclude that it is impossible.[22]

## Qur'ānic Verses that may suggest extraterrestrial life

As they explain Qur'ān 42:29 and Qur'ān 16:8, many exegetes go further to say that the Qur'ān may actually be suggesting that extraterrestrial life does, in fact, exist.

> And from His signs is His creation of the heavens and the earth all of the walking-creatures (*dābbah*) that He has scattered *in both of them* [i.e., in the heavens and the earth]. (Qur'ān 42:29)

The significant part of this verse is 'in both of them' because it implies the existence of walking creatures in both the Earth and the heavens. We can easily understand what it means for there to be walking creatures (*dābbah*) on Earth, but what does it mean for there to be walking creatures in the heavens? Exegetes such as al-Rāzī note that angels are not considered walking creatures because they are celestial beings, but perhaps this verse is saying that they do, in fact, walk somewhere outside of Earth. Then he puts forth another possibility, saying, 'It is not farfetched to say that He Most High has created different kinds of living

[22] Al-Ālūsī, *Rūḥ al-Ma'ānī*, 28:143.

things in the heavens that walk as humans walk on Earth.'[23] Abū al-Su'ūd echoes al-Rāzī and adds that the verse 'and He creates what you don't know'[24] may also be hinting at the existence of such extraterrestrial life.[25]

Although these are possible interpretations, the more likely interpretation, according to the Sunnī exegetes, is to eliminate the 'problem' of extraterrestrial life by:

1. Figuratively interpreting *dābbah* as 'living thing' (now the living things in the heavens are the angels), or
2. Saying that the statement 'there are walking creatures in the heavens and the earth' should be understood as 'the heavens and the earth as a whole' (now the existence of walking creatures on Earth is enough for this to be a true statement, and there is no need for there to be walking-creatures outside of Earth).[26]

Both of these interpretations are based on the assumption that intelligent extraterrestrial life does not exist. If we had scientific information on the existence of intelligent extraterrestrial life, then it is possible that, with this new piece of information, the exegetical methods of the Sunnī scholarly tradition would lead us to conclude that the verse is, in fact, referring to extraterrestrial life. This is important because it illustrates how scientific information on the existence of intelligent extraterrestrials might help us more clearly understand the theological information that we receive through the Qur'ān. I will return to this point in the third section when I summarize the findings of this chapter.

But intelligent extraterrestrials have not yet been discovered, and so we cannot yet say that these verses are, in fact, referring to them. What we can, however, conclude is that the Sunnī scholarly tradition has always been open to the possible existence of intelligent extraterrestrial life because they understand that it is revelatorily possible for intelligent extraterrestrial life to exist. And that is our second piece of theological information:

> **Theological Information 2**: It is revelatorily possible for intelligent extraterrestrials to exist and also for them not to exist.

[23] Al-Rāzī, *Al-Tafsīr al-Kabīr*, 9:599.
[24] Q. 16:8. See Moamer Khalayleh's chapter in this volume.
[25] Abū al-Su'ūd, *Irshād al-'Aql al-Salīm*, 8:32.
[26] Ibid.

## The Sunnī scholarly tradition on human specialness

But while the scholars of the Sunnī scholarly tradition affirmed that revelation is open to the possible existence of intelligent extraterrestrials, they also affirmed that human beings are the most special kind of being that God has created. The ḥadīth scholar Muḥammad ʿAbd al-Raʾūf al-Munāwī (d. 1622) wrote in his influential ḥadīth commentary:

> Allah has surely honoured the human being more than everything else that He has created: he is the cream, the quintessence, and the purpose (*al-thamara*) of the universe; He is the one for whom He has subjugated everything in the heavens and earth; and he is the greatest vicegerent. So whenever human beings purify themselves from the impurities of their souls and bodies, they are superior to the angels.[27]

And al-Kh̲aṭīb al-Shirbīnī (d. 1570) wrote in his Qurʾānic commentary:

> Ibn al-ʿArabī said, 'Allah Most High has not created anything more beautiful than the human being, for He Most High has created him as someone who is (1) alive, (2) knowledgeable, (3) powerful, (4) volitional, and as someone who (5) speaks, (6) hears, and (7) sees. This is what is expressed by his (Allah bless him and give him peace) saying, 'Verily, Allah Most High created Adam on His form.'"[28]

Al-Shirbīnī is interpreting the divine form in the ḥadīth as the seven existent attributes of God (*ṣifāt al-maʿānī*) that are mentioned in Sunnī *kalām* manuals.[29] He is saying that by giving human beings contingent 'shadows' of His own non-contingent attributes, He has enabled them to know Him and worship Him more than any other created thing, and that is the greatest honour that God can give to any of His creatures.

Because both of these scholars are prominent and widely cited in the late Sunnī scholarly tradition, their positions reflect the position of the late Sunnī scholarly tradition as a whole. Since our goal in this chapter is to ascertain the position of the late Sunnī scholarly tradition on extraterrestrial life, these citations give us our third piece of theological information about the existence of intelligent extraterrestrials:

27 Al-Munāwī, *Fayḍ al-Qadīr*, 5:380.

28 Muslim: 2612 and 2841; al-Shirbīnī, *Al-Sirāj al-Munīr*, 4:644.

29 See, for example, al-Bajūrī, *Hāshiyat al-Imām al-Bayjūrī*, 120–44. Muslim: 2612 and 2841.

> **Theological Information 3:** If intelligent extraterrestrials exist, they have been less honoured by God than human beings.

These kinds of statements are common in the Sunnī scholarly tradition, particularly in its late period.

Someone might object that these statements do not specifically mention that human beings have been honoured more than intelligent extraterrestrial life. Rather, they are general statements that were made without considering the possibility of intelligent extraterrestrial life. These kinds of absolute statements were, therefore, not intended as absolute statements but were only meant to include the kinds of beings that Sunnī scholars thought existed in those times, namely humans, jinn and angels. Subsequently, it is possible for intelligent extraterrestrial life to be more honoured than human beings.

The response to this objection is that the second section have shown that the Sunnī scholarly tradition was investigating the question of intelligent extraterrestrials centuries before the modern age, that it affirmed the possibility of their existence and that it even said that some Qur'ānic verses might be suggesting their existence. Scholars working from within the Sunnī tradition were, therefore, considering intelligent extraterrestrial life when they made such absolute statements. Thus, intelligent extraterrestrials are included in their absolute statements.

In the subsections that follow, we will glean some further theological information by delving a little deeper into some of the reasons why the Sunnī scholarly tradition made these absolute statements.

## The Qur'ān on human specialness

The Sunnī scholarly tradition's position is based on one of the central themes of the Qur'ān, namely that God has singled out human beings for His distinctive honour. Right at the beginning of the Qur'ān, God addresses human beings and tells them that He has prepared the Earth and the heavens *for you*[30] (*lakum*). Shortly afterwards, He says that He is the one who 'made everything in the earth *for you*'.[31] It repeatedly exhorts human beings to be thankful for the blessings of rain, wind, clouds, rivers, vegetation, animals, flatlands, mountains, the day, the night, the sun, the moon and the stars because all of these things have been

30 Q. 2:22.
31 Q. 2:29.

made *so that human beings might benefit from them*.[32] Everything in the universe has been made so that human beings might use it to their advantage: 'Don't you see that surely Allah has subjugated to you [to use for your benefit] *everything in the heavens and everything in the earth*, and that He has showered His blessings upon you, both outwardly and inwardly?'[33] This means that God's purpose for everything in the universe is for it to serve the interests of human beings. Any honour that anything else in the universe might have, then, is for the higher purpose of honouring human beings, and human beings have therefore been more honoured by God than anything else that He has created.

The distinctive honouring of mankind is mentioned in many other ways throughout the Qurʾān. That is why, for example, God says that He made the first human being 'with My own two hands',[34] which Sunnī exegetes have understood as a figurative expression of God's 'complete concern for his (i.e., the first human's) creation . . . which entails that he should be venerated and revered'.[35] This is also why the first human being was created in Paradise and encouraged to enjoy himself as he wished in Paradise,[36] even though other intelligent beings, such as the angels, were created to continuously worship God.[37] And that is also why, when the first human being came down from Paradise to Earth, God commanded His angels – the purest, most obedient, the most worshipful beings imaginable – to lower themselves to him in prostration.[38] The Sunnī scholarly tradition has understood these verses as an absolute honouring of human beings above all other creatures (that is where the citations in the previous section are coming from).

But someone might object that the honouring of mankind that has been mentioned in some of the verses earlier can be consistently affirmed alongside the existence of intelligent extraterrestrials that have been honoured even more. For example, the honouring of the first human being and the obligation of angels to venerate him can be consistently affirmed alongside the existence of intelligent extraterrestrials whom God has honoured even more.

That means that we have two possible interpretations. The first is the interpretation of Sunnī scholarly tradition, namely that if intelligent extraterrestrial life exists, it has not been honoured more than human beings.

32 Q. 13:3, 14:32–3, 16:5–8, 16:12, and 25:48.
33 Q. 31:20.
34 Q. 38:75.
35 Abū al-Suʿūd, *Irshād al-ʿAql al-Salīm*, 7:236.
36 Q. 2:35.
37 Q. 21:20.
38 Q. 2:34.

The second is the interpretation that is proposed in the objection, namely that if intelligent extraterrestrial life exists, it has been honoured more than human beings.

We can see which of the two interpretations is stronger by examining the rhetorical purpose of these verses. The rhetorical purpose of all of the verses that describe how much God has honoured human beings is to exhort human beings to be grateful. When humans realize how much God has honoured them, that will lead them to be grateful. And when they are grateful, that will drive them to worship Him alone. For example, right at the beginning of the Qurʾān, after describing how God prepared the Earth and the heavens for human beings to benefit from, the Qurʾān says, 'So don't set up any partner-gods with Allah.'[39] Now that we understand the rhetorical purpose, we can compare the rhetorical force of these verses in each of the two possibilities under consideration.

If the second possibility is the case (i.e. if some intelligent extraterrestrial life has been honoured more than human beings), then human beings' lower honouring will lead to less gratitude, which will lead to a relatively weaker motivation to worship God alone. If, on the other hand, the first possibility is the case (i.e. if human beings have been honoured more than all other creatures), then human beings' higher honouring will lead to more gratitude, which will lead to a stronger motivation to worship God alone. In other words, the rhetorical force of the first possibility (i.e. the interpretation of the Sunnī scholarly tradition) is stronger than the rhetorical force of the second possibility.

The Qurʾān is recognized by Muslims to be miraculously eloquent. If an exegete consistently sees the highest levels of eloquence in Qurʾānic expressions and is then faced with two interpretive possibilities for a verse, one of which has more rhetorical force than the other, then it will be reasonable for him to conclude that the interpretation with greater rhetorical force is the one that was intended. This is, in fact, an agreed-upon interpretive principle in the Sunnī scholarly tradition. Abu al-Suʿūd, for example, says, 'No one has any doubt that it is obligatory to interpret the Magnificent Expression according to the most beautiful and complete meanings.'[40]

If we apply this interpretive principle to the two interpretive possibilities that we are considering, it follows that the interpretation of the Sunnī scholarly tradition is the correct one and that the verses mentioned in this section are

[39] Q. 2:22, 14:32–4, and 16:14–22.
[40] Abū al-Suʿūd, *Irshād al-ʿAql al-Salīm*, 1:40.

theological information from the Qurʾān that no intelligent extraterrestrial life has been honoured more than human beings.[41]

## Scientific reasoning about intelligent extraterrestrials

I began this chapter by observing that the *mutakallimūn* would investigate the existence of intelligent extraterrestrials by gathering information through metaphysical reasoning, revelatory reasoning and scientific reasoning. I will now conclude this chapter by summarizing all of the theological information on extraterrestrials that has been gathered and then explaining what that means for the scientific search for intelligent extraterrestrial life. I have shown that their metaphysical and revelatory reasoning leads to the theological information that has been summarized as follows:

1. It is metaphysically possible for intelligent extraterrestrials to exist and also for them not to exist.
2. It is revelatorily possible for intelligent extraterrestrials to exist and also for them to not exist.
3. If intelligent extraterrestrials exist, they have been less honoured by God than human beings.

This theological information tells us two things about the scientific search for extraterrestrials. First, Islamic theology affirms that it is possible for intelligent extraterrestrials to exist but that there is no revelatory information that either confirms or denies their existence. The theological qualification of intelligent extraterrestrials being less special than human beings (should they exist) is purely revelatory information that can neither be confirmed nor denied by science. Therefore, whether intelligent extraterrestrials exist is a purely scientific question, and Islamic theological information cannot conflict with any scientific information on this topic. Second, we do not yet have any scientific information on the actual existence or non-existence of intelligent extraterrestrials. But if we ever discover this information, it will give us more accurate theological information from Q. 42:29 and Q. 16:8. That means that the gathering of scientific

[41] The distinctive honouring of human beings by God requires a more detailed and nuanced argument that relates that distinctive honouring to the disagreement among the *mutakallimūn* over the relative superiority of humans and angels, as well as the scholarly consensus over the fact that the Prophet Muhammad (God bless him and give him peace) is the best of creation (see: al-Laqānī, *Hidāyat al-Murīd*, 1:747 and 2:782–4). That discussion has been postponed to a future dedicated article on the detailed revelatory argument for the uniqueness of human beings among God's creation.

information on the existence or non-existence of intelligent extraterrestrials is not just theologically neutral, but it may even be theologically useful.

## Bibliography


Abū al-Suʿūd, Muḥammad ibn Muḥammad. *Irshād al-ʿAql al-Salīm ilā Mazāyā al-Qurʾān al-Karīm*. Lebanon: Dār Iḥyāʾ al-Turāth al-ʿArabī, n.d.

Al-Ālūsī, Abu al-Faḍl Maḥmūd. *Rūḥ al-Maʿānī*. Beirut: Idārat al-Ṭibāʿa al-Munīriyya, n.d.

Al-Bajūrī, Ibrāhīm. *Hāshiyat al-Imām al-Bayjūrī ʿalā Jawharat al-Tawḥīd*. Cairo: Dār al-Salām, 2002.

Al-Bayḍāwī, ʿAbdulla ibn ʿUmar and Abū al-Faḍl al-Kāzarūnī. *Anwār al-Tanzīl wa-Asrār al-Taʾwīl wa-bi-Hāmishihī Hāshiyat al-Kāzarūnī*. Beirut: Dār al-Fikr, n.d.

Al-Bayhaqī, Abū Bakr Aḥmad ibn al-Ḥusayn. *Kitāb al-Asmāʾ wa-l-Ṣifāt*. Lebanon: Dār Iḥyāʾ al-Turāth al-ʿArabī, n.d.

Al-Ghumārī, ʿAbdulla ibn al-Ṣiddīq. *Dalālat al-Qurʾān al-mubīn ʿalā anna al-Nabī Afḍal al-ʿĀlamīn*. Palestine: al-Markaz al-Waṭanī li-l-Buhūth wa-l-Dirāsāt al-Tābiʿ li-l-Bayt, 2016.

Al-Haytamī, Aḥmad ibn Ḥajar. *al-Durr al-Manḍūd fī al-Ṣalāt wa-l-Salām ʿalā Ṣāhib al-Maqām al-Maḥmūd*. Beirut: Dār al-Kutub al-ʿIlmiyya, 2002.

Al-Haytamī, Aḥmad ibn Ḥajar. *Al-Fatāwā al-Ḥadīthiyya*. Cairo: Mustafā Bābī al-Halabī, 1989.

Al-Haytamī, Aḥmad ibn Ḥajar. *Al-ʿUmda fī Sharḥ al-Burda*. UAE: Dār al-Faqīh, 2005.

Al-Haytamī, Aḥmad ibn Ḥajar. *Mablagh al-Arab fī Fakhr al-ʿArab*. Beirut: Dār al-Kutub al-ʿIlmiyya, 1990.

Al-Ijī, ʿAḍud al-Dīn ʿAbd al-Rahmān. *Al-Mawāqif fī ʿIlm al-Kalām*. Beirut: ʿĀlam al-Kutub, n.d.

Al-ʿIrāqī, ʿAbd al-Raḥīm ibn al-Ḥusayn. *Maḥajjat al-ʿArab ilā Maḥabbat al-ʿArab*. Riyad: Dār al-ʿĀṣima, n.d.

Al-ʿIzz ibn ʿAbd al-Salām. *Bidāyat al-Sūl fī Tafḍīl al-Rasūl*. Damascus: Dār al-Fikr al-Muʿāṣir, 1999.

Al-Laqānī, Burhān al-Dīn Ibrāhīm. *Hidāyat al-Murīd li-Jawharat al-Tawḥīd*. Cairo: Dār al-Basāʾir, 2009.

Al-Munāwī, Muḥammad ʿAbd al-Raʾūf. *Fayḍ al-Qadīr Sharḥ al-Jāmiʿ al-Ṣaghīr min Aḥādīth al-Bashīr al-Nadhīr*. Beirut: Dar al-Kutub al-ʿIlmiyya, 2006.

Al-Qunawī, Ibn al-Tamjīd and al-Bayḍāwī. *Hāshiyat al-Qunawī ʿalā tafsīr al-Bayḍāwī wa-bi-Hāmishihī Hāshiyat ibn al-Tamjīd*. Istanbul: Al-Maktaba al-Maḥmūdīyya, n.d.

Al-Rāzī, Fakhr al-Dīn. *Al-Tafsīr al-Kabīr li-l-Imām al-Fakhr al-Rāzī*. Lebanon: Dār Iḥyāʾ al-Turāth al-ʿArabī, 2001.

Al-Shirbīnī. *Al-Sirāj al-Munīr fī al-ʿĀnati ʿalā Maʿrifa baʿḍ Maʿānī Kalām Rabbinā al-Ḥakīm al-Khabīr*. Beirut: Dar al-Kutub al-ʿIlmiyya, 2004.

Al-Sūyūṭī, Jalāl al-Dīn ʿAbd al-Rahmān. *Al-Itqān fī ʿulūm al-Qurʾān*. Beirut: Dār al-Nadwa al-Jadīda, n.d.

Al-Sūyūṭī, Jalāl al-Dīn ʿAbd al-Rahmān. *Tadrīb al-Rāwī fī Sharḥ Taqrīb al-Nawāwī*. Riyad: Dār al-ʿĀsima, 2003.

Al-Sūyūṭī, Jalāl al-Dīn ʿAbd al-Rahmā, Jalāl al-Dīn al-Maḥallī and Sulaymān ibn ʿUmar al-Jamal. *Al-Futūḥāt al-Ilāhīyya bi Tawḍīḥ tafsīr al-Jalālayn li-l-Daqāʾiq al-Khafīyya*. Beirut: Dār al-Fikr, n.d.

Al-Taftāzānī, Masʿūd ibn ʿUmar et al. *Sharḥ al-ʿAllāma al-Muḥaqqiq al-Ḥabr al-Fahhāma al-Mudaqqiq Saʿd al-Dīn ʿalā al-ʿAqāʾid al-Nasafiyya*. Cairo: al-Maktaba al-Azhariyya li-l-Turāth, n.d.

Ibn al-Subkī, ʿAbd al-Wahhāb and ʿAbdulla ibn ʿUmar al-Bayḍāwī. *Al-Ibhāj fī Sharḥ al-Minhāj*. Mecca: al-Maktaba al-Makkiyya, n.d.

Ibn Kathīr, Abu al-Fidāʾ Ismāʿīl. *Al-Bidāya wa-l-Nihāya*. Damascus: Dār Ibn Kathīr, 2013.

Ibn Kathīr, Abu al-Fidāʾ Ismāʿīl. *Tafsīr al-Qurʾān al-ʿAẓīm*. Riyad: Dār Ṭayba li-l-Nashr wa-l-Tawzīʿ, 1999.

Karamali, Hamza. *The Madrasa Curriculum in Context*. Abu Dhabi: Kalam Research and Media, 2017.

Muslim ibn al-Hajjāj. *Saḥīḥ Muslim*. Riyad: Dār al-Salām, 1999.

Ramaḍān, al-Kastalī and al-Khayālī. *Al-Majmūʿa al-Saniyya ʿalā Sharḥ al-ʿAqāʾid al-Nasafiyya*. Lebanon: Dār al-Nūr al-Sabāḥ, 2012.

2

# Does the Qur'ān affirm extraterrestrial life?

## A hermeneutic analysis of Sūrat al-Naḥl (Q. 16:8)

Moamer Khalayleh

## Introduction

Given recent developments in modern astronomy, scientists may be able to answer the question of the existence of extraterrestrial life in the not-too-distant future. It may no longer be a hypothetical discussion in exegetical studies. Considering the relevance of this issue, the scriptural compatibility of the existence of life outside of Earth is one that necessitates theological study as it has many religious implications. For example, one of the primary reasons some Muslims leave Islam is a perceived incompatibility between modern science and revelatory claims in the Qur'ān or ḥadīth tradition.[1] This epistemological doubt means a rejection of the belief that the Qur'ān is of divine origin and, as a result, an epistemological source of objective truth about the world. If the Qur'ān claims to be the word of the necessarily existent Creator of the universe, then there should be no discrepancies between statements made in it about the natural world and reality. Whether the Qur'ān affirms or denies the existence of life outside Earth is, therefore, a relevant topic of inquiry.

In the Islamic ontology of species, the scope of intelligent life is said to be comprised of angels, jinn and humans.[2] Beyond these three, the topic of extraterrestrial life was not previously discussed in theological discourse due to limitations in scientific understanding. With concrete empirical evidence suggesting the existence of multiple planets beyond our own, and the promise of further advancements in the study of exoplanets, it is important to study scriptural sources to ascertain their compatibility with the potentiality of life beyond Earth.

[1] Cottee, *The Apostates*, 31–2.

[2] Murata and Chittick, *The Vision of Islam*, 98, 102, and 270–1.

At the end of a verse in Q.16:8 is an ambiguous statement which may indicate the possibility of the existence of extraterrestrial life: 'horses, mules, and donkeys for you to ride and use for show, and other things you know nothing about'. The end of this verse – 'and other things you know nothing about' – is the part that is of exegetical interest in relation to extraterrestrial life. To understand the meaning of this phrase, this chapter analyses and compares ten major exegetical works in Sunnī Islam to determine the possible interpretations of this verse. There are five interpretations of the statement 'and other things you know nothing about'. The most widely accepted takes the verse at face value as an open declarative statement with no qualifications: that God has made creatures that human beings have no knowledge of, independent of where or when they may have been created. A second opinion suggests the verse is alluding to life on Earth, including land and sea creatures. Other opinions appeal to the traditions of the Prophet Muḥammad and make more specific interpretations. The first is that the verse refers to God's creations in Paradise and Hellfire. Another suggests that the beings indicated are angels created in the heavens. Of the more extraordinary interpretations are those which reference a ḥadīth attributed to the Prophet Muḥammad in which he states that there exist sentient creatures a great distance away who know not that God is disobeyed, meaning that they have no concept of sin, nor are they aware of the existence of Adam or Iblīs (Satan). The ḥadīth does not specify a location nor whether they are of Adamic origin. The authenticity of this ḥadīth is dubious because of its weak transmission history. A significant conclusion of this study is that of all the interpretations under consideration, none deny the possibility of the existence of extraterrestrial life.

The structure of this chapter is organized as follows. It begins by elucidating the theological significance of the topic of the possible existence of extraterrestrial life. Subsequently, the methodology of study of the verse is explained. This is followed by an exposition of five distinct interpretations. Finally, there is a discussion of Fakhr al-Dīn al-Rāzī's opinion on the topic of extraterrestrial life.

## Religious significance

Sunnī Islam's conception of God is that of a necessarily existent, omnipotent and omniscient Creator and sustainer of the universe.[3] Muslims also hold, as a

[3] Al-Bājūrī, *Tuḥfat al-Murīd*, 104–13.

tenet of faith, that the Qur'ān is the unaltered word of God.[4] Additionally, any statements soundly attributed to the Prophet Muḥammad are also accepted as a secondary source of revelatory knowledge and play a central role in Qur'ānic exegetical studies.[5] The ḥadīth corpus encapsulates the prophetic traditions.[6] The Sunnī exegetical tradition, as described by Ghazālī in his *Fayṣal al-Tafriqa Bayna al-Islam wa-l-Zandaqa* (*On the Boundaries of Theological Tolerance in Islam*), assumes a literal meaning to scripture as a first assumption unless there is sufficient reason to justify other types of interpretation, such as a figurative reading of the text.[7] Were Muslims able to assume other than literal meanings to scripture as a default position, it would render any claims in the Qur'ān regarding the existence of extraterrestrial life to be of little importance, since they may always be interpreted as allegorical.

The mainstream Qur'ānic exegetical tradition also affirms and assumes an exoteric (non-allegorical) interpretation as a general rule.[8] Therefore, any information found in the Qur'ān or any soundly attributed statement in the ḥadīth tradition regarding the existence (or lack thereof) of extraterrestrial life should reflect reality.[9]

Due to continual and rapid advances in the fields of astronomy and astrobiology, it is becoming evident that the question of whether human beings are alone in the universe could be answered within our lifetimes.[10] One such example is the recently deployed James Webb Space Telescope (JWST) which offers humanity a technological leap that may provide some important clues to the existence of life outside of Earth.[11] Since the discovery of the first exoplanets in the early 1990s, scientists have since detected more than 5,000 planets outside of our solar system. Many of these are rocky planets much like our own and within the habitable zone of their host stars.[12] Through an analysis of the light passing through their atmospheres, it is possible to find evidence of gases and molecules, such as carbon, methane and water, that are important biological signatures for life. A recent study even suggests that it may be possible to detect

[4] Ibid., 160.
[5] Abdul-Raof, *Schools of Qur'ānic Exegesis Genesis and Development*, 33; Brown, *Ḥadīth*, 3.
[6] Ibid.
[7] Ghazālī, *Fayṣal al-Tafriqa*, 61–6.
[8] Abdul-Raof, *Schools of Qur'ānic Exegesis Genesis and Development*, 14.
[9] Ibid.
[10] Tillman, 'We'll Find Alien Life'.
[11] Brenon, 'Can We Find Life?'
[12] Christiansen, 'Five Thousand Exoplanets'.

the presence of artificial light from exoplanets, which may indicate the existence of sentient life.[13]

Scientific advances demonstrate that the question of the existence of extraterrestrial life may no longer be a hypothetical discussion in exegetical studies. On the contrary, it is an issue that should be of great import to people of faith, Muslims included. An exploration of these ideas according to Sunnī interpretative methods on whether the Qur'ān affirms or denies the existence of life outside Earth is, therefore, a relevant topic of scholarly inquiry. After all, modern scientific theories and discoveries have had a profound impact on religious beliefs throughout the centuries.[14] Whereas a few decades ago, an in-depth discussion about what scripture informs us about alien life could have been dismissed as a frivolous pursuit, it is certainly no longer the case.

## The verse in context (Q. 16:8)

Before exploring the interpretation of the verse, it is useful to look at the context in which it is found. The statement under discussion is located in the Chapter of the Bee (*Sūrat al-Naḥl*), which also has the name, the Chapter of Blessings (*Sūrat al-Niʿam*).[15]

> He created the heavens and earth for a true purpose, and He is far above whatever they join with Him! He created man from a drop of fluid, and yet man openly challenges Him. And livestock – He created them too. You derive warmth and other benefits from them: you get food from them; you find beauty in them when you bring them home to rest and when you drive them out to pasture. They carry your loads to lands you yourselves could not reach without great hardship – truly your Lord is kind and merciful – *horses, mules, and donkeys for you to ride and use for show, and other things you know nothing about*. God points out the right path, for some paths lead the wrong way: if He wished, He could guide you all.[16]

We can see that the verse comes after a long passage on the signs of God in creation, with a particular focus on living creatures, both human and animal.

13 Loeb, 'Detection technique'.
14 The theory of evolution is a prime example of this. For an Islamic perspective on the topic, see Malik, 'Islam and Evolution'.
15 Al-Biqāʿī, *Naẓm al-Durar*, 4:243.
16 Q. 16:4-10.

The benefits of animals as a source of food, clothing and means of transport are listed and pointed to as signs and blessings from God.

The verse is unique in that it is perhaps the most comprehensive statement that may be related to the topic of life outside of Earth. As we will see, Qur'ānic exegesis will use other parts of the Qur'ān as a source of interpretation. The ḥadīth is also employed as a second source of interpretation. A general statement in one surah may be qualified in another. Ḥadīths may also be used to qualify, explain and delineate commandments, set certain conditions or specify particular propositions in the Qur'ān.[17] Outside of revelatory knowledge, linguistic analysis may be utilized. For the reasons mentioned earlier, it remains useful to explore this one verse in the Qur'ān since such a general statement will include in its interpretation other verses in the Qur'ān and ḥadīth. If there are clear exceptions, examples or qualifications in scripture, then collectively, we should expect that scholars will include them in their interpretations. In other words, we should find that exegetes will incorporate any relevant information on the meaning of a given verse in their works.

## Methodology survey of ten major exegetical works in Sunnī Islam

The study of the verse will reference ten classic exegetical works in Sunnī Islam, spanning over 600 years of scholarship. In more concise books of interpretation, scholars will often mention the most dominant interpretation of the given verse, while in lengthier works, authors include multiple possible interpretations and will usually indicate what they view as the strongest opinion. Normally, that would be the opinion of the majority of exegetes (*al-jumhūr*). The exegeses consulted in this study are summarized in Table 2.1.

As mentioned earlier, there are five possible interpretations of Q. 16:8 mentioned and discussed by these scholars. Most will mention more than one opinion, and most affirm the first position as the most likely. The following sections will explain these interpretations and how they may or may not relate to extraterrestrial life.

[17] For example, the Qur'ān gives a general injunction to Muslims to pray but does not provide instructions on the method of prayer. These particulars are found in the ḥadīth tradition. See al-Dhahabī, *Al-Tafsīr wa-l-Mufasirūn*, 1:31–7.

**Table 2.1** A Summary of Interpretations for Q. 16:8

| Interpretation of Q. 16:8 | Referenced Exegete |
|---|---|
| An open statement without qualifications | ʿAbd Allāh ibn Aḥmad al-Nasafī, ʿAlī ibn Muḥammad al-Māwardī, Muḥammad ibn Muḥammad Abū al-Suʿūd, Muḥammad ibn Aḥmad al-Qurṭubī, ʿAbd Allāh ibn ʿUmar al-Bayḍāwī, Jalāludīn al-Maḥallī and Jalāludīn al-Sayūṭī (al-Jalālayn), Burhān al-Dīn al-Biqāʿī, Fakhr al-Dīn al-Rāzī, and Sharaf al-Dīn al-Ṭībī[a] |
| Life on earth | Muḥammad ibn Aḥmad al-Qurṭubī and al-Ḥusayn ibn Masʿūd al-Baghawī[b] |
| Paradise and Hellfire | Abū al-Suʿūd, al-Bayḍāwī, al-Ṭībī, and al-Ḥusayn ibn Masʿūd al-Baghawī.[c] |
| Angels | Fakhr al-Dīn al-Rāzī, Muḥammad ibn Muḥammad Abū al-Suʿūd, Muḥammad ibn Aḥmad al-Qurṭubī, and ʿAlī ibn Muḥammad al-Māwardī.[d] |
| Sentient creatures | Fakhr al-Dīn al-Rāzī, Muḥammad ibn Muḥammad Abū al-Suʿūd, Muḥammad ibn Aḥmad al-Qurṭubī, and ʿAlī ibn Muḥammad al-Māwardī.[e] |

[a] Al-Biqāʿī, *Naẓm al-Durar*, 4:247; al-Maḥalli and al-Suyūṭī, *Tafsīr al-Jalālayn*, 2:284; al-Nasafī, *Tafsīr al-Nasafī*, 2:204; Al-Rāzī, *Al-Tafsīr al-Kabīr*, 19:236; al-Bayḍāwī, *Anwār al-Tanzīl*, 2:253; al-Māwardī, *Al-Nukat wa-l-ʿUyūn*, 3:180; Abū al-Suʿūd, *Irshād al-ʿAql al-Salīm*, 3:338; al-Qurṭubī, *Al-Jāmiʿ li-Aḥkām al-Qurʾān*, 12:288; al-Ṭībī, *Futūḥ al-Ghayb*, 9:86.

[b] Al-Qurṭubī, *Al-Jāmiʿ li-Aḥkām al-Qurʾān*, 12:288; al-Baghawī, *Tafsīr al-Baghawī*, 5:11.

[c] Al-Ṭībī, *Futūḥ al-Ghayb*, 9:87; Abū al-Suʿūd, *Irshād al-ʿAql al-Salīm*, 3:339; al-Bayḍāwī, *Anwār al-Tanzīl*, 2:253; al-Baghawī, *Tafsīr al-Baghawī*, 5:11.

[d] Abū al-Suʿūd, *Irshād al-ʿAql al-Salīm*, 3:339; al-Rāzī, *Al-Tafsīr al-Kabīr*, 19:236; al-Qurṭubī, *Al-Jāmiʿ li-Aḥkām al-Qurʾān*, 12:288–9; al-Māwardī, *Al-Nukat wa-l-ʿUyūn*, 3:180.

[e] Ibid.

## Interpretation 1: An open statement without qualification

This interpretation is mentioned in nine of the ten works.[18] The most widely accepted interpretation takes the verse at face value as a general declarative statement with no mention of any qualifications: that God has created entities that human beings have no knowledge of independent of what, where or when they may have been created. Al-Qurṭubī offers a concise interpretation by stating,

[18] These are al-Nasafī, al-Māwardī, Abū al-Suʿūd, al-Qurṭubī, al-Bayḍāwī, al-Jalālayn, al-Biqāʿī, al-Rāzī and al-Ṭībī. This position is mentioned by some scholars explicitly, such as Al-Māwardī or al-Bayḍāwī, who say that what is meant is that God created from creation (*min al-khalq*) that which we have no knowledge of. Qurṭubī and Al-Māwardī also state that this is the dominant opinion of scholars. Other scholars hold this position but mention it implicitly, such as al-Rāzī saying that God has created creatures that we are unable to fully know and comprehend. See al-Biqāʿī, *Naẓm al-Durar*, 4:247; al-Maḥalli and al-Suyūṭī, *Tafsīr al-Jalālayn*, 2:284; al-Nasafī, *Tafsīr al-Nasafī*, 2:204; al-Rāzī, *Al-Tafsīr al-Kabīr*, 19:236; al-Bayḍāwī, *Anwār al-Tanzīl*, 2:253; al-Māwardī, *Al-Nukat wa-l-ʿUyūn*, 3:180; Abū al-Suʿūd, *Irshād al-ʿAql al-Salīm*, 3:338; al-Qurṭubī, *Al-Jāmiʿ li-Aḥkām al-Qurʾān*, 12:288; al-Ṭībī, *Futūḥ al-Ghayb*, 9:86.

**Table 2.2** Referenced Exegetical Works

| Exegete | Date of Death | Name of Exegesis |
|---|---|---|
| ʿAlī ibn Muḥammad al-Māwardī | 1058 | *Al-Nukat Wal-ʿUyūn Fī Tafsīr al-Qurʾān (The Points and Sources of the Exegesis of the Qur'an)* |
| Al-Ḥusayn ibn Masʿūd al-Baghawī | 1122 | *Maʿālim al-Tanzīl* (*The Landmarks of Revelation*) |
| Fakhr al-Dīn al-Rāzī | 1210 | *Mafātīḥ al-Ghayb* (*Keys to the Unseen*) |
| Muḥammad ibn Aḥmad al-Qurṭubī | 1273 | *Al-Jāmiʿ li-Aḥkām al-Qurʾān* (*The Compendium of Qur'ānic Rulings*) |
| ʿAbd Allāh ibn Aḥmad al-Nasafī | 1310 | *Madārik al-Tanzīl wa-Ḥaqāʾiq al-Taʾwīl (The Meanings of Revelation and the Realities of Interpretation)* |
| ʿAbd Allāh ibn ʿUmar al-Bayḍāwī | 1319 | *Anwār al-Tanzīl wa-Asrār al-Taʾwīl (The Lights of Revelation and the Secrets of Interpretation)* |
| Sharaf al-Dīn al-Ṭībī | 1342 | *Fatuḥ al-Ghayb fī al-Kashf ʿan Qanāʿ al-Rayb (Ḥāshiya al-Ṭībī ʿalā al-Kashshāf) (The Opening of the Unseen in Unveiling the Ambiguity (the commentary by al-Ṭībī on al-Kashshāf))* |
| Burhān al-Dīn al-Biqāʿī | 1480 | *Naẓm al-Durar fī Tanāsub al-Āyāt wa-l-Suwar (The Arrangement of Pearls Regarding the Harmony of Verses and Chapters [of the Qurʾān])* |
| Jalāludīn al-Maḥallīand Jalāludīn al-Sayūṭī | 1460/1505 | *Tafsīr al-Jalālayn* (*The Commentary of the Two Jalāls*) |
| Abū al-Suʿūd | 1574 | *Irshād al-ʿAql al-Salīm* (*Guidance of the Sound Mind*) |

'The majority [of scholars] said: [it is] from the creation.' Al-Bayḍāwī elaborates further by saying, 'And it may be to inform [people] that He [Allah] has from the creation that which is unknown to us.' And al-Nasafī also says, 'And He created from His creatures species that you do not know.'[19]

The existence of living beings is not specified at a particular place or at a particular time. The verse could apply to Earth or to other planets, be they in other solar systems, galaxies or realms of existence beyond empirical observation. This interpretation is the most comprehensive and does not contradict any of

[19] Ibid.

the other interpretations discussed by scholars; rather, it includes them all. If we take this opinion as is and if there is no other scriptural information that conveys to us the scope of what God has created, then it would be fallacious to deny the possible existence of extraterrestrial life. Indeed, it would be necessary to take a stance of theological non-commitment on the matter, a term in Islamic theological exegesis called *tawaqquf*.[20] This position follows logically from the idea that the absence of evidence is not to be confused with evidence of absence.[21] It would be presumptuous to assume that if revelation does not discuss life outside of Earth that it does not exist.

## Interpretation 2: Life on Earth

The second opinion holds that the verse is referring to living creatures on Earth, including land and sea animals. This interpretation is mentioned by al-Qurṭubī and al-Baghawī.[22] They narrate an opinion that this position is alluding to insects and vermin living deep underground and in the oceans that humans have never seen nor heard of.[23] Al-Baghawī quotes Qatāda, an early scholar and exegete, who says, 'which means weevils in plants and worms in fruits'.[24] Meaning that the living things which we are not aware of refer to weevils in plants and worms found in fruit. Al-Qurṭubī gives a broader interpretation by saying that the end of the verse means, '[from] among the types of insects and creatures in the depths of the earth, land, and sea, which humans have not seen or heard of'.[25] This understanding, while referring specifically to life on Earth, does not repudiate the possibility of life elsewhere. Interestingly, the interpretation has held up quite well.[26] Scientists are continually discovering new species, with some estimating up to 18,000 new species discovered annually. It is also noteworthy, given Qatāda's reference to insects, that there is an inverse correlation between the size and the diversity of animals discovered. There are a greater variety of living creatures as they get smaller and new species are being found every year.[27]

20 See David Solomon Jalajel's chapter in this volume; Zaʿatra, 'Maʿnā al-Tawaqquf ʿinda al-Usuliyyīn'; Malik, 'Islam and Evolution', 251–5.
21 See David Solomon Jalajel's chapter in this volume.
22 Al-Qurṭubī, *Al-Jāmiʿ li-Aḥkām al-Qurʾān*, 12:288; al-Baghawī, *Tafsīr al-Baghawī*, 5:11.
23 Al-Qurṭubī, *Al-Jāmiʿ li-Aḥkām al-Qurʾān*, 12:288.
24 Al- Baghawī, *Tafsīr al-Baghawī*, 5:11
25 Al-Qurṭubī, *Al-Jāmiʿ li-Aḥkām al-Qurʾān*, 12:288.
26 Josh Davis, 'Museum Scientists Described 351 New Species in 2022'; Science Museum of Virginia, 'How Many Species Are Left to Be Discovered?'; Conniff, 'How Many Species Can We Find Before They Disappear Forever?'
27 Ibid.

## Interpretation 3: Paradise and Hellfire

The third opinion holds that the verse refers to creations in Paradise and Hellfire. This interpretation is mentioned by five scholars: Abū al-Suʿūd, al-Bayḍāwī, al-Ṭībī, al-Qurṭubī and al-Baghawī.[28] This position is evidenced by Qurʾānic and ḥadīth statements that attest to the unknown nature of the blessings created for believers in Paradise. Al-Qurṭubī states:

> And it is said: 'And He creates what you do not know', among what Allah has prepared in Paradise for its people and in Hellfire for its people, of what the eye has not seen, the ear has not heard, and has not occurred to the human heart.[29]

Abū al-Suʿūd likewise says, 'He creates for you in Paradise other blessings besides what has been mentioned of worldly blessings, that which you do not know, meaning that which is not within your capacity to know.'[30]This opinion refers to a famous ḥadīth that states that God has prepared for his righteous servants what 'which no eye has seen, no ear has heard, and it has never crossed the mind of man'.[31] The Qurʾān also mentions this explicitly in the verse: 'Now no person knows what delights of the eye are kept hidden (in reserve) for them – as a reward for their (good) deeds.'[32]

According to Islamic theology, Paradise and Hellfire are, respectively, existent places of perpetual reward and punishment in the afterlife.[33] Those who believe and do good works are people of Paradise, and those who disbelieve and sow corruption on Earth will be people of Hellfire. The Qurʾān and ḥadīth traditions describe both abodes in detail, with much being said about the physical and spiritual pleasures of Paradise and the torment of the Hellfire.[34] Ultimately, as we have seen in the traditions quoted earlier, the true nature of these abodes is beyond human comprehension, and the verse may be referring to the creations of God therein.

## Interpretation 4: Angels

In the Islamic tradition, belief in angels is an article of faith. They are understood to be subtle bodies, meaning unseen, made of light.[35] They are neither male

28 Al-Ṭībī, *Futūḥ al-Ghayb*, 9:87; Abū al-Suʿūd, *Irshād al-ʿAql al-Salīm*, 3:339; Al-Bayḍāwī, *Anwār al-Tanzīl*, 2:253; al-Baghawī, *Tafsīr al-Baghawī*, 5:11; al-Qurṭubī, *Al-Jāmiʿ li-Aḥkām al-Qurʾān*, 12:288.
29 Al-Qurṭubī, *Al-Jāmiʿ li-Aḥkām al-Qurʾān*, 12:288.
30 Abū al-Suʿūd, *Irshād al-ʿAql al-Salīm*, 3:339.
31 Ibn Mājah et al., *English Translation of Sunan Ibn Mājah*, 5:416.
32 (Q. 32:17).
33 Al-Bayjūrī, *Tuḥfat al-Murīd*, 298–300.
34 Ibid.
35 Ibid., 217–18.

nor female, though they may take the form of human beings. Angels are living creatures that are pure and sinless, according to Islamic belief.[36] They do not eat or sleep and reside both in the heavens and on Earth.[37] Muslims believe that angels are bound to do God's command and serve a variety of functions, including the worship and contemplation of God, the recording of human actions, guarding over people and the taking of souls at death, to name but a few. A number of angels are named or described in the Qur'ān, including Gabriel, the angel who brings divine revelation to prophets, Harūt and Marūt, and Isrāphīl, who blows the trumpet to bring about the day of resurrection.[38]

The fourth interpretation says that the verse refers to angels created in the heavens and is mentioned by four scholars: al-Rāzī, Abū al-Suʿūd, al-Qurṭubī and al-Māwardī.[39] This opinion is taken from a narration attributed to ʿAbd Allah ibn ʿAbbās (d. 687), a companion of the Prophet Muḥammad and an authority on Qur'ānic exegesis, who says:

> On the right of the throne is a river of light as large as the seven heavens, the seven earths and the seven seas. Gabriel, peace be upon him, enters it before dawn and bathes therein. He increases in light in addition to his own light and beauty upon his own beauty. Then he shudders, and God creates from every drop that falls from his feathers so and so thousand angels, seventy thousand of whom enter into the Bayt al-Maʿmūr, and in the Kaaba, another seventy thousand who do not return to them until the day of judgement.[40]

Al-Rāzī, Abū al-Suʿūd, al-Qurṭubī and al-Māwardī all reference the earlier ḥadīth nearly verbatim with little commentary afterwards. It should be noted that while this statement is not attributed to the Prophet Muḥammad, but rather one of his companions, scholars will often treat such narrations as though they came from the Prophet Muḥammad.[41] This is because the information that is conveyed is narrated by a companion, who is considered a trustworthy source, and the information could only be known through prophetic revelation. They conclude that if a companion of the Prophet provides such knowledge, then he must have heard it from the Prophet Muḥammad directly or have heard from another companion who narrated the information from the Prophet

[36] Murata and Chittick, *The Vision of Islam*, 174–9.
[37] Ibid.
[38] Ibid., 87.
[39] Abū al-Suʿūd, *Irshād al-ʿAql al-Salīm*, 3:339; al-Rāzī, *Al-Tafsīr al-Kabīr*, 19:236; al-Qurṭubī, *Al-Jāmiʿ li-Aḥkām al-Qur'ān*, 12:288–9; al-Māwardī, *Al-Nukat wa-l-ʿUyūn*, 3:180.
[40] Al-Rāzī, *Al-Tafsīr al-Kabīr*, 19:236.
[41] Jalajel, *Islam and Biological Evolution*, 25–30.

Muḥammad.[42] Another opinion is that the companions narrate opinions from Jewish and Christian sources, named the *Isrā'īlīyāt*, which would relegate the statement as speculative.[43] It would be impossible to attribute the statement to the Prophet Muḥammad. A third opinion is a more nuanced approach which will only consider matters of legal opinion as those of definite prophetic origin, whereas other narrations regarding the unseen or past history may have been taken from *Isrā'īlīyāt*.[44] Regardless, this hadith demonstrates that the verse, if it is referring to angels, does not exclude the possibility of the existence of other living beings created by God.

## Interpretation 5: Sentient creatures

This interpretation is mentioned by al-Qurṭubī and al-Māwardī.[45] It is of the more extraordinary interpretations which reference a ḥadīth attributed to the Prophet Muḥammad.

> The Prophet (peace be upon him) said: 'It is a white land, the journey of the sun over it is thirty days, and it is inhabited by a creation who does not know that Allah the Most High is disobeyed on earth.' They asked: 'O Messenger of Allah, are they from the descendants of Adam?' He replied: 'They do not know that Allah created Adam.' They asked: 'O Messenger of Allah, where is Iblis among them?' He replied: 'They do not know that Allah created Iblis.' Then he recited the verse: 'And He creates that which you do not know'.[46]

Here the Prophet says that the end of verse, 'And He creates that which you do not know', is referring to a white land filled with living beings, in which the sun travels across its sky for thirty days.[47] He states that these sentient creatures know not that God is disobeyed and they know not of Adam or Iblis (Satan).[48] We can suppose that the companions of the Prophet listening to this also assumed that the Prophet was talking about sentient creatures because they asked if they were human beings, to which the Prophet answered in the negative, denying that they even had knowledge of who Adam, the first human being, was.

The ḥadīth does not specify a location; rather, it describes it. The phrase in the ḥadīth 'the journey of the sun over it is thirty days' has been interpreted to

[42] Ibid; 'Itr, *'Ulūm al-Qur'ān*, 75; Sirāj al-Dīn, *Sharḥ al-Manẓūma*, 72–6.
[43] Jalajel, *Islam and Biological Evolution*, 25–30.
[44] Ibid.
[45] Al-Qurṭubī, *Al-Jāmi' li-Aḥkām al-Qur'ān*, 12:289; al-Māwardī, *Al-Nukat wa-l-'Uyūn*, 3:181.
[46] Al-Qurṭubī, *Al-Jāmi' li-Aḥkām al-Qur'ān*, 12:289.
[47] Ibid.
[48] Ibid.

mean that a day lasts for thirty of our days.[49] This is certainly a compelling ḥadīth in that it demonstrates at least the possibility that the location in question may be extraterrestrials. It is common knowledge in modern astronomy that there are countless other planets outside of our solar system, each rotating at different speeds around their own axes. It is, therefore, highly probable that there exist planets with days that are in length many times the length of one day on Earth.

While it would be easy to get carried away with such a narration as a compelling sign that there are extraterrestrials affirmed in Islamic scripture, the authenticity of this ḥadīth is dubious because of its weak chain of transmission. Several sources claim the ḥadīth is, in fact, fabricated and not attributable to the Prophet Muḥammad. Additionally, Qurṭubī is of the opinion that it may be referring to a place beyond Andalusia to the West, perhaps across the Atlantic Ocean. His evidence for this is another ḥadīth of undetermined origins, which he says refers to the same people.[50]

Abu Nuʿaym al-Isfahānī, scholar and hagiographer, relates a similar ḥadīth in his book *Adornment of the Saints and the Ranks of the Elite* (*Ḥilyat al-Awliyāʾ wa-Ṭabaqāt al-Aṣfiyāʾ*) which includes a name and description of the creation in question. He narrates that the creatures are named the *rawḥāniyyūn* and are created of light.[51] It is noteworthy that neither Qurṭubī nor al-Māwardī objects to the content of the ḥadīth. In other words, even if we assume that the ḥadīth is fabricated, it is scripturally conceivable, at least in principle, that God could have created sentient creatures in places unknown to human beings. The location of these creatures may be on Earth, or it may be on other planets in our galaxy, or in domains beyond our comprehension.

## Fakhr al-Dīn al-Rāzī's opinion on extraterrestrial life

Fakhr al-Dīn al-Rāzī is not only a Qurʾānic exegete, but he is also among the most influential Ashʿarī theologians in Islamic history.[52] His considered opinion on the topic is therefore significant. Additionally, al-Rāzī addresses the subject of life outside of Earth explicitly in his *Al-Tafsīr al-Kabīr*. We have seen in the previous sections that Fakhr al-Dīn al-Rāzī includes two interpretations of the end of *Sūrat al-Naḥl* (Q. 16:8). The first is an implicit affirmation that the verse

49 Murtaḍā, *Takhrīj Ahādīth Iḥyāʾ ʿUlūm al-Dīn*, 6:459.
50 Al-Qurṭubī, *Al-Jāmiʿ li-Aḥkām al-Qurʾān*, 12:289.
51 Murtaḍā, *Takhrīj Ahādīth Iḥyāʾ ʿUlūm al-Dīn*, 6:459.
52 Cooper, 'Al-Razi, Fakhr al-Din'.

is a general statement with no qualifications and that it is not referring to any particular creation. The second is that the verse refers to the creation of angels. Later on in his exegetical work, in his interpretation of *Sūrat al-Shūrā* (Q. 42:29), he offers a pertinent and rather interesting opinion on the possible existence of extraterrestrial life in his commentary on the following verse: 'Among His signs is the creation of the heavens and earth and all the living creatures He has scattered throughout them: He has the power to gather them all together whenever He will.'[53]

First, al-Rāzī states a number of possible opinions (none of them decisive) for the meaning of the term *scattered throughout them*.[54] The most prominent opinion, he says, is that the term *throughout them* (*fīhimā*) ostensibly refers to both the heavens and the Earth but is actually a reference only to the latter. In other words, the verse is saying that God has spread living creatures throughout Earth and that the verse is not referring to the heavens. This is because the Arabic language allows for an action attributed to one to be attributed to a group that one is a part of. According to al-Rāzī, this is one possible meaning.[55] However, he goes on to state that it is still possible that the pronoun *fīhimā* refers to both the heavens and the Earth.[56] And, therefore, if one were to take this position, it would include the existence of extraterrestrial life. On this, al-Rāzī makes this rather extraordinary statement: 'It would not be farfetched to say that He [God] almighty created in the heavens living beings that walk as humans do upon the earth.'[57]

This tells us that for al-Rāzī, there were no scriptural or rational limitations on the existence of living things outside of Earth – a point that is affirmed in the dominant opinion of the interpretation of Sūrat al-Naḥl (Q. 16:8). The only difference here is that al-Rāzī is stating this point explicitly. Note, al-Rāzī makes no distinction between sentient or non-sentient living things, meaning the verse could be referring to both. Additionally, the heavens here include celestial objects such as planets and moons. According to this interpretation, al-Rāzī would seem to suggest that alien life may very well exist. Moreover, the notion that the universe is abundant with life and not limited to just planet Earth is a scripturally sound concept.

53 Q. 42:29.
54 Al-Rāzī, *Al-Tafsīr al-Kabīr*, 27:172.
55 Ibid.
56 Ibid.
57 Ibid.

## Conclusion

None of the interpretations of Sūrat al-Naḥl (Q. 16:8) denies the possibility of the existence of extraterrestrial life. Indeed, according to the most dominant opinion, it may very well be possible. We may also conclude that any clear indication in the Qurʾān or ḥadīth tradition for the existence of life outside of Earth would have been made apparent in the exegesis of ten of the most prominent Qurʾānic scholars in Islamic history. Similarly, none of the scholars argues, whether because of scriptural evidence or through rational argument, that the verse specifically refers to living things on Earth alone nor negates the possible existence of extraterrestrial life. This remains the case were we to take any of the five opinions as the decisive interpretation.

It is also noteworthy that in none of the works under discussion is any denial of the possible existence of life outside of Earth, sentient or otherwise. Theologically, Muslims believe that there is no compulsion upon God to reveal such information. One sees no mention of prehistoric animals in the Qurʾān because it is not pertinent to the function of the Qurʾān as a source of guidance. If we were to wake up tomorrow to the news that astronomers have detected life outside of our planet, it would indeed be one of the greatest discoveries in all of human history. Such an event is bound to raise questions for people of faith. For Muslims, according to the positions covered in these exegetical books, it should come as no surprise either way. Scripturally, Islam has, as it were, no commitment to any particular position. The existence or not of life beyond our own planet is a question that is theologically neutral, and its answer lies within the domain of scientific inquiry.

## Bibliography

Abdel Haleem, M. A. S. *The Qurʾān*. Reprint with corrections. Oxford: Oxford University Press, 2010.

Abdul-Raof, Hussein. *Schools of Qur'ānic Exegesis: Genesis and Development*. Abingdon: Routledge, 2010.

Abū al-Suʿūd, Muḥammad ibn Muḥammad. *Irshād al-ʿAql al-Salīm ilā Mazāyā al-Qurʾān al-Karīm*. Riyadh: Makatabat al-Riyāḍ al-Ḥadītha, 2009.

Al-Baghawī, Ḥusayn ibn Masʿūd. *Tafsīr al-Baghawī, Maʿālim al-Tanzīl*. Riyadh: Dār Ṭayba, 1988.

Al-Bayḍāwī, ʿAbd Allāh ibn. *Anwār al-Tanzīl wa-Asrār al-Taʾwīl wa-bi-Hāmishihi Ḥāshiyat al-Kāzarūnī*. Beirut: Dār al-Rashīd, 2000.

Al-Bayjūrī, Ibrahīm. *Tuḥfat al-Murīd ʿalā Jawharat al-Tawḥīd*. Cairo: Dār al-Salām, 2002.

Al-Biqāʿī, Burhān al-Dīn. *Naẓm al-Durar fī Tanāsub al-Āyāt wa-l-Suwar.* Beirut: Dār al-Kutub al-ʿIlmiyya, 1995.

Al-Dhahabī, Muḥammad Ḥusayn. *Al-Tafsīr wa-l-Mufassirūn*. 8th edn. Cairo: Maktabat Wahbah, 2003.

Al-Ghazālī, Abū Ḥāmid. *Fayṣal al-Tafriqa Bayna al-Islām wa-l-Zandaqa*. Jeddah: Dār al-Minhāj, 2017.

Al-Maḥallī, Jalāl al-Dīn and Jalāl al-Dīn al-Suyūṭī. *Tafsīr al-Jalālayn*. Beirut: Dār al-Jīl, n.d.

Al-Māwardī, ʿAlī ibn Muḥammad. *Al-Nukat wa-l-ʿUyūn fī Tafsīr al-Qurʾān, Tafsīr al-Māwardī*. Beirut: al-Kutub al-Thaqāfiyya and Dār al-Kutub al-ʿIlmiyya, n.d.

Al-Nasafī, ʿAbd Allāh ibn Aḥmad. *Tafsīr al-Nasafī, Madārik al-Tanzīl wa-Ḥaqāʾiq al-Taʾwīl*,. Beirut: Dār al-Kalim al-Tayyib, 1998.

Al-Qurṭubī, Muḥammad ibn Aḥmad. *Al-Jāmiʿ li-Aḥkām al-Qurʾān*. Beirut: al-Risāla, 2006.

Al-Rāzī, Fakhr al-Dīn. *Al-Tafsīr al-Kabīr li-l-Imām al-Fakhr al-Rāzī*. Beirut: Dār al-Fikr, 1981.

Al-Ṭībī, al-Ḥusayn ibn ʿAbd Allāh. *Futūḥ al-Ghayb*. Dubayy: Jāʾizat Dubayy al-Duwaliyya li-l-Qurʾān al-Karīm, 2013.

Brenon, Pat. 'Can We Find Life?'. *Exoplanet Exploration: Planets beyond Our Solar System*. https://exoplanets.nasa.gov/search-for-life/can-we-find-life/ (accessed 30 September 2022).

Brown, Jonathan A. C. *Hadith: Muhammad's Legacy in the Medieval and Modern World*. Oxford: Oneworld Publications, 2009.

Christiansen, Jessie L. 'Five Thousand Exoplanets at the NASA Exoplanet Archive'. *Nature Astronomy* 6, no. 5 (2022): 516–19.

Conniff, Richard. 'How Many Species Can We Find Before They Disappear Forever?' *Smithsonian Magazine*, April 2014. https://www.smithsonianmag.com/science-nature/how-many-species-can-we-find-they-disappear-forever-180950184/.

Cooper, John. 'Al-Razi, Fakhr al-Din (1149–1209)'. In *Routledge Encyclopedia of Philosophy*. London: Routledge, 2016. https://doi.org/10.4324/9780415249126-H044-1.

Cottee, Simon. *The Apostates: When Muslims Leave Islam*. London: Hurst, 2015.

Davis, Josh. 'Museum Scientists Described 351 New Species in 2022'. *Natural History Museum*, 30 December 2022. https://www.nhm.ac.uk/discover/news/2022/december/natural-history-museum-scientists-describe-351-new-species-in-2022.html.

Ibn Mājah, Muḥammad ibn Yazīd, Abū Ṭāhir Zubayr ʿAlī Zaʾī, N. Khattab, H. Khattab and Abū Khalīl. *English Translation of Sunan Ibn Mājah*. Riyadh: Darussalam, 2007.

ʿItr, Nūr al-Dīn. *ʿUlūm al-Qurʾān*. Damascus: al-Ṣabāḥ, 1996.

Jalajel, David Solomon. *Islam and Biological Evolution: Exploring Classical Sources and Methodologies*. Bellville: University of the Western Cape, 2009.

Loeb, Abraham and Edwin L. Turner. 'Detection Technique for Artificially Illuminated Objects in the Outer Solar System and Beyond'. *Astrobiology* 12, no. 4 (2012): 290–4.

Malik, Shoaib. 'Islam and Evolution: The Curious Case of David Solomon Jalajel'. In *The Muslim 500*, edited by S. Abdallah Schleifer, 251–5. Amman: Royal Islamic Strategic Studies Society, 2020.

Murata, Sachiko and William C. Chittick. *The Vision of Islam*. New York: Paragon House, 1994.

Murtaḍā, al-Zubaydī. *Takhrīj Ahādīth Iḥyā' 'Ulūm al-Dīn*. Riyadh: Dār 'Āṣima, 1987.

Science Museum of Virginia. 'How Many Species Are Left to Be Discovered?' *Science Museum of Virginia*, 31 May 2018. https://smv.org/learn/blog/how-many-species-are-left-be-discovered/.

Sirāj al-Dīn, 'Abd Allāh. *Sharḥ al-Manẓūma al-Bayqūniyya fī Muṣṭalaḥ al-Ḥadīth*. Aleppo: Dār al-Falaḥ, 2009.

Tillman, Nola Taylor. 'We'll Find Alien Life in This Lifetime, Scientists Tell Congress'. Space.com, 24 May 2014. https://www.space.com/26000-alien-life-prediction-congress-hearing.html.

Za'atra, Ayman 'Īsa. 'Ma'nā al-Tawaqquf 'inda al-Usuliyyīn'. *Dirāsāt* 46, no. 1 (2019): 159–71.

3

# Islamic sacred resources on extraterrestrials and their possible eschatological implications

Mohammad Mahdi Montasseri

## Introduction

While I am penning this chapter, no certain evidence has ever been provided to demonstrate the existence of extraterrestrial living entities. There are hopes, however, that the prospective surveys of NASA's James Webb Space Telescope might confront us with, at least, signs of life outside of planet Earth. At the same time, nonetheless, according to the expanse of the universe and the countless plurality of space objects, scientists estimate that there might be numerous planets, especially in the habitable zones, bearing the susceptibility to life and even intelligent living creatures.[1]

Nevertheless, it is worth noting that research on extraterrestrial life is not confined to scientific approaches; rather, it is also investigated by scholars from the humanities, including arts, archaeology, sociology, religious studies and so on.[2] Although the existence of alien creatures has been investigated from the perspective of some religions,[3] Islamic reports and ideas about the subject remain unappreciated in recent scholarship.[4] Scrutiny in Islamic authentic texts and narratives reveals interesting reports about how God has created other intelligent living creatures. Accordingly, Islamic resources, according to some understandings, have informed us that we are not alone in the universe and

[1] See, for instance, Mayr, 'The Probability of Extraterrestrial Intelligent Life'; and Basalla, *Civilized Life in the Universe*.

[2] For example, see George, *Christianity and Extraterrestrials?*; Maxwell and Rivas, *UFOs and Aliens in Ancient Art*; Moffitt, *Picturing Extraterrestrials*.

[3] See Thigpen, *Extraterrestrial Intelligence and the Catholic Faith*; Childress, *Extraterrestrial Archaeology*; Ariel B. Tzadok, *Aliens, Angels, & Demons*; Carter, *Alien Scriptures*; and Goudsward, *UFOs in the Bible*, to name just a few.

[4] One of the unique exceptions is Determann, *Islam, Science Fiction and Extraterrestrial Life*, although this work has not properly investigated the original scriptures of the Islamic tradition.

there were, there are and there will be other animals (including intelligent ones) in the universe.

This chapter consists of two major parts. The first part will survey the Qurʾān and ḥadīths largely from Sunnī and Shīʿī perspectives but is more primed by sources found in Twelver Shīʿism (*Ithnā ʿAshariyya*). Twelver Shīʿism distinguishes itself from other schools of thought by claiming that twelve Imams from Prophet Muḥammad's lineage are the true political and spiritual leaders after him, starting with his nephew, adopted son, son-in-law and spiritual brother,[5] ʿAlī ibn Abī Ṭālib (d. 600). The importance of the Imams' narrative traditions for Shīʿism is that the Imams are considered to be spiritually on par with the Prophet himself, with the exception that the Imams received no revelation (*waḥy*). Therefore, as Shīʿism holds, the speech and knowledge of an Imam are infallible as that of the Prophet of Islam.[6]

The second part of this chapter puts forward the eschatological implications of taking extraterrestrials into account. Throughout history, the Islamic descriptions of the Day of Judgement (*Yawm al-Qiyāma*) have turned into a popular image reflected in the common understanding of Muslims. This image, whatsoever it is, has not been understood in line with the reports about the existence of the extraterrestrials. If there are intelligent material creatures in the universe and if they are juridically accountable (*mukallaf*), then should we reconsider our mental image of that day? Some of the Islamic reports about aliens seem to bring us to re-examine issues such as the end of the world; the intactness of Paradise and Hell; the everlasting shut of the gates of Paradise and Hell; our coexistence with extraterrestrials in Paradise and Hell; oneness or multiplicity of the Day of Judgement, Paradise and Hell; the very place of the Day of Judgement; and being judged by God on that day, while the extraterrestrials are also witnessing and waiting for judgement. This chapter is neither meant to solve inconsistencies that might occur in Islamic resources and beliefs nor is it about providing a new theological eschatology by taking extraterrestrials into account. Rather the purpose of this chapter is to raise related questions and invite prospective scholars to reimagine the Day of Judgement according to the highlighted reports of Islamic sacred scriptures about intelligent extraterrestrials.

5 According to the reports, when the Prophet ordered his followers to commit the pact of brotherhood (*muʾākhāt*), he chose ʿAlī ibn Abī Ṭālib as his spiritual brother. This incident has been mentioned in both Shīʿī and Sunnī traditions. See Amīnī, *Al-Ghadīr fī al-Kitāb wa-l-Sunna wa-l-Adab*.

6 See, among numerous recourses, al-Shaykh al-Mufīd, *Al-Iʿtiqādāt al-Imāmiyya*, 128; and al-ʿAllāma al-Ḥillī, *Kashf al-Murād*, 500.

Finally, a word about the usage of extraterrestrials. This work is taken to mean biological living creatures that are intelligent and, hence, accountable for their deeds in front of God on the Day of Judgement. Therefore, non-biological creatures, such as angels and jinn, fall out of the scope of this term in this chapter, and creatures of Paradise and Hell will also not properly fit with our understanding of this term here. Furthermore, I am not interested in unintelligent biological creatures such as bacteria and livestock that may be discovered on other planetary bodies.[7]

In the following, I will first survey the history of Qurʾānic interpretations over one of the most explicit verses of the Qurʾān, understood to be referring to extraterrestrials. This will be followed by analyses of the ḥadīth tradition to provide a more detailed account of extraterrestrials and their time and location. Finally, our popular image of different aspects of the afterlife will be illustrated, and the eschatological implications of putting extraterrestrials into this frame will be investigated. As mentioned earlier, the chapter will leave us with questions and doubts about the integrity of the details of popular Islamic beliefs about the Day of Judgement.

## Extraterrestrials in core resources of Islam

Having the Qurʾān as the most important scripture in Islam, this section starts with Qurʾānic verses that may imply the existence of extraterrestrial entities and continues with a detailed report concerning intelligent creatures in the narrations of Prophet Muḥammad and his successors, with a stress on the Twelver Shīʿī tradition.

### Extraterrestrials in the Qurʾān

It is worth noting from the onset that there is no direct reference to extraterrestrials in the Qurʾān, but rather there are some verses that could be explained in a way that indicates the existence of extraterrestrials. These indirect inferences, nonetheless, have not reduced the importance of these verses and their purports for Muslim interpreters of the Qurʾān throughout history. Some of the interpreters argued that, had these verses been understood properly, they would have definite implications for extraterrestrials, while some have left such

7 See Shoaib Ahmed Malik's chapter in this volume.

meanings just in the shadow of probability or have not taken them in such meaning.

Among several verses implying the issue,[8] here I restrict myself to one of the most outright verses, which reads: 'And of His Signs is the creation of the heavens and the earth and the living creatures (*dābba*) that He has spread out in them. He has the power to bring them together when He so wills.'[9] The word *dābba* literally means any materially living creature that keeps its body horizontal as it moves and, in general, refers to beasts of burden.[10] Though this verse indirectly states that there are living creatures both on the Earth and in the heavens, it is up to the interpreter to conceive the word *dābba* and the overall connotation of the verse. A brief survey of exegeses of the Qur᾿ān (from both Shīʿī and Sunnī scholars) reveals seven different understandings of the word *dābba*. Accordingly, Muslim exegetes (*mufassirūn*) can be divided into seven groups.[11] Noteworthily, the names mentioned in the following are the pioneer scholars of each understanding and not necessarily all who have adopted such interpretation.

The first group of interpreters, such as al-Farrā᾿ (d. 822) and al-Zajjāj (d. 923), have comprehended the verse to be referring merely to earthly animals and not any living creatures in the heavens.[12] These interpreters argue that despite the word *dābba* in this verse has been attributed to be spread both in the Earth and heavens, this word has no connection to the word 'heavens' (*samāwāt*).[13] This comes from the prevalence of the word *dābba* mostly or entirely for living creatures on Earth.[14] As a consequence, *dābba* cannot be referring to animals in the heavens. According to this interpretation, this verse has no allusion to extraterrestrials, neither unintelligent creatures nor intelligent nor accountable living entities. This understanding of the verse is, to a large degree, under the influence of the linguistic-rhetorical tradition of Qur᾿ānic interpretation (*tafsīr*) among scholars.[15]

The second understanding of this verse, stated by al-Andalusī (d. 1146) for the first time in the history of *tafsīr*, considers *dābba* as animals and insects

[8] These verses are Q. 1:1, 16:49, 17:44, 50:15 and 65:12, among others.
[9] Q. 42: 29. Translation from Abdullah Yusuf Ali, *The Holy Quran*.
[10] Abel, 'Dābba.'
[11] It is worth noting that this division comes from author's analysis, and there has been no actual classification in this regard between Muslim scholars in the time of composing their works.
[12] Al-Farrā᾿, *Maʿānī al-Qur᾿ān*, 3:311; and al-Zajjāj, *Iʿrāb al-Qur᾿ān*, 1:74.
[13] Al-Samarqandī, *Baḥr al-ʿUlūm*, 3:244.
[14] This is known as the principle of prevalence (*taghlīb*).
[15] For more information, see Leemhuis, 'Origins and Early Development of the *Tafsīr* Tradition.'

in the sky of the Earth,[16] including birds, flies, grasshoppers and so on. Such apprehension comes from the double meaning of the word *samāʾ*, which could be translated to both 'heaven' and 'sky'. The verse, as a result, is referring merely to organisms in the atmosphere, which is above the surface of the Earth and is, in a sense, considered as the *sky*. Although this understanding can bring about a certain connection between the words *dābba* and *samāwāt* (heavens/skies), this interpretation does not entertain extraterrestrials.

The third category of interpretation, expressed by Abū al-Suʿūd (d. 1487) and al-Shirbīnī (d. 1569), uses prophetic ḥadīths to comprehend the word *dābba* as gigantic animals in the heavens. According to a narration from Prophet Muḥammad, there is a sea (*baḥr*) above the seventh heaven, the depth of which is like the distance between the Earth and the sky. There are eight (gigantic) goats above this sea whose legs are as long as the distance between the Earth and the sky, and the Throne of God (*al-ʿArsh*) is, then, above these creatures.[17] One might doubt the materiality of such huge creatures and whether they could be regarded as biological extraterrestrials. It depends to a large degree on how one interprets the seven heavens and what comes above them – either materially or immaterially and literally or abstractly.[18] Moreover, it seems clear that those gigantic goats are not biological in a way that can have movement and spawn or be life and death. They, also, are not in the heavens and, based on this ḥadīth, are located above the seven heavens, in the middle of a sea over there. For this reason, even if we recognize such gigantic creatures as extraterrestrials, in the narrow sense meant in this chapter, they are not in the right place to be conceived as a possible explanation of the word *dābba* in this verse.

The fourth interpretation recognizes *dābba* as animals of Paradise (*janna*). This understanding derives from some Qurʾānic verses indicating the existence of some animals in Paradise[19] and a certain opinion, supported by ḥadīths,[20] states that some animals will be judged on the Day of Judgement and will enter Paradise. Al-Ālūsī (d. 1854), a famous Sunnī scholar from Iraq, has especially put forward this explanation as a plausible meaning of this verse.[21] Despite this understanding, the location of Paradise is a topic of debate, and there is

16 Ibn ʿAtiyya, *Al-Muḥarrir al-Wajīz*, 5:37.

17 See Abū al-Suʿūd, *Irshād al-ʿAql al-Salīm*, 8:32; Al-Shirbīnī, *al-Sirāj al-Munīr*, 3:644. This narration has some minor differences mentioned with the one mentioned in Abū Dāwūd, *Sunan Abī Dāwūd*, 4:231.

18 It is worth noting that in Islamic ontology, seven heavens are located above the earth, and then there are God's Seat (*Kursiyy*) and Throne (*ʿArsh*), which encompass the heavens.

19 Q. 55:21, for instance.

20 See, for instance, al-Majlisī, *Biḥār al-Anwār*, 7:276.

21 Al-Ālūsī, *Rūḥ al-Maʿānī*, 13:39.

no consensus among Muslim scholars about that.[22] Additionally, animals of Paradise and Hell are not to be easily (if ever) understood as biologically living creatures and fall short of the term 'extraterrestrial'.

The fifth interpretation regards angels (*malāʾika*) as indicated by the word *dābba*. This understanding might face a serious objection, however, as angels, according to the common conception, do fly and do not walk. Therefore, identifying them with *dābba* (walking creatures) does not seem to be thoroughly proportional. To defend this objection, al-Ṭabarsī (d. 1153) and al-Nasafī (d. 1310) have argued that it is not improbable for angels to have two kinds of movements: flying and walking. This way, they could also be understood as *dawwāb*.[23] For a further and more technical explanation, Fakhr al-Dīn al-Rāzī (d. 1209) has provided a justification based on the meaning of the origin of the word *dābba*. Deriving from '*dabīb*' (*movement*), *dābba* could be ascribed to angels as well as animals,[24] because we know from Islamic resources that both angels and animals have movement.[25] Another explication elucidates that *life* (*ḥayāt*) is the cause of *dabīb* (movement), and sometimes, in Arabic literature, the name of effect (here, *dābba*) is predicated on the name of cause (here, *ḥayāt*).[26] Therefore, based on this understanding, any living creature (including angels) could be referred to as *dābba*.[27] Regardless of the legitimacy of this interpretation, angels are not to be understood as extraterrestrials, as they are not visible to biological eyes and, according to some scholars of the Islamic world, are not made of matter and do not exist in the planes of time and place.[28]

So far, as we saw, none of the above-mentioned understandings provides us with the possibility of extraterrestrials. As summarized in Table 3.1, they have interpreted *dābba* either as biological living creatures on the Earth (and the earthly sky) or immaterial creatures such as angels or gigantic goats above the seventh heaven.

As for the sixth understanding, the first exegete who raised the possibility of living creatures outside the Earth, as an explanation for this verse, belongs to the eleventh-century scholar, Makkī ibn Ḥammūsh (d. 1045). Although al-Ṭabarānī

[22] While the Qurʾān tells us that Paradise is 'as vast as the heavens and the earth' (Q. 3:133), the place of Paradise is not clarified in the teachings of the Qurʾān.

[23] Al-Ṭabarsī, *Jawāmiʿ al-Jawāmiʿ*, 4:51; al-Nasafī, *Madārik al-Tanzīl*, 4:157. It is also mentioned in al-Rasʿanī, *Rumūz al-Kunūz*, 7:77, and in other exegeses.

[24] Al-Rāzī, *Mafātīḥ al-Ghayb*, 27:599.

[25] For example, see Q. 70:4, and 97:4.

[26] In Arabic, this principle is known as *iṭlāq ism al-musabbab ʿalā ism al-sabab*.

[27] Shaykh-zāde, *Ḥāshiyat Muḥyiʾ al-Dīn Shaykh-zāde*, 7:428. Note that this understanding has later been nullified by al-Ṭabāṭabāʾī (d. 1981), arguing that utilizing the word Dābba for angels is not customary. See al-Ṭabāṭabāʾī, *Al-Mīzān fī Tafsīr al-Qurʾān*, 18:58.

[28] For more information, see Abedi, *Alle Wesen bestehen aus Licht*, 48–54.

**Table 3.1** Summary of the *First Five Positions* That Entertain Non-Extraterrestrial Interpretations of the word '*dābba*' in Q. 42:29

| Understanding | Name of the Scholar(s) | Era (Century) |
|---|---|---|
| Earthly animals | Al-Farrāʾ and al-Zajjāj | Ninth and tenth |
| Animals and insects of Earth's sky | Al-Andalusī | Twelfth |
| Angels | Al-Ṭabarsī, al-Nasafī, and al-Rāzī | Twelfth, thirteenth and fourteenth |
| Gigantic animals in the heavens | Abū al-Suʿūd and al-Shirbīnī | Sixteenth |
| Animals of Paradise | Al-Ālūsī | Nineteenth |

(d. 970) and al-Samarqandī (d. 983) mentioned the possibility of biological living creatures and even humans being in the heavens,[29] their words are not as explicit as that of Makkī. Makkī, as far as we know, was the first to opine: 'Rather, we say: Allah has spread living creatures in the heavens and the earth.'[30] His words, however, are not clear on whether these living creatures include intelligent extraterrestrials or they are merely other unintelligent organisms.

In line with Makkī, other exegetes have argued that God might have created living creatures that we are not aware of. Their Qurʾānic evidence is Q. 16:8, which reads: 'and He creates what you do not know'.[31] So, in contradiction to the majority of the philosophers of the Islamic world,[32] Qurʾānic interpreters such as Ibn Juzayy (d. 1340), al-Thaʿālibī (d. 1479) and Abū al-Suʿūd, to name just a few, see the existence of extraterrestrial species as probable.[33] Their words leave it open whether these probable species are different from those living on the Earth or whether they are the same. So far, no one outrightly considered the word *dābba* as intelligent extraterrestrials.

Finally, for the seventh interpretation, the first Qurʾānic interpreter to raise the possibility of intelligent living creatures is al-Ṭabarsī, who utters: 'And it is not unlikely that there are [living creatures] in the heavens who (*man*) walk therein, as humans walk on the earth.'[34] What distinguishes al-Ṭabarsī from former exegetes is his stress on intelligent extraterrestrial creatures by using the

29 Al-Samarqandī, *Baḥr al-ʿUlūm*, 3:244; and al-Ṭabarānī, *Al-Tafsīr al-Kabīr*, 5:450.

30 Makkī ibn Ḥammūsh, *Al-Hidāya ilā Bulūgh al-Nihāya*, 10:6595.

31 See Moamer Khalayleh's chapter in this volume.

32 The general acceptance of Ptolemy's geocentric model among Muslim philosophers made them have no other room for any living creatures out of the earth. See, for instance, Avicenna, *Al-Shifāʾ*, 1:13–80.

33 Ibn Juzayy, *Al-Tashīl li-ʿUlūm al-Tanzīl*, 2:249; al-Thaʿālibī, *Al-Jawhar al-Ḥisān*, 5:161; and Abū al-Suʿūd, *Irshād al-ʿAql al-Salīm*, 8:32.

34 Al-Ṭabarsī, *Jawāmiʿ al-Jawāmiʿ*, 4:51.

Arabic proposition '*man*' (who/whom), which is used for intelligent entities. Moreover, he has compared those living creatures to human beings, which is a further emphasis on the intelligibility of what stands for the word *dābba* in the concerning verse. The same idea is followed by Fakhr al-Dīn al-Rāzī in his great Qur'ānic work, *Mafātīḥ al-Ghayb* (*Keys to the Unknown*).[35]

These are the views and explanations of the Muslim exegetes before the rise of modernity and the Scientific Revolution. With the emergence of modern astronomy and reports about discoveries in the universe, Muslim scholars have more room for manoeuvring over holding extraterrestrials as the true implication of the verse. Al-Marāghī (d. 1951) seems to be the first one in the modern era to speak of extraterrestrials as a fact mentioned by the Qur'ān, which is approved by modern science (*al-'ilm al-ḥadīth*). He shows too much optimism about life on Mars and, influenced by the scientific approximations of the time, he even claims the existence of Martian intelligent life and civilization.[36] As one can see, this is a divergent approach to understanding the verse, especially compared to medieval interpretations, which were to a very notable extent relying on the internal meanings of Qur'ānic words for explaining the implication of the verse.

All in all, modern exegetes are more confident in speaking of extraterrestrials in explaining the verse, and they are more likely to think this way as well. Al-Mughniyya (d. 1979) paves the way for the possibility of life on other planets without mentioning any detailed examples. He perceives heaven as any supreme (*'ālī*) sphere, including planets and the space itself, and *dābba* is, then, any living creature that dwells either in land, sea, space or a planet.[37] We can simply see how space and other planets have become alternatives for obsolete habitable places of the Islamic Middle Ages. In a further step, Makārim et al. have put forward the existence of aliens as the meaning of the verse without any hesitation.[38] A shift of paradigm is observable in the ontological opinions of Muslim exegetes when al-Qāsimī (d. 1914) casts the geocentric view aside and states that the stars are not merely created to bring pleasure to humans. Putting the connotation of three verses together – Q. 17:44, 42:29 and 55:29 – he concludes that the Qur'ān has previously informed us about the existence of rational animals, like humans, in the heavens.[39]

[35] Al-Rāzī, *Mafātīḥ al-Ghayb*, 27:599.
[36] Al-Marāghī, *Tafsīr al-Marāghī*, 7:118.
[37] Al-Mughniyya, *Al-Tafsīr al-Kāshif*, 6:526.
[38] Makārim et al., *Tafsīr Nemūneh*, 20:438–9.
[39] Al-Qāsimī, *Maḥāsin al-Ta'wīl*, 1:210.

Al-Ṣādiqī (d. 2010) comes to be the first interpreter to use the last part of the verse (Q. 42:29) as clear evidence that declares the existence of intelligent extraterrestrials. This part of the verse reads, 'and He is Most Capable of bringing all [*dābba*] together whenever He wills'. The original Arabic word used for *bringing all together* is '*jam'ihim*', which, according to al-Ṣādiqī, implies that these outsiders are intelligent, because the Arabic pronoun *him* (*them*), in the last part of this word, is grammatically utilized for rational entities.[40]

Another innovative interpretation by Hāshimī Rafsanjānī (d. 2017) pays special attention to the word *baththa* (*spread*) in the verse. Spreading *dābba* on the Earth and in the heavens, he argues, entails that extraterrestrial colonies are not few in number; otherwise, *baththa* would not be a proper word, specifically having the vast expanse of space.[41] Noteworthy is that the change in the interpreters' world view, thanks to modern astronomy, has given rise to new understandings of the verse.

A further step forward is taken by Ayatollah Qurashī (b. 1928) by putting forward the possibility of a prospective meeting between us and extraterrestrials. While previous exegetes used to appreciate the last part of the verse ('and He is Most Capable of bringing all together whenever He wills') as a congregation of living creatures on the Day of Judgement, Qurashī poses that the verse *might* be referring to meeting extraterrestrials before the Day of Judgement, here in the material world.[42] The same idea is expressed by al-Ṣādiqī without uncertainty. The unique unknown aspect for him is the place of this extraordinary meeting.[43] For the Sunnī and Egyptian scholar Ḥawwa (d. 1989), nonetheless, the meeting between the inhabitants of the Earth and extraterrestrials, though overturned, is possible.[44] Table 3.2 summarizes the interpretations that understand the verse as referring to extraterrestrials as understood by the sixth and seventh set of exegetes.

This brief historical survey shows how Q. 42:29 has been interpreted by various exegetes to discuss the potentiality of extraterrestrials. Such interpretations, however, have been brought into question by Darwaza (d. 1984), who believes this verse and similar verses neither imply the existence nor the non-existence of extraterrestrials. Implicitly, he accuses those who write in their Qur'ānic exegeses

[40] Al-Ṣādiqī, *Al-Furqān fī Tafsīr al-Qur'ān bi-l-Qur'ān wa-l-Sunna*, 28:421; al-Ṣādiqī, *Al-Balāgh fī Tafsīr al-Qur'ān bi-l-Qur'ān*, 289.

[41] Hāshimī Rafsanjānī, *Tafsīr Rāhnamā*, 16:406.

[42] Qurashī, *Qāmūs-e Qur'ān*, 1:161.

[43] Al-Ṣādiqī, *Tarjomān-e Furqān*, 3:150 and 5:20; Al-Ṣādiqī, *Setāregān az Dīdgāh-e Qur'ān*, 178–9. This idea is also mentioned in Khurramdel, *Tafsīr Nūr*, 1029.

[44] Ḥawwa, *Al-Asās fī al-Tafsīr*, 9:5104.

**Table 3.2** Extraterrestrial Understandings of Q. 42:29 as Understood by the Sixth and Seventh Interpretations

| Understanding | Name of the Scholar(s) | Era (Century) |
|---|---|---|
| Living creatures outside of the Earth | Al-Ṭabarānī, al-Samarqandī, and Makkī ibn Ḥammūsh | Tenth and eleventh |
| Intelligent living creatures out of the Earth | Al-Ṭabarsī and al-Rāzī | Twelfth |
| Extraterrestrials[a] | Al-Marāghī, al-Mughniyya, Makārim, and Qāsimī | Twentieth |
| Intelligent extraterrestrials | Al-Sādiqī | Twenty-first |
| Numerous colonies of extraterrestrials | Rafsanjānī | Twenty-first |
| Meeting the extraterrestrials in this world | Qurashī | Twenty-first |

[a] From this point, the interpretations have been under the influence of the new astronomy.

about extraterrestrials of trying just to please their readers.[45] This is undoubtedly a pessimistic view towards interpreting the Qur'ān as a source clearly referring to extraterrestrials, and it adopts a neutral position in this regard (*tawaqquf*). However, the majority of contemporary Muslim scholars, as reported earlier, appear to be in favour of understanding the Qur'ān as hinting at the existence of extraterrestrials, while some have remained silent about it.

It is also worth noting that Q. 42:29 is merely one among many Qur'ānic verses that presumably refers to extraterrestrials. Surveying other verses in the interpretation tradition is beyond the scope of this chapter. In what follows, I will illustrate what the ḥadīths have to say about extraterrestrials.

## Extraterrestrials in narrations (al-Ḥadīth)

The narrations, which include the sayings of the Prophet, his companions and Shīʿī Imams,[46] are the second set of authentic resources that we can potentially use to understand Islamic stances on extraterrestrials. As mentioned in the introduction, both Shīʿī and Sunnī resources are used to shed light on the issue. The related narrations contain different contents which are worth being reported. However, it is important to hight that there are a set of narrations

[45] Darwaza, *Al-Tafsīr al-Ḥadīth*, 4:468.

[46] Here it seems necessary to make mention that Sunnī and Shīʿī denominations are not in agreement on who should be regarded as valid sources of narrations. Besides disagreements over the validity of the intermediary narrators, there is no consensus over whose narrations are authentic Islamic sources, especially since the Sunnī party has no theological grounds for appreciating the sayings of Imams, and the Shīʿī party has the same problem with a great deal of companions' sayings.

speaking of creatures that do not seem to be living in a biological sense,[47] which others do inform us about such creatures. Since the latter comes to be more of interest to this survey, I have set aside the former set of narrations and analysed the latter. Four sets of narrations are identified in this survey, each one carrying a distinctive interpretation.

The first set of narrations informs us about former dynasties of intelligent creatures on this very planet, which did not originate from our initial predecessors, Adam and Eve.[48] This might not be thoroughly comprehended as extraterrestrials because those creatures were not living on a different planet or outside the Earth in general. But since they are claimed to be living intelligent creatures out of our ancestry and history, they could be considered aliens, at least in a certain way of understanding. As an example, it is narrated from Imam Muḥammad ibn ʿAlī al-Bāqir (d. 732), the fifth Imam of Twelver Shīʿism, that since the creation of the Earth, God has created seven dynasties of living creatures (*ʿawālim*) from the surface of the Earth (*ʾadīm al-ʾarḍ*) and then accommodated them on the Earth, one after another. Thereafter, He created Adam, the sire of the present humans.[49] According to this narration, there have been seven other genealogies of accountable[50] living creatures before us, who came into existence one after another on this very Earth, and each of them is created from separate origins, not from parents of their kind. The phrase 'one after another' might insinuate the extinction of all of the seven before the rise of the current dynasty of humanity. In short, this narration makes us aware of other intelligent living creatures' dynasties lived on the Earth, and that we are the seventh accountable genealogy created so far in the history of the Earth. Yet, the language of the narration does not suggest that those creatures had been *humans*, since the word human (*bashar*, *insān* or *Ādam*) is missing from the original text and, instead, the word *ʿālam* (creature)[51] is used.

The second set of narrations speaks of alien creatures, this time certainly outside of the Earth, but is yet silent about their quiddity and nature. It is, for instance, narrated from Imam Jaʿfar ibn Muḥammad al-Ṣādiq (d. 765), the sixth

47 Ibn ʿAbbās, to give an instance, has narrated from the Prophet that there are nations that are created like birds and nations that are made out of wind, and above them is the shadow of Throne (*ʿArsh*), where there are 70,000 nations that do not know God has created Adam and his offspring. See the detailed narration in al-Majlisī, *Biḥār al-Anwār*, 54:348.

48 At least according to some Abrahamic religious teachings.

49 Baḥrānī, *Al-Burhān fī Tafsīr al-Qurʾān*, 5:131.

50 The accountability of those creatures comes from this very narration stating that they are already judged and entered their eternal stead in Paradise or Hell. I will discuss this part of the narration in a section on eschatological implication.

51 Although the word *ʾālam* literally means *universe*, the language of the narrations implies that the word means *creatures* in this case.

Imam of the Twelver Shīʿism, that there are forty other suns farther along this Sun, where abundant creatures exist, and there are forty moons farther above this Moon, where copious creatures live.[52] Moreover, it is, also, narrated that there are 7,000 worlds above this green sky, the inhabitants of which are more than the number of humans and the jinn on Earth.[53] Whether these creatures are intelligent or not, and if they are like humans or not, is unknown.

The third set opines on extraterrestrial intelligent living creatures who lived before the creation of this universe and others who will be created after the destruction of our universe (*ʿālam*) and probably in the next universes to come. A ḥadīth is narrated from Imam Muḥammad ibn ʿAlī al-Bāqir that when God demolishes this universe, He will again construct another universe and will create a new creation, the first generation of which is not originated from biological parents (just like Adam and Eve, who were not born from parents). They will be living on an Earth different from this Earth and under a sky different from this one.[54] This narration explicitly speaks of other universes and other sets of creations (*khalq*). Another aspect of this category informs us about the great multiplicity of human creations. As stated in some narrations, God has already created one million (*alf alf*) universes[55] and one million Adams, and we are at the end of this sequence.[56] This specific number (one million) might be referring to a great plurality (though finite) of universes and the creation of human beings, or it could even be understood as an infinite number of universes and human genealogies. The evidence for the perennial creations and destructions of universes by God is the former part of the aforementioned ḥadīth, which remarks the creation of another universe after the destruction of the current one. Moreover, as brought up earlier, a narration from Imam Muḥammad ibn ʿAlī al-Bāqir tells us that, after the destruction of this universe, God will create other accountable creatures on their own Earth to worship and glorify Him.[57] It may imply that the material world was never and will never be free from worshipers of God, and He keeps creating universes and intelligent living creatures for all eternity. Yet, even if the content of this ḥadīth were true, those extraterrestrials are not within our reach, since they initially have no locative relationship to us. They, also, are created in different universes and do not intersect with us,

[52] Al-Ṣaffār, *Baṣāʾir al-Darajāt*, 490.
[53] Ibid., 492.
[54] Baḥrānī, *Al-Burhān fī Tafsīr al-Qurʾān*, 5:131; Ibn Bābawayḥ, *Al-Khiṣāl*, 2:652.
[55] We should recall that the word 'universe' (*ʿālam*) in this literature could be understood as 'set of creatures' as well.
[56] Al-Bursī, *Mashāriq Anwār al-Yaqīn*, 63; and Ibn Bābawayḥ, *al-Khiṣāl*, 2:652.
[57] Baḥrānī, *Al-Burhān fī Tafsīr al-Qurʾān*, 5:131.

especially having the narration speaking of the demolition of a universe and then the creation of another one, which leaves no room for any interconnection between the residents of these universes.

The fourth set of ḥadīths mentions intelligent extraterrestrial creatures that live in our universe and are contemporary to us. As an example, a narration from ʿAlī ibn Abī Ṭālib, the first Imam of Shīʿism, uttered:

> For these stars (*nujūm*) in the sky, there are cities (*madāʾin*) analogous to the cities on the Earth. Each of them is connected (*marbūṭa*) [to others] by a pillar (*ʿamūd*) of light, and the length of that pillar in the sky is the traverse of 250 thousand years.[58]

A few indications in this narration are worth pointing out. First, according to this narration, living creatures are not scattered all over the sky, but rather they live somewhere near other stars.[59] Second, these creatures are not confined to a very small number, because the narration speaks of plural words such as 'stars' and 'cities'. By the same token, this narration does not claim that every star possesses cities around itself. Third, these creatures have cities, which means they have a social life, and, most importantly, they can build cities, which conveys that they are intelligent enough to design and build something as sophisticated as cities. Furthermore, this understanding suggests that they are not at the initial steps of civilization and have reached the level of sedentism and urbanization or possibly even something beyond that which is yet out of the reach of our minds. Or, as another understanding, the word 'cities' can refer to the totality of cities on a planet. This, especially, comes to mind due to the elongated distance between these cities, as mentioned in the narration. This long distance seems unlikely to be for connecting cities of one planet together. As the fourth implication, those extrasolar cities are similar to the cities on the Earth, which, on one comprehension, might mean they are made up of constructions for living, places for work, whereabouts for recreation, paths, alleys and so on; or at least, those cities are made in a way to meet the requirements of living of extraterrestrials. Fifth, these cities, or planets (based on one possible understanding), are connected; so, they seem to be aware of each other, unless that connection is in a way that leads to no awareness at all. Although this narration does not make it clear whether these 'connections' lead the residents of those cities to meet each other in person or they simply are telecommunications, the point,

[58] Al-Qummī, *Tafsīir al-Qummī*, 2:218.

[59] Probably just as we live in the circumstellar habitable zone of the sun. One might, thus, conceive this narration as alluding to extraterrestrials living on extrasolar planets.

according to this understanding, is that we are the lost ones. In other words, while we are still theorizing and searching for any kind of extraterrestrial life, some (if not all) of those extraterrestrial colonies are aware of and even are in touch with each other. *We* are the lost civilization, if so! Sixth, the means for such a connection is a 'pillar of light', which *may* be referring to some kind of electromagnetic means of communication.[60]. Seventh, this pillar of light is in the sky, not on the Earth, which gives us a strong clue that the word 'cities' is referring to *planets* (actually all of the cities of a planet), not just cities. Lastly, the distances between those cities/planets are very far. 'The traverse of 250 thousand years' has been an extraordinary remoteness for the listener of this narration, even if considered as traversing on foot or through livestock. But if the phrase is understood as 250 thousand years of light travelling in the sky, then the distance between those planets would be 250 thousand light years. The problem with the latter understanding, however, is that a 'connection' in which a message takes 250 thousand years to be transmitted seems difficult to comprehend. Whatever the true interpretation of this distance, it implies a very long distance between those planets.

In another narration,[61] Ibn ʿAbbās (d. 687), cousin of Prophet Muḥammad and one of the greatest exegetes of the Qurʾān and narrators of early Islam, has explained Q. 65:12 in a way that explicitly suggests the existence of extraterrestrials. The verse reads: 'Allah is the One Who created seven heavens, and likewise for the earth', which seemingly means there are seven earths as well. Despite different exegeses for this verse, Ibn ʿAbbās, as the narration goes, has uttered: 'There are seven earths, in each of them there is a prophet like your prophet [Muhammad], an Adam like your Adam, an Abraham like your Abraham, a Noah like your Noah, and a Jesus like your Jesus.'[62] This narration approves that there are seven other places, like Earth, where intelligent living creatures are living. While the language of the narration speaks of prophets like Abrahamic prophets on the Earth, one might simply understand it merely implying that the creatures on those earths are similar to us in having prophets analogous to ours, reason, faith, accountability and so on. So, the biological attributions of those creatures remain unclear, and we cannot conclude from the words of this

[60] Although the related phrase of the narration is not free of some ambiguities, one might anachronistically be willing to consider the 'pillar of light' as some sort of parallel amplified electromagnetic radiation that is emitted to make such an interstellar connection possible. Being 'light', on the one hand, might suggest that this means of connection is not made up of substance, and, on the other hand, being 'pillar' means it is concentrated on a certain point, rather than being radiated into a large spectrum of space.

[61] See the chapters of Hamza Karamali, Moamer Khalayleh and Faisal Abdullah in this volume.

[62] Al-Suyūṭī, *Al-Durr al-Manthūr*, 8:211.

narration that those creatures are necessarily humans. Although the narration is prone to other understandings as well, we shall take this consideration seriously and refrain from taking this narration as a justification for alluding to those extraterrestrials (the residents of the other six earths) as humans.

Since Q. 65:12 speaks of seven heavens that have been created and still exist, the seven earths should still exist right now and, hence, should be contemporary to us. We should, also, keep in mind that the verse does not claim that each Earth is located in a different heaven. This specific narration, however, goes far beyond and informs us about similar Abrahamic prophets on each of those earths. One way of understanding this narration is to hold that the histories of civilization on these seven planets are in some way similar to ours. This understanding fits well with the words of this ḥadīth. It could also mean that each prophet mentioned here refers to a level of civilization, as Adam might be perceived as alluding to the creation of intelligent creatures, and then similar developments of civilization have come to pass on each Earth. What fortifies this discernment is the narration merely making mention of five prophets and remaining silent about any other incidents we know happened throughout history. Had we taken such silence to mean something, then it might let us imagine a few similar nodes of history among these earths in which their historical developments are dissimilar.[63] Table 3.3 summarizes the four viewpoints.

The narrative tradition of Islam has a lot more to say about extraterrestrial life that needs an independent survey to be dealt with in detail. The four categories of narrations mentioned briefly earlier can widen our perspectives

**Table 3.3** Extraterrestrials in Ḥadīths

| **Content** | **Source of the Narration(s)** |
|---|---|
| Intelligent creatures living on Earth before us | Imam Muḥammad al-Bāqir |
| Intelligent creatures living in other universes before and after this universe | Imam Muḥammad al-Bāqir |
| Alien creatures contemporary to us (intelligence in question) | Imam Jaʿfar al-Ṣādiq |
| Intelligent extraterrestrials contemporary to us | ʿAlī ibn Abī Ṭālib and Ibn ʿAbbās |

[63] The reliability of this narration has been put in doubt by al-Bayhaqī, arguing that it is merely narrated from Abū al-Ḍuḥā and no one else has ever followed him in this regard. This is while ʿAbd ibn Ḥamīd, Ibn Jarī, Ibn Ḍarīs and Ibn al-Munḍir have narrated Ibn ʿAbbās, saying he will not speak of the interpretation of this verse (Q. 65:12) because the auditor will disbelieve and deny. Al-Suyūṭī, *al-Durr al-Manthūr*, 8:209–10. So, the rareness of this narration could be justified through its unbelievability even in the eyes of Ibn ʿAbbās himself.

about extraterrestrials from the viewpoint of Islam. The first category illustrated other intelligent creatures that lived separately from us on this very planet. The second told us of extraterrestrials while being silent about their essences. The third category provided us with reports about extraterrestrials in other universes, whether existing before or after us. The last category brought forth some detailed information about contemporary extraterrestrials and even their connection with each other.

Having completed this survey of extraterrestrials in the Qurʾān and narrations, I will now assess the eschatological implications of such reports and show how they might require us to change our image of the Day of Judgement.

## Eschatological implications

Our imagination of the Day of Judgement and what comes before and after it originates from the Qurʾān and narrations. Though there is an abundance of various verses and narrations shedding light on both generalities and details of the afterlife, Muslim scholars happened to have numerous divergent readings of those resources. The unrested debate over this issue started from early theologian scholars and continued through narrators (*muḥaddithīn*), philosophers, mystics (*ʿurafāʾ*) and so on. Although Islamic eschatology has been thrashed out in too many different aspects, no one has ever taken extraterrestrials into account for providing an image of the afterlife. This section aims to put Islamic reports about extraterrestrials and eschatology together to show what questions can arise as a result of paying attention to alien life from the prospect of Islam. Without shouldering the burden of responding to these new questions, I will show how different aspects of eschatology need rethinking when extraterrestrials are seriously taken as a part of Islamic belief.

### The end of the world

It is largely believed that the whole world will perish when the angel Raphael (*Isrāfīl*) blows in his trumpet. This teaching of Islam has been mentioned both in the Qurʾān and in narrations. Q. 39:68 informs us that there will be two blows, of which the first will cause the destruction of the universe and the creatures on the Earth and in the heavens but when God wills so. According to a prophetic narration, four archangels, that is, Gabriel, Michael, Azrael and Raphael (*Jibrāʾīl,*

*Mīkāʾīl, ʿIzrāʾīl* and *Isrāfīl*), will survive this blow, and they also will be perished, and God remains alone until the second blow.[64] The second blow will bring about the Day of Judgement, where the creatures will come into existence again and will be judged by the Lord.

This content may, at the first sight, suggest that there will be only two blows, as is largely held by Muslim scholars and believers. However, recall the narrations discussing that God has created about one million universes before us and will continue creating so. One can ask if there are only two blows for all those universes or if each of them will end in the same way. A few possibilities come to mind in response to this question. First, each universe can have its specific blow, and consequently, the Earth and seven heavens will perish, including the four archangels. Then, God will recreate the angels, and all the creatures of that universe will be resurrected to then be judged after the trumpet of *Isrāfīl* is blown for a second time in that world. But if we suppose juridically accountable creatures of the previous universes are already judged and entered Paradise or Hell, though it is a matter of contemplation in its own right, then one can ask if Paradise, Hell and their settlers will also be destroyed and reconstructed. If so, what will be the meaning of 'eternal rest in Paradise'? As mentioned before, this chapter is not about to provide answers to these questions but a probable response will be that the verse (Q. 39:68) simply says: 'The Trumpet will be blown and all those in the heavens and all those on the earth will fall dead, except that Allah wills',[65] and, thus, it is silent about Paradise and Hell, and they might survive the destroying blow of the trumpet.

Second, it could be said that blowing the trumpet is beyond time and has no temporal relation to any of the universes. Rather, the four archangels are in the position of immaterial beings, and their actions, including one single blow of *Isrāfīl*, can simply play the role of an end for all of the countless universes, though they are to be created and demolished one after another.

Third, as some of the narrations told us about different Adams and Eves, there might be a different *Isrāfīl* in and for each of those universes. That way, each universe will have its specific destination and end as well. A potential objection is what will *Isrāfīl* do in each universe after it is perished and is judged. This could be responded with: What is he doing before it?

[64] Ibn Abī al-Ḥadīd, *Sharḥ Nahj al-Balāgha*, 1:95. Note that there are plenty of narrations on this issue, to the extent that makes it an inseparable part of the Islamic faith, though its interpretation might be a matter of debate.

[65] This is only the first part of the verse.

Lastly, why do we have to think that other worlds also are to be perished by the blow of *Isrāfīl*? Although narrations do tell us about the existence of those worlds, *Isrāfīl* and his trumpet might simply be a specification of the present world, and there is no convincing evidence proving that other worlds will be destroyed by the same token. After all, the mentioned details of those worlds in narrations do not necessarily mean that other aspects of these worlds are also one and the same.

These four probable answers are only a few examples to show how diverse the potential responses might be to this question, and it is up to contemporary Muslim scholars to let their readers know about their understanding. What we know for sure is that this question has not been appreciated enough in the history of Islamic intellectual thought.

## Intactness of Paradise and Hell

Do Paradise and Hell exist right now, or will they be created later? Even though there is no consensus over this issue among scholars of the Islamic world, some Islamic sources imply that Paradise and Hell are intact right now, and no accountable person has resided there so far. It seems, based on some narrations, as if one particular person will enter Paradise for the first time, and that has been regarded as a position of excellence and glory for that individual, among others. Both Sunnī and Shīʿī resources consider Prophet Muḥammad as the first entity to enter Paradise, with the exception that Shīʿism sees the family of the Prophet (*Ahl al-Bayt*) as his companions there and then.[66]

Yet, by considering the narrations speaking of numerous universes before and after us, as well as intelligent living there, our imagination of the intactness of Hell and Paradise might face some difficulties. For instance, if other extraterrestrial intelligent creatures have entered Hell and Paradise, as a ḥadīth informs us, they cannot be intact and free from residents who deserve them. This narration tells us that the next universe is created after the inhabitants of Paradise and Hell have resided there, and neither Paradise nor Hell has been free from the souls of believers and wrongdoers since God created the two.[67] That said, how is it possible for the Prophet of Islam to be the first person to enter Paradise?

Another difficulty comes to the fore by reminding the narration from Ibn ʿAbbās about various extraterrestrial prophets (Adam, Noah, Abraham, Jesus

[66] Ibn Ḥajjāj, *Ṣaḥīḥ Muslim*, 188; al-Nuʿmān, *Sharḥ al-Akhbār*, 2:475.
[67] Baḥrānī, *Al-Burhān fī Tafsīr al-Qurʾān*, 5:131; Ibn Bābawayḥ, *Al-Khiṣāl*, 2:652.

and Muḥammad) on seven earths: Does each of these prophets have one instance on the Day of Judgement, or there are seven of each one? If the latter is the case, then which Prophet Muḥammad (among the seven) will enter Paradise first?

As mentioned beforehand, answers to these questions might vary from person to person, but what we know for granted is that Islamic resources about alien entities convey mostly overlooked data that require serious eschatological reconsiderations. These issues are as significant as other eschatological problems, such as the resurrection of animals, the eternity of Hell, bodily versus spiritual resurrection and so on. Therefore, while a declaration of ignorance might be a possible response to these questions, it will not close the way for Muslim theologians to speculate about these questions, especially when taking into account various ideas about the afterlife already put to the fore in the history of Islamic theology.

## Oneness or multiplicity of Paradise and Hell

The popular image of Paradise and Hell implies that there is merely one Paradise and one Hell. The Arabic words used to denote Hell are '*jahannam*' and '*nār*' in the Qur'ān and are always mentioned in the singular form. However, Paradise (*janna*) is mentioned in both singular and plural (*jannāt*) forms, which suggests that there could be more than one Paradise. However, since the word '*janna*' also means garden, the plural form of the word seems to refer to gardens of Paradise, not multiple Paradises,[68] though it does not deny different levels of Paradise.[69]

According to reports on other accountable living creatures before us who have already entered Paradise and on the basis of the narrations saying that Prophet Muḥammad will be the first one to enter Paradise, one might ask whether there is merely one Paradise or there are plenty of them. In other words, if those living creatures have vanished, been judged and entered Paradise, how can the Prophet of Islam be the first one who will open the gate of Paradise and enter it as the first entity? If put evidence together, Muslim scholars might be willing to reconsider the popular image of Paradise regarding the oneness of Paradise. The same reconsideration might be about Hell, especially since there are prophetic narrations which describe the first group of people who enter Hell.[70] Accordingly, one can ask, if extraterrestrials have already entered Paradise

[68] See, for instance, Q. 2:25, 3:15 and 85:11.

[69] These levels of Paradise are referred to in the Qur'ān, such as *Jannāt al-Ma'wā* (Q. 32:19), *Jannāt 'Adn* (Q. 13:23) and *Jannāt Firdaws* (Q. 18:107).

[70] See al-Tirmidhī, *al-Jāmi' al-Ṣaḥīḥayn wa-Huwa Sunan al-Tirmidhī*, 4:319.

and Hell and if, based on a ḥadīth, Paradise and Hell have never been free from the souls of believers and disbelievers since God created them,[71] how can some of the wrongdoers be the first group to enter Hell on the Day of Judgement?

This issue has certain relation with the issue of *the Intactness of Paradise and Hell* and yet is more general than that, as the former might be just a possible answer to the latter. In other words, the supposed multiplicity of Paradise and Hell can justify how some individuals of this human dynasty can be the first to enter Paradise and Hell while other extraterrestrial dynasties are already residing in Paradise and Hell: They are simply in their specific Paradise and Hell. Another possible answer might be that other extraterrestrials (while being wise, accountable and intelligent) are not humans, but rather they have other characteristics and quiddities. Answers to these questions may be a topic of discussion among Muslim theologians, and the chapter, as mentioned recurrently, is not about solving the issue. But whether one holds in the oneness of Paradise, its multiplicity or even prefers a declaration of non-commitment (*tawaqquf*), extraterrestrials force us to reconsider some long-standing beliefs.

## Coexistence with extraterrestrials in Paradise and Hell

Islamic resources tell us about some sort of coexistence of the souls of the accountable creatures in Paradise and Hell. The Qur'ān, to provide examples, has pointed out that residents of the Paradise recline on their jewelled thrones face to face (Q. 56:15-16), have conversations with themselves (Q. 37:50), and even with the inhabitants of Hell (Q. 74:40-42, 7:44 and 37:55-60), and there is some kind of friendship (*rifq*) and companionship between the residents of Paradise (Q. 4:69). There are also conversations between wrongdoers in Hell (Q. 14:22) and even between the residents of Paradise and the residents of the fire (Q. 7:44) mentioned in the Qur'ān. The Qur'ān may also teach us that there is some sort of coexistence between humans and jinn both in Hell and probably in Paradise.[72] This is while other creatures in Paradise accompany human souls – creatures such as houris (*ḥūriyy*) and servants (*ghilmān*, *wildān*) who provide services for the faithful souls of humans and, as a consequence, have coexistence

[71] Baḥrānī, *Al-Burhān fī Tafsīr al-Qur'ān*, 5:131.

[72] On the one hand, Satan (*Shayṭān*), who is a Jinn according to the Qur'ān, has conversations with the residents of Hell (Q. 14:22), and on the other hand, Q. 72:14 might be admitting that the Jinn will also enter Paradise, though there are doubts cast on this understanding as well. There are no straightforward Qur'ānic verses acknowledging that the jinn will enter Paradise, while the exegetical (*tafsīr*) tradition has a lot to discuss on this issue.

with them.[73] There are even few animals, at least according to the Shīʿī faith, which lived once on Earth and will enter Paradise due to the outstanding acts they committed during their lives.[74]

The popular image of Paradise provides no more than humans (limited to the offspring of Adam and Eve), the jinn and the creatures of Paradise. But, taking into account that some narrations admit the existence of extraterrestrial accountable creatures, capable of entering Paradise and Hell, and with the supposition that there may be only one Paradise in which all of the accountable creatures will finally gather together, the popular image of Paradise among Muslims seems to be in need of reconsiderations. The same, needless to say, goes for Hell.

Here, one can ask if the residents of Paradise can have conversations with anyone in their comfort among other residents, or if their conversations are merely confined to those they already know of. If the former is the case, then, one might ask: Can they have coexistence and conversation with righteous extraterrestrials as well? In such a case, we can probably share pieces of knowledge and experiences from the life we lived in our bodies and find friends who once lived on the other side of the universe. In general, while there is no evidence directly admitting the coexistence of extraterrestrials with us in the afterlife, the overall context of resources leaves us with such a possibility and, as a consequence, invites Muslim scholars to reconsider the issue.

## The place and oneness of the Day of Judgement

The popular understanding is that there is only one Day of Judgement, which is when all humans will rise from their graves and wait to be judged by God. Verses of the Qurʾān have always spoken of one Day of Judgement,[75] and the ḥadīths also mention the same.[76] Yet, these authentic sources of Islam are silent about extraterrestrial accountable entities and their place on the Day of Judgement. Besides, the location of the Day of Judgement is also a matter of question. Muslim scholars have fallen short of any consensus about the place of this grand event.[77] To name just a few, some scholars believe that the afterlife is beyond any material place and, as an immaterial event, encompasses even the time and place,[78] while

[73] See Q. 52:24, 56:17, 44:54, 52:20 and 76:19.

[74] Al-Qummī, *Tafsīir al-Qummī*, 2/33. This includes, for instance, *al-Raqīm*, the dog that guarded the Seven Sleepers (*Aṣḥāb al-Kahf*).

[75] See, for instance, Q. 1:4, 17:19, 69:1–3, 7:187, 79:34, 88:1, 101:1, 29:36, 85:2, 11:26, 40:15, 40:18, 30:56, 64:9 and 37:20.

[76] See, for instance, al-Nasāʾī, *al-Mujtabā min al-Sunan*, 231.

[77] Al-Rāzī, *Al-Arbaʿīn fī Uṣūl al-Dīn*, 2:55–64.

[78] Al-Ṭūsī, *Āghāz wa Anjām*, 21–2.

others see this very Earth we live on as the place of the Day of Judgement.[79] Still, others see somewhere else as the arena where the Day of Judgement will take place.[80] Despite these disagreements, taking extraterrestrials into account might add more complexity to two issues of oneness and place of that day and might have us rethink the image we have in our minds from the Day of Judgement.

One might also contemplate over the oneness or multiplicity of the Day of Judgement. As discussed earlier, some narrations infer that some accountable extraterrestrials have already lived their share of life, and their time has totally traversed long ago. Other extraterrestrials, according to another narration, are living in parallel in our time as our contemporaries.[81] The question, then, is if we will be resurrected and judged in the same place and day besides those extraterrestrials. In other words, will we have one single Day of Judgement where all accountable creatures rise and will be judged? The question poses difficulty if we consider the narrations claiming that some antecedent extraterrestrials are judged and entered Paradise and Hell before us.[82] Is it possible, one may want to know, that some extraterrestrials have already been judged and entered Paradise and Hell, and we can still believe in one unique Day of Judgement for every accountable person? That will undoubtedly be a very long Day of Judgement, which lasts almost as long as eternity. Or are there different Days of Judgement for other extraterrestrials? There could be too many different responses to these questions according to different fundamental ideas and principles among Muslim scholars. But the main issue is that we might be required to take extraterrestrials into account when we are about to come up with an image of the Day of Judgement.

The place of that day is also a matter of consideration. If there is only one Day of Judgement, where should it be, and how will that place contain all accountable creatures, including all accountable extraterrestrials, which seem to be infinite in number? It might not be a big deal for those who think of the Day of Judgement as an immaterial event or those who see it in an arena other than the Earth. But for those who believe in the Day of Judgement as a material happening that takes place on this very terrestrial Earth, it might be more complicated. This is especially true if they simultaneously believe in only one Day of Judgement throughout the universe and in the existence of extraterrestrial accountable agents who will be resurrected and judged by God. In such circumstances, we

79 Ṭayyib, *Aṭyab al-Bayān fī Tafsir al-Qur'ān*, 13:200.
80 Al-Ghazālī, *Iḥyā' 'Ulūm al-Dīn*, 1898.
81 Al-Qummī, *Tafsīir al-Qummī*, 2:218.
82 Baḥrānī, *Al-Burhān fī Tafsīr al-Qur'ān*, 5:131; Ibn Bābawayḥ, *Al-Khiṣāl*, 2:652.

can ask if this Earth will be the unique place where the Day of Judgement will come about. And, having the proposed oneness of the Day of Judgement in mind, why should extraterrestrials be resurrected on this Earth and not vice versa?

Such issues require rethinking our image of the Day of Judgement. If verses and narrations permit the existence of intelligent, accountable extraterrestrial beings, then do they coexist with us on the Day of Judgement or not (which can imply other multiple Days of Judgement)? Either way, as a result, reports about extraterrestrials in Islamic resources can call upon Muslims to reconsider the image of the Day of Judgement.

## Conclusion

This chapter was an attempt to clarify two points. First, what do sacred resources of Islam (i.e. the Qur᾿ān and ḥadīths) have to state about the existence of alien living creatures? Second, what are the eschatological implications of what Islam tells us about extraterrestrials, and how might they change the popular image of the Day of Judgement in the minds of the followers of Islam? By extraterrestrials, I meant intelligent biological creatures so that to cast aside angels, jinn and alike. The scope of the research incorporates both Sunnī and Twelver Shīʿī resources.

The Qur᾿ān has no outright allusion to extraterrestrials, but there are at least six verses that could be understood in a way to imply the existence of alien living creatures. This chapter limited itself to surveying the Qur᾿ānic exegetical (*tafsīr*) scholarship regarding Q. 42:29 to show how the tradition has come to comprehend the verse as a hint to extraterrestrials. The survey shows the *possibility* of the verse referring to extraterrestrials was first put forward in the tenth century by al-Ṭabarānī and al-Samarqandī, after which the verse has been understood in a certain voice as Qur᾿ānic evidence of extraterrestrials in the next century by Makkī ibn Ḥammūsh. None of these scholars, however, has uttered a word about the intelligence of extraterrestrials; Al-Ṭabarsī, in the twelfth century, was the first exegete to provide such understanding. With the rise of modern astronomy, we then see how exegetes of the Qur᾿ān tend to appropriate the verse as an explicit suggestion about intelligent extraterrestrials. Although some have put such understanding severely under question, numerous contemporary scholars have taken this understanding for granted. Some even have understood from the verse that God has informed us in the Qur᾿ān that we will reach and meet the aliens in the future. The nature and physical characteristics of those aliens cannot be determined either from these exegeses of the Qurʾān or from the Qurʾān itself.

Unlike the Qurʾān, ḥadīths (especially in Shīʿism) are more definite about extraterrestrial life. By casting aside narrations that do not seem to be referring to biological extraterrestrials, the rest of the related narrations are presented in four categories to illustrate what this tradition has to say about extraterrestrials. The first category claims six genealogies of creatures created, lived and annihilated before us on this very Earth. They might not be alien in an exoplanet sense, but since they are outside of our genealogy and history, I prefer to consider them extraterrestrials in a loose sense. The second category speaks of extraterrestrials outside of the Earth while telling us nothing about them being accountable or intelligent or not. The third category deals with intelligent creatures living not only outside of the Earth but also in another universe. As stated in these narrations, God has created so many universes before this universe and will continue creating many others after the present one is demolished, and these universes contain intelligent living creatures. Paradise and Hell, according to some of these ḥadīths, have never been free from the souls of believers and disbelievers since God created the two. Finally, the last category alludes to accountable, intelligent creatures outside of the Earth who are contemporary to us. In this category, they live somewhere near the stars, have cities and are connected to each other through pillars of light, the length of which is as long as the traverse of 250 thousand years.

A few points, here, are worth noting: first of all, the Qurʾān and the narrations have never spoken of extraterrestrial humans. In other words, although the Qurʾān might, and the ḥadīths are alluding to extraterrestrials, the nature of those extraterrestrials was never claimed to be human or human-like, but rather they are introduced as *dābba*. A further point is that most of the related narratives come from the Shīʿī resources, and I could not come across more than one ḥadīth from the Sunnī narrative tradition, though such scarcity is not reflective of Sunnī interpreters of the Qurʾān. As the last point, if there are other planets containing extraterrestrials, and if (according to the fourth category of narrations) they are connected to each other through pillars of light, then *we* are the lost civilization among others, that is, *we* are the civilization that has not yet found the others and probably is not yet been found by other extraterrestrials.

The second aim of this chapter was to examine the eschatological implication of the Islamic reports on extraterrestrials. In pursuit of this aim, I have recognized five implications, starting with the issue of the end of the world. If there are several universes created by God containing extraterrestrials, as narrations go, the way they will perish and resurrect appears to be a matter of contemplation.

Muslims' popular image of the Day of Judgement has neglected the existence of extraterrestrials and might need reconsideration. The intactness of Paradise and Hell is another matter of reflection. On the one hand, some narrations, from both Shīʿī and Sunnī schools, imply that Paradise and Hell are free from human souls, and even the first groups of people who will enter each of them are determined in some sayings of Prophet Muḥammad. On the other hand, Islamic reports on extraterrestrials suggest that accountable alien creatures who lived before us have already entered Paradise and Hell. The combination of these resources requires rethinking as well. The third implication considers the oneness and multiplicity of Paradise and Hell. The popular image of the Day of Judgement sees each of Paradise and Hell as a single place for those who deserve them, while the existence of accountable extraterrestrial creatures might call for rethinking this issue. Supposed coexistence with extraterrestrials in Paradise and Hell, as the fourth issue, is a further matter of meditation, because the popular image of Paradise and Hell does not consider any kind of coexistence with aliens in the afterlife. Lastly, Islamic reports on extraterrestrials invite us to rethink the place of the Day of Judgement. Are there many places for the Day of Judgement, where each genealogy of intelligent creatures will be resurrected, or is there only one? If the latter is the case, where will it be? On the Earth, on another planet, or would it be in an immaterial arena?

This chapter, needless to say, does not aim to respond to these problems; rather, it is merely about showing that, by taking Islamic perspectives on extraterrestrials, a set of questions will be brought to the fore. Responses to these questions, just like most other issues in Islam, depend to a large extent on the school of thought an eschatologist might come from, and there is no standard response to them. Although the declaration of non-commitment (*tawaqquf*) is a possible answer to all of these questions – which is by no means unpopular among Muslim scholars, especially among some Sunnī schools of thought – what Islamic resources teach us about extraterrestrial life seem to affect our image of the afterlife, whether consciously or unconsciously.

## Bibliography

Abdullah Yusuf Ali. *The Holy Quran: English Translation of the Meanings*. San Francisco: Blurb, 2016.

Abedi, Zohre. *Alle Wesen bestehen aus Licht: Engel in der persischen Philosophie und bei Suhrawardi*. Marburg: Tectum, 2018.

Abel, A. 'Dābba'. In *Encyclopaedia of Islam, Second Edition*, edited by P. Bearman, Th. Bianquis, C. E. Bosworth, E. van Donzel and W. P. Heinrichs. Leiden: Brill, 2012.

Abū al-Suʿūd. *Irshād al-ʿAql al-Salīm ilā Mazāyā Qurʾān al-Karīm*. Beirut: Dār Iḥyāʾ al-Turāth al-ʿArabī, 1983.

Abū Dāwūd. *Sunan Abī Dāwūd*. Edited by Muḥammad Muḥyi-l-Dīn ʿAbd al-Ḥamīd. Beirut: Ṣaydāʾ, 2006.

Al-ʿAllāma al-Ḥillī. *Kashf al-Murād fī Sharḥ Tajrīd al-Iʿtiqād (Revealing the Meaning: Explanation of Abstraction of Creed)*. Qom: al-Nashr al-Islāmī, 2008.

Al-Ālūsī, Maḥmūd ibn ʿAbd Allāh. *Rūḥ al-Maʿānī fī Tafsīr al-Qurʾān al-ʿAzīm wa-l-Sabʿ al-Mathānī*. Edited by ʿAlī ʿAbd al-Bārī ʿAṭiyya. Beirut: Dār al-Kutub al-ʿIlmiyya, 1994.

Al-Bursī, Rajab ibn Muḥammad. *Mashāriq Anwār al-Yaqīn fī Asrār Amīr al-Muʾminīn*. Beirut: Aʿlamī, 2001.

Al-Farrāʾ, Yaḥyā ibn Ziyād. *Maʿānī al-Qurʾān*. Edited by Muhammad Ali Najjar and Ahmad Yusuf Nahati. Cairo: al-Hayʾa al-Miṣriyya al-ʿĀmma li-l-Kitāb, 1980.

Al-Ghazālī, Muḥammad ibn Muḥammad. *Iḥyāʾ ʿUlūm al-Dīn*. Beirut: Dār ibn Ḥazm, 2005.

Al-Majlisī. *Biḥār al-Anwār al-Jamiʿa li-Durar Akhbār al-Aʾimma al-Aṭhār*. Beirut: Dār Iḥyāʾ al-Turāth al-ʿArabī, 1982.

Al-Marāghī, Aḥmad Muṣṭafā. *Tafsīr al-Marāghī*. Beirut: Dār al-Fikr, n.d.

Al-Mughniyya, Muḥammad Jawād. *Al-Tafsīr al-Kāshif*. Qom: Dār al-Kutub al-Islāmī, 2003.

Al-Nasafī, ʿAbd Allāh ibn Aḥmad. *Madārik al-Tanzīl wa-Ḥaqāʾiq al-Taʾwīl*. Beirut: Dār al-Nafāʾis, 1995.

Al-Nasāʾī, Aḥmad ibn Alī. *Al-Mujtabā min al-Sunan*. Amman: Bayt al-Afkār al-Duwaliyya, n.d.

Al-Nuʿmān, Al-Qāḍī. *Sharḥ al-Akhbār fī Faḍāʾil al-Aʾimma al-Aṭhār*. Qom: Jāmiʿat al-Mudarrisīn, 1988.

Al-Qāsimī, Jamāl al-Dīn. *Maḥāsin al-Taʾwīl*. Beirut: Dār al-Kutub al-ʿIlmiyya, 1997.

Al-Qummī, ʿAlī ibn Ibrāhīm. *Tafsīir al-Qummī*. Qom: Dār al-Kitāb, 1984.

Al-Rasʿanī, ʿAbd al-Razzāq ibn Rizq Allāh. *Rumūz al-Kunūz fī Tafsīr al-Kitāb al-ʿAzīz (Mysteries of the Treasuries: Interpretation of the Chary Book*. Edited by ʿAbd al-Malik ibn Dahīsh. Mecca: Maktab al-Asadī, 2008.

Al-Rāzī, Fakhr al-Dīn. *Al-Arbaʿīn fī Uṣūl al-Dīn*. Cairo: Maktaba al-Kulliyyāt al-Azhariyya, 1986.

Al-Rāzī, Fakhr al-Dīn. *Mafātīḥ al-Ghayb*. Beirut: Dār Iḥyāʾ al-Turāth al-ʿArabī, 1999.

Al-Ṣādiqī, Muḥammad. *Al-Balāgh fī Tafsīr al-Qurʾān bi-l-Qurʾān*. Qom: Maktaba Muḥammad al-Ṣādiqī al-Ṭahrānī, 1998.

Al-Ṣādiqī, Muḥammad. *Al-Furqān fī Tafsīr al-Qurʾān bi-l-Qurʾān wa-l-Sunna*. Qom: Farhang Islāmī, 1985.

Al-Ṣādiqī, Muḥammad. *Setāregān az Dīdgāh-e Qurʾān*. Tehran: Omīd-e Fardā, 2006.

Al-Ṣādiqī, Muḥammad. *Tarjomān-e Furqān*. Qom: Shukrāneh, 2009.

Al-Ṣaffār, Muḥammad ibn al-Ḥasan. *Baṣāʾir al-Darajāt fī Faḍāʾil Āl Muḥammad*. Qom: Maktaba Āyatullāh al-Marʿashī, 1983.

Al-Samarqandī, Naṣr ibn Muḥammad. *Baḥr al-ʿUlūm*. Edited by ʿUmar ʿAmrī. Beirut: Dār al-Fikr, 1995.

Al-Shaykh al-Mufīd. *Al-Iʿtiqādāt al-Imāmiyya (The Creeds of Imāmiyya)*. Qom: Congress of al-Mufīd, 1993.

Al-Shirbīnī, Muḥammad ibn Aḥmad. *Al-Sirāj al-Munīr*. Edited by Ibrahim Shams al-Din. Beirut: Dār al-Kutub al-ʿIlmiyya, 2004.

Al-Suyūṭī, ʿAbd al-Raḥmān ibn Abī Bakr. *Al-Durr al-Manthūr fī Tafsīr al-Maʾthūr*. Beirut: Dār al-Fikr, 2011.

Al-Ṭabarānī, Sulaymān ibn Aḥmad. *Al-Tafsīr al-Kabīr (The Great Interpretation)*. Irbid: Dār al-Kutub al-Thaqāfī, 2008.

Al-Ṭabarsī, Faḍl ibn Ḥasan. *Jawāmiʿ al-Jawāmiʿ*. Edited by Abū al-Qāsim Gorjī. Qom: Seminary of Qom, 1991.

Al-Ṭabāṭabāʾī, Muḥammad Ḥusayn. *Al-Mīzān fī Tafsīr al-Qurʾān*. Beirut: al-Aʿlamī, 1970.

Al-Thaʿālibī, ʿAbd al-Raḥmān ibn Muḥammad. *Al-Jawhar al-Ḥisān fī Tafsīr al-Qurʾān*. Beirut: Dār Iḥyāʾ al-Turāth al-ʿArabī, 1997.

Al-Tirmidhī, Muḥammad ibn ʿĪsā. *Al-Jāmiʿ al-Ṣaḥīḥayn wa-Huwa Sunan al-Tirmidhī*. Cairo: Dār al-Ḥadīth, 1998.

Al-Ṭūsī, Naṣīr al-Dīn. *Āghāz wa Anjām*. Tehran: Ministry of Culture and Islamic Guidance, 1995.

Al-Zajjāj, Ibrāhīm ibn al-Sarī. *Iʿrāb al-Qurʾān*. Edited by Ibrahim Abyari. Qom: Dār al-Tafsīr, 1995.

Amīnī, ʿAbd al-Ḥusayn. *Al-Ghadīr fī al-Kitāb wa-l-Sunna wa-l-Adab*. Qom: Markaz al-Ghadīr li-l-Dirāsāt al-Islāmiyya, 1995.

Avicenna. *Al-Shifāʾ: Al-Riyāḍiyyāt*. Qom: Maktaba Āyatullāh al-Marʿashī, 1984.

Baḥrānī, Sayyid Hāshim ibn Sulaymān. *Al-Burhān fī Tafsīr al-Qurʾān*. Qom: al-Biʿtha, 1995.

Basalla, George. *Civilized Life in the Universe: Scientists on Intelligent Extraterrestrials*. Oxford: Oxford University Press, 2006.

Carter, Michael J. S. *Alien Scriptures: Extraterrestrials in the Holy Bible*. Amazon: Emin Elle Literary, 2019.

Childress, David Hatcher. *Extraterrestrial Archaeology*. Kempton: Adventures Unlimited Press, 2021.

Darwaza, Muḥammad ʿIzzat. *Al-Tafsīr al-Ḥadīth: Tartīb al-Suwar Ḥasab al-Nuzūl*. Beirut: Dār al-Gharb al-Islāmī, 2000.

Determann, Jörg Matthias. *Islam, Science Fiction and Extraterrestrial Life: The Culture of Astrobiology in the Muslim World*. London: I.B. Tauris, 2021.

George, Marie I. *Christianity and Extraterrestrials? A Catholic Perspective*. New York: iUniverse, 2005.

Goudsward, Ken. *UFOs in the Bible*. Prince George: Dimensionfold, 2021.

Hāshimī Rafsanjānī, ʿAlī Akbar. *Tafsīr Rāhnamā*. Qom: Būstān Kitāb, 2007.

Ḥawwa, Sa'īd. *Al-Asās fī al-Tafsīr*. Cairo: Dār al-Salām, 2003.

Ibn Abī al-Ḥadīd. *Sharḥ Nahj al-Balāgha*. Qom: Maktaba Āyatullāh al-Mar'ashī, 1983.

Ibn 'Atiyya, Abū Muḥammad 'Abd al-Ḥaqq. *Al-Muḥarrir al-Wajīz fī Tafsīr Kitab al-'Azīz*. Edited by Muhammad 'Abd al-Salām 'Abd al-Shāfi. Beirut: Dār al-Kutub al-'Ilmiyya, 2001.

Ibn Bābawayḥ, Muḥammad ibn 'Alī. *Al-Khiṣāl*. Qom: Jāmi'a al-Mudarrisīn, 1983.

Ibn Juzayy, Muḥammad ibn Aḥmad. *Al-Tashīl li-'Ulūm al-Tanzīl*. Edited by 'Abd Allāh al-Khalidī. Beirut: Dār al-Arqam, 1995.

Khurramdel, Muṣṭafā. *Tafsīr Nūr*. Tehran: Iḥsān, 2005.

Leemhuis, F. 'Origins and Early Development of the *Tafsīr* Tradition'. In *Approaches to the History of the Interpretation of the Qur'ān*, edited by Andrew Rippin, 13–30. Oxford: Clarendon Press, 1988.

Makārim, Nāṣir, et al. *Tafsīr Nemūneh*. Tehran: Dār al-Kutub al-Islāmiyya, 1992.

Makkī ibn Ḥammūsh. *Al-Hidāya ilā Bulūgh al-Nihāya*. Sharjah: University of Sharjah, 2008.

Maxwell, Jordan and Colin Rivas. *UFOs and Aliens in Ancient Art: Before and After Christ*. Amazon Digital Services LLC - KDP Print US, 2020.

Mayr, Ernst. 'The Probability of Extraterrestrial Intelligent Life'. In *Extraterrestrials: Science and Alien Intelligence*, edited by Edward Regis Jr, 23–30. Cambridge: Cambridge University Press, 1985.

Moffitt, John Francis. *Picturing Extraterrestrials: Alien Images in Modern Culture*. New York: Prometheus Press, 2003.

Muslim ibn Ḥajjāj. *Ṣaḥīḥ Muslim*. Beirut: Dār al-Kutub al-'Ilmiyya, 1991.

Qurashī, 'Alī Akbar. *Qāmūs-e Qur'ān*. Tehran: Dār al-Kutub al-Islāmiyya, 2002.

Shaykh-zāde, Muḥyi' al-Dīn. *Ḥāshiyat Muḥyi' al-Dīn Shaykh-zāde 'alā Tafsīr al-Qāḍī al-Bayḍāwī*. Edited by Muḥammad 'Abd al-Qādir Shāhīn. Beirut: Dār al-Kutub al-'Ilmiyya, 1998.

Ṭayyib, Sayyid 'Abd al-Ḥusayn. *Aṭyab al-Bayān fī Tafsir al-Qur'ān*. Tehran: Islam, 1999.

Thigpen, Paul. *Extraterrestrial Intelligence and the Catholic Faith: Are We Alone in the Universe with God and the Angels?* Charlotte: TAN Books, 2022.

Tzadok, Ariel B. *Aliens, Angels, & Demons: Extraterrestrial Life in Judaism/Kabbalah & Its Vital Relevance for Modern Times*. Chicago: Independently Published, 2020.

4

# Extraterrestrials and moral accountability

## Non-human moral personhood through the lens of classical Sunnī theology and law

David Solomon Jalajel

## Introduction

Personhood, for a class of beings,[1] is commonly grounded in that class's potential for moral agency,[2] or at least personhood is seen as the locus of its moral culpability,[3] which, in turn, is taken to hinge on the attributes of self-awareness and the faculty of reason.[4] Hacker explains:[5]

> While *human being* is a biological category, person is a moral, legal and social one. To be a person is, among other things, to be a subject of moral rights and duties. It is to be not only an agent, like other animals, but also a moral agent, standing in reciprocal moral relations to others, with a capacity to know and to do good and evil. Since moral agents can act for reasons, and can justify their actions by reference to their reasons, they are also answerable for their deeds.

1 This chapter will keep discussions of moral accountability to the level of 'class of beings'. This is because individual members of the class may not fully realize the attributes of reason and self-awareness that typify the class, but personhood, or at least its basic entitlements, is generally conferred on all members thereof, even if an individual, due to childhood, insanity or mental handicap, may not be held morally accountable.

2 See Locke, 'Personhood and Moral Responsibility', 40; and Boeker, *Locke on Persons and Personal Identity*, 55.

3 Vilhauer 'Free Will Skepticism', 499.

4 Boeker, *Locke on Persons and Personal Identity*, 55, quotes John Locke defining a person as 'a thinking intelligent Being', while also characterizing a person by 'a Forensic Term, appropriating Actions and their Merit; and so belongs only to intelligent Agents capable of a Law, and Happiness and Misery'. By contrast, Vilhauer, 'Free Will Skepticism', 500, who sees personhood as merely the locus of moral deserts, nevertheless gives the minimum conditions of personhood as 'hav(ing) the ability to do things for reasons'.

5 Hacker, *Human Nature*, 4.

Whereas the attributes of reason and self-awareness can, at least in theory, be confirmed for a class of beings through empirical means, the theological possibility of non-human moral accountability before God might hinge on unobservable considerations of human uniqueness. According to religious doctrine, are humans unique? Is moral accountability one of the ways in which human beings are unique? Does moral accountability hinge upon other attributes, or is it an independent attribute? Many claims for human uniqueness have been made in the Islamic tradition, from the capacity for reason to something as simple as eating with one's hands.[6] There are two important factors in assessing such claims. The first is whether they are grounded in experience or in revelation. The second is, to the extent that they are grounded in revelation, are the conclusions reached to be taken as theologically binding doctrine?

Regarding the first consideration, certain traits lend themselves to empirical observations, and claims about their exclusivity to human beings can at least hypothetically be negated by empirical evidence. Claims concerning the possession of language, rational faculties, eating with the hands and self-awareness would be falsified if unquestionably observed in non-human entities. Therefore, empirical evidence can negate a claim of human exclusivity for a given trait through clear examples of non-human entities possessing the trait in question. On the other hand, positive proof for a claim that a particular trait is unique to humans would require the impossible condition of a comprehensive survey of all entities in the universe so it would remain empirically uncertain in perpetuity due to the possibility that there are beings who possess that trait existing elsewhere in the universe who are unknown to us.[7] Therefore, empirical means can potentially negate particular claims of human uniqueness, but those means can never positively affirm such claims. This can be seen in Table 4.1.

Some traits cannot, by their nature, be verified through observation. For instance, the favour and esteem God confers upon an entity or species and whether they have immortal souls. These are purely theological questions

[6] Ibn ʿAbbās suggests that the honour the Qurʾān refers to in Q. 17:70: 'And indeed We have honoured the Children of Adam' is that everything eats with its mouth while the children of Adam eat with their hands. Al-Rāzī, *Mafātīḥ al-Ghayb*, 21:11; al-Bayḍāwī, *Anwār al-Tanzīl*, 3:262.

[7] The possibility of other beings in the universe that are unknown to us stands in the absence of direct scriptural evidence declaring them non-existent, due to the Sunnī doctrine that God has the power to do whatever He pleases. See al-Rāzī, *Mafātīḥ al-Ghayb*, 13:165–6, where he discusses Q. 6:133: 'If He wishes, He could do away with you and make to succeed after you anything He wishes.' Al-Rāzī supports the view that God is declaring in this verse His power to create a third or fourth class of beings other than humans and jinn, that these other beings could be more obedient, and that they too could have a share in His mercy. Also, in *Mafātīḥ al-Ghayb*, 27:147, while commenting on Q. 42:29, he says: 'It is not far-fetched to say that God could create in the heavens types of animals that walk in the way humans walk on Earth.' See the chapter of Moamer Khalayleh, this volume.

**Table 4.1** Traits and Their Potential to Be Verified in Non-Human Entities by Empirical Evidence

| Claim for Uniqueness | Can Empirical Means Negate the Uniqueness Claim? | Can Empirical Means Affirm the Uniqueness Claim? |
|---|---|---|
| A place of honour with God | No | No |
| Possessing a soul | No | No |
| Moral accountability | ? | No |
| Possessing reason | Yes | No |
| Possessing language | Yes | No |
| First-person perspective | Yes | No |
| Eating with one's hands | Yes | No |

relating to the Unseen (*ghayb*) and must be approached as such. The Unseen are aspects of God's creation that are not available to our senses, like the existence of heaven and hell and the existence of angels. As discussed later, within a Sunnī theological framework, Unseen matters can only be determined by direct scriptural evidence.

This chapter will focus on Sunnī Islam, as the largest branch of Islam, representing an estimated 85–90 per cent of the world's Muslims. Three distinct theological schools developed within the tradition: the Ashʿarī, Māturīdī and Salafī schools. The first two schools appeared in the early tenth century and came as a challenge to the perceived rationalistic excesses of the Muʿtazilīs, an earlier scholastic (*kalām*) theological tradition. The Ashʿarī school was founded by the Iraqi theologian Abū al-Ḥasan al-Ashʿarī (d. 936), while the Māturīdī school developed after the Samarqandī theologian Abū Manṣūr al-Māturīdī (d. 944). These two schools are referred to as the Sunnī *kalām* schools.[8] The Salafī school has its origins in Traditionism (Atharism), an anti-scholastic tendency that called for strict adherence to received prophetic traditions. Its most prominent early figure was Aḥmad ibn Ḥanbal (d. 855). The fourteenth-century theologian Taqī ad-Dīn Aḥmad ibn Taymiyya (d. 1328) responded to the dominant Ashʿarī school in his day with a rational and formal theological defence of Atharī teachings as he understood them and, in doing so, put forth a fully developed formal theological school.[9] Sunnī Islam also developed four closely affiliated legal schools, the Ḥanafī, Mālikī, Shāfiʿī and Ḥanbalī schools, all of which ground normative law in the scriptural authority of the Qurʾān, prophetic traditions (Sunnah) and consensus of the Muslim community.

[8] Leaman, 'The Developed Kalām Tradition', 84–9.
[9] Jackson, *Islam and the Problem of Black Suffering*, 135–6.

The chapter will first explore the theological aspects of whether extraterrestrials could be recognized as morally accountable persons. This theological exploration will begin with the question of whether morally accountable personhood can be determined empirically from qualities observed in a class of entities. The second question is whether there is scriptural evidence limiting moral personhood to humans alone or to humans along with the jinn, who are another class of intelligent beings mentioned in the Qurʾān. Finally, this will be followed by an exploration of the consequences that various theological conclusions would have for the legal status of intelligent extraterrestrials.

## The empirical determination of moral personhood

Can a theological stance on the moral accountability of a class of beings be determined on empirical grounds? The answer to this question hinges on whether that status is intrinsically linked to reason and self-awareness, as prerequisites to volition, so that whenever those traits are observed, the class of entities possessing them is theologically acknowledged to be moral persons. In other words, the presence of these traits is enough; revelation does not need to separately and explicitly establish moral personhood for the class of entities. The Māturīdī school holds this stance, which is grounded in its moral realism.[10] This realism makes the ethical quality of acts discernible to reason,[11] and this is actualized by a self-aware agent through a divinely created attribute of potency (*quwwa*/*istiṭāʿa*),[12] enabling a volitional act grounded in reason and responding to circumstances.[13] Significantly, for Māturīdīs, belief in God does not hinge on revelation. They argue that the signs in nature are so evident that anyone possessing a modicum of reason will arrive at the knowledge of God, and moreover, people will be held morally accountable to believe in God and liable for punishment in the Hereafter for disbelieving, even if they never received revelation.[14]

The latter proposition proves especially problematic for the Ashʿarī school, which holds that moral accountability is exclusively grounded in scripture so that there is no moral index outside of revelation. Abū Ḥāmid al-Ghazālī (d. 1111)

[10] Harvey, *The Qurʾān and the Just Society*, 34–5.
[11] Ibid., 36.
[12] Al-Māturīdī, *Kitāb al-Tawḥīd*, 342–5.
[13] Ibid., 249; Pessagno, '*Irāda, Ikhtiyār, Qudra, Kasb*', 181.
[14] Abū ʿAdhaba, *Al-Rawḍa al-Bahiyya*, 59.

argues that even if a person realizes through reason alone that the world must have a Creator, how does reason take them further to conclude that they are morally accountable to believe in and thank that Creator and then conduct themselves according to some moral standard on Earth?[15] How do they know that the Creator cares what they believe or what they do or that He would want them to focus on Him rather than their worldly benefit?[16] Recognition of the existence of a Creator does not logically entail, for Ashʿarī theologians, an obligation to thank that Creator and act morally. This stance is grounded in the Ashʿarī doctrine that nothing is obligatory upon God, so He is not obligated to reward and punish His creatures for their faith and their actions. He is not required to demand belief from them. He is, therefore, not required to confer the status of a morally accountable agent upon an entity simply because He creates it with the capacity to reason. Likewise, God could, in principle, hold a non-reasoning entity morally accountable, since Ashʿarīs, famously, and in contrast to the other Sunnī theological schools, hold that God can burden with moral accountability those who are unable to carry out that burden (*taklīf mā lā yuṭāq*).[17]

By contrast, Māturīdī theologians argue that God's wisdom dictates the world has the purpose of revealing God's existence to the rational mind, and therefore reason is tied intrinsically to this purpose. Moral accountability is grounded in reason and inseparable from it. Furthermore, the beings who are aware of their Creator must also be sustained in their existence through moral conduct and not exist merely to perish.[18] Moreover, it is inconceivable from the standpoint of wisdom for God to place benefit and harm, pleasure and pain in the created world except for the moral instruction of those who experience these things and have the rational faculties to morally contextualize them.[19] Therefore, the created world must have rational beings within it, and it would be contrary to the dictates of wisdom for such beings not to be morally accountable persons.

As long as a theological tradition is committed to tying moral accountability positively and negatively to the rational faculty, it would be required to confer the status of moral personhood to any class of non-human rational beings they encounter. This is regardless of any contrary pronouncements scholars working within that tradition may have previously made about the possibility of non-human moral persons. The Ashʿarī tradition, by contrast, would not be

15 Al-Ghazālī, *Al-Iqtiṣād*, 118–19.
16 Ibid., 119.
17 Ibid., 112; Abū ʿAdhaba, *Al-Rawḍa al-Bahiyya*, 82–3.
18 Al-Māturīdī, *Kitāb al-Tawḥīd*, 248.
19 Ibid., 249.

compelled to make such a judgement, so an encounter with non-human rational beings would require them to turn to scripture for an answer.

The Salafī theologian Ibn Taymiyya takes a different approach by foregrounding the innate disposition (*fiṭra*). For him, reason builds upon a person's innate dispositional tendency to have an awareness and love of God, bringing a person to the knowledge of God.[20] It also leads to an innate concept of right or wrong, of perfection and imperfection, which, for Ibn Taymiyya, is essential for recognizing a genuine prophet through the claimant's character.[21] It does not, however, bring full appreciation of the doctrine of monotheism and the knowledge that one needs to obey a moral code. Reason requires contact with divine revelation in order to fulfil the condition of entailing reward and punishment.[22] Rather than reason being the condition for understanding the message, the message is the condition for reason to have its appropriate object. This implies that moral personhood is constituted by reason in conjunction with an innate disposition to recognize God. Then, upon receipt of the divine message via a genuine prophet, the person's innate moral accountability is brought to bear upon the particular requirements of the revealed message. This differs from the Ashʿarī stance described earlier, where reason is merely a precondition to understanding the prophetic message, and God can theoretically hold people accountable, or leave them unaccountable, regardless of whether they know and understand the message.

Since, for Ibn Taymiyya, moral accountability is constituted by the innate disposition to recognize God along with reason and not by reason alone, hypothetically, a rational entity could exist devoid of this innate disposition, and for such an entity, the status of moral personhood would remain unclear from a purely empirical standpoint. Nonetheless, the presence of this disposition is very much an observable phenomenon. It can easily be determined whether a class of rational beings has a tendency to arrive at an awareness of God. This would be if they are observed to conceptualize God on their own without others having to inform them. If they are observed to possess this disposition, then according to the Salafī doctrine, they would have to be recognized as morally accountable persons.

In summary, three positions can be deduced regarding the theological determination of morally accountable personhood from empirical means alone. The Māturīdī stance would be that whenever reason is confirmed for a class of

20 Ibn Taymiyya, *Darʾ Taʿārruḍ*, 8:460–2.
21 Hoover, *Ibn Taymiyya's Theodicy of Perpetual Optimism*, 219.
22 Vasalou, *Ibn Taymiyya's Theological Ethics*, 234.

**Table 4.2** Sunnī Stances on the Empirical Determination of Morally Accountable Personhood

| Theological School | Can Moral Personhood Be Empirically Determined? | Why? |
|---|---|---|
| Ashʿarī | No | God is not obligated to hold anyone morally accountable, regardless of the faculties He creates in them. It is an Unseen matter only knowable through scripture. |
| Māturīdī | Yes | Possession of reason makes one a morally accountable person. |
| Salafi | Yes | Possession of reason along with an innate disposition to recognize God makes one a morally accountable person. |

beings, moral personhood is conferred upon them. The Salafi stance would be that whenever reason along with a tendency towards awareness of God are both found in a class of beings, they would have the status of moral persons. The Ashʿarī stance would be that there is no purely empirical means to determine the moral personhood of any class of beings because God can confer that status on whomever He pleases and withhold it from whomever He wills (Table 4.2).

If empirical means cannot determine morally accountable personhood, then the matter must be determined in another way. As will be discussed later, the only other way to make such a determination in the framework of Sunnī theology is through scripture.

## The scriptural determination of moral personhood

To the extent that moral accountability before God is divorced from empirically discernible factors, its application to a class of beings would require scriptural evidence. This is because reason alone cannot determine it. Whenever a matter does not entail a contradiction, like a 'square circle', reason can only determine its possibility. It remains contingent on God's determination, and God can actualize any possibility He wishes. Therefore, it would be judged logically possible that God might confer the trait of moral accountability upon a certain class of beings or that He might not do so.

Any matter where neither empirical observation nor reason can determine the outcome is a matter of the Unseen known by God alone (like the regard in which He holds someone or whether a class of beings possesses a soul) unless He reveals that knowledge to His prophets. Therefore, Unseen matters can only be known to the religious community through scripture. Al-Ghazālī explains:

> What is known only by way of textual evidence (*samʿ* ) is where one of the rational possibilities is actualized (by God), since it is all permitted by reason. These things are only known by way of revelation and inspiration, and we know about them from the revelation that reaches us, like the resurrection, the gathering of souls, reward and punishment, and the like.[23]

Al-Māturīdī gives a similar explanation while discussing the need for God to send revelation via prophets:

> There are three foundations – impossibility, necessity, and between them contingency – upon which rest all the world's matters. Necessity is where reason does not permit a proposition to assert otherwise. The same goes for impossibility. It can be [otherwise] with contingency, since it vacillates from one circumstance to another, from one hand to another, from one domain to another. Therefore, reason cannot necessitate any tendency or rule it out as impossible. Therefore, the Messengers came to explain what is apposite in each circumstance.[24]

The Māturīdī theologian al-Ṣābūnī (d. 1184) says in the same context:

> Rational premises are three: necessary, impossible, and contingent. Reason makes judgments about the necessary and the impossible, but it must be noncommittal (*yatawaqqaf*) about the possible, so it does not pass judgement, neither negating it nor affirming it.[25]

Ibn Taymiyya says that the Messenger clarified the rational approaches to understanding God's unity and attributes, then informed them explicitly of matters of the Unseen:

> The [Messenger] clarified to them what he came with of religious principles and the rational proofs by which is known what can be known by way of reason, and he informed them of the Unseen which is unknowable by reason alone.[26]

He identifies the Unseen as follows:

[23] Al-Ghazālī, *Al-Iqtiṣād*, 132.
[24] Al-Māturīdī, *Kitāb al-Tawḥīd*, 254.
[25] Al-Ṣābūnī, *Kitāb al-Bidāyā*, 86.
[26] Ibn Taymiyya, *Darʾ Taʿārruḍ*, 7:302–3.

> Of [knowledge] is what those who are not prophets can only know by being informed by a prophet, their report alone being the scriptural (*samʿī*) evidence, like the details of the affairs of God, the angels, the Throne, Paradise, the Fire, and the details of what is commanded and prohibited.[27]

Determining theological doctrine through scripture requires the most rigorous hermeneutical standards. Since reason cannot inform anything about these matters, nothing at all can be assumed or inferred about them. The Ashʿarī theologian Fakhr al-Dīn al-Rāzī (d. 1209) says:

> The Unseen is divided into what is indicated by evidence and what is not indicated by evidence. As for what is not indicated by evidence, God alone knows about it to the exclusion of others. As for what is indicated by evidence, it can be said that we know of the unseen what the evidence indicates.[28]

Ibn Taymiyya's student Ibn al-Qayyim (d. 1350) asserts: 'a claim about God's actions; if it is not established by Him declaring it about Himself, is a claim fabricated against Him without knowledge'.[29] In other words, it is obligatory to assert what God explicitly says about matters of the Unseen, negate what He explicitly negates and remain silent on any detail about which God remains silent. Whenever scripture is silent on a matter, it is an obligation to adopt a stance of theological non-commitment (*tawaqquf*), neither affirming nor negating anything. Therefore, theological hermeneutics requires as much awareness about what scripture is not saying as on what it is saying.

Al-Rāzī addresses the fallacy that 'the absence of proof for something entails its absence', describing such reasoning as arguing from ignorance. He invokes the logical axiom that 'the absence of knowledge about something does not entail the absence of the thing itself'.[30]

As a result, theological hermeneutics, which explores matters of binding religious doctrine, is the strictest hermeneutical register. It is applied to texts that are deemed to bequeath certainty or near certainty in the authenticity of their attribution and in their meaning.

There are two other hermeneutical registers to consider. The first is the legal register for determining the legal implications of textual evidence. Several legal rulings are established with decisive scriptural evidence. However, since Islamic

27 Ibn Taymiyya, *Majmūʿ al-Fatāwā*, 13:158.
28 Al-Rāzī, *Mafātīḥ al-Ghayb*, 2:27.
29 Ibn al-Qayyim, *Shifāʾ al-ʿAlīl*, 2:721–2.
30 Al-Rāzī, *Maṭālib*, 3:221. Also, see Shihadeh, 'Ignorance', 206–14, where he examines in detail al-Razi's 'uncompromising' critique of the argument from ignorance and the theologians who employ it.

Law must address a vast range of practical contingencies, most of which are not directly addressed by scripture, the primary purpose of legal hermeneutics is to navigate uncertain evidence to derive the legal verdict that best represents the divine intent. These hermeneutical methods are painstakingly elaborated in the works of Islamic jurisprudence (*uṣūl al-fiqh*). The other hermeneutical register is the exegetical register, which is evident in the works of Qur'ān exegesis (*tafsīr*) as well as in the works of ḥadīth commentary. Exegetes explore possible and likely meanings of scripture, while ruling out what is false. Since this hermeneutical register explores possibilities, exegetes often permit multiple and even contradictory interpretations to coexist (Table 4.3).

Engaging with theological questions of moral personhood from a scriptural angle is challenging because theologians rarely conduct these hermeneutical explorations in their theological works. This means it is necessary to consult works of exegesis (*tafsīr*) where opinions expressed, even forcefully, are often not intended by their authors to be theologically binding but just their favoured interpretation. One way to partially mitigate this uncertainty is to rely on works of exegesis written by leading theologians. When an exegetical work is authored by a theologian, it can be assumed with confidence that the author regards the ideas they express to be theologically acceptable, unless they identify a particular idea as false. Also, if the author acknowledges more than one idea, or advances an idea tentatively, it can safely be concluded that they do not hold a particular interpretation to be theologically binding. However, if the author puts forth a single opinion, it remains a challenge to determine if they consider that opinion to be theologically binding doctrine unless the author directly says it is or the context strongly indicates that they are speaking on a theological register. This is because their expression of an idea or interpretation does not rule out that they would allow other possible interpretations to be theological admissible.

The Salafī school provides less of a challenge, even though their leading classical theologians did not author exegetical works. This is because their

**Table 4.3** Hermeneutical Registers and Their Epistemological Demands

| Register | Purpose | Minimum Epistemological Demand |
|---|---|---|
| Theological | Determining binding doctrine (ʿ*aqīda*) | Certainty/near certainty |
| Legal | Determining legal rulings (*sharīʿa*) | Preponderance of uncertain evidence |
| Exegetical | Determining what the scriptures convey (*tafsīr*) | Possibility |

leading theologian, Ibn Taymiyya, regardless of the context he is writing in, is consistently strict about interpreting scripture on a theological register where matters of the Unseen are concerned.[31] Indeed, he describes speculating about these matters beyond what is explicitly stated in the scriptures as a 'useless pursuit'[32] and 'of no benefit to the believers'.[33]

## Verses indicating moral personhood as a distinctive human feature

Three verses in the Qurʾān can be viewed as singling out human beings for moral accountability: the verse of the succession (*khilāfa*) on Earth (Q. 2:30), the verse of the Trust (Q. 33:72) and the verse of the witnessing (Q. 7:172).

### Verse of the succession (khilāfa) on Earth (Q. 2:30)

This verse speaks about the creation of Adam as follows: 'And when your Lord said to the angels, indeed I am placing a successor (*khalīfa*) on Earth.' This could suggest a singular status for him and, in turn, for his descendants.

The Ashʿarī theologian al-Rāzī declares that the term refers to 'one who succeeds after another'[34] and then discusses the various opinions about the identity and status of this successor. The first is that it is Adam himself, and there are two reasons why commentators say he is referred to with this epithet. The first is that he was placed on Earth after the jinn were expelled from it. The second is that he is appointed to judge between the morally accountable beings of his kind (*al-mukallafīn min khalqihi*). The other opinion is that it refers to Adam's descendants since they come after each other in successive generations. He attributes these various opinions to their proponents among the Companions and Successors and does not indicate a preference for one interpretation over another. He is clearly not speaking on a theological register, as indicated by his willingness to mention the story of the expulsion of the jinn, which is not established by scriptural evidence.

A later Ashʿarī theologian and exegete, al-Bayḍāwī (d. 1319), says that the successor is 'one who succeeds another and acts in their stead'.[35] He identifies

31 Ibn Taymiyya, *An Introduction to the Principles of Tafsīr*, 46.
32 Ibid., 47.
33 Ibn Taymiyya, *Majmūʿ al-Fatāwā*, 13:367.
34 Al-Razi, *Mafātīḥ al-Ghayb*, 2:152, for this statement and the discussion that follows.
35 Al-Bayḍāwī, *Anwār al-Tanzīl*, 1:68, for this statement and the discussion that follows.

this status with Adam alone, since God appointed him to act in His stead on Earth, adding that this is the case for all of God's prophets since they 'are appointed by God to cultivate the Earth, govern the people, perfect them, and execute His orders among them'. So, for al-Bayḍāwī, the status refers to the office of prophethood and not to humanity in general.

Al-Māturīdī relates various exegetical opinions about the succession: (1) Adam specifically, in that he succeeds the angels and jinn who preceded him on Earth, (2) or Adam and all of his descendants until the Day of Judgement in the sense that they succeed each other from one generation to the next, or (3) that they were created to inhabit the Earth and establish the religious rulings therein.[36] He does not indicate that he favours one opinion over another.

A similar approach is seen with later Māturīdī theologians in their exegetical works. For instance, Abū al-Ḥafṣ al-Nasafī (d. 1142) presents the same set of exegetical opinions without comment.[37] He sees that Adam and his descendants are either the successors of the angels whom God is addressing since they were on Earth beforehand or that it refers to Adam being God's prophet, like the other prophets that will come after him.[38]

Turning to Salafi theologians, Ibn Taymiyya cites the verse in the context of arguing that the successor is superior to the one who is being succeeded, who in this case is the angels.[39] He shows this in two ways. First, some angels were the inhabitants of the Earth beforehand, and therefore the successor on Earth is preferable to the angels who were on the Earth. Second, he argues that the angels petitioned God to place the succession with them instead when they appealed: 'Will you place therein those who will make mischief therein and shed blood?' Ibn Taymiyya asserts: 'Had the succession not been a high station, higher than theirs, they would not have sought it and been covetous of its possessor.'[40] This discussion comes in the context of the question of whether the believers, in particular, are preferable to the angels, not humanity as a whole. This means that Ibn Taymiyya is applying the station of the successor to humanity as a whole and the superiority of that station only to those who conduct themselves with righteousness.

Ibn al-Qayyim asserts that the station of successor gives preference to Adam over the angels, that this preference is one of the knowledge God gave to Adam

[36] Al-Māturīdī, *Ta'wīlāt al-Qur'ān*, 1:77.
[37] Al-Nasafī, *Al-Taysīr*, 2:51.
[38] Al-Nasafī, *Madārik al-Tanzīl*, 1:79.
[39] Ibn Taymiyya, *Majmū' al-Fatāwā*, 4:367–8.
[40] Ibid., 4:368.

and not to the angels and that the attribution of the successor to Adam expresses a special devotion to Him even before he was created.[41]

In any event, these Salafī theologians are not specifically linking the station of successor to moral accountability, just to a general station of honour above the angels. However, Ibn Taymiyya links this preference to belief and righteousness, an outcome of moral agency, so it suggests a link between this distinction and moral accountability. The same goes with Ibn al-Qayyim's connecting it with knowledge, a precondition for moral agency. This would imply that the type of moral agency possessed by humans is at least part of the reason why righteous humans are superior to angels. It would not, however, negate the possibility of moral agency to other classes of beings for two reasons. The first is there is nothing to prohibit that other beings unknown to us can also enjoy a status above the angels. The second is that other beings could be moral persons without their particular accountability making them excel the angels in preference. Interestingly, Ibn Abī al-ʿIzz (d. 1390) disagrees with his two Salafī predecessors about the preference of humanity over the angels. He says:

> Our duty is to believe in the angels and the prophets, not to believe one group is better. Had that been our duty, there would be a text making that clear to us. God said: 'Today I have completed for you your religion' and 'Your Lord does not forget'. It is authentically related: 'God has obligated things, so do not neglect them. He has set limits, so do not break them. He has remained silent about things as a mercy to you, not out of forgetfulness, so do not ask about them.' So, silence in asserting or negating something about this matter is best.[42]

He then engages with the various verses that are cited to argue for the preference of humans over the angels and conclude that they merely indicate the honour which humans enjoy, not preference over others.[43]

## Verse of the Trust (Q. 33:72)

The second verse that singles out human beings for mention is 33:72, which reads: 'Indeed, We presented the Trust to the heavens and the earth and the mountains, and they declined to carry it and feared it; but the human being carried it. Indeed, he is unjust and ignorant.'

41 Ibn al-Qayyim, *Kitāb al-Fawāʾid*, 65.
42 Ibn Abī al-ʿIzz, *Sharḥ al-ʿAqīda al-Ṭaḥāwiyya*, 2:474.
43 Ibid., 2:475.

The early Ashʿarī theologian and exegete Ibn Fūrak (d. 1015) understands the presentation of the Trust to the heavens, Earth and the mountains to be a parable depicting the weightiness of fulfilling one's trusts and that God, in this way, 'makes its high status clear by how those things, despite their size, would have feared it, had it been presented to them, and had they possessed knowledge of it'.[44] He mentions another opinion that the presentation was made to the angels inhabiting the heavens, the Earth and the mountains, and that they refused to ever fail to deliver it, an interpretation accommodated by the Arabic phrasing of the verse, but then he says that the stronger interpretation is to understand it as a parable.[45]

Al-Rāzī understands the Trust to refer to moral accountability (*taklīf*), and he contrasts this with nature (*al-ṭabīʿa*).[46] The heavens, Earth and mountains are incapable of the kind of accountability to which humans are held because they behave only in the way they are created, and nothing else can be demanded of them. As for angels, their compliance with God's commands and prohibitions is to them what eating and drinking are to us.

Likewise, al-Bayḍāwī summarized his account of the verse by saying the Trust refers to the rational faculty (*ʿaql*) and moral accountability (*taklīf*). In this sense, the offering of the Trust to the inanimate objects refers to how it relates to their capacity for it, and their refusal is merely their nature which is not susceptible to such meanings. For these Ashʿarī theologians, the Trust refers to human moral agency as seen in contrast to the inanimate world. This understanding of the verse does not rule out the existence of other moral agents who are animate entities.

Abū Manṣūr al-Māturīdī (d. 944) says it is unclear what the Trust refers to and criticizes other commentators for going to unnecessary, superfluous lengths in commenting on it, then says: 'It is not necessary to go to such lengths in the commentary of what it is, since it is unclear and can only be known by way of a text from God saying it is such. It is obligatory to make this a matter that is hidden and for which commentary is not given.'[47] Al-Māturīdī then discusses at greater length four opinions commentators have offered regarding the meaning of the presentation to the heavens, Earth and the mountains without favouring any of them.[48] He then explains what he sees as important, the reference to humanity's

44 Ibn Fūrak, *Tafsīr*, 2:126.
45 Ibid., 2:127.
46 Al-Razi, *Mafātīḥ al-Ghayb*, 25:202, for this statement and the brief discussion that follows.
47 Al-Māturīdī, *Taʾwīlāt al-Qurʾān*, 11:393–4.
48 Ibid., 11:395.

injustice and ignorance, as opposed to those other details.[49] He concludes this discussion on injustice and ignorance by saying: 'How this is understood is just as we mentioned at the start that the Trust is not to be provided commentary, nor the modality of how it was presented to the heavens, Earth, and mountains, and their refusal and fear. God best knows what He intends by that.'[50]

Abū Ḥafṣ al-Nasafī mentions various opinions and narrations about each of the elements of the verse without criticism, followed by the expression of his own opinion, which is to define the Trust as 'the works that the Muslims are commanded to perform and not abandon, and it is incumbent upon every Muslim to refrain from cheating a Muslim or one with whom there is a covenant'.[51] He holds that the presentation of the Trust is the disclosure that 'in fulfilling it there is reward and in squandering it there is punishment', and the refusal is due to fear of punishment.[52] He clarifies that the term 'human' here is a collective noun for 'Adam and His children' and then mentions that the epithets of injustice and ignorance must be understood in that context to refer only to the unbelievers, since it is impermissible to apply them to Adam himself.[53] Abū al-Barakāt ʿAbd Allāh al-Nasafī (d. 1319) briefly affirms that the Trust is obedience to God, and the 'carrying' of the Trust is the failure to render that Trust to its rightful recipient, citing the linguistic precedent for that. He does not elaborate further, nor does he discuss any other view. So, for him, the distinction is only in the occurrence of disobedience from humanity. He understands carrying the Trust in broad terms of obedience.

We see with these Māturīdī exegetes a reluctance to interpret the Trust beyond the bare minimum of the sense it carries of obedience and duties, so it is understood to refer to moral accountability of human beings in some general way or to specific duties imposed on them. The verse is understood to negate this status, or at least those duties, to inert objects incapable of reason and volition.

The Salafī theologian Ibn Taymiyya does not give this verse exclusive treatment. Nevertheless, it is possible to determine his position on the Trust and its relationship to the human being from the numerous references he makes to the passage in question. Ibn Taymiyya understands the verse to be conveying an obligation to acquire knowledge and act justly.[54] He also uses the verse to argue that beneficial knowledge and good works are foundational to the constitution

[49] Ibid., 11:396.
[50] Ibid.
[51] Al-Nasafī, *Al-Taysīr*, 12:214.
[52] Ibid., 12:216.
[53] Ibid., 12:217.
[54] Ibn Taymiyya, *Majmūʿ al-Fatāwā*, 22:252.

of human righteousness, saying: 'Good works are the totality of justice, and what God has forbidden people is the totality of injustice.'[55] Ibn Taymiyya attributes the determination of these criteria to knowledge 'since justice and injustice are only known by way of knowledge, so the religion in its entirety is knowledge and justice, which is opposed by injustice and ignorance'.[56] Furthermore, the Trust encompasses actions of the heart as well as outward deeds since deeds encompass both acts of worship and matters of doctrinal faith, and the basis for all works is the actions of the heart.[57] Therefore, the Trust encompasses both actions of the heart and of the body, which are informed by knowledge and which, in turn, realize justice. Failure to fulfil the Trust is always related to ignorance and brings about injustice. Moreover, justice and knowledge exist in an essential dynamic relationship, as do their opposites.

Ibn Taymiyya understands the attribution of injustice and ignorance as a description of humanity, since they are susceptible to 'the whims of Satan that no member of the human species can conceivably be free of'.[58] This is crucial for Ibn Taymiyya, since he repeatedly links this verse to the importance of repentance, which is the 'utmost aim' of the God-fearing.[59]

His student Ibn al-Qayyim also affirms that the verse refers to the universal state of humanity[60] and that repentance, therefore, is an essential aspect of human worship.[61]

Finally, for Ibn Taymiyya, the consequence of fulfilling this Trust, which is grounded in the success or failure of upholding truth and justice in all actions, and which in turn stems from the heart, is reward or punishment in the Hereafter.[62]

Therefore, Ibn Taymiyya understands the Trust to constitute the active practice of the faith, encompassing both belief in the religion's tenets as well as carrying out its commands and prohibitions, and the foundation for this is knowledge. The failure or refusal to acknowledge the truth and to act according to religious injunctions emanates from a dynamic interplay of injustice and ignorance, qualities which all human beings are susceptible to by their created natures and which they must actively strive against, repent from and overcome in order to

[55] Ibid., 16:65.
[56] Ibid., 28:181.
[57] Ibid., 28:178.
[58] Ibid., 28:54, 3:378 and 29:46.
[59] Ibid., 28:34, 11:256, 15:51 and 17: 514.
[60] Ibn al-Qayyim, *Zād al-Maʿād*, 2:374; Ibn al-Qayyim, *Maʿārij al-Sālikīn*, 1:209 and 3:482.
[61] Ibn al-Qayyim, *Maʿārij al-Sālikīn*, 1:453.
[62] Ibn Taymiyya, *Majmūʿ al-Fatāwā*, 10:294.

attain eternal bliss in the Hereafter. Therefore, the Trust is intrinsically linked to moral agency and the constituents of the human make-up that realize it.

## Verse of the witnessing (Q. 7:172)

This verse reads: 'And when Your Lord took from the Children of Adam, from their loins, their descendants and made them bear witness upon themselves: "Am I not your Lord", they said: "Indeed! We bear witness", lest you say on the Day of Resurrection: "We were oblivious of this"'.

This verse, along with some prophetic traditions,[63] is often understood to indicate a primordial covenant taken with all the Children of Adam, where all his descendants were brought forth at once. The idea of a primordial covenant is not commonly presented as a tenet of creed in works of Ashʿarī theology. Turning to exegesis, we find the Ashʿarī theologian al-Rāzī provides a detailed treatment of the issue, identifying two widely held opinions on it: (1) a covenant taken from humanity after a primordial constitution of all of Adam's descendants and (2) a covenant taking place during the worldly lives of Adam's descendants by their minds being compelled to recognize the signs of God's existence around them.[64]

He then shows that the wording of the verse does not indicate the extraction of Adam's descendants from the body of his person, but rather that all people are brought forth from Adam's descendants through the natural process of successive generations, so the proof for God for each person is what they experience of signs during their natural life.[65] He concludes: 'As for His bringing forth the descendants all at once from within Adam, nothing in the verse's wording indicates anything to affirm it, nor does anything in the verse indicate what would negate it.'[66] He then argues that some prophetic traditions explicitly establish the primordial covenant[67] and argues that 'there is no contradiction'

[63] For instance: It is narrated from ʿUmar ibn al-Khaṭṭāb that he was asked about this verse and said he heard God's Messenger say: 'God created Adam then He wiped his back with His right hand and brought forth his descendants from him and said: "I created these for the Fire and they will work the deeds of the denizens of the Fire. And I created these for the Garden, and they will do the deeds of the denizens of the Garden"' [al-Sijistānī, *Sunan Abī Dāwūd* (4703), 589].

[64] Al-Rāzī, *Mafātīḥ al-Ghayb*, 15:39. He later mentions a third opinion, which he dismisses as unnecessarily obtuse, which makes the matter one of humans having primordial spirits that precede their bodies and that are constituted with an innate and essential recognition of God (15:44).

[65] Al-Rāzī, *Mafātīḥ al-Ghayb*, 15:43.

[66] Ibid.

[67] One explicit tradition narrated from Ibn ʿAbbās relates that the Prophet said, 'God took the covenant from the loins of Adam at Arafat, bringing forth from his backbone every seed that he would sow. He scattered them before him and then He spoke to them as they stood before Him, saying: "Am I not your Lord?" They said: "Indeed, we bear witness." Lest you say on the Day of Resurrection: "We were unaware of this"' (7:172) [*Musnad Aḥmad* (2455)].

between the verse and those traditions, 'nor do they cancel each other out, so it is obligatory to adopt both together, and in this way uphold both the verse and the traditions from criticism as much as possible'.[68]

Al-Rāzī here clearly requires belief in what the traditions say when those traditions are neither in contradiction with the Qurʾān nor with reason. At the same time, as individual-narrator traditions related by a limited number of transmitters, he would not, as an Ashʿarī, consider those traditions strong enough to establish religiously binding doctrine.

Al-Bayḍāwī approaches verse 7:172 entirely on the basis of a worldly covenant, where our minds are compelled to recognize God through His signs. He demonstrates this through a careful analysis of the verse's wording. For instance, he glosses 'and made them bear witness upon themselves', saying: 'It means He established for them proofs of His Lordship and placed in their minds what would call them to recognise those [proofs].'[69]

Al-Māturīdī rejects the idea of a primordial covenant. Beyond the linguistic structure of the verse pointing to Adam's descendants and not Adam, he argues in his exegesis that the purpose of the witnessing mentioned in the verse is to be proof against the people on the Day of Judgement and asks how can God make this the case 'knowing that not a single one of them would have any memory of it, nor would any kind of reminder cause them to recall it?'[70] The witnessing must therefore be the signs that God places in Creation during our lives, so 'this is what the covenant is to all of the descendants and the witnessing that they are made to bear upon themselves'.[71] Harvey (2022) says that al-Māturīdī's denial of the primordial covenant in favour of a 'naturalistic reading' aligns with that theologian's 'commitment to ground human accountability within our intersubjective and rationally accessible worldly lives, rather than a pre-life event that can only be known through revealed scripture or spiritual unveiling'.[72]

Later Māturīdī theologians began to adopt the primordial covenant, easily seen in the many Māturīdī commentaries on the summary of the creed composed by al-Ṭaḥāwī (d. 933), which mentions it.[73] However, al-Māturīdī is followed in rejecting the primordial covenant by his student Abū al-Ḥasan al-Rustughfānī (d. ca 956), so this theological stance was sustained beyond al-Māturīdī

[68] Al-Rāzī, *Mafātīḥ al-Ghayb*, 15:43.
[69] Al-Bayḍāwī, *Anwār al-Tanzīl*, 2:41.
[70] Al-Māturīdī, *Taʾwīlāt al-Qurʾān*, 6:104.
[71] Ibid., 6:103.
[72] Harvey, *Transcendent God, Rational World*, 112.
[73] Al-Turkistānī, *Sharḥ al-ʿAqīda al-Ṭaḥāwiyya*, 116–17; al-Ghaznawī, *Sharḥ al-ʿAqīda al-Ṭaḥāwiyya*, 95.

himself.[74] Moreover, the pivotal classical-period Māturīdī authority Abū al-Yusr al-Bazdawī (d. 1100) asserts that while the majority of Sunnī Muslims affirm the primordial covenant, nevertheless, the belief 'that the covenant did not happen is the position of some *Ahl al-Sunna wa-l-Jamaʿa*, including Abū Manṣūr al-Māturīdī'.[75] He is saying that both opinions are regarded as legitimate within Sunnī Islam, the one affirming the primordial covenant and the one rejecting it, so neither stance is taken as a tenet of creed.

As for the Māturīdī theologians who affirm the primordial covenant, many of them stress the need to maintain theological non-commitment (*tawaqquf*) on its modality and details. Al-Turkistānī (d. 1333) says, 'They asserted the taking of the covenant but did not speak about its modality (*kayfiyya*), since they counted it from the ambiguous matters (*al-mutashābiha*). They asserted belief in its truth since it appears in the Qurʾān, but they did not busy themselves with its modality, since there are multiple possible ways to interpret it.'[76] Likewise, Sirāj al-Dīn al-Ghaznawī (d. 1372) says: 'The scholars affirm the taking of the covenant, but they do not speak about its modality, since it is from the ambiguous matters.'[77]

Turning to the classical Salafī theologians, they consistently reject the notion of a primordial covenant. Ibn Taymiyya says the verse merely refers to people's innate dispositional tendency for awareness of God and that the traditions that explicitly mention a primordial covenant are not sound enough.[78] Ibn al-Qayyim emphasizes that the verse says nothing about people being addressed and bearing witness to their Lord.[79] He argues that people could only be damned to perdition for breaking a covenant that they could remember, so it has to refer to reason and innate disposition.[80] Furthermore, he rejects the primordial covenant because of what it implies 'that souls precede the[ir] bodies with a continuous, stable precedence'[81] which would be the case if all people were genuinely extracted on that primordial occasion and then returned somewhere, awaiting their later re-emergence. He further argues that even if the traditions are taken as authentic, they could only mean that God 'gave form to the population and predetermined their creation, their lifespans, and their works, and then brought forth their forms from their substance and then returned them to it'. In other words, it would have involved their outward forms and not their souls. Therefore, there

[74] Harvey, *Transcendent God, Rational World*, 112.
[75] Al-Bazdawī, *Uṣūl al-Dīn*, 218.
[76] Al-Turkistānī, *Sharḥ al-ʿAqīda al-Ṭaḥāwiyya*, 116–17.
[77] Al-Ghaznawī, *Sharḥ al-ʿAqīda al-Ṭaḥāwiyya*, 95.
[78] Ibn Taymiyya, *Jāmiʿ al-Rasāʾil*, 1:11.
[79] Ibn al-Qayyim, *Kitāb al-Rūḥ*, 386.
[80] Ibid.
[81] Ibid., 385–6.

was no covenant for individuals at that time, but God merely predetermined when their appointed times of creation would be.[82]

The Salafī theologian Ibn Abī al-ʿIzz affirms the Salafī stance in his commentary on Abū Jaʿfar Aḥmad al-Ṭaḥāwī's creed, where it says, 'The covenant that God took from Adam and his descendants is true.' He reaffirms Ibn al-Qayyim's opinion on the extent of what the traditions can mean, rejects the notion of a primordial witnessing and argues that the covenant mentioned in the verse refers to the innate disposition.[83]

The verse clearly establishes moral accountability for human beings to believe in God by declaring: 'lest you say on the Day of Resurrection: "We were oblivious of this".' The question is how this accountability is acquired. Those who reject the primordial covenant, like al-Māturīdī, al-Rustughfānī and the Salafis, hold that it is simply grounded in the faculty of reason, or reason accompanied by the innate disposition, which is their respective schools' stance on moral accountability. Those who uphold the primordial covenant see it as an experiential event that establishes this accountability. Even on that interpretation, there are two reasons why it would not exclude the possibility of moral accountability for non-human entities. The first is that asserting such a covenant for Adam's children on Earth does not negate a similar primordial covenant for other beings elsewhere. Secondly, those who accept that God can hold people accountable for a covenant they cannot remember, which is certainly not a problem for Ashʿarīs, would accept that God can hold beings accountable without enacting a primordial covenant for them at all.

## Verses indicating the moral personhood of the jinn

There are a number of verses of the Qurʾān that indicate the jinn are morally accountable agents. The 72nd chapter of the Qurʾān, entitled 'The jinn', relates how some jinn heard the Qurʾān and believed in it. Significantly, verses Q. 72:15-16 have these jinn declaring: 'And among us are Muslims, and among us are the unjust. And whoever has become Muslim – those have sought out the right course. But as for the unjust, they will be fuel for Hell.' Another passage is Q. 46:29-32. These verses show not only the capacity for belief and disbelief but also the decision to believe and disbelieve, as well as facing moral consequences

[82] Ibid.
[83] Ibn Abī al-ʿIzz, *Sharḥ al-ʿAqīda al-Ṭaḥāwiyya*, 1:371–3.

for doing so.[84] Likewise, Q. 7:179 says that many jinn will be consigned to Hell, as will many humans.

The moral accountability of the jinn is a point of agreement among Sunnī theologians, who also agree that it is firmly established by the Qurʾān.[85] Al-Ṭaḥāwī establishes this point in his *Creed*, saying: 'He [Muḥammad] is an emissary to all of the jinn and the whole of humanity, with truth and guidance, light and radiance.'[86] In his commentary on this passage, al-Turkīstānī asserts: 'He only says this because of the decisive [scriptural] evidence that necessitates this knowledge.'[87] Significantly, this means that Q. 2:30, Q. 7:172 and Q. 33:72 discussed earlier cannot be understood to indicate that humans are the only moral persons. Those verses make no mention of the jinn, so if their wording or context implied exclusivity to human beings, this would entail a contradiction with the verses that discuss the jinn as moral persons. Consequently, those verses, to the extent that they assert moral personhood as a distinctive feature of Adam's descendants, cannot indicate exclusivity for them.

There remains the question of whether moral personhood might be restricted to humans and jinn to the exclusion of other beings. There are indeed a number of verses that address the 'assembly of jinn and humans', like Q. 6:130: 'O assembly of jinn and humans, have not messengers from yourselves come to you relating to you My signs?' Al-Rāzī explains here that the word 'assembly' (*maʿshar*) refers to 'every group whose affair is the same'.[88]

Two verses have particular relevance to this question. One of these is Q. 51:56: 'I did not create jinn and humans except to worship Me.' This verse clearly shows that both classes of beings share the same purpose in life and that purpose is a moral one. Al-Rāzī makes it clear that this verse does not imply exclusivity, saying, "The angels are also from the classes of morally accountable beings, but God does not mention them, though the greatest benefit in His bringing them into existence is [His] worship.'[89]

The other is Q. 55:31, which reads: 'We will turn to you with our full attention, o you two weighty multitudes.' Humans and jinn are referred to in this verse as 'the two weighty multitudes' (*al-thaqalān*).[90] The event being described is the

84 Ibn Taymiyya, *Ibn Taymiyah's Essay on the Jinn*, 20–1, 32, 36.
85 Al-Rāzī, *Mafātīḥ al-Ghayb*, 28:200; al-Māturīdī, *Taʾwīlāt al-Qurʾān*; 5:216 and 14:155; al-Ghaznawī, *Sharḥ al-ʿAqīda al-Ṭaḥāwiyya*, 73; Ibn Taymiyya, *Ibn Taymiyah's Essay on the Jinn*, 17–18, 20–1, and 24; Ibn Abī al-ʿIzz, *Sharḥ al-ʿAqīda al-Ṭaḥāwiyya*, 1:250.
86 Al-Ṭaḥāwī, *The Creed of Imam al-Ṭaḥāwī*, 54.
87 Al-Turkistānī, *Sharḥ al-ʿAqīda al-Ṭaḥāwiyya*, 93.
88 Al-Rāzī, *Mafātīḥ al-Ghayb*, 13:159.
89 Ibid., 28:198.
90 Ibid., 29:99; al-Bayḍāwī, *Anwār al-Tanzīl*, 5:173; al-Nasafī, *Madārik al-Tanzīl*, 4:312.

judgement in the Hereafter, where promised rewards and consequences will be meted out.[91]

What is crucial here is the significance of referring to humans and jinn as 'the two weighty ones'. Al-Rāzī mentions three opinions: (1) they are two classes of beings weighed down with sins, (2) they are classes of beings who weigh down upon the Earth and (3) they are two classes who have considerable importance.[92] Al-Bayḍāwī mentions that it could be referring to the weightiness of their opinion and rank or that they are weighed down with the burden of moral accountability (*taklīf*).[93]

Abū al-Ḥafṣ al-Nasafī elaborates on these latter two notions, saying: 'Jinn and humans are called this because the weight has substance and rank, and these two groups have greater rank over others due to reason, discernment, and carrying the Trust and moral accountability.'[94] Therefore, one interpretation is that the term is intended to refer to moral accountability and its preconditions, which set humans and jinn apart from other creatures. Yet, neither this interpretation nor any of the others, in the verse's context, connotes the exclusivity of these traits for these two classes, or that this judgement of humans and jinn is the only possible judgement God will ever carry out for any beings.

Therefore, if scripture is the sole source for determining the moral accountability of any beings, it can be confirmed with doctrinal authority that human beings and jinn are morally accountable entities. However, the texts do not indicate that this is for them to the exclusion of any other possible beings. In other words, there is no scriptural assertion of exclusivity. This means that the moral accountability of other possible rational beings can neither be affirmed nor denied by scripture. For Ashʿarīs, who require direct scriptural evidence to establish moral personhood, the status of such rational entities remains undetermined. It becomes obligatory for them to remain theologically non-committal on the matter. On the one hand, if we encounter a higher intelligence other than humans and jinn, we cannot negate that they are morally accountable persons like ourselves. Nevertheless, on Ashʿarī principles, we would not be able to establish as binding doctrinal truth that they actually enjoy that status with God.

In that case, how should those beings be treated? What rights do they have? What obligations? To answer these questions, a different hermeneutical register must be adopted, that of Islamic Law.

91 Al-Bayḍāwī, *Anwār al-Tanzīl*, 5:172; al-Māturīdī, *Taʾwīlāt al-Qurʾān*, 14:270.
92 Al-Rāzī, *Mafātīḥ al-Ghayb*, 29:99.
93 Al-Bayḍāwī, *Anwār al-Tanzīl*, 5:173.
94 Al-Nasafī, *Al-Taysīr*, 14:199.

## The legal determination of moral personhood

Islamic Law does not require certainty but preponderance of evidence (*rājiḥ*) to establish the most likely ruling for practical action. Its hermeneutical logic commonly grapples with navigating uncertainties to answer questions of practical importance that need an answer even though decisive scriptural evidence is rarely present. Islamic legal theory (*uṣūl al-fiqh*) and the discipline of legal axioms (*al-qawāʿid al-fiqhiyya*) provide frameworks for jurists to achieve practical legal rulings in the face of such uncertainty.[95]

Two legal principles are important here. The first is that rulings are according to what is manifest (*al-ḥukm bi-l-ẓāhir*). This is an overarching principle that is used in many aspects of the law. One important application is upholding the various rights, duties and rulings of Muslims, People of the Book and other non-Muslims. It is impossible to know the state of anyone's heart. Instead, it is obligatory to act on what is apparent. Due to its implications for establishing the legal ruling of belief and disbelief, this principle is mentioned in theological books, like al-Ṭaḥāwī's *Creed*, where he says: 'We also do not accuse any of them of disbelief, idolatry, or hypocrisy, as long as none of that manifests from them. We resign their inner states to God, the Sublime and Exalted.'[96] Al-Ghaznawī comments on this passage as follows: 'This is because we judge by what is manifest, and God judges the inner state, since it is impermissible for us to attest to what we do not know.'[97] Likewise, al-Turkistānī says: 'He [God] is the one who is privy to this [their inner state], not the servants, so it is obligatory to consign that matter to God.'[98] Ibn Abī al-ʿIzz concurs: 'We are commanded to judge according to what is manifest, and we are prohibited from speculation and from pursuing what we do not know.'[99]

The fact that this principle is applied by theologians in the determination of who is identified as a believer, and not just by legal scholars, stresses the importance of its application for determining such matters. Therefore, if a class of rational, self-aware entities is encountered that shows the ability to understand right and wrong and to conceptualize and believe in God, it would be obligatory to treat that class of entities as moral persons in all practical dealings. This would be the case even for Ashʿarīs who might nevertheless not consider their personhood status to be

95 Hallaq, 'Was the Gate of Ijtihad Closed?', 4–5.
96 Al-Ṭaḥāwī, *The Creed of Imam al-Ṭaḥāwī*, 68.
97 Al-Ghaznawī, *Sharḥ al-ʿAqīda al-Ṭaḥāwiyya*, 128.
98 Al-Turkistānī, *Sharḥ al-ʿAqīda al-Ṭaḥāwiyya*, 142.
99 Ibn Abī al-ʿIzz, *Sharḥ al-ʿAqīda al-Ṭaḥāwiyya*, 2:575.

established with doctrinal certainty. Since it cannot be known how God regards the inner state of these beings, Ashʿarīs will be forced to treat them according to what they outwardly manifest of the conditions of moral agency.

The second legal principle is that avoiding the forbidden takes precedence whenever the forbidden is implicated with something permissible.[100] A related principle is that it is necessary to do whatever is required to abstain from what is unlawful.[101] There is a prophetic tradition that provides a practical application of this principle regarding ambiguity about an entity's personhood status. It is reported that the Prophet informed the people that some jinn in Medina could appear in the form of snakes, saying: 'There are a group of jinn in Medina who have accepted Islam, so if you see any of these snakes, request it to leave thrice. If it appears after that, kill it, for it is a devil.'[102]

Ibn Taymiyya explains that the reason it is forbidden to kill these snakes is that people are obligated to point out the error of wrongdoers before exacting punishment, and this right extends to the jinn: 'They should be ordered to be righteous and to abstain from evil just as is done with humans, based on God's statement: "We will not punish [the wayward] until a messenger has been sent [to them]".'[103] He adds: 'killing a jinn without a just cause is as forbidden as killing a human without a just cause.'[104]

Since the Prophet informed them that jinn in Medina can appear as snakes, this means that it is impossible to determine whether the entity in the person's home is a jinn and therefore a morally accountable person whose life is inviolable and who has commensurate rights in that regard or a dangerous animal that certainly has rights in Islam but of a different order. Since this is impossible to ascertain, it is required to err on the side of caution and treat the entity as a morally accountable person and order it repeatedly to leave, affording it the chance to do so. If the entity refuses to leave, it is one of the following: (1) a wilful and dangerous morally accountable trespasser who can be fought and killed in self-defence or (2) a dangerous animal that can be killed to protect the safety of oneself and one's family. This would apply to any class of entities we encounter whose personhood status is suspected but scripturally unconfirmable. Mistakenly conferring upon them the rights of moral persons entails, at worst, giving them some benefits they

100 For instance, al-ʿAynī, *Al-Bināya*, 12:145, involves this principle while discussing lawful and unlawful exposure of parts of the body and 12:431 while discussing the unlawfulness of game where a hunting dog and another dog are implicated in the kill.

101 Al-Zarkashī, *Al-Baḥr al-Muḥīṭ*, 1:258.

102 Ibn Ḥajjāj, *Ṣaḥīḥ Muslim* (2236), 1665.

103 Ibn Taymiyya, *Ibn Taymiyah's Essay on the Jinn*, 49–50.

104 Ibid., 52.

might not be entitled to, leading to a possible loss for others. On the other hand, denying their rights could entail the gravest degree of unlawful oppression if these entities are, in God's estimation, morally accountable persons.

## Conclusion

There are no theological, doctrinal or scriptural grounds to negate the possibility that God created morally accountable beings elsewhere in the universe. Therefore, if another class of rational beings is ever encountered that exhibits the qualities of volition and discretion, it will be impossible to deny that the members of that class have the status of moral agents and, through that denial, treat them as non-persons.

Furthermore, in the Māturīdī and Salafi theological traditions, moral accountability is connected to the faculty of reason as an imperative of God's wisdom, with Salafis including the innate disposition to recognize God as an additional condition. Therefore, if the requisite qualities are established for a class of beings, they would be taken as morally accountable persons without question. In the Ashʿarī tradition, however, it could be argued that moral accountability before God is a matter of the Unseen, and it is not obligatory upon God to hold all created rational entities morally accountable. Consequently, it is not possible to assert as theological doctrine that a class of rational beings is morally accountable before God merely on the grounds that its members possess reason and self-awareness.

Nevertheless, they would still have to confer upon such beings the legal status of morally accountable persons, due to the obligation to act upon what is manifest, since an intelligence that exhibits volition and discretion has all the appearances of a morally accountable entity, especially if it refers to itself as such. This is crucial since there are no theological grounds to deny it that status. Moreover, it would be obligatory to err on the side of caution and uphold their rights as morally accountable agents, since if they genuinely have this status with God, and that status is denied them, it would constitute a sinful transgression against morally accountable persons.

## Bibliography

Abū ʿAdhaba, al-Ḥasan ibn ʿAbd al-Muḥsin. *Al-Rawḍa al-Bahiyya fīmā bayna al-Ashāʿira wa-l-Māturīdiyya*. Beirut: ʿĀlam al-Kutub, 1989.

Al-ʿAynī, Badr al-Dīn. *Al-Binaya Sharḥ al-Hidāya*. Beirut: Dār al-Kutub al-ʿIlmiyya, 2000.

Al-Bayḍāwī, ʿAbd Allāh. *Anwār al-Tanzīl wa-Asrār al-Ta'wīl*. Beirut: Dār Iḥyāʾ al-Turāth al-ʿArabī, 1998.

Al-Bazdawī, Abū al-Yusr. *Uṣūl al-Dīn*. Cairo: al-Maktaba al-Azhariyya li-l-Turāth, 2011.

Al-Ghazālī, Abū Ḥāmid. *Al-Iqtiṣād fī al-Iʿtiqād*. Beirut: Dār al-Kutub al-ʿIlmiyya, 1988.

Al-Ghaznawī, Abū Haff. *Sharḥ al-ʿAqīda al-Ṭaḥāwiyya*. Cairo: Dar al-Hafaz, 2009.

Al-Māturīdī, Abū Manṣūr. *Kitāb al-Tawḥīd*. Edited by Bekir Topaloğlu and Muḥammad Aruci. Istanbul: Maktabat al-Irshād, 2010.

Al-Māturīdī, Abū Manṣūr. *Taʾwīlāt al-Qurʾān*. Edited by Bekir Topaloğlu, Ahmet Vanlıoğlu, Mehmet Boynukalın, Ertuğrul Boynukalın et al. Istanbul: Dār al-Mīzān, 2006.

Al-Nasafī, Abū al-Barakāt ʿAbd Allāh. *Madārik al-Tanzīl wa-Ḥaqā'iq al-Taʾwīl*. Beirut: Dār al-Nafā'is, 1996.

Al-Nasafī, Abū al-Ḥafṣ. *Al-Taysīr fī al-Tafsir*. Istanbul: Dar al-Lubab, 2019.

Al-Rāzī, Fakhr al-Din. *Al-Maṭālib al-ʿĀliya min al-ʿIlm al-Ilāhiyya*. Beirut: Dār al-Kitāb al-ʿArabī, 1987.

Al-Rāzī, Fakhr al-Din. *Mafātīḥ al-Ghayb*. Beirut: Dār al-Kutub al-ʿIlmiyya, 2000.

Al-Ṣābūnī, Nūr al-Dīn. *Kitāb al-Bidāyā min al-Kifāyā fī al-Hidāyā fī Uṣūl al-Dīn*. Edited by Fatt Allāh Khuayf. Alexandria: Dār al-Maʿārif bi-Maṣr, 1969.

Al-Sijistānī, Abū Dāwūd. *Sunan Abī Dāwūd*. Riyadh: Dār al-Ḥaḍāra lil-Nashr wa-l-Tawzīʿ, 2010.

Al-Ṭaḥāwī, Abū Jaʿfar. *The Creed of Imam al-Ṭaḥāwī*. Translated by Hamza Yusuf. Berkeley: Zaytuna Institute, 2009.

Al-Turkistānī, Shujāʿ al-Dīn. *Sharḥ al-ʿAqīda al-Ṭaḥāwiyya*. Amman: Dār al-Nūr, 2014.

Al-Zarkashī, Badr al-Dīn. *Al-Baḥr al-Muḥīṭ*. Kuwait: Wizārat al-Awqāf wa-l-Shuʾūn al-Islāmiyya, 1992.

Boeker, Ruth. *Locke on Persons and Personal Identity*. Oxford: Oxford University Press, 2021.

Hacker, P. M. S. *Human Nature: The Categorial Framework*. Malden: Blackwell, 2007.

Hallaq, Wael B. 'Was the Gate of Ijtihad Closed?' *International Journal of Middle East Studies* 16, no. 1 (1984): 3–41.

Harvey, Ramon. *The Qurʾān and the Just Society*. Edinburgh: Edinburgh University Press, 2018.

Harvey, Ramon. *Transcendent God, Rational World: A Maturidi Theology*. Edinburgh: Edinburgh University Press, 2021.

Hoover, Jon. *Ibn Taymiyya's Theodicy of Perpetual Optimism*. Leiden: Brill, 2007.

Ibn Abī al-ʿIzz, ʿAlī. *Sharḥ al-ʿAqīda al-Ṭaḥāwiyya*. Beirut: Muʾassasat al-Risāla, 2003.

Ibn Fūrak, Muḥammad. *Tafsīr al-Qurʾān al-ʿAẓīm*. Mecca: Umm al-Qurā University, 2009.

Ibn Ḥajjāj, Muslim. *Saḥīḥ Muslim*. Published with al-Nawawī's commentary. Beirut: Dār Ibn Ḥazm, 2002.

Ibn Qayyim al-Jawziyya, Muḥammad. *Kitāb al-Fawāʾid*. Beirut: Dār al-Kutub al-ʿIlmiyya, 1973.
Ibn Qayyim al-Jawziyya, Muḥammad. *Kitāb al-Rūḥ*. Damascus: Dār Ibn Kathīr, 2002.
Ibn Qayyim al-Jawziyya, Muḥammad. *Maʿārij al-Sālikīn*. Riyadh: Dār Ibn Khuzayma, 2003.
Ibn Qayyim al-Jawziyya, Muḥammad. *Shifāʾ al-ʿAlīl*. Beirut: Dār al-Kitāb al-ʿArabī, 1998.
Ibn Qayyim al-Jawziyya, Muḥammad. *Zād al-Maʿād fī Hadī Khayr al-ʿIbād*. Beirut: Muʾassasat al-Risāla, 1994.
Ibn Taymiyya, Aḥmad. *An Introduction to the Principles of Tafsīr*. Translated by Salim Abdallah lbn Morgan. Sydney: Islamic Centre for Islamic Studies, 2001.
Ibn Taymiyya, Aḥmad. *Darʿ Taʿāruḍ al-ʿAql wa-l-Naql*. Riyadh: al-Imām University Press, 1991.
Ibn Taymiyya, Aḥmad. *Ibn Taymiyah's Essay on the Jinn (Demons)*. Translated by Abu Ameenah Bilal Philips. Riyadh: International Islamic Publishing House, 1989.
Ibn Taymiyya, Aḥmad. *Jāmiʿ al-Rasāʾil*. Dār al-Madanī, 1984.
Ibn Taymiyya, Aḥmad. *Majmūʿ al-Fatāwā*. Medina: King Fahd Printing Complex, 1995.
Jackson, Sherman. *Islam and the Problem of Black Suffering*. Oxford: Oxford University Press, 2009.
Leaman, Oliver. 'The Developed Kalām Tradition'. In *The Cambridge Companion to Classical Islamic Theology*, edited by Tim Winter, 77–96. New York: Cambridge University Press, 2008.
Locke, Lawrence A. 'Personhood and Moral Responsibility'. *Law and Philosophy* 9, no. 1 (1990): 39–66.
Pessagno, J. Meric. '*Irāda, Ikhtiyār, Qudra, Kasb*: The View of Abū Manṣur al-Māturīdī'. *Journal of the American Oriental Society* 104, no. 1 (1984): 177–91.
Shihadeh, Ayman. 'The Argument from Ignorance and its Critics in Medieval Arabic Thought'. *Arabic Sciences and Philosophy* 23, no. 2 (2013): 171–220.
Vasalou, Sophia. *Ibn Taymiyya's Theological Ethics*. Oxford: Oxford University Press, 2015.
Vilhauer, Benjamin. 'Free Will Skepticism and Personhood as a Desert Base'. *Canadian Journal of Philosophy* 39, no. 3 (2009): 489–512.

5

# Classical Muslim thought and the theological implications and possibility of non-human intelligence

Faisal Abdullah

## Introduction

As human beings begin their initial forays into outer space and efforts are now in order to detect signs of life beyond Earth, relevant questions have emerged for believers of universalist religions in light of the possible existence of intelligent life elsewhere in the universe. Can one's religious ethics, moral vision and religious cosmology incorporate a new class of intelligent being outside of our planet, or are these limited to the earthly human experience and thus challenged by the existence of new sentients? This chapter attempts to show how discussions from within Islam's rich intellectual heritage might consider the existence of novel classes of intelligent beings, focusing primarily on premodern examples reflective of the classical Sunnī tradition. Muslim thinkers of the past could not only conceive of intelligent non-human and other-worldly beings existing in God's vast creation, but a handful also engaged in theological and legal discourses that considered the relevancy of Islam for non-human entities. This chapter will first present an Islamic cosmology of the heavens and the Earth based on Qur'ānic ideas found in the Muslim exegetical tradition before delving into legal and theological discussions that relate to the relevancy of Islam for non-human intelligent beings. The latter section will engage mainly with the writings of three respected scholars of the premodern Muslim world, Abū al-Ḥasan al-Māwardī (d. 1058), Taqī al-Dīn al-Subkī (d. 1355) and Jalāl al-Dīn al-Suyūṭī (d. 1505). Al-Māwardī appears to be the first Muslim scholar to formally consider whether the message of the Prophet Muḥammad could be extended to intelligent beings of other 'earths', while al-Suyūṭī and al-Subkī offer us several broad arguments for why this message was universal and applicable for non-human angels and jinn, arguments which theoretically could be used to extend the universality of the Prophet's message to additional classes of non-human intelligent beings.

## Classical views on the heavens, earth(s) and other-worldly beings

Someone approaching the Qur'ān for the first time will be quick to note the significance that the heavens play within Islamic cosmology. The Qur'ān is replete with verses that pair mention of the heavens with our more familiar earthly abode and which note the presence of ambiguous beings in the heavens, as on Earth, who are devoted to God. Again and again the Qur'ān proclaims that it is the heavens *and* the Earth that are encompassed by God's dominion,[1] knowledge[2] and the passing of His divine command.[3] It is a place that was given some divine *purpose* worthy of our contemplation.[4] If God has a relationship with our earthly domain because of His status as divine, the same applies in the heavens as well, for 'It is He who is God in the heaven and God on Earth'.[5]

In a set of striking verses confirming the Prophet's message of Islam (literally surrendering to God in Arabic) as the only way to salvation and the primordial religion that continues the message of prior prophets, the Qur'ān uses derivations of the Arabic verbal root of *islām* to signify that Islam is applicable to 'Everyone in the heavens and earth', all of whom ultimately engage in surrendering (*aslam*) to God:

> Do they seek other than the religion/way (*dīn*) of God? Everyone in the heavens and the earth surrenders [Arabic: *aslam*] to God willingly or unwillingly; they will all be returned to Him. . . . If anyone chooses a religion/way (*dīn*) other than to surrender [to God] (*islām*), it will not be accepted from him: he will be one of the losers in the Hereafter.[6]

The idea that beings exist in the heavens, as suggested by the ambiguous language of 'Everyone in the heavens' in the aforementioned verse, is present in several other verses of the Qur'ān, some of which also convey the sense that these

1 Q. 2:107.
2 Q. 3:5.
3 Q. 65:12 and 41:12.
4 Q. 3:190–1, 12:105 and 21:16.
5 Q. 43:84 and 6:3.
6 Q. 3:81–5.

beings are in devotion to God and will be brought together in a final gathering on the Judgement Day just as earthly humans: 'Among His signs is the creation of the heavens and earth and all the living creatures (*dābbah*) He has scattered throughout them both. He has the power to gather them all together whenever He will.'[7] And elsewhere, it says: 'The seven heavens and the earth and everyone in them glorify Him. There is not a single thing that does not celebrate His praise, though you do not understand their praise: He is the most forbearing, most forgiving.'[8]

Qur'ānic verses making open-ended reference to beings or creatures in the heavens as in the earlier examples, or others that reference God's unfathomable creative ability,[9] His Lordship over undefined *worlds* or *domains of existence* (*ʿālamīn*),[10] a possible allusion to the existence of several 'earths',[11] God's ability to replace humans with an ambiguous 'new creation'[12] and a verse that left open the possibility that God created other entities more favoured then mankind,[13] lent themselves to imaginative possibilities regarding God's limitless creative ability and the possibility of other-worldly beings. For example, while Qur'ānic references to beings in the heavens were generally interpreted within the

7 Q. 42:29.

8 Q. 17:44. See also Q. 19:93–6.

9 For example, Q. 16:8. See the chapter of Moamer Khalayleh in this volume regarding this verse.

10 The term *ʿālam* found in many verses of the Qur'ān may refer to a domain of existence and does not necessarily mean a *physical* universe or world. It could be used, for example, to say the *ʿālam* of humans or the *ʿālam* of jinn, that is, the universe or world of humans or that of jinn – not in a physical sense. Of the many verses that reference God's Lordship over various domains of existence, see Q. 1:2, 45:36 and 26:192.

11 Q. 65:12, which was referenced earlier but which will be discussed shortly.

12 Q. 35:15–17 and 14:19–20.

13 Q. 17:70 states that humans have been favoured over *many* of God's creations, leaving open the possibility that they were not favoured exclusively: 'We have honoured the children of Adam and carried them by land and sea; We have provided good sustenance for them and favoured them specially *above many of those We have created*.'
This verse was referenced in a well-known Muslim debate on the relative merits of angels and humans and whether one was superior to the other. As the premodern jurist Ibn Ḥazm (d. 1064) states, angels were the only beings the verse could be alluding to as superior to humans because the other *available* options were clearly less favoured by God: jinn (considered as a class to be inferior to humans), animals that were incapable of producing intelligent speech and non-animals (e.g. plants). Given that these were the only beings known to exist, the possible superiority to humans alluded to by this verse was *practically* limited to angels within premodern Muslim discourse, even though a hypothetical 'other' intelligent being may fulfil this role as well. In fact, we find that some of the arguments made in these discussions in favour of angel superiority over humans could be employed, in theory, for other theoretical beings. If angels were considered more favoured by virtue of their worshipping more than humans, it is also possible that another intelligent being could worship God more faithfully than humans. Notably in these discussions, though, even if the angels were considered superior to humans, the Prophet – a human – was assumed the greatest of all beings, though the modern Salafī scholar Ibn al-ʿUthaymīn questions whether there is a textual basis for this claim. For a detailed overview of the referenced debate, see al-Suyūṭī, *Al-Ḥabāʾik*, 203–40; al-Ḥalīmī, *Al-Minhāj*, 1:303–15; al-Rāzī, *Mafātīḥ al-Ghayb*, 21:375; al-Māturīdī, *Tafsīr al-Māturīdī*, 7:86–8; Ibn Ḥazm, *Al-Faṣl*, 5:18. For Ibn al-ʿUthaymīn's remarks, see transcripts from his lecture series: *Liqāʾ al-Bāb al-Maftūḥ*. Lecture 53.

tradition to be angels, the explicit mention in Q. 42:29[14] of creatures (*dābba*) dispersed throughout *both* the heavens and the Earth raised other possibilities, since the Arabic signified a creature that steps and walks. While such stepping creatures made sense on Earth, they did not in the heavens, where angels were the only presumed residents and for whom this word was not applied. Some exegetes resorted to non-apparent interpretations of the verse to conclude that these entities were only on Earth, despite the verse explicitly stating that God had dispersed them throughout *both* the heavens and the Earth. Others argued that the Arabic word referred to beings with general movement, in which case angels could also be intended. However, the apparent wording of the verse ultimately also led to express admissions that there could be walking entities in the heavens that were not necessarily angels, as was made by al-Zamakhsharī[15] (d. 1143), al-Rāzī[16] (d. 1210), al-Nasafī[17] (d. 1310) and others.[18] Al-Zamakhsharī states:

> It is not a far-off possibility that God created in the heavens a living being (*ḥayawān*) that walks therein like a human does on Earth. Glory be to God, who creates what we know and that which we do not know from different types of creation.[19]

Elsewhere is a Qurʾānic reference to The Frequented House (*al-bayt al-maʿmūr*).[20] It was explained by the Prophet in a ḥadīth considered authentic as a sacred space in the highest heaven wherein 70,000 angels pray every day[21] and described in separate reports of lesser status as a heavenly mirror of the earthly Kaʿba physically located above the earthly one.[22] This sacred space in the heavens was the basis of popular ideas of a sacred Kaʿba existing in *every* one

[14] See earlier reference. Q. 16:49 could also be read as a reference to creatures existing in the heavens just as on earth, though the specific wording used in that verse is less explicit than Q. 42:29.
[15] Al-Zamakhsharī, *Al-Kashshāf*, 5:225.
[16] Al-Rāzī, *Mafātīḥ al-Ghayb*, 27:599.
[17] Al-Nasafī, *Madārik al-Tanzīl*, 3:256.
[18] See the chapter of Muhammad Montasseri, this volume, which engages with this verse in light of additional exegetical works. As he points out, Makkī ibn Abī Ṭālib (d. 1045), who is even earlier than al-Zamakhsharī, confirms the apparent import of the verse that creatures were spread by God in both the heavens and the earth, in opposition to non-apparent interpretations of this verse that attempted to limit the location of these creatures to just earth. He subtly acknowledges that these beings may be of a type unknown to us by citing Q. 16:8: 'and He creates what you do not know'. Abī Ṭālib, *Al-Hidāya*, 10:6594–5; al-Andalusī, *Al-Baḥr al-Muḥīṭ*, 9:338; al-Sharbīnī, *al-Sirāj*, 3:542. The modern Saʿīd Ḥawwā (d. 1989), a leading member of the Muslim Brotherhood in Syria, references this verse and this interpretation in his exegetical work as Qurʾānic recognition of extraterrestrial life should it be discovered on another planet at some point. See Ḥawwā, *Al-Asās*, 9:5105.
[19] Al-Zamakhsharī, *Al-Kashshāf*, 5:225; Al-Rāzī suggests that it could be *varieties* of living beings. See al-Rāzī, *Mafātīḥ al-Ghayb*, 27:599.
[20] Q. 52:4.
[21] Al-Bukhārī, *Al-Jāmiʿ al-Musnad al-Ṣaḥīḥ*, 4:109 and 5:52; Ibn al-Ḥajjāj, *Ṣaḥīḥ Muslim*, 1:145 and 149.
[22] Ibn Kathīr, *Tafsīr*, 7:428–9.

of the seven heavens above, frequented and worshipped in by the *people* of that heaven (*ahluhā*), a vague reference that might include non-angels as well.[23]

Verses that referred to God as the Lord of the 'worlds' or 'domains' (*ʿālamīn*) resulted in speculation as to how many of these 'domains' existed and what they contained. Some early Muslim views held that these were domains on our physical Earth, while others saw them as far more encompassing. For example, while Saʿīd ibn al-Musayyib (d. 715) reportedly said that God had 1,000 such domains – 600 in the ocean and 400 on land – two other early Muslim figures, Wahb ibn Munabbih (d. 728) and Abū Saʿīd al-Khudrī (d. 693), apparently held that there were 80,000 or 40,000 such domains, respectively, and that the entirety of the closer realm that humans inhabit (*al-dunyā*) made up only *one* of those.[24] Elsewhere, we find that Ibn ʿAbbās (d. 687), the cousin of the Prophet and authoritative early exegete of the Qurʾān, reportedly held that the realm of humans and jinn made up only one domain, the angels another, and 70,000 other domains existed apart from those, the reality of which only God was aware.[25] Clearly, God's creation was unfathomable and could very well contain creatures of various types unfamiliar to us, including some that may walk like us.[26]

It was also acknowledged that God could theoretically create beings comparable to humans or even greater. In Qurʾānic verses such as Q. 35:15-17, God speaks to His ability to replace humans with a new creation. Al-Zamakhsharī comments that the verses signify God's ability to replace humans with other humans or even an alternate class of being that does not resemble the human form.[27] Fakhr al-Dīn al-Rāzī transmits the view of some Muʿtazilī scholars that the verse is more likely to be referencing God's ability to create a non-human or non-jinn being (as opposed to a known class of being), because such an interpretation would be more indicative of God's creative power and thus more in line with the message of the verse. It is God's mercy that He hasn't replaced the present group of humans with other beings when He is fully capable of doing so. And al-Rāzī himself states in the context of these verses that God could replace humans with

[23] Ibid., 7:428.
[24] Al-Thaʿlabī, *Al-Kashf*, 7:662–3.
[25] Ibn al-Wardī, *Kharīdat al-ʿAjāʾib*, 421.
[26] Earthly creatures believed to bear a semblance to humans were not unheard of in antiquity, but the notion of non-angelic beings that walked like humans in the heavens as found in the Muslim sources is noteworthy. Regarding the former type, al-Masʿūdī (d. 956) describes the existence of various communities (*umam*) believed to have existed on Earth prior to Adam, some described with humanoid features and possibly borrowed from Greek mythology and legends. See al-Masʿūdī, *Akhbār al-Zamān*, 32–3.
[27] Al-Zamakhsharī, *Al-Kashshāf*, 1:574 and 2:547–8.

a greater, more complete, more beautiful creation that also worships better.[28] The theoretical possibility was therefore granted.

A handful of premodern discussions also affirm the possibility of concurrent non-human intelligent life and, in at least one fascinating case, even formally consider whether the religious call of the Prophet was extendable to communities of beings outside of our earthly domain. The following verse was the source of discussion regarding several possible 'earths' that may contain other beings: 'God is the One who created seven heavens and of the earth the like of it. His command descends throughout them so that you should realize that He has power over all things and that His knowledge encompasses everything.'[29]

The phrase 'and of the earth the like of it' was interpreted by several authorities to mean that the Earth came as seven, just as the heavens. The Andalusian scholar and exegete al-Qurṭubī (d. 1273), seemingly borrowing also from the statements of the earlier Shāfiʿī jurist al-Māwardī (d. 1058), summarized the majority scholarly position as being that there were seven earths that existed in layers (one above the other), but separated by a vast distance, and that in each Earth were resident beings (*sukkān*) from the creation of God. A separate position held that the 'earths' were layered but were physically attached (with ours on top).[30] A prophetic ḥadīth considered authentic declared that the one who unjustly took a piece of land from another would be punished on Judgement Day by sinking down or being strangled by seven earths.[31] This report was used as evidence that the seven earths alluded to in the verse were layered, an interpretation that was also supported by another more explicit prophetic tradition, which, however, unlike the first tradition, was not to the same standards of authenticity but indicated that the land we are presently on is the top of seven layers of Earth under the heavens, each over the other and separated by a distance of 500 years.[32] While the notion of different 'earths' being arranged in layers was the most widely held one and most in line with some known prophetic reports, there was also a position that these seven 'earths' represented geographically separate lands (*aqālīm*) on the same surface.[33]

Given that the possible existence of several earths was recognized in the tradition, it was not surprising to find the acknowledgement that these earths

28 Al-Rāzī, *Mafātīḥ al-Ghayb*, 13:156, 26:230 and 28:63.
29 Q. 65:12.
30 Al-Qurṭubī, *Al-Jāmiʿ*, 18:174–5; al-Māwardī, *Tafsīr*, 6:36–7.
31 Al-Bukhārī, *Al-Jāmiʿ al-Musnad al-Ṣaḥīḥ*, 3:130; Ibn al-Ḥajjāj, *Ṣaḥīḥ Muslim*, 3:1230–2.
32 See the editor Aḥmad Muḥammad Shākir's footnotes regarding the reliability of the narrators of this report in Ibn Ḥanbal, *Musnad*, 2:375–8. See also al-Tirmidhī's comments on the report in al-Tirmidhī, *Al-Jāmiʿ al-Kabīr*, 5:256–7. Also, see Ibn Kathīr, *Tafsīr*, 7:7–8.
33 See Ibn Kathīr, *Tafsīr*, 8:156; al-Qurṭubī, *Al-Jāmiʿ*, 18:175.

contained actual beings, as we just encountered in al-Qurṭubī and al-Māwardī's summations of scholarly opinions regarding the seven earths.[34] According to the early Muslim scholar Qatāda ibn Diʿāma (d. 736), in reference to the earlier cited verse, 'in every one of the heavens and in every earth exists God's created beings, His command, and His divine decree'.[35] The Shāfiʿī exegete of Mosul al-Kawāshī (d. 1281) additionally stated that just as there were angels in every one of the heavens who glorified and praised God, there were people (*ahl*) in every one of the earths who had their own 'marvellous physical characteristics and qualities',[36] which appears to be a transmission of a position noted in earlier Islamic centuries as well.[37] A prophetic report considered inauthentic by Muslim scholars of ḥadīth yet circulated in many works has the Prophet describe an earth/land (*arḍ*), detailed variously as existing 'in the west' and, in another tradition, 'behind your earth/land', where beings are described as existing that engaged in constant worship of God without sin. The Prophet reportedly describes them as ignorant of the existence of Satan and of even Adam when asked whether they are from Adam's descendants, implying they are non-humans. In one version of the report, they are ignorant of angels as well (negating the possibility that they were angels, which one might conclude from their being sinless).[38] And in perhaps the most well-known Muslim tradition regarding the possibility of beings existing on the several 'earths', the Prophet's cousin and most famous of early Qurʾānic exegetes, Ibn ʿAbbās, reportedly stated that in each of these earths there exist prophets just as the prophets in our known earth: 'In each earth, a prophet like your Prophet [i.e., Muḥammad], an Adam like your Adam, a Noah like your Noah, an Abraham like your Abraham, a Jesus like your Jesus.'[39] In another transmission of his statements, 'In every earth, the equivalent of Abraham, and likewise of all the creatures on the earth', and according to one transmitter, Ibn ʿAbbās stated, 'In every heaven, an Abraham'.[40] Though the

[34] The Ottoman Sufi scholar Ismāʿīl Ḥaqqī (d. 1715) made a similar assertion in his exegetical work. See Ḥaqqī, *Rūḥ al-Bayān*, 10:43.

[35] Al-Ṣanʿānī, *Tafsīr*, 3:318; al-Zamakhsharī, *Al-Kashshāf*, 4:561.

[36] Ḥaqqī, *Rūḥ al-Bayān*, 10:44.

[37] The view that these earths contained beings with unique features and had unique names is also mentioned by Ibn Ṭāhir al-Maqdisī (d. 966). See al-Maqdisī, *Al-Badʾ*, 2:41–2.

[38] See the chapter of Moamer Khalayleh, this volume. The referenced report would suggest that the beings known as *Rawḥāniyyūn* are distinct from the angels, though the *Rawḥāniyyūn* are elsewhere believed to be a *class of* angels (their being made of light in the report also suggests a similarity with the angels). Al-Aṣbahānī, *Kitāb al-ʿAẓama*, 4:1428, 1440, and 1442; Al-Māwardī, *Tafsīr*, 3:180–1; Ibn Kathīr, *Tafsīr*, 8:157. Al-Samʿānī, *Tafsīr al-Qurʾān*, 3:162; al-Kirmānī, *Gharāʾib al-Tafsīr*, 1:99. Al-Qurṭubī, *Al-Jāmiʿ*, 10:80.

[39] See the chapter of Hamza Karamali, this volume. Also, see al-Rāzī, *Tafsīr*, 10:3361.

[40] Al-Ṭabarī, *Jāmiʿ al-Bayān*, 23:469. According to an interesting statement attributed to Ibn ʿAbbās regarding this verse, he reportedly also said that if he were to reveal the exegesis of this verse, it

report was questioned by later Muslim authorities on account of it bearing a remarkable truth claim that could not be confirmed by an authentic statement of the Prophet himself,[41] its attribution to the foremost early exegete Ibn ʿAbbās, even if that attribution was occasionally doubted,[42] bestowed the idea of different earths populated with beings and prophets a degree of credibility that allowed it to be transmitted in authoritative exegetical works. The Ottoman Sufi exegete Ismāʿīl Ḥaqqī (d. 1715), in defending Ibn ʿAbbās's interpretation from the charge that it may have been sourced from questionable lore, suggests that the idea of multiple prophets mirroring our own was in fact in line with the popularly held view that in every heaven was a Kaʿba circumambulated by *its people* (mentioned earlier), and that this was the case likewise in every one of the earths.[43] Al-Kawāshī interpreted Ibn ʿAbbās's statement to indicate that in each of the earths were created beings whose leaders (*sādah*) fulfil the role (*maqām*) that the prophets fulfilled for us on our Earth.[44] This raises the possibility that the Muḥammadan message might not necessarily extend to these

would cause people to disbelieve since they would reject the truth of it. In other words, the exegesis would be deemed highly controversial.

41 The exegete Ibn Kathīr held that if the statement of Ibn ʿAbbās was in fact what he said, it might reflect Isrāʾīlī lore of questionable origin. The ḥadīth scholar al-Sakhāwī (d. 1497), citing Ibn Kathīr's statements, added that such information should be rejected if not authentically traceable to the mouth of someone infallible. That is, it was not a statement of the Prophet and thus couldn't be accepted given its import. The Ottoman Sufi exegete Ismāʿīl Ḥaqqī rejected al-Sakhāwī's dismissal of Ibn ʿAbbās's statements as reflecting questionable lore by affirming Ibn ʿAbbās's status as the foremost exegete of the Qurʾān by Muslim consensus. See Ibn Kathīr, *Al-Bidāya*, 1:22; al-Sakhāwī, *Al-Maqāṣid al-Ḥasana*, 103; Ḥaqqī, *Rūḥ al-Bayān*, 3:105.

42 According to the ḥadīth scholar al-Bayhaqī (d. 1066), while the report ascribed to Ibn ʿAbbās had a sound chain of transmission (an indication of the report's technical authenticity based on the merits of the individual narrators of a report as narrators), he deemed it anomalous (*shādhdh*) and pointed out that to the best of his knowledge, it lacked additional lines of transmission to corroborate the narrator reporting directly from Ibn ʿAbbās. In other words, there was only one direct recipient of the report which might leave some room for doubt about its attribution to him. See al-Bayhaqī, *Al-Asmāʾ*, 2:267–8. Note that the declaration that a report was anomalous by a ḥadīth scholar could also be an indication that the report had a problematic *meaning* which might imply its unreliable transmission. Al-Dhahabī (d. 1347), also an expert ḥadīth scholar, affirmed that the narrators for one of the transmissions of the report were all reliable transmitters and, regarding a separate transmission, recognized that while two of the transmitters had some laxity associated with them in their ability to transmit ḥadīth material accurately, this was not at the level where their reports should be rejected. He acknowledged the challenging import of this report, however, saying that it baffles the one who hears it, and added that it is one of those matters where a person should simply hear and remain silent. Al-Dhahabī, *Al-ʿUluww*, 75; Abū Ḥayyān al-Andalusī (d. 1344), apparently very sceptical of the provenance of the report, declared it an obvious fabrication and something from the narrations of the highly impugned early Muslim historian al-Wāqidī (d. 823), though it is not clear whether al-Wāqidī ever reported this tradition from Ibn ʿAbbās. Al-Andalusī, *Al-Baḥr al-Muḥīṭ*, 10:205.

43 Ismāʿīl Ḥaqqī also relates the idea of multiple 'earths' to an interesting premodern conception of a multiverse, referencing the Ottoman Sufi Sheikh Mehmed Muḥyiddīn Uftāda (d. 1580), who once told his disciple Azīz Maḥmūd Hudāyī (d. 1628) that there were many universes (*ʿawālim*) wherein many Uftādahs and Hudāyīs were talking at the same moment that they were. Ḥaqqī, *Rūḥ al-Bayān*, 3:105.

44 Al-Kawāshī, *Tafsīr*, folio 385.

other communities, which would have their own prophets. Regarding the verse's mention that 'His command descends throughout them', al-Kawāshī offers as one possible interpretation of 'His command' descending between the heavens and the earths that Gabriel comes down with divine inspiration (*al-waḥy*) from the seventh heaven to the under Earth (*al-arḍ al-suflā*).[45] The early Muslim jurist ʿAṭāʾ ibn Abī Rabāḥ (d. 733) similarly interpreted the command to be God's inspired revelation (*al-waḥy*), which was being sent to 'God's creation in every earth, and in every heaven'.[46] Inspired revelation, *al-waḥy*, is the basis of religious scripture, and so this *might* imply a separate set of religious commands for these alternative beings, though, importantly, these interpretations do not make that explicit. Given the incredible nature of Ibn ʿAbbās's claims and his high status in the Muslim tradition, it was unsurprising that some additional statements are attributed to him on the topic of these other worlds. In one of these attributions that lacks a transmission history (and therefore a dubious ascription) al-Zamakhsharī relays from Ibn ʿAbbās an actual *description* of the beings residing in the second of the earths as sinless humanoids that bear the face and body of a human, a mouth resembling a dog, legs and ears like a cow and hair like a sheep.[47] And in case one was wondering whether all the earths were equal in status, a tradition transmitted by Abū Saʿīd al-Dārimī (d. 894) has Ibn ʿAbbās declare that the greatest of the various earths (*sayyid al-araḍīn*) is the one that *we* inhabit.[48] And in the Shīʿī tradition,[49] we have Ibn ʿAbbās reportedly state that God created hundreds of other worlds (*ʿālamīn*) wherein beings that don't sin against God and who are unaware of Adam and his descendants exist (i.e. they themselves are not humans), using similar language to the prophetic report encountered earlier.[50]

[45] Ibid. Note that the text found in the manuscript for the relevant section appears to differ slightly from the text as referenced in Ismāʿīl Haqqī's transmission, found in his *Rūḥ*, 10:44. Ismāʿīl Haqqī's reference to al-Kawāshī's text does not include the earlier passage.

[46] Al-Wāḥidī, *Al-Tafsīr*, 21:522.

[47] Al-Zamakhsharī, *Rabīʿ al-Abrār*, 1:167. Also referenced in Ḥaqqī, *Rūḥ al-Bayān*, 4:13.

[48] Al-Dārimī, *Al-Radd*, 60.

[49] See Muhammad Montasseri's chapter, this volume, which engages heavily with Shīʿī reports. The Shīʿī tradition appears to have preserved more explicit reports regarding the existence of other-worldly domains and seemingly intelligent non-human entities. Shīʿī recognition of select members of the Prophet's family as recipients of secret knowledge is one contributing factor for why such reports appear to have been accepted with greater currency in the Shīʿī sources, as this type of knowledge of the unseen (*ʿilm al-ghayb*) tended to be met with scepticism when reported from sources other than the Prophet in the Sunnī tradition (and thus the noted scepticism regarding the Ibn ʿAbbās tradition).

[50] See al-Majlisī, *Biḥār*, 54:322. Another Shīʿī report has ʿAlī report on an intelligent and worshipping non-human (*laysū bi-ins*) existing on the earth prior to Adam. Al-Makkī, *Samṭ*, 1:77.

## The Muḥammadan message and other-worldly beings: Initial musings from al-Māwardī

Given the predominant understanding documented by al-Qurṭubī earlier of the Earth being one among seven, wherein other beings were imagined or reported to exist, a question that naturally may have arisen was whether the Prophet's message was universally applicable to other intelligent beings if earthly Muslims were to make contact. While the universality of Islam for all of God's creation was a given based on the Qur'ānic paradigm referenced earlier, what about the specific message of Islam as delivered by the Prophet to us humans on this Earth? This was formally considered by at least one well-known jurist and authority, the previously mentioned al-Māwardī (d. 1058), in his work in Qur'ānic exegesis dealing with the verse just looked at. Given the physical restraints and believed inaccessibility between the seven 'layered' earths as they were believed to be arranged, he comments that the religious call of the Prophet would be limited to the people of the top Earth only (i.e., ours), and not the others, 'even if there exists on [those earths] discerning creatures who bear intelligence' (*man ya'qilu fīhā min khalqin mumayyizin*). But what if contact was possible between the 'earths'? Al-Māwardī considers this. A tradition attributed (likely dubiously) to Ibn 'Abbās has the seven 'earths' existing on the same surface but separated by oceans and thus possibly accessible. In this alternative arrangement which interestingly resembles the separation between the Old World and the New World, al-Māwardī maintains that if the other 'earths' (here, geographically separated lands) were unreachable, then the call of Islam would similarly not apply to those beings – the example would be the same as the earths that were layered and unreachable. However, if the other geographies *could* be reached (e.g. by crossing the sea), he offers two possible solutions without providing a clear selection, given the novel and speculative nature of the discussion from his vantage point:

1. One is that the call of the Prophet may possibly be binding on them upon contact since 'the separation by seas, if traversable, does not stop the obligation of that which has a broad ruling' (*lā yamna'u min luzūmi mā 'amma ḥukmuhu*).[51]
2. The second option he gives is that it is possible that 'the call of Islam would not be binding on them [in this case], because if it were, then there

[51] Al-Māwardī, *Tafsīr*, 6:37.

> would have been a [scriptural] text on the matter, and the Messenger [i.e., the Prophet] would have been commanded with it [i.e. carrying the message of Islam to them]'.[52]

The first scenario would imply that the Islamic message should be carried to intelligent and discerning beings on other 'earths'. The second considers the possibility that the Prophet's message was not universal off the face of our own Earth because nothing is known about the Prophet's message being binding elsewhere.[53] This latter view *may* accord with a statement made by the highly regarded legal theorist al-Juwaynī (d. 1085), who, in a rebuke against a Jewish sect that claimed the Prophet was sent by God to only the Arabs and not to other nations, stated that it was established based on mass transmission from the Prophet (*tawāturan minhu*) that his religious call was for all those on the expanse of the Earth (*basīṭ al-arḍ*). However, it is not clear whether al-Juwaynī intended to literally restrict the universality of the Prophet's message to our Earth or whether his reference to the 'expanse of the earth' was merely to exaggerate its universality for the purpose of his specific argument about the message applying for Arabs and non-Arabs.[54]

As should be obvious, al-Māwardī's speculative discussion is highly transferable in the event of actual contact with extraterrestrial entities from other planets, even if the concept of layered earths might not apply, and his remarks offer some initial considerations for Muslim theologians, including the possibility that the prophetic message might not be universally binding off our Earth to other beings.[55] Notably, al-Māwardī does not reference the report of Ibn 'Abbās concerning other-worldly prophets and therefore does not have to speculate on the implications of human contact with a community that may have its own set of prophets and religious laws which may raise its own set of concerns. After offering these possible positions, he affirms that 'God is most knowing of the truth of [matters] that He alone has knowledge of, and what is correct from that which is obscure to His creation'.[56] Given the rather unprecedented and speculative nature of the possibilities he discusses, and perhaps also the

52 Ibid.

53 To the best of my knowledge, this latter possibility was never considered upon discovery of the New World.

54 Unfortunately, I am unable to find the original reference, only its documentation in Taqī al-Dīn al-Subkī, *Fatāwā*, 2:610 and 621.

55 Interestingly, al-Māwardī's comments are broadly about intelligent, discerning creatures that are on geographically cut-off regions and could have also applied to humans living in the 'new world' but was never cited to restrict the universality of the religious message upon discovery of the Americas as far as I'm aware.

56 Al-Māwardī, *Tafsīr*, 6:36–7.

problematic suggestion that the Prophet's message was not applicable for beings off of this 'Earth', it is not surprising that al-Māwardī stops short of choosing an actual answer and wraps up his discussion of this verse seeking forgiveness for delving into matters that are doubtful and obscure. It is noteworthy that when he considers what 'His command descends throughout them' means from the verse, he makes sure to stop short of the interpretations made by ʿAṭā' ibn Abī Rabā and al-Kawāshī mentioned earlier, which allowed for God's command to possibly refer to revealed inspiration (*al-waḥy*) – the basis of scriptural revelation – descending throughout the various earths. Al-Mawārdī states that if we accept that the command in the verse refers to revealed inspiration, then *that* only descends from the highest heaven to *our* Earth (not the earths below), but if it means God's divine decree and predetermination, then this is all-inclusive, from the lowest Earth to the highest heaven.[57]

## Islamic moral responsibility for non-human intelligent beings

Al-Māwardī's novel comments lead us to consider an additional discussion in the Islamic tradition that would help us navigate potential contact with an intelligent non-human. The notion of *taklīf* or 'moral accountability' was understood as the technical quality needed in a being for it to be considered responsible for belief in God and for following God's legislative commands and thus also a being that was subject to divine punishment and entitled to divine reward. It was generally held that to be morally charged (*mukallaf*), one had to possess the intelligence and discernment to allow for the comprehension of moral responsibility.[58] It is for this reason that al-Māwardī considered the ramifications of contact with an other-earthly being that was intelligent and discerning, as opposed to one that was not. Among created entities, it was largely believed that morally accountable beings included only angels,[59] jinn[60] and humans, the latter of which also needed to have reached adulthood and be mentally sane. This was to the

57 Ibid. This passage is quite significant and should be consulted in full; also transmitted in al-Qurṭubī, *al-Jāmiʿ*, 18:175–6; al-Nuʿmānī, *Al-Lubāb*, 19:181; Ḥaqqī, *Rūḥ al-Bayān*, 4:321.

58 See David Jalajel's chapter in this volume.

59 A position that the angels are not *mukallaf* is ascribed to a Ḥanbalī scholar who stated that this was the main position of the scholars, but Jalāl al-Dīn al-Suyūṭī (d. 1505) interprets his comments to mean that the angels were not bound to the *Sharīʿa* of the Prophet as humans and jinn are, not that they are not *mukallaf*, which in fact *is* the main position of the scholars, and is granted by the fact they receive commands that they obey. See al-Suyūṭī, *Al-Ḥabāʾik*, 255–6.

60 Badr al-Dīn al-Shiblī (d. 1367) notes that one solitary exception to this understanding may have been the early anthropomorphist movement known as the *Ḥashawiyya*, which apparently claimed that the jinn did not have free will and thus were not *mukallaf*. See al-Shiblī, *Ākām al-Marjān*, 5.

exclusion of other living creatures (*ḥayawān*) that were believed not to have higher intelligence and thus lacked moral accountability.[61] While the criterion here for excluding other living beings was primarily their perceived lack of higher intelligence, some stipulated that the being be contractually charged with a moral code by God, which the Qurʾān[62] suggests was primordially done between God and humans. Because this further requirement was not known to be present within non-human animals, this position would argue that even if a creature were found that exhibited higher intelligence, moral responsibility (and moral responsibility to a religious law) might not apply.[63]

As we encountered in al-Māwardī's discussion, additional possibilities of *mukallaf* beings outside of humans, jinn and angels were occasionally considered, and these examples may serve as analogues that could be applied to an intelligent extraterrestrial or other non-human intelligent being. One of these is a position that has been documented but with seemingly few (named) adherents that held that non-human creatures were in fact morally accountable (*mukallaf*), based on verses like Q. 6:38, which states that birds and creatures of the Earth are *communities* like us;[64] Q. 35:24 in which it is proclaimed that every *community* was the recipient of a divine warner;[65] verses of the Qurʾān which describe an intelligent and seemingly morally accountable hoopoe bird in the counsel of the Prophet Solomon;[66] and a prophetic ḥadīth[67] which seemed to suggest some form of moral accountability for animals as well.[68] ʿAmr ibn Maymūn (d. ca. 693–4), an early Muslim convert, apparently also witnessed a

61 For example, al-Bāqillānī, *Al-Taqrīb*, 1:236–8. See additional pages after this section for further discussion. The requirement for a human to be an adult in order to be morally accountable was also based on a prophetic ḥadīth.

62 Q. 7:172 was believed by Muslim exegetes to refer to a primordial contract made between humans and God before humans were brought to exist in their physical forms on earth.

63 Al-Taftazānī, *Sharḥ al-Talwīḥ*, 2:322.

64 Q. 6:38.

65 Q. 35:24.

66 In Q. 27:21 Solomon threatens to punish a bird in his royal counsel if it doesn't provide a valid excuse for its absence from his counsel. Being suitable for receiving punishment could be understood as evidence of moral accountability, and the bird's statements found in verses 22–26 demonstrate intelligence and the ability to recognize the reality of monotheism, *tawḥīd*, the central credal point of Islam.

67 The Prophet witnessed two sheep fighting one another and stated that God ultimately knows why they are fighting and would judge between them. See Ibn Ḥanbal, *Musnad*, 35:345.

68 Al-Māwardī states that a group interpreted Q. 6:38 literally to mean that the beasts of the earth and birds are like humans in the quality of being morally responsible. They also paired this with the ḥadīth concerning the two fighting sheep (see prior footnote) to derive this meaning. The discussion is in al-Māwardī's *Tafsīr*, 2:111–12. According to the famous fourth-century theologian Abū Manṣūr al-Māturīdī (d. 944), the verses regarding the hoopoe bird in Solomon's counsel, paired with the two verses mentioned earlier (Q. 6:38 and Q. 35:24), were taken by a party of Muslims to imply that animals may bear some form of moral accountability, at least for some commands. Al-Māturīdī, *Tafsīr*, 8:108–9; al-Zarkashī, *Al-Burhān*, 2:179; al-Kirmānī, *Gharāʾib al-Tafsīr*, 1:358.

group of monkeys in Yemen implement what he regarded as legislative stoning (*rajm*) as a punishment for illicit intercourse among themselves, and said, 'I truly witnessed stoning [practised] among other than the Children of Adam [i.e. among non-humans]!' This report might imply a possibly early view among some Muslims that divine laws were also observed by non-human animals, though 'Amr ibn Maymūn's reading of the event in question was very strongly rejected by later Muslim authorities: monkeys may be intelligent to an extent but not like humans, and they were certainly not *mukallaf*, so 'Amr ibn Maymūn was clearly mistaken in his interpretation of what he witnessed.[69]

As a final example of an internal Muslim discussion that considered the possibility of non-humans as morally charged beings was a highly speculative discussion predominantly among jurists of the Shāfiʿī school about the religious status of intelligent humanoid creatures theoretically born to non-human parents or to a human and a non-human parent. Examples given included an intelligent human-like creature born to two sheep, a being born to a human and a fish and one born to a human and a ritually impure animal like a pig. These interspecies lineages were selected for their relation to pre-existing Islamic legal precepts: if Islamic law considered sheep as permissible to eat once ritually slaughtered, fish to be eaten in all cases and pigs considered ritually filthy, how would those laws pertain to a being that also featured human characteristics?

For the purposes of our discussion, the jurists who engaged in this theoretical discussion generally accepted that if intelligent and capable of producing intelligent speech, the being would be treated as morally accountable by analogy to humans and thus responsible for following the message of Islam. This being might even lead (human) Muslims in prayer. However, some specific rulings as relate to their non-human lineage and their sheep-ness, fish-ness or pig-ness were argued by some of the discussants to bear some separate rulings for these beings.[70] We see from all of these cases that while on the one hand, three classes of beings were explicitly acknowledged as being *mukallaf* – the angels, *jinn* and humans – premodern Muslims were also willing to entertain the possibility that

[69] See Ibn Ḥajar al-Asqalānī's (d. 1449) comments on the report. It was argued that the monkeys may have thrown stones out of innate jealousy but not as an implementation of divine law, or perhaps they were repeating behaviour seen from a prior group of apes that were in fact transformed humans (see Q. 2:65), or perhaps they were jinn in the form of monkeys. Refer also to Ibn Ḥajar's comments regarding a separate report about mice that were reported to be implementing biblical law. The possibility that they may *actually* have been *mukallaf* or implementing a divine law as ʿAmr ibn Maymūn suggests was not accepted. See al-Asqalānī, *Fatḥ al-Bārī*, 7:160.

[70] Al-Qalyūbī and ʿUmayra, *Ḥāshiyatā Qalyūbī wa-ʿUmayra*, 1:79; al-Anṣārī, *Al-Ghurar al-Bahiyya*, 1:40; al-Haytamī, al-Shirwānī, and al-ʿAbbādī, *Tuḥfat al-Muḥtāj*, 1:290–1. See al-ʿAbbādī's (d. 1584) comments on whether the outward human form is relevant for a being's status as *mukallaf*.

additional beings could bear the privileged status of being morally accountable, and thus subject to a moral or legal code, with the primary consideration for this status generally being higher intelligence and the ability to comprehend moral responsibility. An extraterrestrial being, therefore, would not necessarily have to fear being labelled a lower life form by virtue of not being part of the pre-existing human-jinn-angel paradigm of *mukallaf* beings and thus may also be subject to a religious law and message.

## Al-Subkī and al-Suyūṭī's arguments for the universal relevancy of the Muḥammadan message

We now turn to the writings of Taqī al-Dīn al-Subkī (d. 1355) and Jalāl al-Dīn al-Suyūṭī (d. 1505) who both engaged with the universality of the Prophet's message. While al-Māwardī left open the possibility that the Prophet's message may be limited to earthly beings, some of the arguments cited by al-Subkī and al-Suyūṭī could serve as a blueprint for extending that universality to *all mukallaf* beings, whether on Earth or elsewhere. Among the three widely recognized *mukallaf* beings, angels, humans and jinn, only humans and jinn were generally believed to be bound to the message of the Prophet and the *Sharīʿa* or divinely based laws and moral system that he brought, whereas it was believed that angels only followed commands directly from God.[71] This would imply that any hypothetical entity that was *mukallaf* was not necessarily bound to accept the message or *Sharīʿa* of the Prophet. A verse of the Qurʾān that stated the Prophet was a warner for all the worlds (*al-ʿālamīn*)[72] might have implied otherwise but was not taken to mean such: as Fakhr al-Dīn al-Rāzī stated, Muslims were in agreement that the Prophet was *not* sent as a messenger to the angels, and so the verse's implication was restricted to only humans and jinn.[73] While al-Rāzī believed there was agreement on this point, al-Suyūṭī points out that the later Taqī al-Dīn al-Subkī and another Shāfiʿī jurist, Sharaf al-Dīn al-Bārizī (d. 1338), held an opposing view that the Prophet was in fact sent to the angels as well, with al-Bārizī extending the argument to *all* creatures (even the non-*mukallaf* ones)

71 Al-Ḥalīmī, *al-Minhāj*, 1:303–4.

72 Q. 25:1.

73 Both al-al-Suyūṭī and al-Asqalānī (see references in next footnote) interpreted al-Rāzī's statements as a declaration of a Muslim consensus on the matter (*ijmāʿ*), given that he uses the related verb to describe Muslim agreement on the matter (*ajmaʿnā*). However, as the later Ibn Ḥajar al-Haytamī (d. 1567) says, al-Rāzī doesn't appear to be making a formal declaration of a theological consensus with his usage of this verb as others proclaimed. See al-Rāzī, *Asrār*, 142; al-Haytamī, *Al-Durr al-Manḍūd*, 59.

along with inanimate objects, on account of certain traditions about a lizard, rock or tree bearing witness to the Prophet's status.[74] That angels were bound to the message of the Prophet was also al-Suyūṭī's own position, and he articulates the argument at length in a dedicated treatise on the subject as a rebuke of the predominant scholarly position.[75]

Among the various pieces of evidence he cites in support of his position included a ḥadīth wherein the Prophet states that he was 'sent to all of creation' (*ursiltū ilā al-khalqi kāffatan*),[76] the verse cited earlier stating he was a warner for all the worlds and other verses like it,[77] a verse revealed to the Prophet believed to contain an address to angels (implying his message was to them as well),[78] a verse wherein the Prophet is told to say that he was given the Qur'ān to broadly warn 'whomever it reaches'[79] and traditions that suggest the angels engaged in the same worship as that of the Muḥammadan community and thus were bound to the Muḥammadan *Sharī'a* in some form (e.g. angels were known to pray like the believers prayed and also joined humans in their prayers, as the Prophet lead the angels in prayer on his Night Journey). Al-Suyūṭī also references disputed traditions stating that the Prophet's status as God's messenger was written throughout Paradise and the heavens as further evidence of the Prophet being a messenger for all the worlds and even concludes that he was, therefore, also sent as a messenger to the known residents of Paradise, such as the Eternal Maidens mentioned in the Qur'ān (the *Ḥūr al-'Ayn*). Interestingly, given that the Eternal Maidens are a non-human class of beings which Muslim tradition understands to be intelligent and sentient in some way,[80] and existing in an Eternal Paradise presently existing somewhere outside our Earth,[81] they would *technically* classify

[74] Al-Suyūṭī, *Al-Ḥabā'ik*, 256. It is for this reason that Ibn Ḥajar al-'Asqalānī, in his dedicated work on identifying the technical Companions of the Prophet (understood to be those who accepted the Prophet's message, died as believers and were in his company for some period of time), notes that if one considers the angels to be bound to the Prophet's *Sharī'a* as Taqī al-Dīn al-Subkī did, they would be considered companions as well. See al-'Asqalānī, *al-Iṣāba*, 1:158.

[75] The dedicated treatise, entitled *Tazyīn al-Arā'ik fī Irsāl al-Nabī Ṣallā Allāh 'alayhi wa Sallam ilā al-Malā'ik* (*The Adornment of the Raised Couches: On the Prophet – May God Bless Him and Grant Him Peace – Being Sent to the Angels*), is included in the printed version of al-Suyūṭī, *al-Ḥāwī*, 2:168–77.

[76] Ibn al-Ḥajjāj, *Ṣaḥīḥ Muslim*, 1:371.

[77] For example, Q. 21:107. Note that there are several other verses, such as Q. 6:90, 12:104, 38:87 and 81:27, which declare that the message of the Qur'ān was a reminder for the worlds/domains of existence.

[78] See Q. 21:29, believed to be regarding angels, promising them punishment if they claimed divinity.

[79] Q. 6:19.

[80] Ibn Ḥazm states that all Muslims are aware that the *Ḥūr al-'Ayn* are intelligent beings able to produce higher speech. In other words, they seem to bear the characteristics of a *mukallaf* being. See Ibn Ḥazm, *al-Iḥkām*, 7:81; Ibn Ḥazm, *al-Faṣl*, 3:146.

[81] Some early exegetes understood the Eternal Paradise promised to believers as existing somewhere in the heaven above, as implied by Q. 51:22, which mentions the heaven as where the believers

as extraterrestrial intelligent beings and, given al-Suyūṭī's position, would be a case where the Muslim tradition accepted an additional non-human *mukallaf* entity as bound to the message of the Prophet.

While some of his listed arguments are specific to angels, many of them are broad enough to extend the religious message to additional classes of beings. What is remarkable about al-Suyūṭī's treatise is that it was an attempt by a major scholar of the tradition to extend the relevancy of the Prophet's message to a *new* class of being that was not acknowledged as a recipient of the Muḥammadan message by a majority of Muslim scholarship, and in doing so, he has provided an outline of a theological argument that could be employed for including additional intelligent beings should they be discovered. Not only that, but the position he adopted also had legal ramifications. He notes that al-Subkī built a legal position in the *Shāfiʿī* school of jurisprudence whereby a Muslim could enact the congregational form of prayer even when he is the sole human, with the belief that angels are praying behind him as was indicated in prophetic reports.[82]

Much earlier than al-Suyūṭī, in a lengthy treatise written in 1338 as a response to a question he received while in Cairo, Taqī al-Dīn al-Subkī lays out arguments for the accepted Islamic creedal point that the jinn are bound to the Muḥammadan message and *Sharīʿa* just as humans are.[83] The treatise is significant for our purposes because while al-Subkī lists evidences that are specific to the jinn,[84] he also provides ones that are broad enough that they are relevant for all *mukallaf* beings, which he also acknowledges. Referencing Q. 6:19 noted earlier, wherein the Prophet is told to say that he was given the Qurʾān to broadly warn whomever it reaches, and the similarly unrestricted nature of God's command to the Prophet to simply give warning,[85] al-Subkī suggests that it is hermeneutically the best to interpret these commands given to the Prophet to mean that his message was meant for as many recipients of this warning as possible because doing so would confirm the Prophet's ableness to deliver the

will get what they are promised. See interpretations in al-Ṭabarī, *Jāmiʿ al-Bayān*, 22:421; perhaps differing from this interpretation, Q. 3:133 was taken as evidence that Paradise was *outside* of the universe since its size *encompasses* the heavens and our earth (though in all cases it is somewhere off our earth).

[82] See al-Suyūṭī, *al-Ḥāwī*, 2:168–77. For al-Subkī's referenced legal position, see al-Subkī, *Qaḍāʾ al-Arab*, 340–3.

[83] See al-Subkī, *Fatāwā*, 2:594–625. Because of the length of his response, he dedicates it as a separate treatise that he names *al-Dalāla ʿalā ʿUmūm al-Risāla* (*Proof of the Universality of the Message*).

[84] Some of this evidence included Qurʾānic verses specifically about the jinn, such as those found in Q. 72 in which a party of jinn had become believers and who heard and accepted the message of the Prophet. See also Q. 55:31, understood to be a reference to humans and jinn. Refer to al-Subkī's treatise for further evidence from ḥadīth as well, in ibid., 2:598–600.

[85] Q. 74:2.

message he was charged with to all and also confirm his status as the most caring and concerned for the welfare of all of God's creation. As al-Subkī states, he would not leave behind anyone from this warning, nor any time period, nor any geographic location. Thus, al-Subkī states that the command to the Prophet to be a warner applies to *all* who may benefit from this warning (and would even apply to communities *before* he even existed, had he been alive). The jinn had among them those who were astray and foolish and thus in need of warning, and they were also *mukallaf*, meaning they could receive this warning and turn away from misguidance through it, and thus they were from among those whom the Prophet's care would include.[86] As should be apparent, this broad argument could easily apply to other non-human intelligent beings.

With the prior framing, al-Subkī then makes an important assertion regarding the many Qurʾānic verses involving commands, prohibitions and the like that are directed to *believers* (*al-muʾminūn*) or disbelievers (*al-kāfirūn*). He says that these terms should not be read as addressed to just humans 'but rather *mukallaf* beings, [which] is broader than the class of humans or jinn'.[87] He then states that using this logic, countless verses of the Qurʾān would then not only apply to humans but also to jinn (and we may infer, though he does not argue it, *other mukallaf* beings). He pairs this with a discussion of the authenticated ḥadīth noted earlier, in which the Prophet declared that he was sent to all of creation to further prove the universality of his message to the non-human class of jinn.[88] Citing an incident in the life of the Prophet, he makes a subtle point to advance his position. In the event in question, the Prophet was reciting the Qurʾān but was reportedly not aware that his recitation was being heard by a group of jinn, nor did he see them. He was later informed via revelation that they heard his message and accepted it, which is narrated in the opening verses of Q. 72.[89] Al-Subkī pulls from the particularities of this incident an interesting conclusion, namely that it shows the Prophet's message was ultimately binding on all those

[86] Al-Subkī, *Fatāwā*, 2:596.

[87] Ibid.

[88] Al-Bukhārī, *Al-Jāmiʿ al-Musnad al-Ṣaḥīḥ*, 1:95. The ḥadīth, noted earlier as being narrated in the *Ṣaḥīḥ* of Muslim ibn al-Ḥajjāj, was often juxtaposed with a separate report in which the Prophet states he was sent to all humans (*al-Nās*). However, al-Subkī argues that the two are not contradictory in meaning and they are in fact statements made by the Prophet on separate occasions given the difference in text and lines of transmission. He addresses this variant ḥadīth and verses that speak specifically to people (*al-Nās*) in al-Subkī, *Fatāwā*, 2:597–8 and 602–3.

[89] For the event in question, see Ibn Ḥajjāj, *Ṣaḥīḥ Muslim*, 1:331. Ibn 'Abbās reports the incident and is the one who comments that the Prophet did not recite to the jinn or see them (which al-Subkī states is regarding this incident only since the Prophet could witness them on other occasions). As al-Subkī also points out, the version found in al-Bukhārī's *Ṣaḥīḥ* does not include this statement from Ibn ʿAbbās. See al-Bukhārī, *Al-Jāmiʿ al-Musnad al-Ṣaḥīḥ*, 1:154 and 6:160.

that it reached, *whether he was aware of its delivery or not*. He makes this point to refute the hypothetical argument that the Prophet would've needed to intend delivery of his message to the jinn if he was in fact a messenger for them. In the incident in question, it was confirmed by the Qurʾān that the delivery of his message was fulfilled even though the Prophet was unaware of it himself, just as the delivery of his message is similarly fulfilled when it reaches humans that are on the far reaches of the Earth who hear his message even without him physically reaching them himself.[90] Though he doesn't use these arguments in the treatise to extend the universality of the Prophet's message to other classes of *mukallaf* beings aside from humans and jinn on Earth, it should be clear that this same argument could, in theory, apply to any *mukallaf* being, including a theoretical intelligent extraterrestrial. Even if the Prophet did not specifically intend to share the message with some community of beings, this would not bar his message from applying to them once it reached them (just as it did with the jinn in the incident in question). Similarly, his status as a prophet sent to all of creation would open the message to more than just humans and jinn.[91]

The laws and *Sharīʿa* of the Prophet were also believed to apply to the jinn in some form by virtue of them being bound to his message. If one were to extend al-Subkī's arguments for the universality of his mission to additional classes of *mukallaf* beings, it would mean that these laws would likewise apply to them as well. But how did this religious law apply to the jinn,[92] and how could it be for a novel class of being? Given the available textual evidence, al-Subkī was of the position that the jinn followed the same religious laws as humans, that is, they were expected to follow the same rules regarding ritual purity, prayer and so on. The rules of the Qurʾān would apply to them equally except in cases where they might not have an analogue. Could the jinn have unique laws that might have been tailored for them by the Prophet? While this was widely believed to be the case based on a particular ḥadīth that seemed to suggest the Prophet allowed them to consume bones while humans could not, al-Subkī didn't believe the wording of the report was clear in supporting

[90] Al-Subkī, *Fatāwā*, 2:598–600.

[91] Ibid., 610 and 621.

[92] For discussion of some of the human laws that relate to jinn, see Badr al-Dīn al-Shiblī's (d. 1367) dedicated work on the topic, *Ākām al-Marjān fī Aḥkām al-Jānn*. Some interesting legal discussions include the possibility of a human praying behind a jinn or forming a congregational prayer with jinn (pp. 61–2), the prohibition from killing jinn and possible blood money that would be paid out (pp. 63–4) and the ruling on marriage with a jinn (pp. 65–75). Some interesting cases are also noted, including an incident where an eighth-century Muslim judge apparently adjudicated on access rights to a well between a jinn and a human (p. 86). Rulings that relate to the interspecies interaction between humans and jinn may bear relevance in the event of contact with an intelligent extraterrestrial.

this.[93] It was a *possibility*, but he didn't believe there was clear textual evidence proving that the jinn had a unique set of laws. He also explores whether it was possible that the jinn could follow laws that they received prior to the Prophet, say from past jinn prophets,[94] which the Prophet then confirmed and let continue specifically for them. Al-Subkī's own position was that the Prophet's *Sharīʿa* abrogated all laws that came prior and that no other *Sharīʿa* from a prior prophet had currency.[95] But if he did give a verdict that was in agreement with a law of another past prophet, it would ultimately be from his *Sharīʿa* anyways, so it wouldn't make a difference.[96] This case, in particular, bears some relevance in the event that some novel intelligent being was the recipient of its own divine message and law in the past. Could the Prophet's *Sharīʿa* confirm aspects of those laws, especially laws that may be pertinent to this being, in a way that wouldn't make sense for humans? While this wouldn't be in line with al-Subkī's own position, several prominent Muslim legal theorists held that it was from the completeness of the Prophet's *Sharīʿa* that it continued laws that came from prior (albeit human) prophets as well, and thus those other laws were not necessarily abrogated but could, in theory, be a *source* of Islamic law for Muslim jurists.[97] Thus, extending al-Subkī's arguments, the Muḥammadan *Sharīʿa* could hold applicability for novel *mukallaf* beings in cases where there was an analogue for them (just as jinn are expected to follow the same rules as humans do). However, in legal cases that were unique to their experience, if an extraterrestrial being had access to its own authentic and divinely originating scripture and law, that law might theoretically be a source for extending the

93 See ibid., 623 and onward. It was believed that the jinn maintained some unique laws based on a ḥadīth where the Prophet was asked by a party of jinn regarding their provision, to which the Prophet replied, 'For you is every bone that the name of God has been recited. It will fall in your hands full of flesh. And the animal dung will be fodder for your animals.' From this, the Prophet told his Companions not to use either of these objects to clean themselves after relieving themselves, 'for they are the food of your brothers'. See Ibn al-Ḥajjāj, *Ṣaḥīḥ Muslim*, 1:332. While understood by many to be an example of the Prophet establishing separate rules for the jinn (the allowed consumption of bones), al-Subkī says the text isn't clear enough to derive this conclusion, since the report doesn't use language that would demonstrate the Prophet gave a legal verdict, since it is alternatively possible the Prophet was merely praying for them in the event they were in a state of need (i.e. praying that meatless bones be full of meat for them) or some other alternative. Though he doesn't deny the possibility that they were given some specific laws related to them being non-human. See al-Subkī, *Fatāwā*, 2:600–1, 609 and 617.

94 This was considered a minority position espoused by the early exegete al-Ḍaḥḥāk (d. ca. 724) based on the apparent meaning of Qurʾān 6:130, though rejected by others. See Ibid., 2:609 and 618–19.

95 Ibid., 2:601–2 and 608–9.

96 Ibid., 2:609, 618–21, and 623. See also his separate but analogous discussion elsewhere about a hypothetical scenario where the Prophet lives in the time of a prior prophet and adjudicates with laws that match theirs. Ibid. 1:40-41.

97 Abdullah, 'Pre-Muḥammadan Law', 12–84.

relevancy of the Muḥammadan *Sharīʿa* given the aforementioned scholarly position.

## Conclusion

The above overview analysed several discussions from within the classical Muslim scholarly tradition from the fields of exegesis, theology and law. These discussions demonstrated the ability of classical Muslim scholarly thought to consider additional classes of intelligent non-human beings within an Islamic cosmology. The language of specific Qurʾānic verses allowed for interpretations where God's vast universe could contain many earths apart from our own and possibly other-worldly beings. As proclaimed in earlier cited Qurʾānic verses, Islam, the religion of surrender to God the Creator, is observed on Earth as anywhere else.

As for the relevancy of the *earthly* revealed Muḥammadan message of Islam for novel classes of intelligent beings perhaps elsewhere in the universe, we came across premodern Muslim discussions offering us possible answers. The eleventh-century scholar al-Māwardī considered both the possible limitation of the Muḥammadan message to our specific earthly domain and also its possible universality. Al-Suyūṭī and al-Subkī provided broad arguments for the universality of the Prophet's message for the non-human classes of angels and jinn based on Qurʾānic verses and prophetic tradition and, in doing so, showed us how the Muḥammadan message may be relevant for non-humans as well from an Islamic theological perspective.

## Bibliography

Abdullah, Faisal. 'Pre-Muḥammadan Law and the Muḥammadan Sharia: Muslim Theories and Implementation of Biblical Law and the Laws of Prior Religious Communities'. PhD diss., UCLA, 2020.

Al-Andalusī, Abū Ḥayyān Athīr al-Dīn. *Al-Baḥr al-Muḥīṭ fī al-Tafsīr*. Edited by Ṣidqī Muḥammad Jamīl. Beirut: Dār al-Fikr, 1999/2000.

Al-Anṣārī, Zakariyyā ibn Muḥammad. *Al-Ghurar al-Bahiyya fī Sharḥ al-Bahja al-Wardiyya*. Cairo: Al-Maṭbaʿa al-Maymaniyya, n.d.

Al-Aṣbahānī, Abū al-Shaykh. *Kitāb al-ʿAẓama*. Edited by Riḍāʾ Allāh al-Mubārakpūrī. Riyadh: Dār al-ʿĀṣima, 1987/1988.

Al-ʿAsqalānī, Ibn Ḥajar. *Al-Iṣāba fī Tamyīz al-Ṣaḥāba*. Edited by ʿĀdil Aḥmad ʿAbd al-Mawjūd and ʿAlī Muḥammad Miʿwaḍ. Beirut: Dār al-Kutub al-ʿIlmiyya, 1994/1995.

Al-ʿAsqalānī, Ibn Ḥajar. *Fatḥ al-Bārī: Sharḥ Ṣaḥīḥ al-Bukhārī*. Edited by Muḥibb ad-Dīn al-Khaṭīb. Beirut: Dār al-Maʿrifa, 1959/1960.

Al-Bāqillānī, Abū Bakr. *Al-Taqrīb wa-l-Irshād (al-Ṣaghīr)*. Edited by ʿAbd al-Ḥamīd ibn ʿAlī Abū Zunayd. 2nd edn. Beirut: Muʾassasat al-Risāla, 1998.

Al-Bayhaqī, Abū Bakr. *Al-Asmāʾ wa-l-Ṣifāt*. Edited by ʿAbd Allāh ibn Muḥammad al-Ḥāshidī. Jeddah: Maktabat al-Sawādī li-l-Tawzīʿ, 1993.

Al-Bukhārī, Muḥammad ibn Ismāʿīl. *Al-Jāmiʿ al-Musnad al-Ṣaḥīḥ (Ṣaḥīḥ al-Bukhārī)*. Edited by Muḥammad Zuhayr ibn Nāṣir al-Nāṣir. Dār Ṭār al-Najāh, 2001.

Al-Dārimī, Abū Saʿīd. *Al-Radd ʿalā al-Jahmiyya*. Edited by Badr ibn ʿAbd Allāh al-Badr. 2nd edn. Kuwait: Dār Ibn al-Athīr, 1995.

Al-Dhahabī, Shams al-Dīn. *Al-ʿUluww li-l-ʿAlī al-Ghaffār fī Īḍāḥ Ṣaḥīḥ al-Akhbār wa-Saqīmihā*. Edited by Abū Muḥammad Ashraf ibn ʿAbd al-Maqṣūd. Riyadh: Maktabat Aḍwāʾ al-Salaf, 1995.

Al-Ḥalīmī, Abū ʿAbd Allāh. *Al-Minhāj fī Shuʿb al-Īmān*. Edited by Ḥilmī Muḥammad Fawda. Beirut: Dār al-Fikr, 1979.

Al-Haytamī, Ibn Ḥajar. *Al-Durr al-Manḍūd fī al-Ṣalāh wa-l-Salām ʿalā Ṣāḥib al-Maqām al-Maḥmūd*. Edited by Bū Jumʿa ʿAbd al-Qādir Makrī and Muḥammad Shādī Muṣṭafā ʿArbash. Jeddah: Dār al-Minhāj, 2005/2006.

Al-Haytamī, Ibn Ḥajar, ʿAbd al-Ḥamīd al-Shirwānī and Aḥmad ibn Qāsim al-ʿAbbādī. *Tuḥfat al-Muḥtāj fī Sharḥ al-Minhāj maʿa Ḥāshiyatā ʿAbd al-Ḥamīd al-Shirwānī wa-Aḥmad ibn Qāsim al-ʿAbbādī*. Egypt: Al-Maktaba al-Tijāriyya al-Kubrā, 1983.

Al-Kawāshī, Muwaffaq al-Dīn Abū al-ʿAbbās. 'Tafsīr Al-Kawāshī'. MS Arabic 400. 418 fols. Istanbul/Fatih: Süleymaniye Kütüphanesi.

Al-Kirmānī, Tāj al-Qurrāʾ Burhān al-Dīn. *Gharāʾib al-Tafsīr wa-ʿAjāʾib al-Taʾwīl*. Jeddah: Dār al-Qibla li-l-Thaqāfa al-Islāmiyya, n.d.

Al-Majlisī, Muḥammad Bāqir. *Biḥār al-Anwār*. 3rd edn. Beirut: Dār Iḥyāʾ al-Turāth al-ʿArabī, 1983.

Al-Makkī, ʿAbd al-Malik ibn Ḥusayn. *Samṭ al-Nujūm al-ʿAwālī fī Anbāʾ al-Awāʾil wa-l-Tawālī*. Edited by ʿĀdil Aḥmad ʿAbd al-Mawjūd and ʿAlī Muḥammad Miʿwaḍ. Beirut: Dār al-Kutub al-ʿIlmiyya, 1998.

Al-Maqdisī, al-Muṭahhir ibn Ṭāhir. *Al-Badʾ wa-l-Tārīkh*. Būr Saʿīd: Maktabat al-Thaqāfa al-Dīniyya, n.d.

Al-Masʿūdī, Abū al-Ḥasan. *Akhbār al-Zamān*. Beirut: Dār al-Andalus li-l-Ṭibāʿa wa-l-Nashr wa-l-Tawzīʿ, 1996.

Al-Māturīdī, Abū Manṣūr. *Tafsīr al-Māturīdī (Taʾwīlāt Ahl al-Sunna)*. Edited by Majdī Baslūm. Beirut: Dār al-Kutub al-ʿIlmiyya, 2005.

Al-Māwardī, Abū al-Ḥasan. *Tafsīr al-Māwardī*. Edited by al-Sayyid ibn ʿAbd al-Maqṣūd Ibn ʿAbd al-Raḥīm. Beirut: Dār al-Kutub al-ʿIlmiyya, n.d.

Al-Nasafī, Abū al-Barakāt ʿAbd Allāh. *Madārik al-Tanzīl wa-Ḥaqāʾiq al-Taʾwīl*. Beirut: Dār al-Kalim al-Ṭayyib, 1998.

Al-Nuʿmānī, Abū Ḥafṣ Sirāj al-Dīn al-Ḥanbalī al-Dimashqī. *Al-Lubāb fī ʿUlūm al-Kitāb*. Edited by ʿĀdil Aḥmad ʿAbd al-Mawjūd and ʿAlī Muḥammad Miʿwaḍ. Beirut: Dār al-Kutub al-ʿIlmiyya, 1998.

Al-Qalyūbī, Aḥmad Salāma and Aḥmad ʿUmayra. *Ḥāshiyatā Qalyūbī wa-ʿUmayra*. Beirut: Dār al-Fikr, 1995.

Al-Qurashī, Ibn Kathīr. *Al-Bidāya wa-l-Nihāya*. Edited by ʿAlī Shīrī. Beirut: Dār Iḥyāʾ al-Turāth al-ʿArabī, 1988.

Al-Qurashī, Ibn Kathīr. *Tafsīr al-Qurʾān al-ʿAẓīm (Tafsīr Ibn Kathīr)*. Edited by Sāmī ibn Muḥammad Salāma. 2nd edn. Riyadh: Dār Ṭayba li-l-Nashr wa-l-Tawzīʿ, 1999.

Al-Qurtubī, Abū ʿAbd Allāh. *Al-Jāmiʿ li-Aḥkām al-Qurʾān*. Edited by Aḥmad al-Bardūnī and Ibrāhīm Aṭfīsh. 2nd edn. Cairo: Dār al-Kutub al-Maṣriyya, 1964.

Al-Rāzī, Fakhr al-Dīn. *Asrār al-Tanzīl wa-Anwār al-Taʾwīl*. Edited by ʿAbd al-Raḥmān ʿUmayra and ʿAbd al-Munʿim Faraj Darwīsh. Cairo: Rikābī li-l-Nashr wa-l-Tawzīʿ, n.d.

Al-Rāzī, Fakhr al-Dīn. *Mafātīḥ al-Ghayb*. 3rd edn. Beirut, Lebanon: Dār Iḥyāʾ at-Turāth al-ʿArabī, 1999.

Al-Rāzī, Ibn Abī Ḥātim. *Tafsīr al-Qurʾān al-ʿAẓīm li Ibn Abī Ḥātim*. Edited by Asʿad Muḥammad al-Ṭayyib. 3rd edn. Maktabat Nizār Muṣṭafā al-Bāz, 1419 AH.

Al-Sakhāwī, Shams al-Dīn. *Al-Maqāṣid al-Ḥasana*. Edited by Muḥammad ʿUthmān al-Khust. Beirut: Dār al-Kutub al-ʿIlmiyya, 1985.

Al-Samʿānī, Abū al-Muẓaffar. *Tafsīr al-Qurʾān*. Edited by Yāsir ibn Ibrāhīm and Ghunaym ibn ʿAbbās ibn Ghunaym. Riyadh: Dār al-Waṭan, 1997.

Al-Ṣanʿānī, Abū Bakr ʿAbd al-Razzāq. *Tafsīr ʿAbd al-Razzāq*. Edited by Maḥmūd Muḥammad ʿAbduh. Beirut: Dār al-Kutub al-ʿIlmiyya, 1998/1999.

Al-Sharbīnī, Shams al-Dīn al-Khaṭīb. *Al-Sirāj al-Munīr fī al-Iʿāna ʿalā Maʿrifat Baʿḍ Maʿānī Kalām Rabbinā al-Ḥakīm al-Khabīr*. Cairo: Maṭbaʿat Būlāq al-Amīriyya, 1285AH.

Al-Shiblī, Badr al-Dīn. *Ākām al-Marjān fī Aḥkām al-Jānn*. Edited by Aḥmad ʿAbd al-Salām. Beirut: Dār al-Kutub al-ʿIlmiyya, n.d.

Al-Subkī, Taqī al-Dīn. *Fatāwā al-Subkī*. Beirut: Dār al-Maʿrifa, n.d.

Al-Subkī, Taqī al-Dīn. *Qaḍāʾ al-Arab fī Asʾilat Ḥalab*. Edited by Muḥammad ʿĀlim ʿAbd al-Majīd al-Afghānī. Mecca: Al-Maktaba al-Tijāriyya, 1413 AH.

Al-Suyūṭī, Jalāl al-Dīn. *Al-Ḥabāʾik fī Akhbār al-Malāʾik*. Edited by Muḥammad al-Saʿīd ibn Basyūnī Zaghlūl. Beirut: Dār al-Kutub al-ʿIlmiyya, 1985.

Al-Suyūṭī, Jalāl al-Dīn. *Al-Ḥāwī li al-Fatāwā*. Beirut: Dār al-Fikr, 2004.

Al-Ṭabarī, Muḥammad ibn Jarīr. *Jāmiʿ al-Bayān fī Taʾwīl al-Qurʾān*. Edited by Aḥmad Muḥammad Shākir. Muʾassasat al-Risāla, 2000.

Al-Taftazānī, Saʿd al-Dīn Masʿūd ibn ʿUmar. *Sharḥ al-Talwīḥ ʿalā al-Tawḍīḥ*. Egypt: Maktabat Ṣabīḥ, n.d.

Al-Thaʿlabī, Abū Isḥāq. *Al-Kashf wa-l-Bayān ʿan Tafsīr al-Qurʾān*. Edited by Abū Muḥammad ibn ʿĀshūr. Beirut: Dār Iḥyāʾ al-Turāth al-ʿArabī, 2002.

Al-Tirmidhī, Abu ʿĪsā Muḥammad. *Al-Jāmiʿ al-Kabīr (Sunan al-Tirmidhī)*. Edited by Bashshār ʿAwād Maʿrūf. Beirut: Dār al-Gharb al-Islāmī, 1998.

Al-Wāḥidī, Abū al-Ḥasan. *Al-Tafsīr al-Basīṭ*. ʿImādat al-Baḥth al-ʿIlmī bi-l-Jāmiʿa al-Islāmiyya, 2009.

Al-Zamakhsharī, Abū al-Qāsim. *Al-Kashshāf ʿan Ḥaqāʾiq Ghawāmiḍ al-Tanzīl*. 3rd edn. Dār al-Kitāb al-ʿArabī, 1407 AH.

Al-Zamakhsharī, Abū al-Qāsim. *Rabīʿ al-Abrār wa-Nuṣūṣ al-Akhbār*. Beirut: Muʾassasat al-Aʿlamī, 1412 AH.

Al-Zarkashī, Badr al-Dīn. *Al-Burhān fī ʿUlūm al-Qurʾān*. Edited by Muḥammad Abū al-Faḍl Ibrāhīm. Beirut: Dār Iḥyāʾ al-Kutub al-ʿArabiyya / Dār al-Maʿrifa, 1957.

Ḥaqqī, Ismāʿīl. *Rūḥ al-Bayān*. Beirut: Dār al-Fikr, n.d.

Ḥawwā, Saʿīd. *Al-Asās fī al-Tafsīr*. 6th edn. Cairo: Dār al-Salām, 2003/2004.

Ibn Abī Ṭālib, Makkī. *Al-Hidāya ilā Bulūgh al-Nihāya*. Sharjah: Jāmiʿat al-Shāriqa, 2008.

Ibn al-Ḥajjāj, Muslim. *Ṣaḥīḥ Muslim*. Beirut: Dār Iḥyāʾ al-Kutub al-ʿArabiyya, n.d.

Ibn al-ʿUthaymīn, Muḥammad. *Liqāʾāt al-Bāb al-Maftūḥ*. Transcription of Audio Lectures, n.d. https://audio.islamweb.net/audio/index.php?page=FullContent&audioid=111503#

Ibn al-Wardī al-Maʿarri al-Ḥalabī, Sirāj al-Dīn ʿUmar ibn al-Muẓaffar. *Kharīdat al-ʿAjāʾib wa-Farīdat al-Gharāʾib*. Cairo: Maktabat al-Thaqāfa al-Islāmiyya, 2008.

Ibn Ḥanbal, Abū ʿAbd Allāh. *Musnad al-Imām Aḥmad ibn Ḥanbal*. Edited by Aḥmad Muḥammad Shākir. Cairo, Egypt: Dār al-Ḥadīth, 1995.

Ibn Ḥanbal, Abū ʿAbd Allā. *Musnad al-Imām Aḥmad ibn Ḥanbal*. Edited by Shuʿayb al-Arnaʾūṭ and ʿĀdil Murshid. Muʾassasat al-Risāla, 2001.

Ibn Ḥazm, Abū Muḥammad ʿAlī. *Al-Faṣl fī al-Milal wa-l-Ahwāʾ wa-l-Niḥal*. Cairo: Maktabat al-Khānjī, n.d.

Ibn Ḥazm, Abū Muḥammad ʿAlī. *Al-Iḥkām fī Uṣūl al-Aḥkām*. Edited by Aḥmad Muḥammad Shākir. Beirut: Dār al-Āfāq al-Jadīda, n.d.

6

# Extraterrestrial intelligent life and Islamic beliefs

## Investigating six potential conflicts

Shoaib Ahmed Malik

### Introduction

With accelerating advancements in astronomy, there have been plenty of *scientific* speculations regarding the existence of alien life forms, otherwise called extraterrestrials, on planets apart from our own.[1] This has advanced all kinds of conjectures regarding the possibility or probability of extraterrestrial life (*that* extraterrestrials exist). What conditions are needed for life to exist? Would they need to be similar to the conditions and history of the Earth, or could they differ? Such questions link the study of extraterrestrials to the theory of evolution, as it is presumed that forces that govern the origins of life and species on Earth might also be responsible for life and species elsewhere. These things are being explored and discussed in astrobiology. The next question relates to their potential characteristics (*what* kind of extraterrestrials could exist). If extraterrestrials do exist, could they speak? Could they have a language? Can they possess consciousness? Might they have a soul? Intelligence? Ethics? Religion? Questions like these strike at the core of theological anthropology, that is, the discourse of human *nature* and *uniqueness*,[2] and they have captured the popular imagination.[3]

1 This is opposed to mere (non-empirical) speculations about the existence of life on other planets that took place before modern science. See Ashkenazi, *Foundations of Xenology*; Basalla, *Civilized Life in the Universe*; Connes, *History of the Plurality of the Worlds*; Dick, *The Biological Universe*; Jakosky, *Search for Life in the Universe*; Dick, *Space, Time, and Aliens*; Wilkins, *Search for Extraterrestrial Intelligence*.

2 Cortez, *Theological Anthropology*; Farris, *Introduction to Theological Anthropology*.

3 It has been done in many ways, ranging from science fiction, doomsday scenarios, societal impacts to conspiracy theories. See Allnutt, *Infinite Encounters*; Basalla, *Civilized Life in the Universe*;

The Abrahamic traditions have traditionally conceived humans to be a unique and important creation of God.[4] However, if extraterrestrials exist and possess faculties that we generally and uniquely prescribe to human beings, how might this affect theological perspectives? Such questions are being addressed in the growing field of exotheology.

The current discourse is overwhelmingly saturated with Christian perspectives,[5] with other religious views being marginal, and Islam has been no exception.[6] This chapter looks at exotheology broadly from an Islamic lens, specifically looking at potential conflicts between extraterrestrials and Islamic thought. It does this by taking a cue from an article written by C. A. McIntosh and Tyler Dalton McNabb, ingeniously called *Houston, Do We Have a Problem? Extraterrestrial Intelligent Life and Christian Belief.*[7] In there, they identify and address six potential conflicts between Christianity and the existence of extraterrestrial intelligent life (ETI):

1. Conflict with theism – does ETI contradict God's existence?
2. Conflict with scripture – does ETI contract the Bible?
3. Conflict with Christian doctrine – does ETI contract the teachings of Christianity?
4. Conflict with Christian tradition – does ETI contradict any past beliefs held by the ecclesiastical community?
5. Conflict with the problem of evil – does ETI exacerbate the problem of evil?
6. Conflict with the Christian narrative – in addition to 1–5, does ETI conflict with anything else for Christians?

They categorically conclude that there is no conflict in any of these areas. This article addresses the same concerns from an Islamic perspective. Some of the preceding conflicts have been modified accordingly:

Jakosky, *Search for Life in the Universe*; Weldon and Levitt, *UFOs: What on Earth is Happening*; Lewis and Shreckhise, *UFO: End-Time Delusion*; Robertson, *UFOs, Conspiracy Theories and the New Age*; Thompson, *Angels and Aliens*; Wilkinson, *Aliens, The X-Files and God*; Traphagan, *Extraterrestrial Intelligence and Human Imagination*; Wilson and Weldon, *Close Encounters*.

[4] Peters, 'Introducing Astrotheology', 3–26; Weintraub, *Religions and Extraterrestrial Life*, 1–7.

[5] Connes, *History of the Plurality of the Worlds*; Crowe, *The Extraterrestrial Life Debate*; Dick, *Many Worlds*; Dick, *Plurality of Worlds*; Peters, *Astrotheology*; Parkyn, *Exotheology*; Rosato and Vincelette, *Extraterrestrials in the Catholic Imagination*; Vainio, *Cosmology in Theological Perspective*.

[6] At the time of writing this chapter, only three known references were published in English in the academic literature. Determann, *Islam, Science Fiction, and Extraterrestrial Life*; Iqbal, 'Islamic Theology Meets ETI'; Weintraub, *Religions and Extraterrestrial Life*, 161–8.

[7] McIntosh and McNabb, 'Extraterrestrial Intelligent Life and Christian Belief'.

C1. Conflict with theism – does ETI contradict God's existence?
C2. Conflict with Islamic scripture – does ETI contract the Qur'ān and ḥadīths?
C3. Conflict with Islamic doctrine – does ETI contract the teachings of Islamic beliefs?
C4. Conflict with Islamic tradition – does ETI contradict any beliefs held by the Muslim scholarly community in the past?
C5. Conflict with the problem of evil – does ETI exacerbate the problem of evil?
C6. Conflict with the Muslim narrative – after clearing 1–5, does ETI conflict with anything else for Muslims?

Given the many different intellectual streams within Islam,[8] for the sake of transparent positionality, this chapter is written from the perspective of the Sunnī strand of Islam and Ashʿarī theology in particular.[9] The conclusions, however, are not necessarily exclusive to Ashʿarism or Sunnism.

Finally, it will be helpful at this stage to clarify the way ETI is being understood here. The Islamic tradition acknowledges three kinds of creations that are usually situated in the higher ranks or degrees of creation (*marātib al-makhlūqāt*). These are humans (*insān/bashar*), angels (*malāʾika*)[10] and jinn.[11] Though they have a spiritual component, humans are considered terrestrial beings because they seem to be designated to planet Earth.[12] Angels and jinn interact with human beings through what might be expressed as other dimensions. For instance, the Islamic tradition acknowledges that two angels are sitting on the shoulders of each human being, one recording the good deeds and the other bad.[13] Similarly, jinn influence humans towards immoral behaviour and can also possess human beings.[14] However, such beings are not strictly visible to humans; they are metaphysical and definitely not what is being referred to as ETI. The term 'extraterrestrials' is the broad term used for a set of biological entities that live on other planets apart from our own in this universe, *whatever* and *wherever* that may be.[15] The mere idea of there being extraterrestrial life is scientifically

[8] Jackson, *Islam and the Problem of Black Suffering*; Schmidtke, The *Oxford Handbook of Islamic Theology*.
[9] This can be seen as a continuation of my earlier work. See Malik, *Islam and Evolution*; Malik and Muhtaroglu, 'How Much Should or Can Science Impact Theological Formulations?'.
[10] Burge, *Angels in Islam*.
[11] El-Zein, *Islam, Arabs, and the Intelligent World of the Jinn*. See also Richard Playford's chapter in this volume.
[12] Q. 2:30–40.
[13] Q. 50:16–18.
[14] Rassool, *Evil Eye, Jinn Possession, and Mental Health Issues*, 75–184.
[15] Ashkenazi, *What We Know About Extraterrestrial Intelligence*; Dick, *Space, Time, and Aliens*; Dick, *The Biological Universe*.

interesting. However, what motivates the theological inquiry, in particular, are extraterrestrials that possess human-like qualities, for example, intelligence, spirituality, moral accountability or physical superiority, be they matching them or superseding them.[16] It is this class of beings that is referred to as ETI, and it is how this term is to be understood in the remainder of this chapter.

## C1. Conflict with theism

There are many different forms of theism. The one that is characteristic of the Abrahamic traditions is monotheism. In Ashʿarī theology, God is understood as a volitional being that is omnipotent and omniscient.[17] God's existence is usually proved by one of two cosmological arguments: (1) the *kalām* cosmological argument (*dalīl al-ḥudūth*) or (2) the contingency argument (*dalīl al-imkān*).[18] Both arguments use contingencies, be they temporal or mere *possibilia*, to establish a necessary being (*wājib al-wujūd*) that is identified with God through further argumentative steps.[19] Given these kinds of arguments, it is difficult to see how ETIs can conflict with God's existence.

One could consider the argument of New Atheists who use evolution to deny the existence of God. According to Richard Dawkins, the theory of evolution operating through natural selection does not need God:

> I am continually astonished by those theists who, far from having their consciousness raised in the way that I propose, seem to rejoice in natural selection as 'God's way of achieving his creation'. They note that evolution by natural selection would be a very easy and neat way to achieve a world full of life. God wouldn't need to do anything at all! Peter Atkins, in the book just mentioned, takes this line of thought to a sensibly godless conclusion when he postulates a hypothetically lazy God who tries to get away with as little as possible in order to make a universe containing life. Atkins's lazy God is even lazier than the deist God of the eighteenth-century Enlightenment: *deus otiosus* – literally God at leisure, unoccupied, unemployed, superfluous, useless. Step by step, Atkins succeeds in reducing the amount of work the lazy God has to do until he finally ends up doing nothing at all: he might as well not bother to exist.[20]

16 Peters, 'Introducing Astrotheology', 7–8.

17 Al-Ghazālī, *Al-Iqtiṣād fī al-ʿItiqād*, 71–97; al-Ghazālī, *Moderation in Belief*, 83–104; Malik and Muhtaroglu, 'How Much Should or Can Science Impact Theological Formulations?', 13–16.

18 Al-Rāzī, *Maʿālim Uṣūl al-Dīn*, 191–202; Fawda, *Bayna al-Mutakallamīn wa-l-Falāsifa*, 215–318.

19 Al-Ghazālī, *Al-Iqtiṣād fī al-ʿItiqād*, 46–9; al-Ghazālī, *Moderation in Belief*, 27–40.

20 Dawkins, *God Delusion*, 118.

In other words, a scientific explanation for the origins of life and species on Earth makes God a redundant explanation. This argument has been very influential.[21] By extension, if life did exist on other planets, and if ETI were to exist, evolution would be the presumed causal explanation, further reifying the redundancy of God.[22]

Moreover, others ascribed some agency to the complexity found in the biological make-up of the world. For instance, the famous molecular biologist Francis Crick, also an atheist, entertained the possibility of ETI interfering with the evolutionary history on Earth, what he referred to as Directed Panspermia:

> Could life have started on Earth as a result of infection by microorganisms sent here deliberately by a technological society on another planet, by means of a special long-range unmanned spaceship? To show that this is not totally implausible we shall use the theorem of detailed cosmic reversibility; if we are capable of infecting an as yet lifeless extrasolar planet, then, given that the time was available, another technological society might well have infected our planet when it was still lifeless.[23]

According to this thesis, life on Earth could have been influenced by ETI, which also potentially renders the explanation of God as creating life and species on Earth useless.

Both arguments have and can be used to question the necessity of God's existence. However, both explanations are contingent realities and, therefore, would still require a necessary being. From the Ashʿarī perspective, contingent realities can, in one sense, be explained by other contingent realities (which is what science uncovers). However, contingent explanations are not exhaustive; all contingencies are grounded by a necessary being and are thus categorically different explanations. So even if such explanations were true, they do not conflict with God's existence.[24] Subsequently, the existence of ETI poses no conflict with theism.

## C2. Conflict with Islamic scripture

Islamic scripture consists of two primary sources that are the Qurʾān and the ḥadīths. The former is a foundational scriptural, and its historical veracity has

[21] Barnes et al., 'Accepting Evolution Means You Can't Believe in God'.
[22] Peter, *Science, Theology, and Ethics*, 130.
[23] Crick and Orgel, 'Directed Panspermia', 343.
[24] A contingency-predicated world view avoids the false disjunction of God *or* scientific explanation(s). Instead, it sees the relationship as a conjunction: God *and* scientific explanation(s). See Malik and Muhtaroglu, 'How Much Should or Can Science Impact Theological Formulations?', 26–7 and Malik, *Islam and Evolution*, 179–211.

been maintained as a statement of fact in the Islamic tradition.[25] The ḥadīths, however, vary, and ḥadīth scholars have developed a variety of principles to differentiate weak ḥadīths from strong ones, with only rigorously authenticated ḥadīths being usable in matters of theology (*ʿaqīda*) and jurisprudence (*fiqh*).[26]

Apart from the mention of supernatural entities like angels (*malāʾika*) and jinn, Islamic scripture has, for the most part, remained silent on the issue of ETI. This could be taken as an argument against the existence of ETI and, thus, a potential conflict. An analogue can be found in the discussion of Islam and evolution. One position in this particular discourse is Adamic exceptionalism, which states that Adam's descendants could have interbred with other coexisting pre-Adamic or co-Adamic hominins.[27] One potential pushback against this position is scriptural silence. Since scripture does not mention this, it must be rejected. However, the counter-response to this is that the absence of evidence does not entail the evidence of absence.[28] If scripture is silent about a particular issue, it cannot be used to deny or affirm an option; it remains moot, which leaves both possibilities hermeneutically open (*tawaqquf*).[29]

Indeed, there is no explicit mention of ETI, but two essential scriptural references are important to highlight here.[30] One is Q.16:4-8:

> He created man from a drop of fluid, and yet man openly challenges Him. And livestock – He created them too. You derive warmth and other benefits from them: you get food from them; you find beauty in them when you bring them home to rest and when you drive them out to pasture. They carry your loads to lands you yourselves could not reach without great hardship – truly your Lord is kind and merciful – horses, mules, and donkeys for you to ride and use for show, and *other things you know nothing about* (*wa yukhluqu mā lā tʿalamūn*). (Italics for emphasis)

Another is a ḥadīth which states:

> There are seven earths, and in each of them, there is a prophet like your prophet [Muhammad], an Adam like your Adam, an Abraham like your Abraham, a Noah like your Noah, and a Jesus like your Jesus.[31]

25 Brown, *Hadith*, 69–134.
26 Ibid., 162–95; al-Ghazālī, *Fayṣal al-Tafriqa*; al-Ghazālī, *Al-Mustaṣfā min ʿIlm al-Uṣūl*, 1:374–504.
27 Malik, *Islam and Evolution*, 133–6.
28 Al-Rāzī, *Al-Maṭālib al-ʿĀliya*, 3:221.
29 Al-Ghazālī, *Iḥyāʾ ʿUlūm al-Dīn*, 4:23.
30 There are, of course, others, for example, the word *dābba* or its plural form *dawābb* mentioned in the Qurʾān raises interesting questions about potential scriptural space for ETI. For further details, see the chapters of Moamer Khalayleh, Mohamed Montasseri and Faisal Abdullah in this volume. Also see Tlili, 'The Meaning of the Qur'anic Word "*dābba*"'.
31 Al-Bayhaqī, *Kitāb al-Asmāʾ wa-l-Ṣifāt*, 389–90.

The Qurʾānic verse has an unqualified statement which has left open the hermeneutic possibility of ETI.[32] The ḥadīth is very interesting, as it explicitly mentions there being human copies entities on other 'earths'. If it is assumed that 'earths' entail other planets, this could very well be considered a scriptural affirmation of ETI. However, the only problem with this ḥadīth is that its authenticity has been questioned, and it seems to be part of a ḥadīth genre known as the Isrāʾīlīyāt. Ḥadīths from this genre are considered dubious and therefore do not carry theological weight.[33] Subsequently, there is no conflict between Islamic scripture and ETI.

## C3. Conflict with Islamic doctrine

Several treatises discuss Islamic doctrines from basic to advanced levels,[34] but the most basic and notable one is *The Creed of Ṭaḥāwī* (*Aqīda al-Ṭaḥāwī*) by Abū Jaʿfar Aḥmad ibn Muḥammad ibn Salama (d. 933).[35] There is nothing in these treatises that conflicts with the idea of there being ETI. However, this space provides an opportunity for comparing important Islamic and Christian doctrines.

There are three key theological doctrines in Christianity that are of importance: (1) the Fall, (2) the Incarnation and (3) the Atonement. According to Christian belief, the Fall refers to the moment when Adam and Eve disobeyed God in the Garden of Eden by eating from the forbidden tree of knowledge. This act of disobedience introduced sin, which is inherited by humans from Adam and Eve (original sin), and suffering, evil and death into the world and distanced humanity and God. Christians believe that all human beings are born with a sinful nature as a result of the Fall and are in need of salvation.[36] Christ fulfils the need for this salvation, which leads us to the Incarnation.

The Incarnation refers to the Christian belief that God became human in the person of Jesus Christ. According to the Bible, Jesus was born of a virgin, lived a sinless life and died on the cross for the sins of humanity. Christians believe that

[32] See Khalayleh, this volume. Also, see Q. 21:16 for another possibility in the Qurʾān: 'We did not create the heavens and the earth *and everything between* them playfully' (*wa mā khalaqnā al-samāʾa wa-lʾarḍ wa mā baynahumā lāʿibīn*) (italics for emphasis).

[33] Ibn Kathīr, *Al-Bidāya wa-l-Nihāya*, 1:22.

[34] Al-Ṭaḥāwī, *The Creed of Imam Al-Ṭaḥāwī*; Al-Taftazānī, *Sharḥ al-ʿAqāʾid*; *Al-*Ghazālī, *Al-Iqtiṣād fī al-ʿItiqād*; Al-Rāzī, *Al-Maṭālib al-ʿĀliya*; Al-Rāzī, *Maʿālim Uṣūl al-Dīn*.

[35] Al-Ṭaḥāwī, *The Creed of Imam Al-Ṭaḥāwī*.

[36] Stump, *Four Views on Creation, Evolution, and Intelligent Design*.

Jesus is fully God and fully human, and that his death and resurrection make it possible for human beings to be reconciled with God and have eternal life.[37]

The Atonement refers to the process by which humanity is reconciled to God through the death of Jesus Christ. Christians believe that because of the Fall, human beings are separated from God and unable to save themselves from sin and death. However, through the sacrificial death of Jesus on the cross, God provided a way for humanity to be forgiven and reconciled to him. Christians believe that by putting their faith in Jesus and accepting his sacrifice, they can receive salvation and have eternal life.[38]

Two considerations are important when analysing these axioms in light of ETI. The first is to do with the scope of the agents involved: is the concern human-centric or intelligence-centric? The former is a subset of the latter, given the existence of other intelligent beings. The second dimension has to do with the physical boundaries of the event: is the concern an Earth-bound event, or can it be extended to the universe? Put together, a few important questions arise. Was the fall just on Earth, or were there multiple falls on other planets with ETI? Was there just the one Incarnation on Earth, or could there be multiple ones on other planets? Finally, is the Atonement just for human beings? Or is ETI atoned for through the one on Earth? If not, is there space for pluralistic conceptions of the Atonement? Christian scholars have disagreed over these matters.[39] Depending on how wide or narrow the scope of these axioms is entertained (human-centric versus intelligence-centric or Earth-bound versus universe-bound), Christian doctrines may have issues with their being ETI, particularly ones that can have a relationship with God.

Suffice it to say that none of these – the Fall, Incarnation and the Atonement – are axioms in Islamic thought. While there is an understanding of the Fall in Islam, in that Adam and Eve did sin by eating from the tree and thus fell from The Garden, this is not the source of sin, evil and suffering, and nor does it call the need for a saviour in Islamic thought.[40] Acting upon sin is a personal endeavour, and repentance and salvation are achieved through one's personal actions, intentions and God's mercy.[41] Accordingly, the need for the Incarnation and, thus, Atonement is not required in the Islamic framework. Therefore, while

[37] Ware, *Perspectives on the Doctrine of God.*

[38] Beilby and Eddy, *The Nature of the Atonement.*

[39] Parkyn, *Exotheology*, 52–125; Peters, *Science, Theology, and Ethics*, 121–38; Wilkins, *Search for Extraterrestrial Intelligence.*

[40] Malik, *Islam and Evolution*, 100.

[41] Q. 6:14: 'Say, "Should I seek a Lord other than God, when He is the Lord of all things?" *Each soul is responsible for its own actions; no soul will bear the burden of another.* You will all return to your Lord in the end, and He will tell you the truth about your differences.'

these ideas may cause some tension for some Christian thinkers, they would not be problematic for Muslims in the slightest, given the difference in the theological systems.

The question that does arise from a theological standpoint is the eschatological salvation of ETI. Will ETI get judged on the Day of Judgement? Could we see ETI in Hell or Heaven?[42] Given that their very existence is not acknowledged in Islamic scripture, it is best not to speculate about such matters. They may be, or they may not be. Neither option poses any conflict for Islamic thought. That said, Muzaffar Iqbal seems to suggest some ideas:

> It is not beneficial to speculate, but the basic Qur'ānic framework of accountability (*taklīf*) may suggest a fruitful way to frame this question. God imposes obligations on his creatures which subject them to his command; their final fate depends on how well they discharge these obligations. Thus, if we encounter ETI who are granted the resource and freedom to be governed by his Law of obligation and accountability (i.e., they are *mukallaf*), then, strictly speaking, there would be resurrection and judgement for them, just as for humans.[43]

In other words, for Islamic law (*Sharīʿa*) to be applicable, one must be a responsible agent (*mukallaf*).[44] If ETI fit the criteria, they may be judged in the eschaton. Interestingly, by extension, it may be a communal duty (*farḍ kifāya*) upon Muslims to invite them to the message of Islam, as anyone recognized as a responsible agent should be informed and invited to the faith.[45]

## C4. Conflict with Islamic tradition

There is one specific debate in the Islamic tradition that potentially intersects with ETI, particularly when ETI could be deemed superior to human beings. It is the discussion of the best or the most superior of creation (*afḍal al-khalq*). Muslim scholars disagreed over the superiority of humans as opposed to angels. There are three recorded opinions on this issue: (1) humans are superior to angels, (2) angels are superior to humans and (3) no commitment, as scripture does not decisively affirm one over the other.[46] Each position has its necessary

[42] See Muhammad Montasseri's chapter in this volume.
[43] Iqbal, 'Islamic Theology Meets ETI', 226.
[44] Al-Ghazālī, *Al-Mustaṣfā min ʿIlm al-Uṣūl*, 1:222–9.
[45] See the chapters of David Solomon Jalajel and Faisal Abdullah in this volume.
[46] Al-Madhūn, 'Al-Malkāʾika wa-l-Jinn', 101–4; Al-Ramlī, *Fatāwa al-Ramlī*, 4:381–2. Also, see al-Rāzī, *Al-Maṭālib al-ʿĀliya*, 7:405–28; Al-Rāzī, *Maʿālim Uṣūl al-Dīn*, 531; Ibrahim, 'The Questions of

pieces of scriptural evidence. The details of this issue do not matter to us here. What concerns us is the implication of each position for ETI.

For those opting for human superiority,[47] the kinds of ETI that could exist might be limited. Depending on how superiority is understood (intelligence, spiritual, ethical or physical strength, among others), there will be a limit to the kind of ETI that could be encountered. However, if there actually is ETI that shows superiority in some way and goes against what this position deems to be superior, it may conflict with this position. This potential conflict does not appear with the other two positions. For those adopting the superiority of angels, ETI may be the second best and humans as third or ETI as third best and humans as second. The position of non-commitment has no actual position on this issue, and so it can potentially entertain ETI occupying the most superior rank. This position situation is best summarized by Iqbal:

> if we were to encounter ETI of superior physical abilities, who are not endowed with higher spiritual qualities, that would not demote humans from their creational rank, but an encounter with ETI superior in intelligence and spiritual receptivity indeed would. The latter scenario would mean that God, who is the *Exalter of Ranks* (*darajāt*) (Q 40:15), created a cosmos in which there exists a creation superior to humankind. It should be noted that Q 17:70 also states that humans *are preferred greatly over many of those We created*, but it does not grant an absolute or exclusive superiority to humankind.[48]

In short, depending on where thinkers stand in the traditional discussion of the superiority between humans and angels (*afḍal al-khalq*), a conflict may or may not arise.[49]

## C5. Conflict with the problem of evil

The problem of evil is a ubiquitous concern for religious believers. If an omnipotent, omniscient and omnibenevolent God (hereon referred to as the omni-God) exists, then why is there evil to begin with? There are two forms of the problem. The *evidential problem of evil* is an argument that suggests that the

the Superiority of Angels and Prophets'. I would like to thank Samuel Ross for sharing the PhD Dissertation by al-Madhūn with me.

47 See the chapter of Hamza Karamali in this volume.

48 Iqbal, 'Islamic Theology Meets ETI', 225. For a similar point by al-Bayḍāwī, see Ibrahim, 'The Questions of the Superiority of Angels and Prophets', 73.

49 To be sure, further subdivisions were discussed as well, for example, messengers of humanity versus general people. For more details, see al-Taftazānī, *Sharḥ al-ʿAqāʾid*, 112–14.

existence of evil in the world constitutes evidence against the existence of an omni-God. The argument is based on the idea that if such a God exists, then he would have the power to prevent evil, the knowledge to know that evil exists and the desire to eliminate evil. However, since evil does exist in the world, it is argued that either God is not omnipotent, not omniscient or not omnibenevolent.[50]

The evidential problem of evil differs from the *logical problem of evil*, which argues that the existence of any evil whatsoever is logically incompatible with the existence of an all-powerful, all-knowing and perfectly good God. The evidential problem of evil, on the other hand, does not claim that the existence of evil is logically incompatible with the existence of God, but rather that the existence of evil makes it less likely that God exists. Proponents of the evidential problem of evil often argue that the sheer amount and intensity of evil in the world, especially gratuitous or pointless suffering, is difficult to reconcile with the existence of an omnipotent, omniscient and omnibenevolent God.[51]

The two kinds of evil are prevalent in the literature. *Moral evil* refers to the evil that is caused by human beings, such as murder, theft and war. It is considered to be the result of human free will, where individuals make choices that result in harm to themselves or others. By contrast, natural evil refers to evil that is not caused by human beings but rather by natural events or phenomena, such as natural disasters, disease and animal predation. Examples of natural evil include earthquakes, tsunamis, hurricanes and cancer. *Natural evil* is the result of natural processes that operate independently of human choice or action. The distinction between moral and natural evil is important because they may require different explanations and responses. Moral evil may be attributed to human moral responsibility and the misuse of free will, whereas natural evil may be seen as an inevitable consequence of the laws of nature.[52]

More recently, prompted by evolutionary biology, Yujin Nagasawa identified what he refers to as the *systemic problem of evil*:

> The problem of evil standardly focuses on specific events that are considered evil (e.g. the Holocaust, the Rwandan Genocide, the Boxing Day tsunami in Southeast Asia, etc.) or the specific types of events (e.g. wars, murders, rapes, earthquakes, floods, etc.). But the problem in question suggests that not only that are specific events or specific types of events are evil, but the entire biological system which nature is based is fundamentally evil, too. Hence, I call it the 'problem of systemic evil'. The problem of systemic evil is more forceful

[50] Meister and Moser, *Cambridge Companion to the Problem of Evil*, 1.
[51] Ibid., 3.
[52] Ibid., 2.

> than the standard problem of evil because, again, it is focused on something more fundamental than specific events or type of events that are deemed evil.[53]

Given that 99 per cent of all species that ever existed are extinct, and hence went through horrendous suffering,[54] Nagasawa believes evolution provides a new category of evil, one that is not momentary but systemic throughout the process of evolution. Accordingly, this exacerbates the problem of evil. Similarly, McIntosh and McNabb discuss how ETI aggravates the problem of evil:

> If there are extraterrestrial intelligent species, then presumably they would also be like us in those respects which mean they can suffer: they have bodies, they are self-conscious, and can experience physical and emotional pain. So if ETI exists in great number, then presumably there is a lot more suffering in our universe than we have imagined. Insofar as suffering conflicts with Christian belief, ETI would therefore exacerbate that conflict.[55]

In other words, if ETI exists and are the products of evolution on other planetary bodies, this leads to a combinatory amplification of *moral*, *natural* and *systemic* evil that extends to ETI living on other planetary bodies, potentially the entire universe. For lack of a better term, this will be referred to as *astrobiological evil*.

Muslims have developed a variety of theodicies in trying to tackle the problem of evil and its varieties.[56] In the Ashʿarī perspective, the problem of evil is not really an issue that needs to be dealt with, as God can impose any obligations and create whatever reality that He pleases, filled with evil and suffering or not. Abū Ḥāmid al-Ghazālī (d. 1111), one of the foremost Ashʿarī scholars, highlights this in no uncertain terms:

> We claim that it is possible for God (Exalted is He) not to assign obligations to His servants, that it is possible for Him to assign obligations to them beyond their ability, that it is possible for Him to bring suffering upon them without compensating them and through no fault of theirs, that it is not obligatory for Him to care for their well-being, that it is not obligatory for Him to reward obedience and punish disobedience, that nothing is made obligatory for a person by virtue of reason but only by virtue of the revelation.[57]

53 Nagasawa, 'The Problem of Evil for Atheist', 153–4.
54 Murray, *Nature Red in Tooth and Claw.*
55 McIntosh and McNabb, 'Extraterrestrial Intelligent Life and Christian Belief', 114.
56 Chowdhury, *Islamic Theology and the Problem of Evil*; Jackson, *Islam and the Problem of Black Suffering.*
57 Al-Ghazālī, *Al-Iqtiṣād fī al-ʿItiqād*, 119; al-Ghazālī, *Moderation in Belief*, 157.

That is, God's creative acts are not bound by any human moral considerations; He is an absolutely free Creator. This is because the Ashʿarī framework prioritizes God's omnipotence over and above any other characteristic.[58]

Relatedly, God is morally amodal and thus is beyond moral categories. Tim Winter summarizes the Ashʿarī position aptly:

> God is . . . not 'morally good' in any human sense but habitually and validly acts according to wisdom . . . Divine acts are unlike human acts, not least because they are not axiologically shaped by the values of obedience and disobedience. On this conclusion, divine omnipotence includes the capacity to impose suffering that by human measuring is certainly unjust or unbearable, but this cannot compromise the principle of divine wisdom.[59]

It is why the Ashʿarī perspective on the problem of evil is referred to as an anti-theodicy, that is, it does not vindicate God of evil and suffering.[60] Consequently, if astrobiological evil were to be true, it poses no issue for the Ashʿarī position.

## C6. Conflict with the Muslim narrative

In this section, McIntosh and McNabb tackle any other outstanding conflicts that do not come under the preceding sections.[61] Two specific issues come to mind from the Islamic perspective. The first is an *existential* or perhaps a *psychological* issue. It could be contended that, if ETI do exist, and the Qurʾān and ḥadīths are meant to be defining books for Muslims, why would God miss out on such an important reference? In other words, the discussion of ETI is of such paramount importance that not acknowledging their existence in Islamic scripture would be seen as a problem. Two things can be said of this.

The purpose of Islamic scripture is not to provide detailed scientific explanations of the world. It is a book that contains insights into metaphysics (God, prophethood, hereafter), epistemology (how we come to know of and believe in God and His messengers) and axiology (values and purpose).[62] If God chose not to mention certain things in scripture, why would it be deemed an issue? It seems that personal estimations of what is considered wise or necessary seem to

[58] Jackson, *Islam and the Problem of Black Suffering*, 75–8.
[59] Winter, 'Islam and the Problem of Evil', 242.
[60] Al-Ghazālī, *Al-Iqtiṣād fī al-ʿItiqād*, 119–35; al-Ghazālī, *Moderation in Belief*, 157–98; Malik, 'Divine Command Theory'; Winter, 'Islam and the Problem of Evil', 243.
[61] McIntosh and McNabb, 'Extraterrestrial Intelligent Life and Christian Belief', 118.
[62] Al-Ghazālī, *Jawāhir al-Qurʾān*, 23–34.

be the real problem here, as they are being used to question God's wisdom in not mentioning realities that might be of significance. To this point, Ashʿarī theology seems to make it clear that God's wisdom is not the same thing as one's personal or human estimations of what is deemed wise;[63] God may not reveal some ideas because there might be no benefit in it or because He simply willed it.[64] The key thing that is stressed in Ashʿarī theology is that God's wisdom is not the same as a human's wisdom; the latter is far more limited and constrained and therefore is not in the position to judge the former.[65] This does not entail that discussions cannot be had on hermeneutic gaps. Rather, the point here is about epistemic humility.[66]

Second, this concern falls back on the hermeneutic principle of theological non-commitment. The questioner may be primed or accustomed to thinking there must always be an affirmative answer in Islamic scripture. However, this is not the case. In scripture, God either affirms realities, for example, prophets of the past and their miracle; negates realities, for example, Jesus not dying on the cross;[67] and neither affirms nor denies something, for example, dinosaurs and ETI, which is why theological non-commitment is considered a valid hermeneutic principle. Accordingly, if there is no discussion of a particular issue, no matter how important it may be regarded by some, lacking mention of that issue in scripture is not a problem, given the hermeneutic validity of theological non-commitment.

The second issue seems more to do with the jurisprudential (*fiqh*) side of things. For example, can humans have relationships or intermarry with ETI? But these are not concerns of conflict per se, as they are more to do with moral conduct and jurisprudence. Muslim theologians will have to do their necessary due diligence in regulating such matters if and when the time comes.[68]

## Conclusion

This chapter took McIntosh and McNabb's article as a template to determine if there are any potential or actual conflicts between ETI and Islamic thought. Six different kinds of questions were examined in this study:

63 See Q. 2:30 for a clear demonstration of this: '[Prophet], when your Lord told the angels, "I am putting a successor on earth," they said, "How can You put someone there who will cause damage and bloodshed, when we celebrate Your praise and proclaim Your holiness?" but He said, "*I know things you do not*" (*ạʿalamu mā lā tʿalamūn*).'

64 An explicit example of this teaching can be found in Q. 18:22.

65 Al-Ghazālī, *Al-Iqtiṣād fī al-ʿItiqād*, 119–35; al-Ghazālī, *Moderation in Belief*, 157–98; Jalajel, 'Presumptions about God's Wisdom'.

66 Al-Ghazālī, *Fayṣal al-Tafriqa*; al-Ghazālī, 'Qānūn al-Taʾwīl'.

67 Q. 4:157.

68 See the chapters of David Solomon Jalajel and Faisal Abdullah in this volume.

C1. Conflict with theism – does ETI contradict God's existence?
C2. Conflict with Islamic scripture – does ETI contract the Qur'ān and ḥadīths?
C3. Conflict with Islamic doctrine – does ETI contract the teachings of Islamic beliefs?
C4. Conflict with Islamic tradition – does ETI contradict any beliefs held by the Muslim scholarly community in the past?
C5. Conflict with the problem of evil – does ETI exacerbate the problem of evil?
C6. Conflict with the Muslim narrative – after clearing 1–5, does ETI conflict with anything else for Muslims?

The answer to all of them was negative. The only exception was C4, which revealed a potential conflict if (1) it is believed that humans beings are the best of all creation based on specific criteria (intelligence, spiritual, ethical, or physical, among others) *and* (2) there actually being ETI that is superior to humans based on the selected criteria. The other two options – believing in angels as the most superior creation or theological non-commitment altogether – discussed in C4 do not necessarily have this potential tension. This is a historical disagreement that very neatly parallels the difference of opinion among contemporary thinkers. Muzaffar Iqbal believes that humans, though highly ranked, are not necessarily the best or the most superior creation and, therefore, can entertain ETI being superior to humans in some or multiple ways, while Hamza Karamali, a contributor to this volume, seems to think the contrary. This discussion will likely take centre stage in the growing discourse of Islamic exotheology and Islamic theological anthropology more broadly.

It was also determined that the Fall, Incarnation and Atonement are essential principles in Christianity. Depending on how they are interpreted, they can have significant implications for Christian perspectives on exotheology. By contrast, there are no equivalents of these ideas in Islam. Despite the conclusions of this article and McIntosh and McNabb's being (largely) similar, it is vital to highlight the different theological underpinnings in each religious tradition.

Finally, this chapter is written from the perspective of the Sunnī strand of Islam and Ash'arī theology in particular. However, the conclusions are not necessarily exclusive to this strand. How much they reflect or align with other intellectual traditions will require additional analyses. This is future work that can be picked up by other scholars interested in looking at ETI's impact on Islamic thought from other Islamic perspectives.

# Bibliography

Al-Bayhaqī, Abū Bakr Aḥmad ibn al-Ḥusayn. *Kitāb al-Asmāʾ wa-l-Ṣifāt*. Beirut: Dār Iḥyāʾ al-Turāth al-ʿArabī, n.d.

Al-Ghazālī, Abū Ḥāmid. *Al-Iqtiṣād fī al-ʿItiqād*. Edited by Inṣāf Ramaḍān. Damascus: Dār al-Qutayba, 2003.

Al-Ghazālī, Abū Ḥāmid. *Al-Mustaṣfā min ʿIlm al-Uṣūl*. Beirut: Dār al-Arqam, 1994.

Al-Ghazālī, Abū Ḥāmid. *Fayṣal al-Tafriqa Bayna al-Islām wa-l-Zandaqa*. Edited by Sulaymān Dunyā. Cairo: Dār Ihyā al-Kutub al-ʿArabiyya, 1961.

Al-Ghazālī, Abū Ḥāmid. *Jawāhir al-Qurʾān*. Edited by Muḥammad Rashīd Riḍā al-Qabbānī. Beirut: Dār ʾIḥyāʾ al-ʿUlūm, 1976.

Al-Ghazālī, Abū Ḥāmid. *Iḥyāʾ ʿUlūm al-Dīn*. Beirut: Dār al-Fikr, 2018.

Al-Ghazālī, Abū Ḥāmid. *Moderation in Belief*. Translated by Aladdin M. Yaqub. Chicago: University of Chicago Press, 2013.

Al-Ghazālī, Abū Ḥāmid. 'Qānūn al-Taʾwīl'. In *Majmūʿatu Rasāʾil al-Imām al-Ghazālī*, compiled and edited by Ibrahīm Amīn Muḥammad, 623–30. Cairo: Al-Maktaba al-Tawfīqiyya, n.d.

Al-Madhūn, May Bint Ḥassan Muḥamamd. 'Al-Malkāʾika wa-l-Jinn – Dirāsat Maqārina fī al-Diyānāt al-Samāwiyya al-Thulāth: Judaism – Christianity – Islam'. PhD diss., Umm al-Qura University, Mecca, 2009.

Al-Ramlī, Shihāb al-Dīn. *Fatāwa al-Ramlī*. Compiled by Shams al-Dīn al-Ramlī. Dubai: Al-Maktaba al-Islāmiyya, n.d.

Al-Rāzī, Fakhr al-Dīn. *Al-Maṭālib al-ʿĀliya min al-ʿIlm al-Ilāhī*. Beirut: Dār al-Kitāb al-ʿArabī, 2010.

Al-Rāzī, Fakhr al-Dīn. *Maʿālim Uṣūl al-Dīn*. Published with the commentary of Ibn al-Tilmasānī. Amman: Dār al-Fatḥ li-l-Dirāsāt wa-l-Nashr, 2010.

Al-Taftazānī, Saʿd al-Dīn Masʿūd ibn ʿUmar. *Sharḥ al-ʿAqāʾid*. Edited by Aḥmad Ḥijāzī al-Saqqā. Cairo: Maktabat al-Kulliyyāt al-Azhariyya, 1987.

Al-Ṭaḥāwī, Abū Jaʿfar Aḥmad ibn Muḥammad ibn Salama. *The Creed of Imam Al-Ṭaḥāwī*. Translated by Hamza Yusuf. Berkeley: Zaytuna Institute, 2007.

Allnutt, Frank. *Infinite Encounters: The Real Force Behind the U.F.O. Phenomenon*. Old Tappan: Spire Books, 1978.

Ashkenazi, Michael. *What We Know About Extraterrestrial Intelligence: Foundations of Xenology*. Dordrecht: Springer, 2017.

Barnes, M. Elizabeth, Hayley M. Dunlop, Gale M. Sinatra, Taija M. Hendrix, Yi Zheng and Sara E. Brownell. '"Accepting Evolution Means You Can't Believe in God": Atheistic Perceptions of Evolution among College Biology Students'. *Life Sciences Education* 19, no. 2 (2020).

Basalla, George. *Civilized Life in the Universe: Scientists on Intelligent Extraterrestrials*. Oxford: Oxford University Press, 2006.

Beilby, James and Paul R. Eddy. *The Nature of the Atonement: Four Views*. Downers Grove: IVP Academic, 2006.

Brown, Jonathon A. C. *Hadith: Muhammad's Legacy in the Medieval and Modern World*. London: Oneworld Academic, 2018.

Burge, S. R. *Angels in Islam: Jalāl al-Dīn al-Ṣuyuṭī's Al-Ḥabā ʾik fī Akhbār al-Malā ʾik*. Abingdon: Routledge, 2012.

Chowdhury, Safaruk. *Islamic Theology and the Problem of Evil*. Cairo: American University of Cairo Press, 2021.

Connes, Pierre. *History of the Plurality of the Worlds: The Myths of Extraterrestrials Through the Ages*. Dordrecht: Springer, 2020.

Cortez, Marc. *Theological Anthropology: A Guide for the Perplexed*. Edinburgh: T&T Clark, 2010.

Crick, Francis H. C. and Leslie E. Orgel. 'Directed Panspermia'. *Icarus* 19 (1973): 341–6.

Crowe, Michael J. *The Extraterrestrial Life Debate, 1750–1900*. New York: Dover Publications, 1999.

Dawkins, Richard. *The God Delusion*. London: Bantam Press, 2006.

Determann, Jörg Matthias. *Islam, Science Fiction and Extraterrestrial Life: The Culture of Astrobiology in the Muslim World*. New York: I.B. Tauris, 2021.

Dick, Steven J. *The Biological Universe: The Twentieth Century Extraterrestrial Life Debate and the Limits of Science*. Cambridge: Cambridge University Press, 1996.

Dick, Steven J., ed. *Many Worlds: The New Universe, Extraterrestrial Life and Theological Implications*. Philadelphia: Templeton Press, 2000.

Dick, Steven J. *Plurality of Worlds: The Extraterrestrial Life Debate from Democritus to Kant*. Cambridge: Cambridge University Press, 1982.

Dick, Steven J. *Space, Time, and Aliens: Collected Works on Cosmos and Culture*. Dordrecht: Springer, 2020.

El-Zein, Amira. *Islam, Arabs, and the Intelligent World of the Jinn*. Syracuse: Syracuse University Press, 2017.

Farris, Joshua R. *An Introduction to Theological Anthropology: Humans, Both Creaturely and Divine*. Grand Rapids: Baker Academic, 2020.

Fawda, Saʿīd ʿAbd al-Laṭīf. *Al-Adilla al-ʿAqliyya ʿala Wujūd Allāh bayna al-Mutakallamīn wa-l-Falāsifa*. Amman: Dār al-Aṣlayn, 2016.

Ibn Kathīr, Abū al-Fiḍāʾ ʿImād ad-Dīn Ismāʿīl ibn ʿUmar. *Al-Bidāya wa-l-Nihāya*. Edited by ʿAlī Shīrī. Beirut: Dār Iḥyāʾ al-Turāth al-ʿArabī, 1998.

Ibrahim, Lutpi. 'The Questions of the Superiority of Angels and Prophets between al-Zamakhsharī and al-Bayḍāwī'. *Arabica* 49, no. 4 (1981): 429–55.

Iqbal, Muzaffar. 'Islamic Theology Meets ETI'. In *Astrotheology: Science and Theology Meet Extraterrestrial Life*, edited by Ted Peters, 216–27. Eugene: Cascade Books, 2018.

Jackson, Sherman A. *Islam and the Problem of Black Suffering*. Oxford: Oxford University Press, 2014.

Jakosky, Bruce. *Science, Society, and the Search for Life in the Universe*. Tucson: University of Arizona Press, 2006.

Jalajel, David Solomon. 'Presumptions about God's Wisdom in Muslim Arguments For and Against Evolution'. *Zygon: Journal of Religion and Science* 57, no. 2 (2022): 467–89.

Lewis, David Allen and Robert Shreckhise. *UFO: End-Time Delusion*. Arkansas: New Leaf Press, 1992.

Malik, Shoaib A. 'Al-Ghazālī's Divine Command Theory: Biting the Bullet'. *Journal of Religious Ethics* 49, no. 3 (2022): 546–76.

Malik, Shoaib A. *Islam and Evolution Al-Ghazālī and the Modern Evolutionary Paradigm*. Abingdon: Routledge, 2021.

Malik, Shoaib A. and Nazif Muhtaroglu. 'How Much Should or Can Science Impact Theological Formulations? An Ashʿarī Perspective on Theology of Nature'. *European Journal of Analytic Philosophy* 18, no. 2 (2022): 5–35.

McIntosh, C. A. and Tyler Dalton McNabb. 'Houston, Do We Have a Problem? Extraterrestrial Intelligent Life and Christian Belief'. *Philosophia Christi* 23, no. 1 (2021): 101–24.

Meister, Chad and Paul K. Moser, eds. *The Cambridge Companion to the Problem of Evil*. New York: Cambridge University Press, 2017.

Murray, Michael J. *Nature Red in Tooth and Claw: Theism and the Problem of Animal Suffering*. Oxford: Oxford University Press, 2008.

Nagasawa, Yujin. 'The Problem of Evil for Atheists'. In *The Problem of Evil: Eight Views in Dialogue*, edited by N. N. Trakakis, 151–75. Oxford: Oxford University Press, 2018.

Parkyn, Joel L. *Exotheology: Theological Explorations of Intelligent Extraterrestrial Life*. Eugene: Pickwick Publications, 2021.

Peters, Ted. ed. *Astrotheology: Science and Theology Meet Extraterrestrial Life*. Eugene: Cascade, 2018.

Peters, Ted. 'Introducing Astrotheology'. In *Astrotheology: Science and Theology Meet Extraterrestrial Life*, edited by Ted Peters, 3–26. Eugene: Cascade Books, 2018.

Peters, Ted. *Science, Theology, and Ethics*. Hants: Ashgate Publishing Limited, 2003.

Rassool, G. Hussein. *Evil Eye, Jinn Possession, and Mental Health Issues: An Islamic Perspective*. Abingdon: Routledge, 2019.

Robertson, David G. *UFOs, Conspiracy Theories and the New Age*. New York: Bloomsbury, 2016.

Rosato, Jennifer and Alan Vincelette, eds. *Extraterrestrials in the Catholic Imagination: Explorations in Science, Science Fiction and Religion*. Newcastle upon Tyne: Cambridge Scholars Publishing, 2021.

Schmidtke, Sabine, ed. *The Oxford Handbook of Islamic Theology*. Oxford: Oxford University Press, 2018.

Stump, James, ed. *Four Views on Creation, Evolution, and Intelligent Design*. Grand Rapids: Zondervan Academic, 2017.

Thompson, Keith. *Angels and Aliens: UFOs and the Mythic Imagination*. New York: Fawcett Columbine, 1991.

Tlili, Sarra. 'The Meaning of the Qur'anic Word "dābba": "Animals" or "Nonhuman Animals"?' *Journal of Qur'anic Studies* 12, no. 1–2 (2010): 167–87.
Traphagan, John. *Extraterrestrial Intelligence and Human Imagination*. Dordrecht: Springer, 2015.
Vainio, Olli-Pekka. *Cosmology in Theological Perspective*. Grand Rapids: Baker Academic, 2018.
Ware, Bruce, ed. *Perspectives on the Doctrine of God: Four Views*. Nashville: B&H Academic, 2008.
Weintraub, David A. *Religions and Extraterrestrial Life How Will We Deal with It?* Dordrecht: Springer, 2014.
Weldon, John and Zola Levitt. *UFOs: What on Earth is Happening?* Irvine: Harvest House Publishers, 1975.
Wilkinson, David. *Alone in the Universe? Aliens, The X-Files and God*. Downers Grove: InterVarsity Press, 1997.
Wilkinson, David. *Science, Religion, and the Search for Extraterrestrial Intelligence*. Oxford: Oxford University Press, 2017.
Wilson, Clifford and John Weldon. *Close Encounters: A Better Explanation*. San Diego: Master Books, 1978.
Winter, Tim. 'Islam and the Problem of Evil'. In *The Problem of Evil*, edited by Chad Meister and Paul J. Moser, 230–48. Cambridge: Cambridge University Press, 2017.

7

# The alien in the lamp? The jinn and alien life in Islamic theology

Richard Playford

## Introduction

Many thinkers have held that, while not incompatible with the existence of God or the truth of the world's major religions, the existence of extraterrestrial intelligence does create a certain awkwardness for followers of those traditions. This awkwardness, rarely made explicit, seems to lie in the multitude of difficult questions about the place of this intelligence in the theology and metaphysics of these faith traditions should they turn out to exist. For example, would intelligent aliens have souls? Could they partake in the afterlife? Would their existence challenge the 'specialness' of human beings? Could their religious beliefs and practices match our own, and would we expect them to? And so on. At the moment, these questions appear to be merely hypothetical ('If aliens exist . . .'). However, should intelligent extraterrestrials be discovered, then these questions would become some of the most difficult and pressing questions we face, in desperate need of answers, both because of their intellectual significance and because of their possible real-world importance where they inform our religious practices. It makes sense, therefore, to prepare our answers in advance.

One potential response to these questions, even *if* we actually discover alien life, is to simply maintain that there are answers even if we can never know them. Per se, this response is perfectly sound; if Islam is true, then these aliens will fit into God's plan in some way or another. After all, according to Q. 46.3, God[1] has

[1] I shall use the English term 'God' rather than the Arabic term 'Allah' for a number of reasons. One, much of what I shall say in this chapter applies to a lesser or greater extent to all three Abrahamic religions. Two, while admiring of certain aspects of Islamic theology and philosophy, I am not Muslim. Three, while 'Allah' is used as the/a name of God in Islam, literally translated it simply means 'God'. That said, if the Muslim reader wants to cross out 'God' and write 'Allah' in its place then I shall have no objection to this as little rests on it.

created everything and has given everything a purpose which will come about. It follows from this that if there are intelligent extraterrestrials, then they must also have been created by God, and they must also fit into his divine plan in some manner or other.

At the same time, it still strikes me as desirable that Muslims should be able to provide us with, if not *the* answer, then at least some *possible* options for how these aliens *might* fit into their theological and metaphysical world view. After all, there are many competing ways of seeing the world, and one of the ways we judge their respective likelihoods is by examining their explanatory scope, parsimony and completeness.

Similarly, if, upon reflection, we discover that Islam cannot accommodate intelligent extraterrestrials, then this puts Muslim believers in a difficult position since the rationality of their faith could be undermined at any moment. After all, given projects like SETI,[2] and the launch of the James Webb Space Telescope, we might discover intelligent extraterrestrials at any moment. Further, even if we stop looking, there is always the possibility that they might discover us! Given that we cannot rule out the possibility of intelligent aliens, the intellectual plausibility of Islam would therefore be in a much better position if it could be demonstrated how such creatures could fit into a Muslim worldview.

It follows that if Muslims can sketch out some options for how aliens might fit into their world view, then this strengthens them from both an intellectual perspective and from an interfaith perspective when trying to engage with, or convert, those of competing world views. In addition to this, while excessive speculation can be dangerous, pondering these sorts of questions allows us to delve more deeply into our own world views and to sharpen our understanding of various related questions. This strikes me as a desirable outcome whether we are alone in the universe or not!

We have now spelt out the 'problem' intelligent extraterrestrials pose to Islam. As a result, this chapter will do a number of different things. I will begin by examining the Muslim concept of the jinn while carefully explicating the difference between jinn, human beings and angels (both Islamic and Judaeo-Christian). I will then demonstrate that the jinn provide Muslims with a useful model with which to consider the questions raised by the possibility of intelligent aliens. Finally, I will sketch out some possibilities for how Muslims

[2] The SETI Institute is a research organization started in 1984 to search for extraterrestrial intelligence and to explore, understand and explain the origin and nature of life in the universe. SETI stands for the 'search for extraterrestrial intelligence'.

might incorporate intelligent aliens into their world view based on their pre-existing belief in the jinn.

## Not quite human, not quite angels: The jinn

The Qur᾿ān attests to the existence of at least three classes of created intelligence: human beings, jinn and angels. For example, Sūrat al-Ḥijr references all three in quick succession: 'the jinn We created before, from the fire of scorching wind. Your Lord said to the angels, "I will create a mortal out of dried clay, formed from dark mud."'[3] Similarly, Sūrat al-Dhāriyāt, " I created jinn and mankind only to worship Me."[4] All three classes of being are referenced throughout the Qur᾿ān, but hopefully these two examples will suffice.

To a Western audience, human beings and angels will sound familiar. We are human beings (so one would hope they sound familiar!), and belief in angels is shared across all three Abrahamic faiths conceived of in similar, although perhaps not identical, terms. The jinn, however, may well be unfamiliar. What are these creatures? And how do they differ from human beings and angels?

As El-Zein has pointed out, when examining Islamic beliefs, there are three major 'layers' or sources of information: orthodox or official Islam, folk or popular Islam and Sufism.[5] Orthodox or official Islam is primarily based on the teaching of the Qur᾿ān and the ḥadīth as well as the teachings and interpretations (of the Qur᾿ān and the ḥadīth) by the great historical Islamic schools of thought. Folk or popular Islam is based on the legends, myths, folktales and popular stories found in the Islamic world. Finally, Sufism is, fairly obviously, based on the teachings and writings of the Sufi tradition, often defined as the mystical aspect of Islam. Primarily, I will try to focus on the official layer of Islamic beliefs since, in principle, these should be more systematized and more creedally binding upon Muslim believers. However, where appropriate, I will refer to other sources from the other two layers, particularly where this fills in 'the gaps' left by official Islam. I will also try to focus primarily on, what we might call, 'mainstream' or classical Islam, that is, Islam as understood and expressed by the major Sunnī and Shīʿī traditions.[6] With that in mind, what do these traditions teach about the jinn?

[3] Q. 15:27–8.

[4] Q. 51:56.

[5] El-Zein, *Islam, Arabs, and the Intelligent World of the Jinn*, xix–xxiii.

[6] The Sunnī and Shīʿī sects are the largest two denominations within Islam. The Sunnī tradition is the larger of the two. The disagreement between the two denominations goes back to the death of Muḥammad and a disagreement about who should succeed him. Sunnī Muslims believe Abu Bakr,

In many ways, the jinn, at least prior to the resurrection, seem to occupy a place somewhere between human beings and angels. Examining various qualities in turn, the jinn, like human beings, have free will and are capable of both good and evil.[7] Further, as a result of their free will, they will also be judged at the resurrection alongside human beings.[8]

Angels, on the other hand, in all three Abrahamic faiths are usually considered to be either totally good or totally bad (i.e. fallen angels, otherwise known as demons). In Judaism and Christianity, angels are traditionally held to have had free will, albeit not in the precise same way that human beings have free will.[9] As a result of their choices at some point in the past or at the moment of their creation they are now either totally obedient to God or evil.[10] With regard to Islamic angels, many thinkers have held that angels do not have free will at all. The Sufi thinker Abd al-Qādir al-Jilānī (d. 1166), for example, wrote, 'Angels have no will, while prophets have no passion, and the rest of humans and jinn have both will and passion, except for certain saints who are free of passion.'[11,12]

The jinn also seem to share with humans a sexual, tribal, phagous (concerned with food and eating) and mortal nature. Taking each in turn, al-Kisāʾī writes of jinn reproduction:

> God created the first jann and called him marij (the mixed one). From him he also created a mate called marijah. Then marij lay with marijah, and she bore him a son called jann, from whom all the tribes of the jinn proceed . . . Jann produced male jinn and female jinn. The males were mated to the females.[13]

Muḥammad's father-in-law, was the rightful successor, while Shīʿī Muslims believe Muḥammad's cousin and son-in-law, ʿAlī, was the rightful successor.

7 Q. 72:11. See also Ibn Taymiyya, *Ibn Taymiyya's Essay on the Jinn (Demons)*, 20–1.

8 Q. 7:38, 55:39, and 72:13–15. See also Ibn Taymiyya, *Ibn Taymiyya's Essay on the Jinn (Demons)*, 40–1; Ibn al-Qayyim al-Jawziyya, *Al-Tafsīr al-Qayyim*, 461.

9 For example, the Catholic Church teaches that 'As purely spiritual creatures angels have intelligence and will: they are personal and immortal creatures, surpassing in perfection all visible creatures, as the splendour of their glory bears witness' (Catholic Church, 330).

10 This debate is fairly technical and goes beyond the scope of this chapter. For our purposes, however, it will suffice it to say that, while they do have free will, angels and demons cannot 'change their mind' when it comes to God. Once they have turned towards (or away from) God, they cannot turn back. See Aquinas, *Summa Theologica*, I: q.59 and 63, for a detailed discussion of this topic.

11 Al-Jīlānī, *Futūḥ al-Ghayb*, 16, as translated in El-Zein, *Islam, Arabs, and the Intelligent World of the Jinn*, 44.

12 This raises interesting questions about whether, within Islam, Satan/Iblīs is a jinn or a fallen angel. If he is a jinn, then it is clear how Iblis could have turned away from God. However, if he is a fallen angel, and angels lack free will, as some thinkers have claimed, it is much less clear how he could have turned away from God. See El-Zein, *Islam, Arabs, and the Intelligent World of the Jinn*, 44–7, for a lengthier discussion of this topic.

13 Al-Kisāʾī, *The Tales of the Prophets*, 19.

In a similar vein, Ibn 'Arabi (d. 1240) explains that 'Just as procreation in human beings involves the scattering of the seed inside the womb, which gives rise to conception and reproduction in the human Adamic species, so procreation amongst jinns involves air being projected into the female womb so that the conception and reproduction of the jinn takes place' adding that their mating is like 'a spiral, as when smoke comes out of a potter's kiln or a kitchen oven; that is how one enters the other and they satisfy each other in this coupling'.[14]

The jinn are also described in numerous places as being organized into tribes or nations. The Qur'ān, for example, addresses the jinn as nations (*umam*). Additionally, the historian al-Ḥusayn ibn ʿAlī al-Masʿūd (d. 956) states that the jinn are divided into twenty-one tribes,[15] although other thinkers disagree with him about the precise number of tribes.

With regard to the jinn consuming food, Ibn ʿArabī writes:

> Due to the dominance of air and fire in jinn, their food is the air content in the fat of the bones. Allah caused them to find sustenance in bones. It is clear for us to see the substance and meat in bones, of which nothing is wasted. On the question of bones the Prophet, peace be upon him, said: 'They are the provisions of your brothers amongst the jinn.' And in another ḥadīth he said: 'Surely Allah put in them [i.e. bones] their sustenance.' I was informed by one of the people of insight (*mukāshifūn*) that he had seen some jinn go up to a bone and sniff at it as wild beasts do. After eating their food, they departed. They ate their food by sniffing it. Glory be to Him, the Subtle, the Well-Informed![16,17]

We find similar attestations to the jinn's appetites in various ḥadīths. For example, in *Saḥīḥ Bukhārī*, Muḥammad prohibits his followers from cleaning themselves using bones or animal dung since they are the food of the jinn.[18]

The jinn, like human beings, are mortal, although the length of their lives is far greater than ours. There is no consensus on precisely how long they live, nor does the Qur'ān offer any definitive answers, but certainly in folk Islam it is agreed that it is immensely long.[19] The jinn can also be killed. There are numerous accounts of the jinn being killed by human beings, either intentionally or by accident. How easy it is to kill them in these various accounts varies. In folk Islam, for example, some stories indicate that they are immensely strong

[14] Ibn ʿArabī, *Al-Futūḥāt al-Makkiyya*, 1:131–4.
[15] Al-Masʿūdī, *Akhbār al-Zamān*, 34.
[16] Ibn ʿArabī, *Al-Futūḥāt al-Makkiyya*, 1:132.
[17] See also Ibn Taymiyya, *Ibn Taymiyya's Essay on the Jinn (Demons)*, 36–8.
[18] Khan, *Saheeh al-Bukhari, (Arabic-English)*, 5:126.
[19] Al-Kisāʾī, *The Tales of the Prophets*, 19; El-Zein, *Islam, Arabs, and the Intelligent World of the Jinn*, 50–1.

and dangerous creatures. In other stories it is implied that they are rather feeble. This inconsistency is exemplified in the story of the 'The Merchant and the Jinni' in *The Arabian Nights*. In the story the titular merchant is eating dates and casually throwing the date seeds away. A passing jinn, invisible to the merchant, is accidentally killed after being struck by one of the discarded date seeds. This seems to suggest they are rather feeble creatures. The slain jinn's father (also a jinn) then appears. However, his threats to kill the accidental jinn slayer are met with fear and bargaining by the terrified human being.[20] This seems to suggest that the jinn are powerful, dangerous creatures. Why else would the merchant be so afraid? In a more scholarly context, the Sunnī theologian Ibn Taymiyya (d. 1328) also affirms that the jinn can be killed again with, what would appear to be, relative ease. He explains that jinn can become angry when 'humans accidentally harm or hurt them by urinating on them, by pouring hot water on them, or by killing some of them'.[21]

Regardless of the finer details, the jinn clearly share a number of characteristics in common with human beings. At the same time, the jinn share with angels an invisible nature. Under normal circumstances, at least, the jinn are invisible to the naked (human) eye.[22] Human beings, on the other hand, at least under normal circumstances, are visible to the naked eye. In this respect, the jinn are more like angels than human beings.

Materiality is an area where the jinn seem to be somewhere between human beings and angels. Human beings are clearly made up of matter, as evidenced by the existence of our physical bodies. This materiality is affirmed in the Qurʾān,[23] as is an additional immaterial element to our composition.[24] Angels, on the other hand, certainly within Christianity, are normally considered to be immaterial. However, this was a topic of some debate in the early Church, with some thinkers arguing for their materiality.[25] Aquinas (d. 1274), however, appears to have settled the debate, at least in the West, in the eleventh century in his *Summa Theologica*, arguing for their immateriality.[26]

20 Haddaway, trans., *The Arabian Nights*, 17 and 43.

21 Ibn Taymiyya, *Ibn Taymiyya's Essay on the Jinn (Demons)*, 44.

22 See, for example, El-Zein, *Islam, Arabs, and the Intelligent World of the Jinn*, 47, and Ibn ʿArabī, *Al-Futūḥāt al-Makkiyya*, 3:367. See also al-Tahānawī, *Mawsūʿat Iṣṭilāḥāt*, 2:264, in which it is argued that humans cannot see jinn because we lack the appropriate sensory organs.

23 Q. 23:12–14 and 15:26.

24 Q. 38:72.

25 See Jacobs, 'Are Created Spirits Composed of Matter and Form? A Defence of Pneumatic Hylomorphism', 81–90 for more details.

26 Aquinas, *Summa Theologica*, I, q.75, a.5.1.

The jinn are described in the Qurʾān as being made of 'scorching fire' (and/or possibly 'scorching wind').[27] Later Muslim thinkers would continue to think of the jinn in relatively materialistic sort of terms with Ibn ʿArabī, for example, arguing that the jinn must be composed not only of air and fire but also water because otherwise they would be incapable of breathing.[28] One could conclude on the basis of this that the jinn, like human beings, are material rather than immaterial. At the same time, many Muslim sources do seem to describe the jinn as being incorporeal and perhaps unembodied.[29] Certainly, as a non-Muslim and European, fire and wind (and, if Ibn ʿArabī is correct, water) strike me as material components or constituents of an entity. Similarly, sexual reproduction and the act of eating both strike me as quintessentially physical and embodied activities. As a result, unless this language is to be taken entirely symbolically, and I see no reason why it should, then it seems to me that the jinn must be seen as material entities. Their 'materiality' may well be very different to ours, but if they are 'made' of something (fire and air) and if they need to eat to survive and to have sex to reproduce, then, it seems to me, that they must be material in *some* sense of the word. As a result, the fact that some Muslims may not see the jinn as material entities lead me to suspect there are slightly different conceptions of what it means to be material at play here. Perhaps when Muslims describe the jinn as immaterial, they simply mean they do not have the same physical limitations and are not bound by the same physical laws as us. Either way, ultimately, it doesn't matter too much for our purposes whether or not the jinn are material, so I will explore this topic no further. It would be *convenient* if the jinn are material since this would increase their similarity to (possible) extraterrestrials, but if they are not, then this does nothing to undermine the overall thesis of this chapter.

The jinn also share with angels a luminous nature. The angels, in the Islamic tradition, are composed of light and thus are luminous when they wish to be. Likewise, the jinn, being composed of fire, are luminous when they wish to be. Finally, the jinn also share with angels the ability to shapeshift.

[27] Q. 15:27.

[28] Ibn ʿArabi, *Al-Futūḥāt al-Makkiyya*, 1:130–4.

[29] El-Zein. *Islam, Arabs, and the Intelligent World of the Jinn*, 47. It is worth noting that El-Zein uses the word 'incorporeal' rather than 'immaterial' and that she uses the word, seemingly intentionally, in an inexact manner, perhaps in opposition to the word 'robust' and more akin to the word 'ethereal'. Perhaps, we can conclude from this that relatively few Muslims have actually held that the jinn are 'immaterial' in the strict metaphysical sense I am attributing to the word. My thanks go to David Jalajel for pointing this out.

There are other factors which we could consider, but this brief discussion nicely illustrates that in many ways, at least prior to the resurrection,[30] the jinn occupy a place somewhere between human beings and angels. To summarize, then, the jinn share with human beings: free will and moral accountability as well as a sexual, tribal, phagous and mortal nature. They share with angels: invisibility, luminosity and the ability to shapeshift. They are also sometimes described as sharing with angels an immaterial nature, although I have argued that the plausibility of this claim will hinge on your definition of (im)materiality.

## Extraterrestrial intelligence and the jinn

Turning now to extraterrestrials, at this moment in time, we can only speculate about the appearance of alien intelligence. Ultimately this is a question for the astrobiologist to consider, but I will make some modest assumptions. I shall assume that such aliens are physical beings and thus subject to the same basic needs and limitations as us. These needs and limitations would include things like being mortal, needing to take in sustenance from one's environment, needing to reproduce and so on. Note, however, that I am entirely prepared to accept that these needs and limitations may manifest themselves in very different ways. For example, I make no claims about the length of their average lifespan or precisely how vulnerable they are to physical damage. There are many possibilities, perhaps they live on average for thousands of years, or perhaps they only live on average for one or two years. However, I assume, given what we know about chemistry and physics, that their bodies can be damaged, undergo decay and so on, and that, as a result, they can be killed. Further, given the volatilities and precarity of the universe as we understand it, not only can they be killed, but it is highly likely that they will perish after a certain length of time. Therefore, even if they are very long-lived, they will technically be mortal.

I will also assume that, alongside their intelligence, comes free will and moral responsibility.[31] There is insufficient space here to consider the nature of intelligence and free will since no uncontentious accounts of these concepts

[30] See El-Zein, *Islam, Arabs, and the Intelligent World of the Jinn*, 21, for a brief discussion of how the powers and abilities of the jinn (and human beings) will change in Paradise.

[31] It is for this reason that I draw the primary comparison between the jinn and possible intelligent extraterrestrials rather than, and to the exclusion of, angels. As we have seen, according to many Islamic sources, angels lack free will. This makes them importantly different from intelligent extraterrestrials (and us!), and this limits their use as models for how Muslims might incorporate aliens into their world view.

exist. However, I will assume that they have intelligence and free will in a manner comparable to our own. As a result, like us, these aliens will also have 'the capacity for such things as: abstract thought . . . language; knowledge of why it does many of the things it does, what Aristotelians call knowledge of finality; the conscious ordering of ends or objectives; development of and adherence to a life plan; reflection, meditation . . . a moral life . . . humour, irony, aesthetic sensibility, the creation and maintenance of families and political societies . . . we all know the sorts of things we rational animals are capable of'.[32] As a result, such intelligent aliens will be, importantly, like us, both physically and intellectually.

Note, again, that this claim is not incompatible with the possibility that they will exercise these shared intellectual (and physical) capacities in a very different way from us. Their sense of humour, for example, may be 'alien', but it is still a sense of humour.[33] Here, it is important to distinguish between having a sense of humour simpliciter and having a particular sense of humour, such as a love of slapstick comedy. All human beings share a capacity for humour (simpliciter), even though our individual tastes vary. An intelligent alien may very well, by human standards, have a very unusual sense of humour which most (all?[34]) of us find unintelligible. However, such an alien would still share with us a capacity for humour (a sense of humour simpliciter). This would be an important shared characteristic.

We now return to the questions posed at the beginning of this chapter. As we shall see, we can now answer the questions raised by the existence of extraterrestrials for Islam using the jinn as a model. To see this, let's rephrase the questions while inserting the jinn in place of intelligent extraterrestrials. When we do this, we shall see that the answers are readily available and that, with one exception, the very same answers can be given for intelligent aliens.

32 Oderberg, 'Could There Be a Superhuman Species?' 216.

33 Here I am assuming that all rational creatures, including extraterrestrials, will have at least the capacity for humour and comedy. I make this assumption because our humour is tied to our intelligence and imagination. As a result, it seems likely that any creature with both intelligence and imagination will also have the capacity for humour. At the same time, I accept that more of an argument is needed in order to justify this assumption. However, due to limits on space, I will have to leave that discussion for another time. Note, however, that I am merely using humour as a possible example of a shared capacity between us and possible intelligent extraterrestrials. As a result, if the reader wants to consider a different example (perhaps art or storytelling) then these examples will also suffice for my purposes.

34 I suspect that if, as I have asserted, humour is tied to our rationality and intelligence, and given intelligent aliens would share our rational and intelligent nature, we would be able to, at the very least, intellectually understand their comedy and sense of humour. It also then seems possible that at least some of us would actually enjoy their comedy and sense of humour. This raises the possibility of sharing a joke with an extraterrestrial. This strikes me as an encouraging possibility!

Taking each in turn, with regard to whether or not the jinn have souls, we can now see that they do. With regard to whether or not the jinn partake in the afterlife, we can now see that they do. With regard to whether or not their existence challenges the 'specialness' of human beings, it is not obvious that it does. Finally, with regard to whether or not their religious beliefs and practices match our own, while we don't know the precise details of the jinn's day-to-day lives, by and large, the answer is yes. The Qurʾān, for example, is sent to both humans and jinn.[35]

With these answers in mind, turning now to intelligent aliens, it seems likely that intelligent aliens would have souls, it seems likely that they would partake in the afterlife and, given the existence of the jinn does not undermine the 'specialness' of human beings, it is unclear why the existence of intelligent aliens should undermine the 'specialness' of human beings.

I will return to the final question momentarily, however, as we can see the very same answers we gave when considering the jinn can be given for intelligent aliens. This makes perfect sense because both intelligent aliens and the jinn are non-human[36] created beings with free will, moral accountability and so on. As a result, both share certain features in common with us while also being distinct from us. Thus, the jinn mirror intelligent aliens in that they are like us in some respects but different from us in others.

We have now answered most of the questions we initially set out to answer. This is an encouraging result. One question, however, remains unanswered: Could their religious beliefs and practices match our own and would we expect them to? As we shall see, the jinn do not provide a useful model for intelligent aliens in this context. To see why, we must first consider where the jinn live compared to where extraterrestrials (intelligent or otherwise) live.

## The invisible realm versus different planets

Within Islamic theology and philosophy, many different thinkers have postulated numerous different cosmologies. One distinction, however, that is

[35] See, for example, Q. 72:1–2, 46:29 and 81:27.

[36] Obviously, this claim depends on how we define human beings. If we define human beings in such a way as to exclude intelligent aliens, then this phrasing is unobjectionable. However, if we adopt Aristotle's definition of man as a rational animal, then intelligent aliens (and potentially the jinn) would also count as human beings. In that case, we can simply rephrase this to make the distinction clear by saying (something like) 'they are both intelligent non-*Homo sapiens* created beings' and so on. There are numerous options, and little rests on which one we pick, so I won't labour this point.

commonly made is between the visible and invisible realms. These two realms are not geographically separate. As a result, even though we cannot see it (at least under normal conditions), and even though we cannot directly interact with it, the invisible realm is 'right here'. It is also important to emphasize that these two realms are not isolated from each other. They are both equally real, they both form an integral part of reality and the two realms can interact with each other. As a result, in a sense, the jinn do live on 'Earth', albeit, under normal circumstances, not in the way that we do.

On the other hand, extraterrestrials, as implied by their very name, do not live on Earth. We don't yet know where they live (if they are out there). It certainly seems highly unlikely that there are any technologically sophisticated aliens in our solar system because we would have spotted them by now. As a result, wherever they are, it is likely a long way away from here. At the same time, such creatures would, like us, live in the visible realm. They, unlike the jinn, are geographically distant from us. In a sense, we can say that the jinn are metaphysically distant from us, because they live primarily in a different realm, whereas extraterrestrials, if there are any, are physically and geographically distant from us.

Either way, regardless of how far away they are, this does raise a particular problem for Islam. The difficulty is that Islam as a religion is tied to both a particular geographical place and particular historical time. The Qur'ān, for example, is very clearly tied to a particular time, place, historical context and, indeed, person. According to Islam, while the Qur'ān itself is eternal it was revealed in seventh century, in the Arabian Peninsula, by a particular human being (the Prophet Muḥammad). It refers to specific (earthly) historical events, and it is written in the Arabic dialect of that time and place. This raises a number of difficult questions. Do these intelligent aliens have access to the Qur'ān? If so, is it the same as our Qur'ān? If so, can they understand it? Do they speak Arabic? Do they understand the events it describes and their implications? If not, and their 'Qur'ān' is different to our Qur'ān, is it really a/the Qur'ān? Is this acceptable, given the importance of the Qur'ān in Islam?

Similarly, do these aliens have prophets? If not, how can they learn about God and about the things they need to do to be saved? If these aliens do have prophets, what is the relationship between their prophets and our prophets, particularly the Prophet Muḥammad? According to Islam, Muḥammad is the final prophet, known as the 'Seal of the Prophets'. This gives him particular importance and authority in Islam. Do these aliens have their own 'Seal of the Prophets'? If so, how does this prophet relate to Muḥammad?

Muslim practices are similarly tied to specific geographical places. They must pray facing Mecca. Must these aliens pray facing Mecca? Is this even practically possible, given the fact that their planet will likely be moving relative to ours? Muslims must also perform the Hajj, a pilgrimage to Mecca, at least once in their lives. Are these aliens expected to perform an earthly Hajj? This seems like an unreasonable ask! Alternatively, perhaps they have their own Mecca and their own Hajj, but, again, this raises more questions than it answers. The point, I think, is becoming clear. Islam is very much an earthly religion – in that, it is tied to the planet Earth historically and geographically. This poses problems for Muslims when they try to imagine it on an interstellar and cosmic scale.

Despite these problems, I want to end this section, and ultimately this chapter, on an optimistic note. None of these problems strike me as insurmountable. Should intelligent alien life be discovered, certain Islamic beliefs may need to be reinterpreted or reconsidered, but I've no doubt that with a bit of thought and a bit of work, answers to these difficult questions can be found. Islam, as a religion, has the intellectual resources needed to find them!

Of course, at this stage, we can only speculate, and the reality of alien life, should we find it, may well surprise us. With that in mind, it is important to clarify that nothing I have said here should be taken as anything more than a speculation, nor should anything I have said here be taken as an attempt to limit the power of God. In Islamic thought, and within the Abrahamic traditions more generally, God is seen to be omnipotent and capable of anything. As a result, there are an almost (actual?) infinite number of ways God could have created and arranged the universe. This includes the different ways he may (or may not) have created intelligent aliens and guided (or not guided) them towards a knowledge of him. As a result, while we can speculate, with regard to the actual answers, we shall simply have to wait and see. Perhaps the answers will be revealed when we discover or make contact with alien life. Perhaps, when this happens, certain questions will cease to be relevant, with entirely new questions emerging in their place. Perhaps, even then, some of these questions will remain unanswered and unanswerable. Perhaps we will find out at the resurrection, perhaps not even then. For now, only God knows the answer to these questions, but it is fun to speculate!

## Could Christians and Jews use this model?

One additional question to consider, before we finish this chapter, is whether or not other faiths could also use the jinn as a model for how intelligent extraterrestrials could fit into their theology. Due to limitations of space, I will limit my discussion to the other two major Abrahamic faiths: Christianity and Judaism. Could Christians and Jews use the jinn as a model for how they might accommodate aliens into their world view?

I think the answer here is strictly speaking *yes* but practically speaking *no*. The reason for this is simple. While 'folk' Christianity and Judaism do often postulate non-human physical intelligences, akin to the jinn, traditional mainstream Christian and Jewish theology does not.[37] At the same time, there is nothing in their respective scriptures or religious traditions that rules out the possibility of such creatures.

This means that, strictly speaking, Christians and Jews could use the jinn as a model for aliens, but in order to do this, they would first have to consider how the jinn would fit into their theology. As a result, if the goal is to work out how aliens could fit into their respective theologies, such an exercise would be pointless. This is because they would have to answer the very same questions when working out how the jinn might fit into their world view as they were aiming to answer for aliens in the first place. To give an example, if the question a Christian was trying to answer concerned alien salvation, then, in order to use the jinn as a model, they would first have to work out how the jinn might be saved within a Christian soteriology, before applying that same answer to aliens. It would be much simpler to just consider how intelligent extraterrestrials might be saved and to ignore the possibility of the jinn altogether. Such a step (that of using the jinn as a model) is simply unnecessary.

As a result, practically speaking, I can see no value for Christians and Jews in using the jinn as a model to understand how intelligent extraterrestrials could fit into their world view. At the same time, I do not think Christians and Jews should be concerned by the possibility of intelligent extraterrestrials. There are numerous ways they might accommodate the existence of such beings and various possibilities have been put forward over time.[38]

[37] This is, of course, a simplification and generalization, and there were noted theologians who did engage with the possibility of non-human physical intelligences. For example, the Christian theologian Ratramnus (d. 868) considered the possibility of dog-headed men: the Cynocephali. He concludes, based on the accounts available to him, that they were in fact rational creatures, and that they did have a part in God's plan for salvation. For more information, see Bruce, 'Hagiography as Monstrous Ethnography: A Note on Ratramnus of Corbie's Letter Concerning the Conversion of Cynocephali'.

[38] For a Christian consideration of how aliens might fit into their world view see Losch and Krebs, 'Implications for the Discovery of Extraterrestrial Life: A Theological Approach'. For a Jewish response see Lamm, 'The Religious Implications of Extraterrestrial Life'.

## Conclusion

Bringing everything together, this chapter has done a number of different things. It began by sketching out the problem raised by the existence of intelligent extraterrestrials for the major world religions. The problem was simply that their existence raises a number of difficult to answer questions, the answers to which may also stand in tension with other doctrines and beliefs. Examples of these questions included: Would extraterrestrial intelligences have souls? Could they partake in the afterlife? Would their existence challenge the 'specialness' of human beings? Could their religious beliefs and practices match our own and would we expect them to? It then applied these questions to Islam in particular and argued that, while the Muslim is not intellectually *obliged* to provide an answer, it is desirable that they do so, both for the sake of intellectual completeness and when engaging with followers of other faiths. It then explored the Muslim concept of the jinn and examined their various features, properties and powers. I demonstrated that although, in a sense, they occupy a position midway between human beings and angels, they have many important features in common with us. I put forward the idea that because the jinn resemble us in some respects, but not others, they provide a model for how we might understand the place of intelligent extraterrestrials within Islam since such beings would also resemble us in some respects but not others. Using the jinn as a model I then re-examined the questions posed by the existence of intelligent extraterrestrials for Islam. I argued that such intelligent aliens would likely possess souls, that they would partake in the afterlife and that their existence would no more challenge the 'specialness' of human beings than the existence of the jinn. Finally, I turned to the question of alien religious beliefs and practices. Here I suggested that there were some difficulties. I argued that because Islam, as a religion, is tied to particular locations, particular languages, particular earthly historical events and particular people, it is difficult to imagine it on, and apply it at, an interstellar or cosmic scale. However, I then ended on a note of optimism arguing that although there are difficulties here, they are not insurmountable. It is in the nature of the world's great religions to adapt and evolve as the context and situation in which they operate changes. Those religions that cannot adapt rarely survive long and are soon confined to the history books. Islam has survived thus far, and I see no reason why that should change anytime soon, whether or not we discover alien life.

# Bibliography

Al-Jīlānī, ʿAbd al-Qādir. *Futūḥ al-Ghayb*. Cairo: Maktabat al-Thaqāfa al-Dīniyya, 2005.

Al-Kisāʾī, Muḥammad ibn ʿAlī. *The Tales of the Prophets*. Translated with notes by W. M. Thackston Jr. Boston: Twayne Publishers, 1978.

Al-Masʿūdī, al-Ḥusayn ibn ʿAlī. *Akhbār al-Zamān*. Beirut: Dār al-Andalus, 1980.

Al-Shiblī, Badr al-Dīn. *Ākām al-Marjān fī Gharāʾib al-Akhbār wa-Aḥkām al-Jānn*. Beirut: Al-Maktaba al-ʿAṣriyya, 1988.

Al-Tahānawī, Muḥammad ibn ʿAlī. *Mawsūʿat Isṭilāḥāt al-ʿUlūm al-Islāmiyya*. Beirut: Dār Khayyāṭ, 1966.

Aquinas, Thomas. *Summa Theologica*. Translated by the Fathers of the English Dominican Province. New York: Benziger Bros, 1948.

Bruce, Scott G. 'Hagiography as Monstrous Ethnography: A Note on Ratramnus of Corbie's Letter Concerning the Conversion of Cynocephali'. In *Insignis Sophiae Arcator: Medieval Latin Studies in Honour of Michael Herren on His 65th Birthday*, edited by Gernot R. Wieland, Carin Ruff and Ross G. Arthur, 45–56. Turnhout: Brepols, 2006.

Catholic Church. *Catechism of the Catholic Church*. Second Edition. Libreria Editrice Vaticana, 1997.

El-Zein, Amira. *Islam, Arabs, and the Intelligent World of the Jinn*. New York: Syracuse University Press, 2017.

Haddaway, Husain, trans. *The Arabian Nights*. New York: W. W. Norton and Company, 1990.

Ibn al-Qayyim al-Jawziyya, Muḥammad ibn Abī Bakr. *Al-Tafsir al-Qayyim*. Beirut: Dār al-Kutub al-ʿIlmiyya, 1978.

Ibn ʿArabī, Muḥyī al-Dīn. *Al-Futūḥāt al-Makkiyya*. Edited by Osman Yahya. Beirut: Dār al- Ṣādir, 1972.

Ibn Taymiyya. *Ibn Taymiyya's Essay on the Jinn (Demons)*. Translated by Abu Ameenah Bilal Philips. Riyadh: International Islamic Publishing House, 1989.

Jacobs, Nathan A. 'Are Created Spirits Composed of Matter and Form? A Defence of Pneumatic Hylomorphism'. *Philosophia Christi* 14, no. 1 (2012): 79–108.

Khan, Muhammad Muhsin. *Saheeh al-Bukhāri (Arabic English)*. Riyadh: Maktaba al-Riyāḍ al-Hadīth, 1981.

Lamm, Norman. 'The Religious Implications of Extraterrestrial Life'. *Tradition: A Journal of Orthodox Jewish Thought* 7, no. 4 / 8, no. 1 (1965/1966): 5–56.

Losch, Andreas and Andreas Krebs. 'Implications for the Discovery of Extraterrestrial Life: A Theological Approach'. *Theology and Science* 13, no. 2 (2015): 230–44.

Oderberg, David. 'Could There Be a Superhuman Species?' *The Southern Journal of Philosophy* 52, no. 2 (2014): 206–26.

Wieland, Gernot, Carin Ruff and Ross G. Arthur, eds. *Insignis Sophiae Arcator: Medieval Latin Studies in Honour of Michael Herren on His 65th Birthday*. Turnhout: Brepols, 2006.

8

# A Qurʾānic ufology? Seven exotheological hypotheses of the Indonesian 'Islamic UFO' community

Ayub and Ilham Ibrahim

## Introduction

The history of interest in unidentified flying objects (UFOs) in Indonesia dates back at least to the 1950s. One of the earliest sightings of a UFO pilot (ufonaut) is reported to have taken place on the island of Alor, East Nusa Tenggara, in 1959. After the appearance of the creature, islanders reported that they saw an unidentified aircraft circle the coast and then fly low over their village.[1] Interest in UFOs was not only among the public, but important government officials were also involved in discussions about UFOs in those early days. One of these important figures was Raden Jacob Salatun. He was the pioneering founder of the National Institute of Aeronautics and Space (LAPAN), the Indonesian counterpart of NASA. One of the important reports prepared by Salatun was on the sighting of unidentified aircraft in the skies over Surabaya and surrounding towns from 18 to 24 September 1964. Observations of the planes were not only via radar, but many residents also claimed to have seen them with their own eyes. They initially thought the strange objects belonged to the British armed forces that at that time were conducting military exercises in the Malaysian region. But upon further investigation, the strange objects emitted bright lights on their undersides, unlike any other aircraft that they had seen.[2] In 1976, Indonesian foreign minister Adam Malik invited J. Allen Hynek, editor of the International UFO Reporter, to lecture at the University of Indonesia and Bosscha Observatory. Although Project Blue Book was discontinued in the United States, leading to a

1 Pratomo, 'Alien Pernah Singgah Di Indonesia?'
2 Jo, 'Sejarah Penampakan UFO Di Indonesia: Disangka Pesawat Canggih Milik Musuh'.

decline in the interest of governments around the world in investigating these extraterrestrial phenomena, in 1977 the Indonesian government gave its support to Granada's prime minister Eric Gairy's proposal to establish a UN agency for the study of UFOs.[3]

By the 1980s, the Indonesian government, which was then focused on development projects, seemed to have lost interest in further research into UFOs. Nevertheless, UFOs still attracted the curiosity of many people; communities of amateur UFO hunters have sprung up in Indonesia. In the 1980s, the UFO Study Indonesia was founded by Jacob Salatun. He also published several books on UFOs, including *Uncovering the Secret of Flying Saucers* (1960) and *UFOs: One of the World's Current Problems* (1982). It is no wonder that UFO enthusiasts in the country have recognized Salatun as the Father of Indonesian UFO studies. In 1997, a community of extraterrestrial investigators known as BETA-UFO was established.[4] One of the major events in which they were involved was the debate around the discovery of crop circles in early January of 2011. BETA-UFO members who conducted the research concluded that the crop circles were not man-made. Meanwhile, the head of LAPAN at the time believed that the crop circles were man-made.[5]

The public discourse on crop circles eventually led to the theological dimension of the issue. There was public speculation that the existence of intelligent extraterrestrials would shake the foundations of many people's faith. As a Muslim-majority country, media outlets that quickly picked up the issue interviewed the chairman of the Indonesian Ulema Council (MUI) on Islam and extraterrestrial intelligent beings. Ma'ruf Amin, the current vice president of Indonesia who was then one of the chairmen of the MUI, said that the Qur᾽ān does mention the existence of living beings in the heavens. However, according to Amin, the verses refer either to angels or jinn. He was not sure whether the verses could be linked to UFOs. On behalf of the MUI, Amin stated, 'We do not understand about UFOs or aliens.'[6] In the same year, an online community called 'Islamic UFO' was established and since then they have been actively discussing UFO and alien phenomena from an Islamic perspective. According to one of its founders, the main reason for the formation of this group was that mainstream ulema in Indonesia do not pay enough attention to UFOs and extraterrestrials.

[3] Determann, *Islam, Science Fiction and Extraterrestrial Life*, 108.
[4] Agustinus and Tri, *Satu Dekade Perjalanan Komunitas BETA-UFO Indonesia Melacak Fenomena UFO*.
[5] Akbar, 'LAPAN: Crop Circle Di Sleman Buatan Manusia'.
[6] Ramdan, 'Misteri UFO Dan Alien Dalam Pandangan Ulama'.

They did not find any satisfactory exotheology from the ulema. The members of this community come from diverse educational backgrounds, and not all of them have a strong foundation in Islamic sciences. However, they are united by their desire to provide a scientific explanation for UFOs that is also acceptable from an Islamic theological perspective. An Islamic ufology, according to this group, is an ufological explanation that is in accordance with the Qur'ān, Sunnah and the opinions of scholars. By referring to these sources, they hope to present an Islamic perspective in ufological discourse.

Islam plays important epistemological roles for the members of the Islamic UFO community. The founders of the group insist that ufology is not a pseudoscience. Following Robert Bigelow, they prefer to describe ufology as a frontier science. Bigelow is an American business mogul who founded Bigelow Aerospace, a research centre significant enough to attract cooperative interest from NASA. Bigelow's efforts, according to one of the group's founders, have elevated ufology from a protoscience to a frontier science. A frontier science is a body of relatively new scientific ideas that are not yet supported by current scientific evidence. They argue that, as a frontier science, there are many uncertainties in ufology, and therefore they need religion to provide a foundation of certainty, which serves to fill in the gaps in ufological data as well as a framework for interpreting verified data. An Islamic perspective is considered very important when interpreting the data, because there are many atheistic interpretations of ufological data that, according to them, would harm the faith (*'aqīda*) of Muslim UFO enthusiasts. Thus, the adjective 'Islamic' in the group name indicates that, for them, there are ufological theories that go against Islamic teachings. One of the founders mentions the Annunnaki theory and various UFO cults as examples of un-Islamic ufologies.[7]

Members of the community call the arguments they put forward 'hypotheses'. In developing the hypotheses, Qur'ānic hermeneutics plays a very important role. One of the active members described their activity as an attempt to develop a 'dialogue between their interpretation of the Qur'ān, and the evidence of Ufological findings'.[8] Although he realized that he did not have the knowledge needed to do proper *tafsīr*, he asserts that if he and his community had not started this discussion, then the exotheological discourse among Indonesian Muslims would not have progressed. He believes that those who are qualified in the religious sciences have no interest in discussing this issue seriously. Since

[7] A co-founder, WhatsApp message to author, 17 January 2022.
[8] Ibid.

the discussion began in 2011, members of this community have developed seven hypotheses. This chapter will discuss these seven hypotheses with a focus primarily on the plausibility of their hermeneutics. It will also explore how ufology shapes their hermeneutical choices and how their understanding of Qur'ānic verses guides their interpretation of ufological findings.[9]

## The hypotheses and their hermeneutical justifications

The main concern of the Islamic UFO community is to provide an Islamically acceptable explanation of UFO sightings. They believe the existence of UFOs is already established, and the question at hand is to determine the identity of the ufonauts. The proposed hypotheses vary and do not necessarily point to extraterrestrial life. One active member of the community divides the hypotheses into three categories: terrestrial hypotheses, which suggest that the ufonauts are earthlings; extraterrestrial that posit they are from other planets; and ultraterrestrial hypotheses, which propose they come from another dimension. In general, the hermeneutical strategy used by the Islamic UFO community to support their hypotheses is to propose a certain reading of a concept or a historical event/story mentioned by the Qur'ān. They introduce new interpretations to provide space for a reading that accommodates their hypotheses. In engaging with their hypotheses, we would examine whether the interpretations they propose are still plausible from the perspective of the *tafsīr* tradition. Therefore, we will attempt to trace whether their interpretations have precedents in both premodern and modern *tafsīr.* In addition, we will also examine their interpretations by adopting the basic procedures commonly used in the *Tafsīr* tradition, namely to examine their interpretation of certain terms in light of the original meanings of the terms' semantic roots and the wording or context of the verses.[10]

[9] As research on an online community, there were two main ways we collected data on their ufological thoughts. First, by collecting status updates from the 'Islamic UFO' Facebook group. The data collected from this Facebook group will be attributed to the person who posted it by mentioning their Facebook account name, which is not necessarily their real name. The second was by conducting interviews through a WhatsApp Group and Zoom. Since the community members we interviewed requested anonymity, we will refer to them by pseudonyms. For example, a proponent of the Banī Adam hypothesis would be called a 'BAH proponent', and a co-founder would simply be called a 'co-founder'.

[10] Haddad, 'Introduction to the Principles of Qur'ānic Exegesis', 106.

## Pre-Adamic Hypothesis (PAH)

The main premise of PAH is that UFOs are a technological product of the civilization of human-like intelligent beings, which God created before Adam. Their mastery of high-level technology is the result of their civilizational development that has been taking place since time unknown. Their civilization is much older than human civilization on Earth. Proponents of this hypothesis support their argument by referring to the narration of the creation of Prophet Adam in Q. 2:30. They are particularly interested in the angels' motives for 'questioning' God's decision to create a new creature. According to Q. 2:30, upon learning that God would create a *khalīfa* on Earth, the angels asked, 'Will You place upon it one who causes corruption therein and sheds blood, while we declare Your praise and sanctify You?'

Proponents of PAH cited Quraisy Shihab's explanation in his *Tafsīr al-Misbāh* that the angel's question indicates three possibilities. Firstly, since they were not the *khalīfh*, the angels assumed that there would be rampant corruption on Earth; secondly, the angels assumed that since the word *khalīfa* means arbiter of disputations, the creation of a *khalīfa* on Earth is an indication that there would be serious conflicts in the future; and thirdly, it is possible that before humans were created, there were already creatures that caused great corruptions and slaughtered each other on Earth. As the name of the hypothesis suggests, PAH proponents conclude that the third possibility is the most acceptable.

To substantiate their argument that the third possibility is the correct one, PAH proponents refute the previous two possibilities. According to them, the first two possibilities assume that angels had certain prejudices against the newly created being. Furthermore, if the first and second possibilities are assumed to be true, then it would mean that angels are guessing at something that has not yet happened beyond their limited knowledge. PAH proponents argue that making assumptions is not the character of Qur᾽ānic angels. They point out that Q. 2:32 states that the angels said, 'Glory to You, we know nothing but what You have taught us; indeed, you are the All-Knowing, the All-Wise.' PAH proponents conclude:

> The verse reveals that the angels are fully aware that they only know what God has taught them, so naturally they would not guess about the nature of Adam and his descendants (who had just been created). As a creature that knows God directly, it is highly unlikely that the angels would doubt the wisdom behind His decision.[11]

[11] Amus, 'UFO: Jejak Mahluk Cerdas Sebelum Adam as.'

They reject the second possibility by arguing that interpreting a term means that the angels made assumptions beyond the knowledge that God has taught them, thereby contradicting Q. 2:32. This verse is also the basis for PAH proponents to believe that the angels specifically mentioned corruption and bloodshedding because of their previous experience with Adam-like creatures that caused these two specific wrongdoings. This line of argument requires PAH to address the issue of ancient hominins. According to them, the pre-Adamites who corrupted and spilt blood on Earth were not the ancient humanoids whose fossils have now been discovered. They argue that the ancient humanoids found so far did not have enough intelligence to develop technology that could cause catastrophic corruption on Earth, damage significant enough to prompt the angels to 'question' Adam's creation.

> As far as we know, early hominin species had low levels of intelligence, and generally only mastered simple technologies for hunting. Their main concern was certainly to survive and maintain their offspring. They did not destroy nature. Even when they shed blood, it was not for the purpose of expansion or greed, but merely as an effort to survive.[12]

Killing or exploiting natural resources for mere survival, for PAH proponents, is unlikely to impress angels. It is not a crime but part of the process of life on Earth as ordained by God. Furthermore, the proponent of PAH points out that from historical experience, the more advanced the technology developed by a society, the greater the destruction of nature and the more horrific the bloodshed they commit. Therefore, they conclude, the creature that caused the devastating destruction and bloodshed on Earth before Adam must have had a very high intellectual capacity. Based on this argument, PAH proponents claim that the pre-Adamites referred to by the angel in Q. 2:30 are not ancient hominins but a race of intelligent beings who, with their advanced technological capabilities, created UFOs as their vehicles.

In their discussions in the Islamic UFO Facebook group, proponents of the PAH developed several arguments to answer objections to their idea. Two important topics make their idea problematic for other members of the group. Firstly, other members of the community consider that this idea robs Prophet Adam of the privilege of being the first human being. One of the group members stated:

[12] Ibid.

> We must be guided by the pillars of faith, one of which is to believe in the prophets. Each prophet has his own characteristics. Prophet Adam was the first man . . . if we don't believe that Prophet Adam was the first man, this is against the pillars of faith.[13]

PAH proponents answer this objection by pointing out that the Qur'ān never explicitly mentions Adam as the first man in the universe. They even go so far as to say that anyone who understands Q. 2:30 as information about the creation of the first human being is mistaken. Furthermore, they also state that such an objection arises from the belief that Prophet Adam and his descendants (banī Adam) are special because of their physical form.

> This opinion is based on a certain understanding of the following verse: 'We created man in the finest state' (Q 95:04). This verse is often understood to mean that humans are unique because they are endowed with the most perfect physical form. Consequently, they think that Q. 02:30 recounts the creation of a creature with an Adamic physical form for the first time in the universe. In fact, Q. 02:30 only states that God appointed Adam as *khalīfah* on Earth, not that this is the first time God has designed a creature with this particular physical form.[14]

In their attempt to answer the objections of other members of the group, PAH proponents effectively entered the debate about the uniqueness of Adam and his descendants. They formulate not only a hermeneutic answer but also a metaphysical argument. PAH supporters answer the question of human uniqueness by stating that only God has the right to be called an absolutely unique entity. They base this argument on one of the attributes of God in the Ashʿarī creed that is widely taught in Indonesia, namely that God does not resemble his creatures (*mukhālafa li-l-ḥawādith*). They argue that only God can be said to have nothing in common with his creatures. Therefore, suggesting that Adam is like other creatures in terms of physical form and intellectual capacity is not theologically problematic. On the contrary, this stance is evidence of a firm commitment to the doctrine of non-resemblance. Proponents of the PAH do not see themselves as undermining the unique status of Prophet Adam and his descendants. They argue that being highly intelligent and physically beautiful is not an advantage to be proud of. By quoting Q. 95:4-6, they assert that despite being created in the best possible state (*aḥsani taqwīm*), human beings may still be the most despicable of God's creatures if they fail to obey His commands.

[13] BAH supporter, Zoom interview with author, 13 November 2022.
[14] Amus, 'UFO: Jejak Mahluk Cerdas Sebelum Adam as'.

To further strengthen the legitimacy of their hypothesis among members of the Islamic UFO group, PAH supporters then justify their reading of Q. 02:30 with ufological data.

> UFOs are often observed to be superior to even the most sophisticated modern fighter jets, yet the phenomenon of UFO sightings have existed for thousands of years, as recorded in cave paintings made by pre-historic societies. Due to this fact, most ufologists would insist that UFOs are not man-made aircrafts . . . So far, there have been at least eight different types of aliens (ufonauts) that have visited Earth. They have different physical forms, but there is one that bears a high resemblance to modern humans, aliens known as Nordics, or Blonds.[15]

Nordics, also known as the Blonds, are a type of ufonaut popularized by George Adamski through photographs he circulated in the 1950s. They are described as having the closest physical similarities to humans, particularly people from Northern Europe. They are tall, blue-eyed and blonde-haired like the Nordic people, hence the name.[16] PAH proponents believe that there is a very high probability that the Nordics inhabited the Earth before Adam, enjoying prosperity and developing advanced technology. Unfortunately, the argument goes, they then misused these advantages by destroying the Earth and waging bloody wars, so God banished them from the Earth. This pre-Adamic then left Earth and created space colonies. Some of those who colonized various planets evolved according to the natural conditions of the planets they inhabited. This evolutionary process explains why they have different physical features than Blonds or Nordics.

The idea of intelligent beings inhabiting the Earth before the Prophet Adam is not foreign to the tafsīr literature. Just like PAH proponents, various exegetes also derive the possibility of such beings from Q. 2:30. One of the earliest commentators, Muqātil ibn Sulaymān (d. 767), cites the story of the inhabitants of the Earth before humans when explaining the meaning of *khalīfa* as successor. According to him, Adam was called *khalīfa* on Earth because before he was created and appointed as vicegerent, the Earth had been inhabited by jinn. The jinn that inhabited the Earth then caused destruction and bloodshed, for which God sent angels, under the leadership of *Iblīs*, to eradicate them. Similar to the PAH, Muqātil indicates that the angels asked God because they had witnessed the inhabitants of the Earth before Adam, the jinn, causing corruption

15 Ibid.
16 Leslie and Adamski, *Flying Saucers Have Landed.*

and bloodshed.[17] The narrative is also cited, with a transmission (*sanad*) that goes back to Ibn ʿAbbās (d. 687), by al-Ṭabarī (d. 923) in his commentary.[18] Throughout the history of the genre, this narrative continued to appear in influential works such as those of Ibn Kathīr (d. 1373),[19] al-Bayḍāwī (d. 1319)[20] and *Tafsīr al-Jalālayn*[21] of al-Maḥallī (d. 1460) and al-Suyūṭī (d. 1505), who also adduces the narration in his own narration-based commentary.[22]

The uniqueness of PAH's reading of Q. 2:30 compared to the Qurʾānic exegetes is that PAH assumes that the angels questioned Adam's creation because of the similarity in physical appearance between Adam and the creatures that previously inhabited the Earth. PAH supporters understand that God's conversation with the angels in Q. 2:30 took place after the creation of Adam, that is, after the angels saw Adam's physical appearance. One of the exegetes who explicitly expresses an explanation that contradicts this reading is Ibn Kathīr. In his exegesis, he states that God informed the angels about Adam before he created him (*qabla ījādihim*).[23] For Ibn Kathīr, this fact shows the nobility of humans, as God mentioned them and their role on Earth to the archangels before the first human was created. In explaining the angels' question, one explanation that often reappears in the *tafsīr* literature is that in the verse, God is teaching His servants to deliberate (*istishār*). Deliberation is only possible if the work has not yet been done. Abū al-Suʿūd (d. 1574) explains that the active participle form (*ism al-fāʿil*) of the verb create (*jāʿil*) in the verse means that the creation of Adam will happen after God informs the angels (*mustaqbal*).[24] PAH's assumption, therefore, finds no precedent in the *tafsīr* tradition and is not linguistically sound.

By considering the ufological data presented by PAH proponents to support their case, one can notice that their interpretation of Q. 2:30 seems to be shaped by their conception of what the ufonauts might look like. They accept Adamski's testimony about the existence of human-like aliens, the Nordics. PAH proponents believe that the angels are likely to have seen the Nordic aliens committing corruption and shedding blood on Earth, so they assume Adam and his descendants would have done the same. On the other hand, most *tafsīr* works emphasize two types of corruption that the jinn had done on Earth before

17 Sulaymān, *Tafsīr Muqātil ibn Sulaymān* 4:521.
18 Al-Ṭabarī, *Jāmiʿ al-Bayān*, 1:450.
19 Ibn Kathīr, *Tafsīr al-Qurʾān al-ʿAẓīm*, 1:281.
20 Al-Bayḍāwī, *Anwār al-Tanzīl wa Asrār al-Taʾwīl*, 1:67–8.
21 Al-Maḥallī and al-Suyūṭī, *Tafsīr al-Jalālayn*, 8.
22 al-Suyūṭī, *Al-Durr al-Manthūr*, 1:11.
23 Ibn Kathīr, *Tafsīr al-Qurʾān al-ʿAẓīm*, 1:216.
24 Abū Suʿūd, *Irshād al-ʿAql al-Salīm*, 1:81.

Adam was created. According to the exegetes, the angels specifically mentioned these two evils – committing corruption and shedding blood – because these were the evils that they witnessed the jinn committing. In this reading, one need not assume the existence of beings with the physical appearance of Adam had existed on Earth before him. The angels are not basing their analogy on the physical appearance of these pre-Adam earthlings but on the specific crimes they committed.

In conclusion, proposing that there were creatures inhabiting the Earth before Adam can still be justified by certain readings of the term *khalīfa*. This reading does not pose any theological problem in the *tafsīr* literature. In fact, they use this particular interpretation to explain away the theological issues that may arise from the angel's question. As mentioned by Fakhr al-Dīn al-Rāzī (606/1209), this verse sparked a debate about whether or not angels can commit sins.[25] By pointing out that angels only analogize between humans and jinn, angels are no longer deemed to doubt God's wisdom. In this respect, PAH proponents share the same motives as the exegetes. According to one PAH proponent, one of the important motives behind PAH is to provide an alternative interpretation to theologically problematic ufological theories for Muslims. One of these is the Ancient Astronaut or Anunnaki theory, which posits the existence of intelligent human-like aliens who used to visit the Earth, and they are the true creators of humanity. In PAH, even if the Anunnaki had been to Earth, they are nothing more than Allah's creations that once inhabited the Earth before Adam, not the creators of mankind.

## Banī Adam Hypothesis

Banī Adam Hypothesis (BAH) proposes that UFOs are flying vehicles created by the descendants of Adam. According to the proponents of this hypothesis, Adam and his descendants had mastered high technology since the early days of his creation, along with being given the mandate as the *khilāfa*. Their advanced technology allowed them to create vehicles capable of space exploration. They even established colonies on many planets. Supporters of BAH also base their opinion on Q. 2:30, but unlike PAH, they conclude that the verse clearly shows that Adam was the first human. The uniqueness of Adam and his descendants is strongly emphasized in this hypothesis.

[25] Al-Rāzī, *Mafātīḥ al-Ghayb*, 2:388.

> Adam is God's perfect creation, both in terms of physical form and his intelligence. There is no other creature in the universe that is equal to the perfection of the descendant of Adam. Because of this perfection, the Children of Adam are the only creatures of God who can master advanced technology.[26]

Furthermore, according to BAH proponents, the statement 'and God taught Adam the names of all things' in Q. 2:31-33 indicates that Adam was bestowed with advanced knowledge of the universe, as he was not only the *khalīfa* of planet Earth but of the entire universe. Therefore, they insist that the term 'earth' (*al-arḍ*) should not be interpreted as just planet Earth but the entire physical universe.[27] Nevertheless, they still believe that Adam lived on planet Earth before his descendants travelled to other planets. They assert that the angels' question mentioned in Q. 2:30 does not indicate that they had prior experience with Adam-like creatures but rather an indication that angels are intelligent beings that can foresee the great corruption mankind is capable of doing.

One of the key points in BAH is that the universe is extremely old. They argue that the angels' inability to mention the 'names of things' (*al-asmā'*) in Q. 2:33 indicates that this event took place very early in terms of the age of the universe. According to the proponents of BAH, angels are God's servants who take care of all His creations, so they should be familiar with the details of each of the creations. Angels could not mention the names because most of the components of the universe had not yet been created at that time.[28] Therefore, one of the key assumptions of BAH is that Adam was already created in his perfect physical form when the universe was just being created. As such, BAH proponents reject both evolutionary theory and Young Earth Creationism. They argue that the universe is very old, and Adam is almost as old. They back up their claim by using a Qur'ānic passage that says Adam was created with *kun*, indicating a spontaneous creation. They also support this argument by explaining that the Qur'ān uses the phrase 'news of the unseen' (*min anbā'i al-ghayb*) in Q. 11:49 to describe the story of Adam and Noah because these events are impossible to know except through revelation. The reason for this impossibility, according to them, is that the period of Adam and Noah is so far in the past that no trace of them can be found in human historical knowledge.[29]

One important reference for BAH is Michael Cremo's *Forbidden Archaeology*. This book is instrumental in helping them to explain their belief that the universe

26 Amus, 'Bani Adam Hypothesis (BAH)'.
27 BAH supporter, Zoom interview with author, 13 November 2022.
28 Amus, 'Bani Adam Hypothesis (BAH)'.
29 BAH supporter, Zoom interview with author, 13 November 2022.

is much older than what mainstream science would suggest. Moreover, they also refer to Cremo to explain that the modern human race has existed on Earth for a long time without undergoing an evolutionary process. Another important connection between BAH and Cremo's approach is their use of ancient mythologies as evidence of the existence of advanced scientific technologies in many ancient civilizations. According to BAH, there are two generational waves of Adam's descendants who are most likely responsible for the UFO phenomenon, namely the direct descendants of Adam and the descendants of Noah, who survived after the global flood. Adam's direct descendants were able to develop technology as sophisticated as UFOs because they were educated directly by Adam. While the descendants of Noah, more specifically the descendants of Japheth, were able to develop technology because they were taught by their father. The Japhetites, according to BAH, managed to develop an extremely advanced civilization on Earth. They were able to build anti-gravity machines enabling them to travel to other galaxies. Japhet's descendants continued to prosper on Earth until the time of Gog and Magog. These creatures are the descendants of Japheth, who caused such great destruction that they were imprisoned by Dhū al-Qarnayn.[30]

Apart from the Qur'ān and ufological findings, BAH's arguments are also heavily based on old mythologies of various civilizations. A prominent member of the Islamic UFO community who supports BAH admits that before considering Islamic sources, he read a lot about what he calls Alien Folklore. Alien Folklores are mythologies which UFO enthusiasts believe recount human and extraterrestrial interactions in the past. However, he faced difficulties in making sense of both the folklore and the ufological data he knew.

> I used to read a lot about alien folklores, but these stories are confusing. Because of them, many UFO enthusiasts actually believed in the Annunaki theory. According to this theory, the first human was created by an alien race that visited earth a long time ago. But then after taking Islam into account, I can finally put information I got from the folklores into a coherent hypothesis.[31]

It is then not surprising that the mythological aspect is one of the main features that distinguishes BAH from other hypotheses. The idea of the Japhetites and their anti-gravity machines, for example, is derived from the story of Japhet in the Bible, the legend of Japetus in Greek mythology and the ancient Nepalese mythology of Javana. Proponents of BAH conclude that although these stories are mythological, the fact that different civilizations across time and space tell

[30] Xeno 101, 'Pilar-Pilar Seth (Nabi Syits AS) Berisikan Pengetahuan Mengenai Anti Gravitasi?' I.
[31] BAH supporter, Zoom interview with author, 13 November 2022.

the same story is an indication that there is a historical truth behind the stories. Moreover, according to them, there is a phonetic similarity between Japheth, Japetus and Javana, so they believe that these names actually refer to the same nation. In these stories, the nation is said to be technologically advanced, and one of their main specialities is that they were able to build flying vehicles. Therefore, they believe these stories are based on the historical fact that there was once a civilization that was so scientifically advanced that they could create an anti-gravity machine.

To further justify their narrative, BAH proponents point out that many Qur'ānic verses tell us to travel the Earth (*al-arḍ*) and look at the traces of past civilizations. They then argue that such verses could be understood to refer to the Japhetites. The significance of their interpretation that *al-arḍ* refers not only to the Earth but the entire physical universe becomes apparent in this line of argument. That is because for them, to truly be able to see traces of past advanced civilizations, we should not just stop at planet Earth but also look across the galaxy. They support this idea by referring to the notion of space as a 'cosmic junkyard' popularized by Corey Goode in a documentary entitled *The Cosmic Secret*. The film was produced by Goode along with David Wilcock, in which they explored various data provided by, among other things, direct communication with extraterrestrials. One of the claims made in the film is that space is scattered with the ruins of extraterrestrial civilizations, making it a cosmic junkyard. According to BAH proponents, this claim confirms their reading of the Japhetite mythology as well as their interpretation of the Qur'ānic verses. The cosmic junkyard is none other than the relics of the ancient civilizations mentioned in many Qur'ānic verses.[32]

BAH proponents believe that these civilizations were not only scientifically advanced, but they were also physically superior to modern humans. BAH believes that the human races that built these advanced civilizations in the past were much larger than modern humans. They state that they follow the interpretation that the people of *ʿĀd* and *Thamūd* were giants. These two nations, according to them, were part of Adam's descendants from the Japhet lineage. They then harmonize this interpretation with information from the biblical story of the Nephilim and other mythologies. Furthermore, BAH supporters believe that their interpretation is validated by the testimony of ufologists such as Goode and Wilcock, who state that the artefacts of advanced civilizations

[32] BAH Supporter, Zoom interview with author, 31 November 2022.

found in the solar system show that whoever created and used them was larger in stature than modern humans.

PAH seeks to show that while there were indeed human-like aliens who lived on Earth before Adam, they were nothing more than creatures of God who were given technological sophistication. They show that, at least hermeneutically, this is not problematic for Muslims. A different strategy is pursued by BAH supporters. Since the uniqueness of Adam is particularly important for them, BAH proponents developed an entirely new narrative of human history that differs from what is commonly suggested by natural science, archaeology and the mainstream narrative of the history of ancient civilizations. Their primary motivation is to establish that Adam's descendants still occupy a unique and superior position in a universe where technologically advanced vehicles such as UFOs exist. The basis of BAH's main argument is also in the series of verses about Adam's creation. They focus on Q. 2:31, particularly the term *al-asmā' kullahā* (*all the names*). In the *tafsīr* tradition, Q. 2:31 is indeed presented to emphasize the exceptionality of human beings. For the proponents of BAH, however, this verse also shows that Adam was created when the universe was young, at which time, most creatures had not yet been created. Angels were unable to mention this because they had not yet been created.

The discussion on whether the objects whose names were taught to Adam were existing objects at that time or objects that had not yet been created also arises in the *tafsīr* tradition. Muqātil states that the objects taught to Adam were those that had already been created. One of the earliest opinions appearing in Muqātil's commentary states that the story serves to prove that the angels' knowledge of what has already been created is limited, let alone their knowledge of the uncreated being, namely Adam.[33] Therefore, this verse is a further explanation of God's answer at the end of Q. 2:30, 'surely I know what you do not know'. Other readings consider this issue to be unimportant, as the significance of this verse is to show Adam's intellectual capacity as an important requirement for being *khalīfa* on Earth. This capacity is shown by his ability to receive knowledge from God and convey it to the angels. So, whether these objects were created or not is irrelevant. The opinion of the supporters of BAH that the objects taught to Adam were objects that had not yet been created, thus, is still acceptable from the perspective of tafsīr. Nonetheless, in general, the exegetes do not take this as a reason that Adam was created when the universe was young.

[33] Sulaymān, *Tafsīr Muqātil ibn Sulaymān*, 1:98.

In their hermeneutical arguments, BAH proponents reinterpret keywords in the Qur'ānic cosmology, particularly Earth (*al-arḍ*) and heavens (*al-samāwāt*). For the latter, Muslim scholars, both modern and premodern, have tended to give it a broader, less literal meaning. This broad, non-literal reading of *al-samāwāt* has become more established and accepted in modern times thanks to modern cosmology. The reinterpretation of the word *al-arḍ*, however, is not common. Within the tafsīr tradition, there is a debate about the scope of the place referred to by the word *al-arḍ* in Q. 2:30. Some commentators claim that *al-arḍ* does not refer to the whole Earth but only to Mecca. Linguistically, both interpretations can still be accommodated; according to al-Rāghib al-Iṣfahānī (d. 1108), the word *al-arḍ* refers to any physical surface facing the heavens.[34] Therefore, the word *al-arḍ* in the Qur'ān should not be interpreted as planet Earth as it is understood in modern astronomy; it can refer to just a particular city.

However, BAH's proponent's idea that *al-arḍ* refers to the entire physical universe is difficult to justify linguistically, unless the word *al-arḍ* is paired with the word *as-samāwāt*. Muhammad Asad (d. 1992) proposed a linguistic argument to show that the Qur'ān uses the pair *as-samāwāt* and *al-arḍ* to refer to the entire universe metonymically.[35] This argument, however, still cannot be used to support the case of BAH's supporters, as their aim is to prove that Q. 2:30 refers to Adam as the *khalīfa* of the entire physical universe, despite the verse only mentioning *al-arḍ*. With the implausibility of *al-arḍ* being interpreted as the entire physical universe, it would also be difficult to accept their reading of the verses containing the commands 'travel the earth' (*sīrū fī al-arḍ*) as a command to explore space. Consequently, their narrative of the space filled with the ruins of past, more sophisticated alien civilizations simply loses its Qur'ānic basis.

## Smart Dābba and the Man Hypothesis

As the name suggests, SDH explores one of the terms used by the Qur'ān in describing God's creatures, namely the term *dābbah*. This term is used in the Qur'ān to describe God's creatures in the heavens (*al-samāwāt*) and on Earth (*al-arḍ*) without specifically mentioning their species, making the term '*dābbah*' an interesting term for those who are looking for clues about extraterrestrials in the Qur'ān. Unlike the previous hypotheses, especially BAH, the *dābbah* hypothesis relies more on the interpretation of the Qur'ānic verses and does not

[34] Al-Aṣfahānī, *Al-Mufradāt*, 73.
[35] Asad, *The Message of the Qur'ān*, 676.

quote much ufological data, let alone ancient mythology, to build their case. Of the verses that mention the term '*dābbah*', Q. 42:29 is the most interesting verse for proponents of this hypothesis. The verse indicates that God created *dābbah* not only on Earth but also in the heavens: 'among His signs is the creation of the heavens and earth and all the *dābba* He has scattered throughout them.' The verse is considered by SDH proponents to establish the first premise for SDH, namely that there is indeed a type of living being, called '*dābbah*', that lives in the heavens. In addition, proponents of this hypothesis also corroborate their opinion by referring to Q. 16:49 and Q. 13:15. Although these verses do not explicitly use the term *dābbah*, they indicate that there are creatures in the heavens that worship God. Both verses refer to these celestial beings with the relative pronoun *who* (*man*). This line of argument has also been developed by other members of the group into the *man* hypothesis.

In the official translation of the Qur'ān published by the Ministry of Religious Affairs of the Republic of Indonesia, *dābbah* is translated as '*hewan melata*', *which* literally means slithering beasts. Since most members of the Islamic UFO community are not well versed in Arabic, this translation presents its own problems to SDH supporters because in the Indonesian language, the word '*hewan*' is only used for non-intelligent creatures. Therefore, their first hermeneutical argument aims to show that *dābbah* is not just an animal but can also be interpreted as an intelligent being. One of the group members in favour of SDH began his lengthy discussion by addressing this issue:

> In this statement I would like to share information about the meaning of *dābbah* which in the Qur'ān can be pronounced *dābbatin*, *dābbatun*, *dawwābatun*, *dāwwabi*, *dābbatin*. In the Arabic-Indonesian translation, this word is translated as slithering beast (*hewan melata*). But what is the real meaning of *dābbah*? We should know that although the Qur'ān has explained in detail about this creature, we must seek its true meaning by understanding one verse in light of other verses . . . by this method we can derive a more comprehensive understanding that is in accordance with the intended meaning of this term. Slithering beast is in fact just one of the meanings of the term.[36]

The first step in the hermeneutical method of SDH proponents is to compile Qur'ānic verses that contain the term *dābbah* or words derived from the same root, such as *dābbatin*, *dābbatun* and *dawwābatun*. With this method, they hope to draw a more comprehensive conclusion. Their main motive was to prove that the *dābbah* is indeed an intelligent being. This strategy is vital to clear up the

[36] Pramana, 'Makhluk Bernama Dabbah'.

confusion caused by the Ministry of Religious Affairs' translation of this term. They conclude that *dābbah* cannot be interpreted as animals or beasts, as the Qur'ān indicates them as intelligent beings. They point to Q. 16:49, Q. 8:22 and Q. 8:55, which attribute evil as well as obedience and disobedience to God (*Kufr*) to *dābbah*. According to them, in the Qur'ānic context, these attributes can only be possessed by intelligent and free-willed creatures.[37]

Furthermore, they also emphasize that just like humans, *dābbah* have various races. In terms of physical variations, *dābbah* are even more varied than humans. For example, the Qur'ān mentions that some *dābbah* walk on two legs, some on four and some even move by slithering. Derived from Q. 35:28 and Q.24:45, they utilize this idea to harmonize their interpretation of the term *dābbah* with the ufological findings they believe to be reliable. These findings mention that the ufonauts have very diverse physical forms. Some have a human-like appearance, but others have a more lizard-like or avian-like physique. However, other members of the Islamic UFO group criticized this interpretation by pointing out that the two-legged *dābbah* in Q. 24:45 is none other than human beings. Therefore, when the Qur'ān speaks of *dābbah* possessing the attributes of intelligent beings, it is referring to humans. In response to this criticism, SDH proponents point out that the Qur'ān mentions humans and *dābbah* separately in Q. 22:18 and Q. 45:4. Such separate mention, for them, is the evidence that humans and *dābbah* are different creatures.[38]

To further support their stance that the term *dābbah* indeed refers to intelligent creatures other than humans, SDH proponents develop revisionist interpretations of historical accounts in the Qur'ān involving *dābbah*. In the story of the death of Prophet Solomon in Q. 34:14, for example, it is mentioned that no one realized that the King-Prophet had died until the *dābbat al-arḍ* ate (*ya'kulu*) his staff. After the staff fell off, Solomon's body collapsed, making all his people, especially the jinn, realize that the Prophet had passed away. Proponents of the smart *dābbah* hypothesis propose a unique interpretation of this story. They believe that the *dābbah* mentioned in the verse is not a type of termite that gnawed on Prophet Solomon's staff, as commonly understood. They believe that the *dābbah* was a member of Prophet Solomon's court, which indeed consisted of various creatures. In this interpretation, *dābbah* played a more significant role than just gnawing on Solomon's staff. *dābbah* was the only member of the court

[37] Ibid.
[38] Ibid.

who was able to notice that the Prophet had passed away. It was also able to convey this news to the jinn, humans and the rest of Solomon's subjects.[39]

According to SDH proponents, the Qur'ānic description of the role of *dābbah* in the story of Prophet Solomon indicates that a type of intelligent *dābbah* that can communicate with humans and jinn once lived on Earth. Furthermore, the level of intelligence of such *dābbah* can surpass jinn and humans, as indicated by their ability to know the death of Prophet Solomon, when jinn and humans could not. Their idea of *dābbah*'s ability to communicate with humans is further developed by referring to Q. 27.82. This verse states that before the coming of the Day of Judgement, *dābbah* will appear and remind people that they have ignored God's warnings. Moreover, they also adduce several ḥadīths that mention the appearance of *dābbah* as one of the signs of the Hour as evidence that *dābbah* and humans can understand each other. Thus, SDH proponents believe that in addition to extraterrestrial *dābbah*, there are also *dābbah* that have lived on Earth and even have had interactions with humans. This second type of *dābbah* is what the Qur'ān calls *dābbah al-arḍ*. However, the exact location of both types of *dābbah* is only known with certainty by God because it is God who guarantees their sustenance, as mentioned in Q. 31:10, Q. 11:56, Q. 11:6 and Q. 29: 60. In short, SDH proponents believe that *dābbah* is a race of intelligent beings who can develop advanced technology and is responsible for the UFO sighting phenomenon. They are the ufonauts.

Another group among the members of the Indonesian Islamic UFO community pursues a similar hermeneutical strategy as the SDH proponents; they select a Qur'ānic term that vaguely refers to the existence of intelligent beings in the heavens and build a whole narrative about the ufonauts around that term. The hypothesis they propose is called the *man* hypothesis because their main basis is the Qur'ānic verses that use the Arabic relative pronoun *who* (*man*) to describe the inhabitants of the heavens. The verse they base their hypothesis on is Q. 13:15, which reads: 'And to God prostrates whoever (*man*) is within the heavens and the earth, willingly or by compulsion, and their shadows (*ẓilāluhum*) in the mornings and the afternoons.'

Proponents of this hypothesis first assert that one of the miraculous features of the Qur'ān is that every word it contains is open to new interpretations in accordance with the development of human knowledge. This hypothesis, for them, is their attempt to demonstrate this feature in the context of ufology. They point out that in Arabic, the relative pronoun *man* is reserved for intelligent

[39] Ibid.

creatures. Meanwhile, in the Qur'ānic narrative, as commonly understood, intelligent beings are only angels, jinn and humans. The main purpose of the hermeneutical effort developed by this group is to demonstrate that *man* in the verse does not refer to either of these beings but rather to another type of intelligent being not mentioned by name in the Qur'ān. Furthermore, based on Q. 13:15, the proponents of TMH argue that the creature the relative pronoun *man* refers to has three main characteristics, namely worshipping God willingly, worshipping Him unwillingly and possessing a shadow. In addition, they also assert that the verse shows that the creatures not only live on Earth but also live in the heavens (*samāwāt*). They argue that the fact that the verse uses the plural form of *al-samā'*, that is, *samāwāt*, means that these creatures live in multiple locations in the heavens.[40]

They then employ the established characteristics to prove that the relative pronoun *man* neither refers to the angel, jinn, Iblīs, nor humans. Q. 13:15 describes that the creatures at times prostrate to God willingly and at times unwillingly, so *man* cannot possibly refer to angels who always obey God or Iblīs who always disobey Him. In addition, both creatures have no shadows. The no shadow argument is also used to eliminate jinn because, although it is possible that jinn obey and disobey God, they do not have shadows. Finally, they argue that the relative pronoun *man* does not refer to humans because humans only live on Earth, while the creatures described in Q. 13:15 also live on other planets (*samāwāt*).

To link their reading with ufology, proponents of TMH argue that the creature may have encountered humans. This conclusion is derived from Q. 42:29 which states that God, if He wills, will bring together the creatures that live on Earth and those that live in the heavens. An advocate of this view concludes:

> The verse indicates the possibility of interaction between heavenly beings to whom *man* refers and humans who live on earth, even the possibility of mating each other, of course according to God's will.[41]

SDH proponents' argument that the term *dābbah* refers to extraterrestrial beings has precedents in both modern and premodern *tafsīr*. Commentaries on the term *dābbah* in the tradition show how the exegetes considered various alternative meanings that are linguistically valid and supported by the context of each verse. Mårtensson argues that the pragmatist semantic paradigm, the

[40] Misbah, 'Al-Qur'ān Mengakui Keberadaan UFO?'
[41] Ibid.

fundamental view that the meaning of every word is always related to its context, is an important link between the Qur᾽ān and the *tafsīr* tradition.[42] In this context, Q. 42:29 poses a unique problem for exegetes; on the one hand, the fundamental meaning of *dābbah* is an animal that treads the Earth, while on the other hand, the verse indicates the existence of *dābbah* in the sky. The solution offered by one of the early authorities in *tafsīr*, Mujāhid ibn Jabr (d. 722), was that the verse refers to angels.[43] However, with linguistic considerations, al-Ṭabarī rejected it; angels who fly with their wings clearly do not fall under the category of *dābbah*.[44]

Al-Zamakhsharī and later al-Rāzī, who chose to be faithful to the linguistic meaning, proposed an alternative reading. According to them, it is not impossible for God to create different kinds of creatures living in the heavens who move like humans on Earth. One could argue that this interpretation, which was reproduced in several premodern commentaries, is a precedent for the SDH reading of Q. 42:29. Al-Rāzī's commentary on Q. 42:29 can even be understood as his affirmation of the possibility of intelligent extraterrestrial beings. He mentions that the meaning of the phrase '*gather them*' (*jam ῾ihim*) at the end of the verse is to gather them in the afterlife to hold them accountable for their deeds (*ḥisāb*).[45]Accountability for one's deeds only applies to intelligent beings. The possibility of interpreting the verse as an affirmation of the existence of extraterrestrial beings is also mentioned by one of the most important modern exegetes, Ṭāhir ibn ῾Āshūr (d. 1973).[46] While one of the pioneers of modern *tafsīr*, Jamāl al-Dīn al-Qāsimī explicitly links this verse to the existence of intelligent beings living on other planets.[47]

An important difference between the exegetes, including those who recognize the possibility of extraterrestrial beings such as al-Rāzī, Ibn ῾Āshūr and al-Qasimi, and the proponents of SDH is that SDH proponents regard the term *dābbah* almost as a species – a species of intelligent beings living on Earth and other planets. The Qur᾽ānic exegetes, on the other hand, following the linguistic meaning of *dābbah*, simply consider it as an umbrella term for all living beings, whether intelligent or not. This interpretation of SDH led them to propose a revisionist interpretation of the story of Prophet Solomon's death in Q. 34:14. According to them, instead of gnawing on the Prophet's staff, the *dābbah* in the story noticed that the Prophet had died and informed the jinn

42 Mårtensson, 'Linguistic Theory in Tafsīr between 100/400 and 700/1000'.
43 Ibn Jabr, *Tafsīr Mujāhid*, 590.
44 Al-Ṭabarī, *Jāmi῾ al-Bayān*, 3:275.
45 Al-Rāzī, *Mafātīḥ al-Ghayb*, 27:599.
46 Ibn ῾Āshūr, *Al-Taḥrīr wa-l-Tanwīr*, 25:97.
47 Al-Qāsimī, *Maḥāsin al-Ta᾽wīl*, 8:369.

and humans. The word used in the verse is '*ya'kul*', the root meaning of which is to reduce something little by little (*al-tanaqquṣ*),[48] which implies that the most likely meaning is gnawing. Moreover, if one considers the variant readings of the Qur'ān (*qirā'āt*), the creatures in the verse are indeed termites (*al-araḍ*); some Qur'ānic readers read it as *dābbat al-araḍ*.[49]

MH supporters also present their arguments in the same manner; they argue that the relative pronoun *man* refers to a particular species of creature. The main basis of MH's argument is that as a relative pronoun, *man* can only be used to refer to intelligent beings. While this is generally the case, it is also grammatically acceptable to use *man* to refer to unintelligent beings, therefore, *man* is used when a sentence mentions both intelligent and non-intelligent beings, and this is the case for Q. 13:15.[50]

## The Jinn Hypothesis (JH) or Iblīs' Trickery Hypothesis (ITH)

Both the *dābbah* hypothesis and the *man* hypothesis presuppose the existence of a kind of intelligent and free-willed creature alluded to by the Qur'ān without explicitly mentioning its name. This assumption is then challenged by the next hypothesis, which asserts that the idea of the existence of intelligent and free-willed beings other than jinn and humans goes against the Qur'ān. According to the proponents of this hypothesis, the ufonauts must be intelligent beings with free will, and the Qur'ān limits only two creatures to these criteria: Jinn and humans. Since the UFOs are clearly not human's vehicles, then the ufonauts are none other than jinn. The advocates of this idea call it the Jinn Hypothesis (JH).[51] The notion that jinn and humans are the only intelligent, free-willed creatures is an important foundation of this argument.

They base their belief that the only intelligent and free-willed beings in the universe are jinn and humans on Q. 55:31. The proponents of this hypothesis cite the Qur'ānic commentators and translators who interpret the term *thaqalān* in this verse as jinn and humans. However, they go further and argue that the Qur'ān calls jinn and humans *thaqalān* because they are the only creature that consists of not only body and spirit but also intellect (*'aql*) and soul (*nafs*). According to them, having these faculties would allow a creature to develop advanced technology, such as UFOs. In developing their argument, JH proponents

48 Ibn Zakariyyā, *Mu'jam Maqāyis al-Lugha*, 1:122.
49 Abū Su'ūd, *Irshād al-'Aql al-Salīm*, 7:126.
50 Abū Zahra, *Zahrat al-Tafāsīr*, 7:3918.
51 Katsujima, 'Jinn Hypothesis'.

specifically criticize the arguments of the *dābbah* hypothesis. According to them, the contactee's and abductee's testimonies about the characteristics of the ufonaut are identical to those of the jinn. One proponent of this hypothesis explains the similarity:

> Just like jinn, aliens like to lie while promising and demonstrating advanced technology (I deduced this from a comparative study of Islamic texts with the Book of Enoch and other records of ancient civilisations). Like jinn, aliens can engage in sexual relations with humans. Aliens have their own civilization, as do jinn. Aliens only show themselves occasionally and only in the presence of certain people, jinns too. Aliens can communicate with contactees through telepathy, jinns too. Aliens like to give misleading information about their existence, and so do jinns. Both jinn and aliens have made claims that they are more advanced in science and technology than humans. Aliens are only visible when they deliberately reveal themselves to humans, jinns too, and just like jinns when they reveal themselves, aliens manifest with physical bodies. This list can go on forever.[52]

One of the questions that other members of Islamic UFO community often ask the proponents of the JH is about the nature of jinn as spiritual beings. If jinn are spiritual beings, then why would they create UFOs as vehicles? The JH proponents' answer leads to their idea also being called the ITH. According to them, even though jinn can actually move from one space to another easily, they deliberately create UFOs and expose them to humans in an attempt to have them doubt the truth of the Qur'ān.

> Hasn't Iblis promised to mislead the Children of Adam right up to the Day of Judgement? The UFO/USO phenomenon, in my view, is part of that plan. With UFOs, they can create the impression of the existence of a 'third intelligent being' who is neither a Jinn nor a human being. This impression will make people doubt the literal meaning of the Qur'ānic verses that indicate that there are only two *Thaqal*.[53]

This answer shows the centrality of the concept of *thaqalān* for JH proponents. Doubting the meaning of *thaqalān* as two intelligent and free-willed beings, jinn and man, for them is tantamount to denying the truth of the Qur'ān. The implication of this answer is that those who promote the *dābbah* and *man* hypotheses are not only erroneous in their understanding of the Qur'ān but also have been deceived by Iblis to deny the truth of God's revelation. Furthermore,

52 Ibid.
53 Ibid.

the supporters of the JH/ITH also appeal to ufology to explain that, indeed, UFOs may come from another dimension, that is, the realm of jinn. This answer is based on an idea developed by Jacques Vallee, namely the interdimensional visitation hypothesis. Vallee argues that the UFO phenomenon is in the same class (and origin) as ancient mythological phenomena, like the gods and goddesses, fairies or ghosts.[54] Thus, the idea that a spiritual being such as a jinn is responsible for the UFO phenomenon is not unheard of in ufology.

Similar to PAH and BAH, the hermeneutic element of JH also relies on the reading of one specific term in the Qur'ān, namely *thaqalān* in Q. 55:31. JH proponents do not explicitly mention the specific commentators they refer to in their interpretation of the term *thaqalān*. However, this interpretation is the mainstream opinion in the tafsīr tradition. Al-Rāzī describes this interpretation as a well-known opinion among exegetes. This opinion is based on a ḥadīth that states that the interaction between the dead in their graves and the angels is heard by all creatures except the *thaqalān* – one narration of this ḥadīth explicitly states 'except jinn and humans'.[55] Based on this ḥadīth, Ibn Kathīr considers that this interpretation is the correct meaning of the word *thaqalān* in Q. 55:31.[56] Ibn Qutayba al-Dīnawarī (d. 889), in his lexical dictionary of the Qur'ān, mentions that jinn and humans are referred to as *thaqalān* because they are *thiql al-arḍ*, the burden of the Earth.[57] Furthermore, the JH proponent's explanation that jinn and humans are called *thaqalān* because they both possess the advantages of having reason is in line with al-Zamakhsharī's analysis that *thaqalān* means those who possess the advantage (*qadr*) of intellect.

Regardless of the linguistic and hermeneutical plausibility of JH proponents' interpretation of the term '*thaqalān*', making this interpretation a criterion for belief in the Qur'ān is problematic. The members of the Islamic UFO community never explicitly mention a particular theological school as a standard for their theological boundaries. However, in Indonesia, Abū Ḥāmid al-Ghazālī (d. 1111) and Ash'arism are commonly followed. Regarding the limits of hermeneutical tolerance in a theological context, al-Ghazālī states that as long as one does not deny the literal meaning (*ẓāhir*), then he can still offer a metaphorical interpretation provided that the interpretation has supporting arguments. Let alone if, linguistically, the meaning is still acceptable. This applies to the SDH interpretation, which becomes the target of JH criticism because it assumes that

54 Vallee and Strieber, *Dimensions*.
55 Al-Rāzī, *Mafātīḥ al-Ghayb*, 29:360–1.
56 Ibn Kathīr, *Tafsīr al-Qur'ān al-'Aẓīm*, 7:496.
57 Al-Dīnawrī, *Gharīb al-Qur'ān*, 22.

the word *dābbah* refers to an intelligent being other than jinn and man. Ibn Manzūr (d. 711) states that the term *dābbah* can refer to both intelligent and non-intelligent beings.[58] Therefore, one may still propose that the word *dābbah* in Q. 42:29 refers to intelligent extraterrestrial beings without being seen as denying the truth of the Qurʾān.

## Permanent Ghayb Hypothesis (PGH)

All the previously mentioned hypotheses assume that one day humans will be able to determine the identity of the ufonauts. However, there are also members of the Indonesian Islamic UFO community who believe that the identity of the ufonauts will never be known. This is a consequence of their understanding of the concept of the unseen (*ghayb*) in the Qurʾān. For them, there are indeed matters that cannot be reached by human knowledge because God deliberately hides them. These matters are referred to as the matters of the unseen (*ghayb*). They believe that the exact identity of aliens or ufonauts belongs to this category. This group specifically refers to Q. 16:8, which states, 'and He created what you know nothing about' (*wa yakhlaqu mā lā taʿlamūn*). They recognize that ufological data might suggest that aliens are intelligent beings, but their true nature is deliberately concealed by God so that we would never discover it.[59]

One could argue that PGH proponents offer a partial reading of Q. 16:8. The sentence structure in Q. 16:5 uses the *al-ishtighāl* pattern where the noun (*ism*) comes before the verb (*fiʿl*), so the animals mentioned are the object of the verb to create (*khalaqa*) in the sentence, 'He created what you do not know.' Therefore, the context of the sentence, 'what you know nothing about' (*mā lā taʿlamūn*), is actually about domesticated animals that can be used as means of transportation. Modern exegetes generally interpret this verse with this context in mind. Saʿīd Ḥawwa (d. 1988), for example, states that the animals mentioned in this verse are means of transportation known at the time of revelation, therefore, there will be other means of transportation that the direct audience of the Qurʾān did not know about.[60] Another modern scholar, Muḥammad Mutawallī al-Shaʿrāwī (d. 1997), explains that all modern means of transport, such as cars, trains, planes and others, fall under the category of 'things that you do not know' (*mā*

[58] Ibn Manẓūr, *Lisān al-ʿArab*, 1:369–70.
[59] Amus, 'Rangkuman Hasil Diskusi'.
[60] Ḥawwa, *Al-Asās fī al-Tafsīr*, 6:2924.

*lā ta'lamūn*).[61] Therefore, in this reading, Q. 16:8 is not discussing the unseen, let alone ufonauts.

However, the PGH proponents' approach to this passage has precedents in premodern as well as modern tafsīr. Al-Zamakhsharī and those who follow one of his alternative interpretations of the word *dābbah* in Q. 42:29, such as Abū Su'ūd[62] (d. 1574) and Ismā'īl Haqqī[63] (d. 1715), use this passage to support their argument about the possibility of extraterrestrial life. This camp includes two important modern commentaries, namely Ibn Ashūr's *al-Taḥrīr wa-l-Tanwīr* and Muḥammad Sayyīd Ṭanṭāwī's (d. 2010) *Tafsīr al-Wasīṭ*.[64] Nonetheless, the PGH emphasis is not on the possibility of ETs; for them, this is already established, and this verse is proof that we will never know the identity of those ETs. This position is difficult to maintain because this uses the negation particle *lā*, which serves to negate something in the past and present. That is why the exegetes who understand this verse in the context of means of transport mention the modern vehicles that are known today, after previously being unknown. PGH's position would only be correct if the verse used the negation particle *lan*, the negation particle for future events. So even though some exegetes relate this verse to ETs, they in no way deny the possibility of us knowing the ETs' identity in the future.

## Conclusion

As a highly religious Muslim-majority country, Islam plays a major role in Indonesia's public discourse on virtually every issue.[65] This was evident when public interest in UFOs and extraterrestrials resurfaced after the appearance of a number of crop circles in several cities in the early 2010s, where the question of the theological consequences of extraterrestrial existence is one of the main talking points. However, the absence of exotheological writings from mainstream scholars led many lay Muslims to formulate their own exotheology. In 2011, a group of Muslim UFO enthusiasts established 'Islamic UFO' as a virtual community with a focus on discussing scientific explanations of UFOs that are also acceptable from an Islamic theological perspective. Their main concern has been to uncover the identity of the ufonauts and the origin of UFOs.

[61] Al-Sha'rāwī, *Tafsīr al-Sha'rāwī*, 17:10943.
[62] Abū Su'ūd, *Irshād al-'Aql al-Salīm*, 8:32.
[63] Haqqī, *Rūḥ al-Bayān*, 8:321.
[64] Ṭanṭāwī, *Al-Tafsīr al-Wasīṭ li-l-Qur'ān al-Karīm*, 8:32.
[65] Tamir et al., 'The Global God Divide'.

One might argue that the community's attempt to find Qur'ānic clues about the identity of the ufonauts, or to provide Qur'ānic justification for established ufological data, is a variation of what Walid Saleh calls scriptural theology, the 'democratisation of theology, a falling back on Qur'ānic terms to recast old concepts and to develop new ones'.[66] According to Saleh, an important feature of this trend is the neglect of scholastic theology (*kalām*) and, therefore, the absence of metaphysical considerations in its hermeneutic endeavours; in fact, its hermeneutic considerations are leading to new metaphysics. This feature is one of the easily recognizable features of the exotheological hypothesis of the Islamic UFO community. They do not start from the metaphysical considerations of a particular school of *kalām*; instead, they start from hermeneutics.

In general, their hermeneutical strategy is to exploit the polyvalency of certain expressions in the Qur'ān, but their choice of interpretive option is often not based on metaphysical or even linguistic considerations but rather informed by their understanding of ufology. This tendency may be comparable to what Malik identifies as hermeneutic scientism in the discourse of the Qur'ān and science in the more mainstream field of evolutionary theory.[67] Perhaps not unlike those who engage in the hermeneutic scientism in mainstream fields, members of Islamic UFO are also driven by a strong desire to show that there is no contradiction between Islam and ufology and that in fact Islam can contribute to the development of the field. They believe that taking Islam into account in ufological discourses will be beneficial to the development of ufology as a 'scientific' discipline and also to the Muslim community. This optimism is based on the idea that UFOs are a real phenomenon that requires serious scientific research. There is great optimism that the world will eventually solve the flying saucer mystery and Muslims should take part in the effort.

Despite stating that 'the opinions of scholars' is one of the references in their discussion, the discussed groups rarely refer to any classical commentator and only made limited reference to an Indonesian commentator, namely Quraish Shihab. One might suspect language barriers to be the reason for the lack of reference from the *tafsīr* tradition, which is predominantly in Arabic. However, apart from Shihab, there are several Indonesian and English commentaries that they could have explored for insight. Therefore, it is possible that this tendency reflects their scepticism that no scholar of Islam has seriously discussed the

[66] Saleh, 'Contemporary Tafsīr'.
[67] Malik, *Islam and Evolution*, 306.

possibility of extraterrestrial beings. Nonetheless, despite the aforementioned tendency, they sometimes come to the same conclusions as Qurʾānic exegetes, both modern and premodern. Therefore, there is a need for a productive dialogue between communities such as Islamic UFOs and traditionally trained Muslim scholars to formulate a more coherent Islamic exotheology.

## Bibliography

Abū Suʿūd, Muḥammad ibn Muḥyī al-Dīn. *Irshād al-ʿAql al-Salīm ilā Mazāyā al-Kitāb al-Karīm*. Beirut: Dār al-Ihyāʾ al-Turāth al-ʿArabī, n.d.

Abū Zahra, Muḥammad bin Aḥmad. *Zahrat al-Tafāsīr*. Cairo: Dār al-Fikr al-ʿArabī, n.d.

Agustinus, Nur and Gatot Tri. *Satu Dekade Perjalanan Komunitas BETA-UFO Indonesia Melacak Fenomena UFO (A Decade Journey of BETA-UFO Indonesia Community in Tracing the UFO Phenomenon)*. Surabaya: BETA-UFO Indonesia, n.d.

Akbar, Cholis. 'LAPAN: Crop Circle Di Sleman Buatan Manusia (LAPAN: Crop Circle in Sleman Are Man-Made)'. Hidayatullah Online. https://hidayatullah.com/iptekes/saintek/2011/01/25/46230/lapan-crop-circle-di-sleman-buatan-manusia.html (accessed 14 January 2023).

Al-Aṣfahānī, al-Rāghib. *Al-Mufradāt fī Gharīb al-Qurʾān*. Damascus: Dār al-Qalam, 1990.

Al-Bayḍāwī, Nāṣir al-Dīn. *Anwār al-Tanzīl wa Asrār al-Taʾwīl*. Beirut: Dār al-Iḥyāʾ al-Turāth al-ʿArabī, 1997.

Al-Dīnawrī, Abū Muḥammad ʿAbd Allāh. *Gharīb al-Qurʾān*. Cairo: Dār al-Kutub al-ʿIlmiyya, 1978.

Al-Maḥallī, Jalāl al-Dīn and Jalāl al-Dīn al-Suyūṭī. *Tafsīr al-Jalālayn*. Cairo: Dār al-Ḥadīth, n.d.

Al-Qāsimī, Jamāl al-Dīn. *Maḥāsin al-Taʾwīl*. Beirut: Dār al-Kutub al-ʿIlmiyya, 1997.

Al-Rāzī, Fakhr al-Dīn. *Mafātīḥ al-Ghayb*. Beirut: Dār al-Iḥyāʾ al-Turāth al-ʿArabī, 1998.

Al-Shaʿrāwī, Muḥammad Matwalī. *Tafsīr al-Shaʿrāwī*. Cairo: Maṭābiʿ Akhbār al-Yawm, 1997.

Al-Suyūṭī, Jalāl al-Dīn. *Al-Durr al-Manthūr fī al-Tafsīr bi-l-Māʾthūr*. Beirut: Dār al-Fikr, n.d.

Al-Ṭabarī, Abū Jaʿfar ibn Jarīr. *Jāmiʿ al-Bayān ʿan Taʾwīl āy al-Qurʾān*. Mecca: Dār al-Tarbiyya wa-l-Turāth, n.d.

Amus, Bayu Yunantis. 'Bani Adam Hypothesis (BAH)'. Islamic UFO Facebook Group, 2013. https://www.facebook.com/notes/islamic-ufo/bani-adam-hypothesis-bah/465518090176325 (accessed 8 April 2023).

Amus, Bayu Yunantis. 'Rangkuman Hasil Diskusi (Summary of Our Discussions)'. Islamic UFO Facebook Group, 2012. https://www.facebook.com/groups/islamicufo/posts/458803970847737/ (accessed 26 August 2023).

Amus, Bayu Yunantis. 'UFO: Jejak Mahluk Cerdas Sebelum Adam as (UFO: Traces of Pre-Adamic Intelligent Creatures)'. Islamic UFO Facebook Group, 2013. https://www.facebook.com/groups/islamicufo/posts/520198051374995/ (accessed 8 April 2023).

Asad, Muhammad. *The Message of the Qur'ān: The Full Account of the Revealed Arabic Text Accompanied by Parallel Transliteration*. Bristol: Book Foundation, 2003.

Determann, Jörg Matthias. *Islam, Science Fiction and Extraterrestrial Life: The Culture of Astrobiology in the Muslim World*. London: I.B. Tauris, 2021.

Haddad, Gibril Fouad. 'Introduction to the Principles of Qur'ānic Exegesis'. *Islamic Sciences* 14, no. 1 (2016): 106–11.

Haqqī, Ismā'īl. *Rūḥ al-Bayān (The Spirit of Elucidation)*. Beirut: Dār al-Fikr, n.d.

Ḥawwa, Sa'īd. *Al-Asās fī al-Tafsīr*. Cairo: Dār al-Salām, 2003.

Ibn 'Āshūr, Tāhir. *Al-Taḥrīr wa-l-Tanwīr*. Tunis: Dār al-Tūnisiyya li-l-Nashr, 1984.

Ibn Jabr, Mujāhid. *Tafsīr Mujāhid*. Cairo: Dār al-Fikr al-Islāmī al-Hadītha, 1989.

Ibn Kathīr, Abū al-Fiḍā' 'Imād ad-Dīn. *Tafsīr al-Qur'ān al-'Aẓīm*. Riyadh: Dār al-Ṭayyiba, 1999.

Ibn Manẓūr, Abū al-Fatḥ Muḥammad. *Lisān al-'Arab*. Beirut: Dār al-Ṣadir, 1993.

Ibn Zakariyyā, ibn Fāris. *Mu'jam Maqāyis al-Lugha*. Damascus: Dār al-Fikr, n.d.

Jo, Hendi. 'Sejarah Penampakan UFO Di Indonesia: Disangka Pesawat Canggih Milik Musuh (History of UFO Sightings in Indonesia: Mistaken for Enemy's Advanced Aircraft)'. Merdeka.com, 2022. https://www.merdeka.com/histori/sejarah-penampakan-ufo-di-indonesia-disangka-pesawat-canggih-milik-musuh.html

Katsujima, Danjiro. '"Jinn Hypothesis: FAQ"'. Islamic UFO Facebook Group, 2013. https://web.facebook.com/legacy/notes/524222427639224/?_rdc=1&_rdr#_=_ (accessed 8 April 2023).

Leslie, Desmond and George Adamski. *Flying Saucers Have Landed*. New York: British Book Centre New York, 1953.

Malik, Shoaib Ahmed. *Islam and Evolution: Al-Ghazālī and the Modern Evolutionary Paradigm*. Abingdon: Routledge, 2021.

Mårtensson, Ulrika. 'Linguistic Theory in Tafsīr between 100/400 and 700/1000: Implications for Qur'ānic Studies'. *Journal of Qur'ānic Studies* 24, no. 3 (2022): 1–45.

Misbah, Dedi. 'Al-Qur'ān Mengakui Keberadaan UFO? (Do the Scripture Affirm the Existence of UFO?)'. Islamic UFO Facebook Group, 2012. https://www.facebook.com/groups/islamicufo/posts/385736211487847/?_rdr%2C&_rdc=2&_rdr0

Pramana, Hadika. 'Makhluk Bernama Dabbah'. Islamic UFO Facebook Group, 2016. https://web.facebook.com/groups/islamicufo/posts/1247984758596317/? (accessed 8 April 2023).

Pratomo, Gito Yudha. 'Alien Pernah Singgah Di Indonesia?' CNN Indonesia. cnnindonesia.com/teknologi/20141031191947-199-9184/alien-pernah-singgah-di-indonesia (accessed 14 January 2023).

Ramdan, Dadan Muhammad. 'Misteri UFO Dan Alien Dalam Pandangan Ulama'. Okezone, 2011. https://news.okezone.com/read/2011/01/25/340/417516/misteri-ufo-dan-alien-dalam-pandangan-ulama (accessed 8 April 2023).

Saleh, Walid A. 'Contemporary Tafsīr: The Rise of Scriptural Theology'. In *The Oxford Handbook of Qur'ānic Studies*, edited by Mustafa Shah and Muhammad Abdel Haleem, 694–702. London: Oxford University Press, 2020.

Sulaymān, Muqātil ibn. *Tafsīr Muqātil ibn Sulaymān*. Beirut: Dār Iḥyā' al-Turāth, 2002.

Tamir, Christine, Aidan Connaughton and Ariana Monique Salazar. 'The Global God Divide'. *Pew Research Center*, 20 July 2020. https://www.pewresearch.org/global/2020/07/20/the-global-god-divide/

Ṭanṭāwī, Muḥammad Sayyid. *Al-Tafsīr al-Wasīṭ li-l-Qur'ān al-Karīm*. Cairo: Dār Nahḍat Miṣr li-l-Ṭibā'a wa-l-Nashr wa-l-Tawzī', n.d.

Vallee, Jacques and Whitley Strieber. *Dimensions: A Casebook of Alien Contact*. Chicago: Contemporary Books, 1988.

Xeno 101. 'Pilar-Pilar Seth (Nabi Syits AS) Berisikan Pengetahuan Mengenai Anti Gravitasi?' Islamic UFO Facebook Group, 2019. https://www.facebook.com/groups/islamicufo/posts/2352187278176054/ (accessed 8 April 2023).

9

# Exotheology in contemporary Egyptian science fiction

## A comparative appraisal

Emad El-Din Aysha

## Introduction

Exotheology is theology applied to a world where man is not the only sentient life form. It poses a double question – if alien life existed in the universe, what consequences would this have for *our* belief system, and what would the theological systems (if any) of these aliens look like? This is akin to the question of religious pluralism. Can you believe that your religion is the one true faith if you acknowledge other faiths as equally valid? Is the God of Christianity the same as Allah in Islam? Are the faithful the chosen people or just one among many chosen peoples? If such questions can be posed within the human fold, then why not on a cosmic scale vis-à-vis alien races?

Fantasy author C. S. Lewis, a devout Christian, struggled with these quandaries in his classic 1958 essay 'Religion and Rocketry'. The Catholic Church has said it has no problem with converting Martians to Christianity.[1] Most recently, NASA has hired a team of expert theologists to 'determine how different religions around the world would react to contact with aliens'.[2] One of these is the reverend Andrew Davison, a biochemist who is also a priest and theologian at the University of Cambridge. Established religions then have shown a certain flexibility to the possibility of exotheology, albeit a situation forced on them by the realities of the space race and the ongoing search for extraterrestrial life. This is faith adapted to the era of science. But how does

[1] Rose, 'The Pope has said that he would Baptise a Martian'.
[2] WION Web Team, 'NASA is Hiring Priests'.

science fiction (SF) deal with these questions, particularly in the case of Islam, the newcomers to the genre? Has SF even dealt with exotheology, East or West? Arabic SF is notoriously hard to generalize about, as Arab sci-fi expert Muḥammad al-Yāsīn reminds us.[3] To circumvent this problem of generalization, it is instructive to focus on exotheological themes in Egyptian SF, especially in its current phase. Egyptian SF is much older than SF, say, in Syria, which began in the 1980s and is profoundly secular.[4] Egyptian SF in the contemporary world, moreover, has overcome some initial handicaps that held back Arabic SF. That is, early Egyptian and Arab SF, while not secular, took a rather hostile view towards modern science – seen as a Western import threatening local identities.[5] Also, while religion and the spiritual side of life were concerns, these themes were mainly dealt with in a terrestrial setting without too many alien encounters, closing down the opportunity to explore exotheology more fully. Egyptian SF, from the 1990s onwards, has transformed itself on several fronts. It has become self-confident as far as science is concerned. It has also gone beyond Earth-bound considerations, far more so at the turn of the century and then the current-phase Egyptian SF is going through. That is, following the Arab Spring revolutions from 2010–11 onwards.[6]

This is a methodological bias on my part, but it also affords us the opportunity for in-depth analysis and personal encounters and interviews with authors, as I am an active member of the Egyptian Society for Science Fiction (ESSF) and know both the older and younger generation of writers. That being said, comparisons with Western SF are called for and anything of an Islamic-themed nature that is of relevance to the topic at hand – how Islam deals with exotheology in the hands of Arab authors.

## Historical trajectories: Exotheology between Western and Arab SF

Sci-fi legend Theodore Sturgeon, while cataloguing SF's concern with religion, found it is almost as old as the genre. It stretches as far back as Lucian of Samosata, imagining himself looking down at mankind from the heavens to pass

[3] Aysha, 'Egypt as a Test', 29.
[4] Al-Yāsīn. Facebook message.
[5] Aysha, 'Science Fiction by, about', 6 and 11–13; Campbell, 'False Gods and Libertarians'; Campbell, 'Science Fiction and Social Criticism'.
[6] Aysha, 'Better Late than Never'.

judgement on men and their follies, to Robert Heinlein's 1961 classic *Stranger in a Strange Land*, dealing with everything from self-serving cults to real Christ-like figures.[7] But what of exotheology specifically? Modern Western SF, with a few notable exceptions, does not tend towards the religious spectrum. Consequently, the existence of sentient life out there is often taken as a nullification *of* religion. Sturgeon himself cites Arthur C. Clarke's short story 'The Star' (1955) and Lester del Rey's novella *For I am a Jealous People!* (1954) in this regard.[8] In Clarke's story, human explorers discover a peaceful people who were wiped out by their sun exploding, in this case, the very Star of Bethlehem, posing the age-old problem of evil. I would add Clarke's classic novel *The Fountains of Paradise* (1979) with a subplot involving an alien race that sent out a messenger probe to explore the galaxy, a device that informs humankind that far more advanced races exist and that they have given up on the notion of God altogether, finally legitimizing atheism on Earth. (The only character in the novel who more or less believes in God is a lonely Buddhist monk who eventually repents by the end.)

As for *For I am a Jealous People!*, the story has two human protagonists caught in the middle of an alien invasion – one a minister, the other an atheist – discovering that God has broken his covenant with man and has made a new covenant with this alien race and called upon them to wipe out mankind once and for all. (And despite this divine mandate, human beings prevail in the end.) Such notions are repeated in a lesser form in movies like *Homeworld* (2008) and rebooted TV series like *Battlestar Galactica* (2004–9), where notions like alien invaders believing in the same God as us or God making a mistake in creating such flawed entities as man are explicitly batted around.

These examples of moral and theological dilemmas are to be expected since Christianity is historically an anthropomorphic and anthropocentric religion.[9] Man was created in God's image, and Adam is the perfect being, the pinnacle of creation. (Witness the frequent references to these notions in Western SF, in movies like *Babylon A.D.* (2008), *The Island of Dr. Moreau* (1996) and *The Island of Lost Souls* (1932).) If sentient life exists out there, then a series of metaphysical quandaries follow: Are the religious beliefs of these aliens equally valid? If they have no religious beliefs at all but are more advanced than us, should we follow their guide? Is the human form superior any longer? Do aliens

[7] Sturgeon, 'Science Fiction, Morals, and Religion', 103, 112.
[8] Ibid., 105.
[9] For the complex relationship between anthropocentrism and anthropomorphism in Christianity please see Ferré and Ferré, 'In Praise of Anthropomorphism'; Simkins, 'The Bible and Anthropocentrism'.

think of themselves as being created in the image of their God? Islam is a very different species of belief, however, since we do not adhere to the belief that Adam was created in God's image. The expression *sayyid al-khalq* (master of creation or best of creation) is a reference to the Prophet Muḥammad, only, and not mankind. Muslims are acutely aware of the existence of other sentient beings that far outweigh us – the jinn (genies) and the angels. The jinn, in particular, bear the same burden we do as believers since they have the power of free will; in the Qur'ān, God explains that He created the jinn and the humans to worship and obey Him, mentioning the jinn first.[10] The jinn themselves have their own prophets, and some even converted to Islam in the presence of the Prophet Muḥammad.[11] Even animals in the Qur'ān are described as worshipping God and having their own kingdoms and empires, hence the Prophet Solomon and his ability to command the animals and speak their languages, along with the jinn. Satan in Islam is actually a jinn, not a fallen angel, someone who sinned through jealousy of man. (God ordered the angels to bow to Adam, and he objected because he was made of fire while man was made from the lowly substance of mud.) In Islamic folklore the jinn inhabited the Earth before man and had incredible magical powers ensuring their dominion was far greater than anything man and human civilization could muster.[12]

This would explain, straight away, the frequent appearance of jinn in works of Arabic and Muslim borderline and soft SF. Saudi author Ibrāhīm ʿAbbās has a novel, *HWJN* (2013), about a jinn by that name who falls in love with a human woman. From Egypt there is Wā'il and Maḥmūd ʿAbd al-Raḥīm's novel *Akwān* (*Universes*, 2017), about parallel universes existing on Earth. The jinn exist in one of these parallel dimensions and are benign entities that try to guard the boundaries between dimensions to make sure a war doesn't erupt between the separate races, a war that would engulf the planet and wipe out humanity in the process. They are so benign, in fact, they do not engage in demonic possession of humans except in the most extreme circumstances and are pious Muslims themselves. Human beings, needless to say, are the least advanced of the races and the most hell-bent on breaching the dimensional boundaries, through their arrogance. A similar set-up emerges in ʿAmmār al-Miṣrī's novel *Ṣadmah Kawniyya: Al-Malāk al-Aswad* (*Cosmic Shock: The Black Angel*, 2021), in which scientists build a portal that allows them to contact other dimensions with

[10] Q. 51:56.
[11] Q. 6:130 and 72:1-2.
[12] El-Zein, *Islam, Arabs, and the Intelligent World of the Jinn*; Al Hosni, 'Black Magic and Djinn in Omani Literature'.

horrendous consequences when monsters creep in from the other side. The jinn exist in one of these dimensions but are also benign and not even shaped in devilish form with horns and hooves and reptilian wings, in contrast to the other monsters on display.

As for hard SF, from the earliest days of Egyptian SF, you have scenarios where human beings travel to alien worlds only to discover that these races hold similar beliefs and legal practices to the Muslim explorers. The classic statement of this is Aḥmad Rāʾif's play *Al-Buʿd al-Khāmis* (*The Fifth Dimension*) – written while he was in political prison in the 1960s – where the human protagonist makes it to Mars only to find them being ruled on the basis of a revealed scripture with decisions based on consensus.[13] Consensus here is a reference to the Islamic principle of *shūrā*, literally translated as consultation and seen as the basis for politics and legitimacy as spelt out in the Qurʾān. A more contemporary example is Dr Ḥusām ʿAbd al-Ḥamīd Al-Zambīlī's *Anṣāf al-Bashar* (*The Half-Humans*, 2001), where Muslim space explorers are entrusted with rescuing a dying breed of aliens related to mankind, and this brings them to the planet of the Seven Hills. The alien race there had travelled the galaxy in its early days and encountered man, in his primitive past, and even mated with some to give birth to the hybrid half-humans, imprisoned on Pluto and slowly dying from the conflict in their genes. (See ancient aliens later in the text.) The Muslim heroes travel to the land of the Seven Hills to find the cure, and when they arrive, meet their noble and wise king, who informs them, unfortunately, that:

> the decision is not mine alone to make. We believe in consultation here . . . You are no strangers to consultation, I am sure. To my knowledge, your great religion – Islam – insisted on it. And so the Council of Elders of our world has the final say. And they decided long ago to never give the medicine to the race of half humans.[14]

The main hero of the story, Sayf al-Dīn (Sword of Religion), even converts an evil alien tyrant at one point in the story, through his bravery and sacrifice in facing off against the tyrant. The people of the Seven Hills may be democratic but sadly their civilization has fallen into moral decay, cutting themselves off from so-called lesser species or even destroying planets that can rival them technologically.

ʿAmmār al-Miṣrī also highlights the centrality of *shūrā* in his Atlantis trilogy, an alien invasion epic where the linux empire attacks Earth. The irony is that the

[13] Determann, *Islam, Science Fiction and Extraterrestrial Life*, 89–90.
[14] Al-Zambīlī, *Anṣāf al-Bashar*, 107.

linux race are actually monotheists, believing in the same God as the humans, but they fell under the rule of a tyrant king who used magical powers entrusted to the linux people by an older (and very angel-like) alien being. The king was a patriot and wanted to revive his ailing empire in the face of other races – who are either pagan or atheist – but his power went to his head, and he failed in the end, thinking that he could do everything by himself. In conversations with ʿAmmār, we learned he was thinking of Muḥammad Ali Basha, who reigned over Egypt from 1805 to 1848; he was a great modernizer but also disempowered the Egyptian people through his monopolization of power. ʿAmmār also explained that the linux are a stand-in for the rise, and decline, of the Ottoman Empire; he even connected them to the lost city of Atlantis and the biblical flood.[15]

Muslim SF authors, moreover, are often fond of books like *Chariots of the Gods*, and publications about the Bermuda Triangle and UFO mythology, with a small Arab cottage industry, churning out everything from serious novels to pulp about everything from the sinking of Atlantis to alien visitations from the times of the pyramid builders. (See authors cited later.) Going from the world of Muslim fiction to facts, Jörg Matthias Determann has amply documented the surprising number of UFO cults and claimed sightings in modern Islamic history, extending as far as diaspora and minority Muslim communities.[16]

*Akwān* is actually set 'in' the Bermuda Triangle, and there are religious themes evident throughout. Not only are the Muslim jinn the valiant guardians of the dimensional divide but the Egyptian scientist, Dr Bilal, trying to open the dimensional gate located in the Triangle is a somewhat lapsed Muslim whose father was a sheikh who used the Qurʾān to fight against evil spirits. In the sequel *Akwān 2*, we are introduced to a parallel human race that is more advanced than us and is also devoutly Muslim, and they are presented in an almost angelic way. A key character in this sequel novel is a scientist, the assistant of Dr Bilal, in fact, but here he follows the guide of the jinn and becomes a sheikh, too, combining religious knowledge with modern science. (A criticism of Dr Bilal in the first novel is that he was not selfless in his pursuits, unlike his father, who cured people for free and warned his son about breaching the dimensional boundaries guarded by the jinn.)

From attending repeated meetings and sessions of the ESSF, I was quite surprised to discover that many an Arab SF author can easily imagine Adam and Eve as extraterrestrials transplanted on Earth with advanced alien races seeding

15 Al-Miṣrī, *Cultural Salon*.

16 Determann, *Islam, Science Fiction and Extraterrestrial Life*, 37, 101, 103–4, 105–13, 115, 117, 120–6, 128–37, and 171–2.

hospitable planets in the universe – see alchemy later in the text. Nobody condemned these unconventional ideas as blasphemous and many a pious and conservative Muslim author, old and young, has penned such epics in their careers as writers. (Aḥmad Rāʾif was associated with the Muslim Brotherhood.) Other examples include prominent literary critic and travel writer Anīs Manṣūr (1924–2011) who wrote novels about alien visitations and the ancient Egyptians among other ancient peoples – *alladhīna habaṭū min al-samāʾ!* (*Those Who Descended from the Heavens*, 1971) and *alladhīna ʿādūailā al-samāʾ* (*Those Who Returned to the Heavens*, 1977). Nihād Sharīf (1932–2011), the dean of Arabic SF, wrote extensively on alien visitations and first contact scenarios stretching from the modern world to the time of the Pharaohs, still a popular theme in Egyptian SF.[17] Even SF written about Muslims, by non-Muslims, attests to this theological flexibility. Blaze Ward's short story 'Assassin' has a devout Muslim imam on an alien world, having converted the natives to Islam.[18] When the imam is confronted by an assassin sent from the Caliphate back on Earth to punish this, among other acts of supposed blasphemy, the imam explains that he converted the aliens for the same reason that he rejected the Caliphate. The new Caliphs insist that the leader of the umma must come from the tribe of Quraysh, the original Meccan tribe of the Prophet Muḥammad, which automatically consigns all other Muslims to the status of second-class citizens. Likewise, hereditary rule means that aliens will also be second-class citizens, something he cannot accept – 'Either Allah loves all of Creation, or he doesn't'.[19]

This open-mindedness towards the possibility of life elsewhere in the universe goes beyond the existence of the jinn. As Determann argues, this is in part in response to the cryptic Qurʾānic description of Allah as the Lord of the 'worlds', implying that there are other worlds and beings we do not know of.[20] From watching religious programmes, from my youth and to this day, you find Islamic scholars and thinkers quoting verses from the Qurʾān that mention creatures that reside on Earth *and* the heavens and reinterpreting verses that in the past seemed to give man an undeserved centrality in the cosmos. The sun and moon are described as being in the service of man, but, in the context of the conquest of space, scholars have speculated that this may be a futuristic reference to human beings actually making use of a stellar phenomenon through technology.

17 Al-Shārūnī, *Al-Khayāl al-ʿIlmī fī al-Adab*, 229–52.
18 You can access the story on Blaze Ward's website, 'Farouk 001 – Assassin', https://www.blazeward.com/product/assassin/.
19 Ward, Facebook message.
20 Determann, *Islam, Science Fiction and Extraterrestrial Life*, 10–11, 57.

Historical context always influences interpretation, and SF is no exception – see the *Black Angel* commentary later in the text.

## Monotheism in perspective: Man as the measure of godliness

There are exceptions, of course, in the tradition of Western SF when it comes to negative or neglectful appraisals of religion. *Contact* (1997), the movie at least, creates a parallelism between religion and science since both depend on faith in the unknown and still unproven – everything from the existence of God to black holes. There is Barry Longyear's novella *Enemy Mine* (1979), where the human protagonist learns from the Drac the teachings of the Talman and comes to see himself as a Drac, because of the universal truths contained within the teachings of the Drac Prophet Shiuzmaat. Philip K. Dick was the great spiritualist and mystic using the Bible alongside the *I Ching* in *The Man in the High Castle* (1962) and the Qur'ān in *The Divine Invasion* (1981). There is even some Sufism in *The Transmigration of Timothy Archer* (1982).[21] Someone predisposed to religious pluralism like him would obviously have no problem when it came to exotheology. Nonetheless Western SF, by and large, is quite secular and is always trying to find moral foundations independent of religion.[22] The very progress of science is presumed to eat away at the foundations of religion since the mysteries of the universe upon which faith is built are explained away by scientific discovery.[23]

If religion is kept at all in the Western SF tradition, it is in purely theological terms, 'to detach religion from God'.[24] Even 'Enemy Mine' is the exception to the rule because the human hero still wonders what lies in the afterlife, as the Talman only covers moral conduct in this life. Theology is noticeably absent, while the principles on how to live one's life are derived in a secular fashion. There are no creation myths and talk of God in this holy scripture that resonates, say, with similar accounts in the Bible. Again, the assumption in much Western SF is that science explains existence, with reference to laws of nature and natural processes, with evolution taking the place of creation.

21 Please see Barlow, 'How Much Does Chaos'; Kinney, 'The Political Gnosis'; Boonstra, 'Final Interview'.
22 Beswick, 'Glimpses of Ecclesiastical Space'.
23 Linford, 'Deeds of Power', 84–5.
24 Ibid., 81.

Even more lessons abound from Lester del Rey's *For I am a Jealous People!*, mentioned earlier. On the surface of it, the story seems radical in its implications, with God changing His mind about mankind and a priest having to change his world perspective as a consequence, and mankind finding itself in a pitched battle with God's new adherents. In actual fact, this perspective is quite commonplace in Western art and literature, such as the movie *Legion* (2010), where an angel is trying to rescue humanity from an army of angels sent by God, a repeat of God's last *failed* attempt to wipe out humanity with the Flood. The newly chosen people in del Rey's story failed to wipe out the human race, after all. The concepts of omnipotence and omniscience do not seem to be as deeply ingrained in the Western imagination as once thought. This places the Judeo-Christian God on a par with Zeus (who can be hoodwinked by his goddess wives) or the debates Greek philosophers had about God's knowledge and if untruths and particulars were beneath God's ability to know them. In pagan faiths gods can grow old and feeble and forget things and be defied by humans or other gods who can steal their power – *The Clash of the Titans* (2010) being a contemporary example of this. Worship and sacrifices for the gods, for the most part, were meant to appease the gods and keep their anger and retribution at bay, which we see clearly in the sequel *Wrath of the Titans* (2012).

There is a hint of exotheology in del Rey's story when a fanatic explains the existence of aliens with reference to John 14:2 about God's house having many mansions. But this is something he thinks up off the top of his head in a defensive mode. It's not told from the perspective of the narrator or the two central characters. Meanwhile the priest is still pondering whether the invasion was an act of God or Satan. It is the atheist in the story who has the last laugh, even after realizing that God does actually exist, just in a malevolent form. Priests quite often are humbled, or humiliated, in Western SF; Sturgeon uses the example of Marion Zimmer Bradley's *Darkover Landfall* (1972) to illustrate this.[25] Even in *Contact* a televangelist-like fanatic blows up the teleportation facility meant to bring mankind to the alien's doorstep.

Also note the setting for Lester del Rey's story, the small town, the 'moral heartland' of the United States, while the atheist (not coincidentally) is a medical doctor, a stand-in for science versus religion. The irony is that what you see in the story is not secularism, per se, not a modernist minimization of religious influence. It is instead an example of religiosity just in the ancient polytheistic mode of thinking. Even Aristotle's more monotheistic Prime Mover

[25] Sturgeon, 'Science Fiction, Morals, and Religion', 109–111.

had restrictions placed on him in terms of knowledge and power, and Aristotle still believed that human beings had to devise their own ethics independent of religion.[26] The priest himself recollects Immanuel Kant's quest for an independent sense of morality – treating other people as ends and not means – and even declares that God has now found a worthy opponent in man.

Looked at from the history of the Scientific Revolution, other curious parallels and paradoxes emerge. As science historian Steven Shapin explains, while Ptolemy's geocentric model of the universe was quintessentially anthropocentric, the heliocentric view that took its place in the seventeenth century could just as easily be accused of placing man on a pedestal above all of God's creation. This is because, again, of the Greek heritage. Scholars in the Middle Ages understood the Bible in distinctly Platonic terms, seeing the Fall not only as a punishment to man's body (growing old, sick and dying) but also as a punishment to the senses and the intellect. When Adam was in heaven, he lived in the world of God and the angels and (by extension) the ideal forms of Plato, only to be consigned to the world of subjectivity and mere appearances on Earth.[27] As the sixteenth-century French essayist Michel de Montaigne put it, the dwelling place of humans was 'the filth and mire of the world, the worst, lowest, most lifeless part of the universe, the bottom story of the house'.[28] Heliocentrism conveniently placed man back into the heavens, with the sun now as the source of illumination – God's knowledge – at the heart of the universe instead of the wretched, imperfect Earth. We can add that this brand of theologically inspired heliocentrism has a long and proud history, going as far back as the Pythagoreans, who not only posited that the Earth went around the sun but also that there was even a counter-Earth behind the sun – a notion Aristotle found offensive to the senses.[29] Needless to say, the Pythagoreans were a philosophical order steeped in austerity and mysticism, almost a cult, positing notions such as the musical harmony of the heavenly spheres.[30]

All that heliocentrism did then was dethrone one kind of anthropomorphism with another. There are reverberations of this species of heliocentrism in Western SF and pop culture, as evidenced by *The Chronicles of Riddick* (2004). The story takes place in the 'Helios' system after all, a planetary system built on tolerance being threatened by the crusader-like Necromongers. An Islamic

26 Please see Defilippo, 'Aristotle's Identification'; McClymont, 'Reading between the Lines'.
27 Shapin, *The Scientific Revolution*, 24–5.
28 Quoted in Ibid., 24.
29 Robinson, *An Introduction to Early Greek Philosophy*, 74–6; Hoskin, 'Astronomy in Antiquity', 34.
30 Hoskin, 'Astronomy in Antiquity', 26–7; Robinson, *An Introduction to Early Greek Philosophy*, 58, 61, and 69–70.

dictum is that the world and everything in it is worth no more than the wing of a mosquito to God.[31] Consequently this whole way of thinking, likening man to God or placing man in contest with God, is *not* found in the folds of Islam. As a rule, Muslims are not allowed to draw God or even imagine God, knowing full well that any such picturing of Him will be fallible and mundane. It could even be argued that such flawed imaginings of God would make us more prone to doubting Him and His abilities and seeing Him as flawed and fallible. We are constantly enjoined to *trust* God and His intentions for us, not see Him as a tempestuous entity that treats us as His harbingers.[32] (In Islam, man is the one who makes a covenant with God, not the other way around.) And, as stated earlier, Islam is not anthropocentric or anthropomorphic, placing it in contrast to the classical Greek stance voiced by Protagoras that sees man as the measure of all things. It is true that we as a nation think of ourselves as a charmed people, our own version of chosenness, but the proper phrasing of the term refers to the services we can give the human race since the emphasis is on encouraging good and forbidding evil.[33] The opening word in the verse moreover says, 'you were' (*kuntum*) in the past tense, emphasizing conditionality. It is the doing of good deeds that benefits mankind and the forbidding of evildoing that harms people that *makes* you better. If Muslims stop behaving this way, they fall from grace, just like previous generations of believers. No surprise, then, that the Qur᾽ān is full of injunctions for us as a people to study the relics and remains of previous civilizations, peoples that perished because of their arrogance, thinking of themselves as divinely charmed also.[34] Even in Sufi thought, where some do consider man to be more exalted than the angels because of the gift of free will (which is not shared by the angels), men only attain this status through piety and *humility*, so they can prevent themselves from exercising this freewill in a way detrimental to themselves and God's creation. We are the stewards of God on Earth, after all. (See Iraj Fazel Bakhsheshi later in the text.) Otherwise, we sink to a level *lower* than the animals, who likewise have no free will but don't have the intelligence to cause as much damage as we can. And not all Sufis see man as the repository of divine wisdom, incidentally.[35]

[31] *Sunan Ibn Majah*, Book 37, Ḥadīth 11, https://sunnah.com/ibnmajah:4110.

[32] In the very chapter where God explains why He created the jinn and the humans, the following verse adds poignantly that: 'I seek no provision from them, nor do I need them to feed Me.' Q. 51:57. Remember that in the movies *Clash* and *Wrath of the Titans* the Greek gods on Mount Olympus *needed* human worship to 'fuel' their immorality.

[33] Q. 3:110.

[34] Q. 27:51, 30:42 and 47:10.

[35] Khafājī, *Al-Adab fī al-Turāth al-Ṣūfī*, 118 and 120–2.

Taking a second look at Blaze Ward's story 'Assassin', you still find traces of the mindset of Western SF towards religion, despite the fact that it is written from a Muslim perspective. When the imam sees the assassin coming in through the saloon door, he is at first surprised the man would come to this blasphemous alien world then notes: 'but Allah's will was not something wise man might sought to deny.' When the aliens are described, moreover, we are told how humanoid they are: 'Allah had obviously made them all in the same image he crafted Humans.'[36] Again hints at anthropomorphism and anthropocentricity. We can add that Protagoras would feel perfectly at home in the modern world of Western SF, especially among the fans and creators of the *Star Trek* franchise that quite explicitly say that humanity is the measure of all things if not God Himself.[37] Even the Q in *The Next Generation* was famously terrified of man and his potential for growth – episode 10, season 1, 'Hide and Q'.

As Muslims, we are brought up to see our intelligence as fallible and highly subjective when it comes to matters of ethics and so always in need of divine guidance and limitation. This is a sentiment *not* shared by Western SF, Frank Herbert's *Dune* being the classic example, decoupling God from both morals and laws.[38] Religion always has a place in Islamically themed SF, if only because of the way we understand God *and* religion – the topic we move to now.

## Lexicon of faith: Worldly affairs, unity and progress

It is often noted, in Western discourse, that in contrast to Christianity, Islam is more than a mere religion to Muslims. To cite sociologist and development theorist Ankie Hoogvelt:

> Islam is more than a religion; it is a complete way of life. It concerns not only God's relationship with His people, but it also orders social relations amongst people including legal, contractual institutions, social and political institutions, and issues of economic propriety and practice.[39]

Subscribing religion to mere theological beliefs or matters of faith is an alien way of thinking to Muslims since religion, to us, specifically means a way of life. Traditionally Muslims don't see it as divorced from everyday concerns, practices

[36] Quotes taken from the downloadable version of the story, 'Assassin: Farouk Al-Hashemi Vol. 1', https://dl.bookfunnel.com/n0gt346rwt.
[37] Asa, 'Classic *Star Trek*', 50.
[38] Hrotic, *Religion in Science Fiction*, 114–15.
[39] Hoogvelt, *Globalisation and the Postcolonial World*, 185.

and dilemmas. In English, for instance, a distinction is made between ethics and morals; morality is theories of right and wrong, whereas ethics is practical rules. In Arabic, however, we lump the two concepts together into words like noble customs (*ādāb*) and ethics (*akhlāq*). Hence religion, as a way of life; what else could it mean, with this usage of language?

This has implications for SF straight away, very different implications than for Christianity and Western SF. As stated earlier, in mainstream SF, morals (and laws) are divorced from God, while God (the question of His existence) is likewise kept isolated from religion. Religion, in all cases, is reduced to faith. In *Contact*, cited earlier, the key issue again was 'faith' – proof of God's existence up against the equally unproven belief in life out there. Muslims, however, when portraying their people's future give religion a much bigger role to play specifically because they understand religion in a more expansive sense. This is also a matter of historical consciousness since religion played a much bigger role in the historical accomplishments of Muslims, as a people, than Christianity did in European history. Muslims at one point in time were united as a nation and empire and consequently modern-day Muslims understand their power and glory – and scientific advancement – in political terms, seeing unity as well as morality as a prerequisite for progress. For a ready example we have Ḥusām ʿAbd al-Ḥamīd Al-Zambīlī's *Al-Kawkab al-ʿAjīb* (*Planet of the Viruses*, 2001). The hero, Dr Salah al-Din, encourages his research team by telling them they are making history and 'bringing enlightenment to the world . . . no different than our heroes and first scientists . . . Abbas Ibn Firnas, the first man to fly . . . Khalid ibn al-Walid . . . the great Muslim military leader . . . Ibn Rushd . . . Ibn Sina . . . Al-Khawarizmi . . . Jabir ibn Hayyan . . . and hundreds like them'. He then reminds them of the decline of Islamic civilization and how this was only turned around when 'we reunited and began once again to light the path for humanity . . . Bringing back to life the values of nobility and chivalry . . . Values that almost disappeared'.[40]

In both *Planet of the Viruses* and *The Half-Humans*, you have the Union of Islamic States, much as he has an Arab-Islamic Union in other novels. In the case of *Planet of the Viruses*, more specifically, you have a scene where Dr Salah al-Din – or Saladin, with obvious connotations – gets into trouble with the authorities for withholding facts from them. He is forgiven, however, since the governing body of the Islamic Union is based (again) on *shūrā*, understood very explicitly to mean democracy, and this allows the ruling body to engage in legal

[40] Al-Zambīlī, *Al-Kawkab al-ʿAjīb*, 119.

innovation or *ijtihad* that relies on the spirit of the law as opposed to the word of the law.[41] *Ijtihād* was a hallmark of Islamic civilization in the past and yet another area where Muslims have fallen behind in the present.[42]

More than this, the word 'Islam' in common Muslim usage, on the one hand, denotes the religion itself – the body of beliefs, practices and scripture – and, on the other, denotes the Muslim nation or umma. The expression 'Islam is in danger' is a reference not to the religion per se but the umma, such as at the time of the Crusades or the Mongol invasions or Western imperialism. In Christianity, however, the co-equivalent term to religion is either faith or church – people of a different church meaning a different religion. In Philip José Farmer's novel *The Lovers* (1961) there is 'The Sturch', where the state and church become one, with all that implies in terms of forceful moral instruction on the model of the inquisition and witch-hunting.[43] (In the dystopian movie *Equilibrium* the secret police force are called 'the cleric' and words like faith are used to justify summary executions without resort to due judicial process.)

Islam doesn't have priests and clergy in the sense of mediators between God and humankind. The faith 'finds its social embodiment in a learned laity where Christianity has priests'[44] – the umma once again.[45] The formative experience of Christianity as a religion is radically different from that of Islam too, since the last Christian ruler who tried to unite Christendom under one banner was Charlemagne. Scientific progress in European history not only came at the expense of religion – or the authority of the Catholic Church – but was also not tied to any kind of unity on the European continent or among Christians, even within the same sect. And with no centralized pan-religious authority like the Vatican in Islamic history, there are no ready equivalents of Galileo's trial. It is certainly true that Muslim state authorities have a history of persecuting intellectuals, on religious pretences. But even here, religious conservatives themselves have suffered at the hands of such rabble-rousers as much as philosophers and radicals did – if not more so. A case in point is Aḥmad ibn

41 Ibid., 97–102.

42 For details and debates about *Ijtihād* in Islam please see Ali-Karamali and Dunne, 'The Ijtihad Controversy'.

43 Interestingly the protagonist in the story, a linguist, is sent to an alien world Earth wishes to colonize to decode their language. He falls in love with a humanoid woman while there (almost a forest nymph) but despite the anatomical similarities they never have any dialogues over similarities or differences between faiths. The hero only comes to question some of his own beliefs through his friendship with one of the aliens on the planet but the woman's religious beliefs never seem to be addressed and the real focus of the narrative is the love/sex story. This is all the more amazing since Philip José Farmer was known to be a devout Catholic.

44 Crone, *From Kavād to al-Ghazālī*, 63.

45 Goldberg, 'Smashing Idols', 6–7 and 11–12.

Ḥanbal (780–855), a staunch Muslim cleric who was imprisoned and tortured over the controversy around the creation of the Qur'ān, and at the hands of the philosophers no less.[46]

The stand-off between science and religion found in much Western pop culture, not least in SF,[47] is noticeably absent in Islam.[48] Not to forget that this reading of European history itself is a caricature given that Christianity did, in fact, play a positive role in scientific history, such as in Protestant lands to the North in Galileo's same era.[49]

This perceived stand-off seems to be unique to the West. It is noticeably absent in India and SF written by Hindus, for instance, as Sami Ahmad Khan has argued – while a Muslim himself.[50] It must also be understood that much of Arabic SF, certainly the Egyptian variety, is premised on reconciling science with religion and, more specifically, modern science originating in the West. The more secular or Marxist-style authors, such as Ṣabrī Mūsā and Ḥusayn Qadrī, are a rarity, and they didn't necessarily see advanced alien life in religious terms.[51] The point is, however, that most Muslims see religion as answering key questions about how people should live their lives, and many see no need to import Western ideologies – socialism, liberalism, anarchism – to answer these self-same questions.

One of the pioneers of Arabic SF, Muṣṭafā Maḥmūd, has everything in his world driven by some spiritual aspiration in his novel *Rajul taḥta al-Ṣifr* (*A Man Under Zero*, 1967), even inanimate objects, since scientists in this future world discover rock formations that are alive and grow and prosper. (See 'spontaneous generation' in *Ḥayy ibn Yaqẓān* later; scientists in Islamic history had misidentified coral as living rocks.) The entire narrative was geared towards people rebelling against the crass materialism of their future Utopia and rediscovering God. Mustafa Mahmoud (an Egyptian) wrote several Sufi and spiritually inspired speculative novels, including *Al-Ankabūt* (*The Spider*, 1967), *Al-Khurūj min al-Tābūt* (*Out of the Coffin*, 1967) and *Al-Afyūn* (*Opium*, 1976), all dedicated to finding a middle path between spiritually arid scientism and spiritualism divorced of the rational faculties.[52] These sentiments coincide, if not overlap, with exotheology in contemporary Egyptian SF, one case in

46 Melchert, 'Aḥmad Ibn Ḥanbal'.
47 Matthew, *Japanese Science Fiction*, 131–2, 237.
48 Yalcinkaya, 'Science as an Ally'.
49 Jacob and Jacob, 'The Anglican Origins'.
50 Khan, 'The Indian Recipe'.
51 Al-Shārūnī, *Al-Khayāl al-'Ilmī fī al-Adab*, 220 and 207.
52 Rāghib, *Zawāj al-'Ilm wa-l-Adab*, 87–93.

point being the novel *Mughāmarat al-Arāḍīn al-Sabʿ* (*The Adventure of the Seven Earths*) (2021) by Ḥusām Ṣalāḥ. The title is an explicit reference to the Qurʾānic notion of seven heavens and, with that, a related theological idea that there are a grand total of seven earths in those heavens, universes in effect with alternate earths in parallel realities. This is precisely what happens in the novel as the scientist hero travels from one version of the Earth to the next, through energy fields and pan-dimensional portals not coincidentally located in or near ancient Egyptian monuments and other famous historical locales in Egypt. In one of these alternate realities, you find that Egypt has become a scientific and industrial powerhouse – a clear patriotic sentiment the author confirmed during a literary event for his book – and with praise heaped on the advanced scientific knowledge of the ancients. The author even explained that there is an apocryphal ḥadīth (saying ascribed to the Prophet) where it is said that just as there are seven earths there are also seven Adams and Muḥammads.[53] The ḥadīth was rejected by the bulk of Muslim scholars, Ḥusām Ṣalāḥ insisted, but some did, in fact, entertain the notion and did not find it to be blasphemous. The mere fact that scholars and theologists were willing to speculate about such outlandish notions (to conventional Muslim sentiments) is evidence of tremendous open-mindedness and theological flexibility in Islamic history.

Imagine their shock at discovering that alchemists in Islamic history believed they could *recreate* Adam and Eve from mere chemical substances. Egyptologist Dr Okasha El-Daly explained this during a lecture on the scholarly study of hieroglyphics in Islamic history; alchemists made these boasts because they'd dedicated their lives to uncovering the secrets of the ancients. The speaker was very right to point out that if somebody in the modern-day Muslim world made such grandiose claims, he'd be outright accused of blasphemy.[54] Again, there was more theological open-mindedness in Islam's distant past, which creates even more room for exotheology in the contemporary context, citing Ḥusām Ṣalāḥ as an example. The alternate realities he outlines in his Seven Earths novel are not perceived as threatening to the Muslim's sense of self, bolstered as it is by scientific accomplishments. The novel even toys around with imagery and motifs from foreign myths, such as the Cyclops. Querying the author, he explained that he was initially thinking scientifically – genetic engineering and mutations in a

[53] See the chapter of Hamza Karamali in this volume.

[54] El-Daly, 'Cairo Lecture'. For additional information on the creation of Adam and Eve, see El-Daly, *Egyptology*, 179.

parallel-universe Earth – but the idea appealed to him subconsciously because of this trademark image we have from Greek mythology.[55]

Returning to the example of *Planet of the Viruses*, it is notable that Muslims have their own version of the internet – the United Islamic Computerised Network – and the scientists and medical doctors of the Islamic Union dedicate themselves to the service of humanity, trying to find a cure to the herpes virus that is turning the world blind. They learn that the virus is actually sentient and infecting the irises of people in an attempt to communicate with mankind, desperately needing their help to return to their planet and overthrow the tyrant who has enslaved their race. These viruses also communicate to the scientists using Arabic letters, and the tremendous favour the humans do to them by answering their call would no doubt make it easier for them to convert!

## The mystical dimension: Differing Muslim contributions to exotheology

Another source of exotheology in Arabic and Islamic SF is the spiritual heritage of Islam, which comes out most clearly in Sufism as well as Shiism. ʿAmmār al-Miṣrī gives a very unique interpretation of the Qurʾān in his novel *Black Angel*, citing a verse in the Qurʾān to mean that humans existed in spirit form before they entered their bodies and actually witnessed God and took their oath of obedience, only to have their memories wiped clean once they enter into their host bodies.[56] He says this thesis explains why the Qurʾānic verse states that they cannot plead ignorance on the Day of Judgement for breaking their sacred vows.[57] That's what drives the scientist hero of the story, Karim, towards his research into the supernatural, hoping to see the spirit world, including the world of the jinn, and unlock secrets about the nature of the soul and man's ultimate fate. (He just got more than he bargained for in the end.) Karim, not coincidentally, is a pious Muslim and devoted husband and very proud of his Islamic identity, frequently getting into debates with his friend and fellow scientist Anas, who is a sceptic and someone enamoured by Western materialist philosophy. (Also, non-coincidentally, the two of them work in an American-owned research facility, where they regularly have East vs. West-type debates).

55 Ṣalāḥ, *Cultural Salon*.
56 Q. 7:172.
57 Al-Miṣrī, *Ṣadmah kawniyya*, 26.

From his appearances at ESSF meetings, ʿAmmār Al-Miṣrī has made it abundantly clear that he is a staunch Sunnī Muslim and not actually cordial to Sufism, the main mystical tradition in Islam. (Al-Zambīlī and the ʿAbd al-Raḥīm brothers are more spiritual in their inclinations.) Nonetheless, his novel found itself in much the same place as the Sufi classic *Ḥayy ibn Yaqẓān*, a being who went through his own spiritual arch whereby he became a devout Muslim and a Sufi, all by himself, even seeing no need for the Qurʾān once he encountered it. (*Ḥayy* originally spoke no language, having been raised by the animals far from the corrupting influence of man. He even found the wording of the Qurʾān leaning too much towards anthropomorphism.)[58] There is an added twist, however, not analogous to ʿAmmār's novel, namely evolution. Sufis believed in alchemy and the evolution of inanimate objects towards sentient life, in the path of attaining divine knowledge, and also believed in spontaneous generation. One account of *Ḥayy*'s genesis had him evolving from mud. Dr El-Daly, in his Egyptology lecture, also noted that Sufis were very interested in deciphering hieroglyphic inscriptions alongside the alchemists. They, too, had no theological reservations over unlocking the secrets inscribed in the 'pagan' temples of this long-lost race. And as further evidence of how theologically open-minded Muslim scholars were back then, we have the example of ʿAbd al-Laṭīf al-Baghdādī, a historian and philosopher who surmised that the reasons the pyramids weren't mentioned in the Qurʾān is that they were built *before* Adam set foot on the Earth![59]

Similar themes and readings of history emerge in Iranian works of SF, such as Iraj Fazel Bakhsheshi's novella *A Message Older Than Time* (2007).[60] Here an ancient race of technologically advanced semi-vertebrates is threatened with extinction by the meteorite that will kill off the dinosaurs. A top biologist is entrusted with leaving a warning message to the future inheritors of the Earth, the apes that will later evolve into the human race. In the penultimate scene the biologist has an apeman captured, to study his neural system, and laments how feeble the creature is with its primitive hands and puny frame. Nonetheless, he knows that his race's superiority is coming to an end as they are draining and polluting themselves into extinction anyway, albeit slowly, leaving you wondering whether biological evolution is the same thing as moral and spiritual evolution. Is mankind any different in its factionalism, racism and classism than

58 *Ḥayy ibn Yaqẓān* is often seen as an example of proto-science fiction, like the Golem myth in Judaism, an early robot story in its own right. Even Mary Shelley's more explicit robot story *Frankenstein* was heavily influenced by alchemy.

59 El-Daly, *Egyptology*, 13–14 and 48.

60 Jannessari-Ladani, 'An Eye on the Past', 133–4.

this older, more evolved species? Will they continue to reign supreme on the Earth if another meteorite strikes the planet, as the semi-vertebrates suspect? Another reason for their hidden message. The objective of the story, then, is to teach man to be humble in the face of creation and realize that man's mission is really to honour his birthplace, Mother Earth, and live in balance with nature. Evolution, in Muslim hands, *dethrones* man and opens up even more possibilities for exotheology.

It's even hinted that at least some of the semi-vertebrates made it to another star system and that they may be on their way back to reclaim their birth right. And the humans who dig up the message left for them are not nearly as technologically advanced as this older race who mastered travel across the light years. Speaking to Bakhsheshi, he confirmed that evolution frequently enters into his novels and short stories.[61] There is more to this than meets the untrained eye. Evolution as a biological concept was mentioned repeatedly in the discourses of Iranian revolutionary thinkers like Ali Shariati and Jalal Al-e Ahmad.[62] Shariati, in particular, was more explicit, openly quoting Charles Darwin on how proto-man became the most evolved of animals because he lost his body hair and tail and became erect. The real turning point, however, came afterwards because this physical evolution stopped, and an 'inner, spiritual' evolution took its place with the 'appearance of the mystical sense', which made him 'properly human' – a bond he sensed 'toward some rocks or toward an idol, the numinous quality he senses in certain things, the mysterious tie with them he feels in his being'.[63] Intelligence in the practical sense of tool-making wasn't what distinguished man but his ability to see behind things in terms of divine causality and the striving to higher things.

This universalist, evolutionist ethos exists even in the theocratic regime ruling the Iran of today. It comes out in debates about 'religious pluralism' – alluded to earlier – arguing that other religions are equally valid to Islam and that Islam is not the only path to the Truth. Abd Al-Karim Soroush, a member of Iran's Council for the Cultural Revolution, once forwarded a paper on religious pluralism entitled Siratha-ye Mustaqim or Straights Paths. In Islamic lexicon, the religion is described in the Qur'ān as the straight path (*al-ṣirāṭ al-mustaqīm*) towards salvation, in the singular. Even so his paper was endorsed by the regime.[64]

[61] Bakhsheshi, Personal email.
[62] Mottahedeh, *The Mantle of the Prophet*, 301.
[63] Shariati, *Marxism and Other Western Fallacies*, 98–9.
[64] Sedgwick, *Against the Modern World*, 252.

Iran and Shīʿism, it emerges, have an interesting history with evolutionary theory.[65] Not that the Arabs and mainstream Sunnī Islam are exempt from evolutionary theory, having long been anticipated in the heyday of Islamic science, most prominently in the works of the great historian and scholar al-Jāḥiẓ. His views on evolution not only encompass what today are called the food pyramid and food chain but even Social Darwinism's genetic ranking of human beings by class and race.[66] Al-Jāḥiẓ, it emerges, was also into alchemy, proudly proclaiming that he could create a living, breathing mouse out of mere substances.[67] (Ḥayy was generated out of mud, after all.)

If religion can evolve independent of revelation, through pure reason, emotional inspiration and biological advance, on Earth, then this can just as readily happen elsewhere in the cosmos with alien races. The author has been told this by another Iranian genre writer (who prefers to go unnamed); that SF authors in Iran are positively *obsessed* with both evolution and the person of Charles Darwin, so this goes far beyond Iraj Fazel Bakhsheshi's writings, one of Iran's top SF authors as he is. Iran's most widely published SF author, Zoha Kazemi, also incorporates evolution into some of her works, most prominently in her novel *Rain Born* (2020), about a post-apocalyptic future where global warming leads to mass flooding.[68] Women who give birth at sea gradually begin to make babies naturally adapted to life in the water, and a penultimate scene in the story has dolphins kidnapping and suckling the baby of the hero and heroine. While a dystopian novel, with a new saviour religion and priesthood taking over in this post-apocalyptic world, the new faith does actually worship and revere nature with prophecies about the said dolphins. Nature is getting its revenge against the technological arrogance of man (the melting of the ice caps), and evolution is one of its tools, so to speak. Admittedly Darwin isn't entirely kosher in the Sunnī Arab world of today, but nonetheless, we have spiritual credentials that put us on more or less the same path. Sunnīs also aren't as radical as Shīʿīs when it comes to religious pluralism, but we do recognize Christianity and Judaism as Godly faiths, so extending this mentality to the stars above is not – and *has* not been – that much of a leap of faith either, as evidenced earlier by Sunnī Arab authors.

65 Aysha, 'Foucault's Iran and Islamic Identity Politics', 387.
66 Please see Bayrakdar, 'Al-Jahiz and the Rise of'; Kéchichian, 'The Father'. For other evolutionary thinkers in Islamic history please see El-Daly, *Egyptology*, 115.
67 El-Daly, 'Cairo Lecture'.
68 Aysha, 'Zoha Kazemi on the Cybernetic Ties'.

Evolution plays a role in this, too, as evidenced by the Indonesian novel *The Trinil Gate* (2014) by Riawani Elyta and Syila Fatar. The story combines prehistory – Pithecanthropus erectus of East Java – and ufology, since the long-lost Pythe nation makes a comeback, returning to Earth from outer space after eons to reclaim their divine birth right and wipe out the Homo sapiens.[69] (Remember *A Message Older than Time*?) Also worth mentioning is Uzbek author Hamid Ismailov and his SF novel *Of Strangers and Bees* (2019), which focuses on the future adventures of Muslim philosopher, medical doctor and Sufi mystic Ibn Sīnā (Avicenna), after he discovers the Elixir of Life. And Ibn Sīnā was the original author of *Ḥayy ibn Yaqẓān*, prior to Ibn Ṭufail, as Mr Ismailov kindly reminds us.[70]

Returning to Egyptian SF, Ḥusām ʿAbd al-Ḥamīd Al-Zambīlī has a new novel, set on Mars, and it is positively teaming with intelligence other than man. Two AI robots migrate to Mars before the human protagonists because they're smarter than humans and have more volition than them. There are crystalline alien intelligence on the red planet – non-organic life forms as in *Man Under Zero* or evolving mud as in *Ḥayy* – and this curious verse from the holy Qurʾān: 'Indeed, We have dignified the children of Adam, carried them on land and sea, granted them good and lawful provisions, and privileged them far above many of Our creatures.'[71] As Dr Al-Zambīlī insists, the verse says God preferred man to 'much' of what He created, not *all* of what He created.[72]

## A concluding word

Islam's theological flexibility in the face of extraterrestrial life is almost a fact acknowledged, of all places, in Western SF itself. We saw a little of this in Blaze Ward's story, but a more substantive example can be found in Harlan Ellison's '*Hadj*', where Earth falls under the purview of a superior alien race. The Earth government sends a roguish tycoon, Wilson Herber, to negotiate terms on their behalf and to prove to the alien masters that humans are their equals – if not inherently superior. The captain of Herber's ship, interestingly, is a Muslim, and he draws his own (religious) comparisons with what is happening:

69 Elyta, 'Raising the Elements', 226–7.
70 Ismailov, 'Hamid Ismailov', 219.
71 Q. 17:70.
72 Al-Zambīlī, WhatsApp message.

The Moslem nodded. He was a huge man, yet he gave the impression of compression, efficiency. And nobility. 'This is almost like a hadj, Mr. Herber.'

'Eh? Hadj? Which is?'

'What my people long ago called a pilgrimage to Mecca, the holy city. Now here we are, the first humans to make the pilgrimage to the new Mecca . . .'

Herber cut him off. 'Listen, old son; just remember this: *we're* the chosen people. Earth is the center, no matter *what* they think. As good as them, probably better: quicker, stronger, cleverer. And they know it, too. Take my word for it. Otherwise they wouldn't have come all that way to solicit us. They came to *us*, remember? They gave us the invitation, not the other way around. So get all those old subservient hadj ideas out of your head. Proud, my boy, be proud. We're coming to establish diplomatic relations, to show them how it should be done.'[73]

These italics are in the original text, mind you. In the end, however, the Muslim's subservient hajj ideas turn out to be correct as they are politely told:

And the answer came back, already translated into English for them. It filled the cabin of the starship that had been built with the science of the Masters for these humans who had come a great distance as equals:

*Please go around to the service entrance. Please go around to the service entrance. Please go around.*[74]

Need we say more?

## Acknowledgements

Special thanks to Farzad, Wāʾil and ʿAmmār.

## Bibliography

Al Hosni, Manar. 'Black Magic and Djinn in Omani Literature: Examining the Myths and Reality'. In *Arab and Muslim Science Fiction: Critical Essays*, edited by Hosam A. Ibrahim Elzembely and Emad El-Din Aysha, 185–93. Jefferson: McFarland, 2022.

Al-Miṣrī, ʿAmmār. *Cultural Salon for the Egyptian Society for Science Fiction*, Nasr City, Egypt, 27 December 2019.

[73] Ellison, '*Hadj*', 114.
[74] Ibid., 116.

Al-Miṣrī, ʿAmmār. *Ṣadma Kawniyya: Al-Malāk al-Aswad*. Al-Qāhira: Dār al-Kanzī lil-Nashr wa-l-Tawzīʿ, 2021.

Al-Shārūnī, Yūsuf. *Al-Khayāl al-ʿIlmī fī al-Adab al-ʿArabī al-Muʿāṣir: Ḥattā Nihāyat al-Qarn al-ʿIshrīn*. Al-Qāhirah: al-Hayʾa al-Miṣriyya al-ʿĀmma lil-Kitāb, 2002.

Al-Yāsīn, Muḥammad. Facebook message, 9 September 2021.

Al-Zambīlī, Ḥusām ʿAbd al-Ḥamīd. *Al-Kawkab al-ʿAjīb: Awwal Ḥiwār maʿa Fayrūs ʿĀqil*. Al-Qāhira: Jamāʿat al-Wasaṭiyya, 2001.

Al-Zambīlī, Ḥusām ʿAbd al-Ḥamīd. *Anṣāf al-Bashar*. Al-Qāhira: Jamāʿat al-Wasaṭiyya, 2001.

Al-Zambīlī, Ḥusām ʿAbd al-Ḥamīd. WhatsApp message, 13 November 2022.

Ali-Karamali, Shaista P. and Fionna Dunne. 'The Ijtihad Controversy'. *Arab Law Quarterly* 9, no. 3 (1994): 238–57.

Asa, Robert. 'Classic *Star Trek* and the Death of God: A Case Study of "Who Mourns for Adonis?"' In *Star Trek and Sacred Ground: Explorations of Star Trek, Religion, and American Culture*, edited by Jennifer E. Porter and Darcee L. McLaren, 33–59. Albany: State University of New York Press, 1999.

Aysha, Emad El-Din. 'Better Late than Never: The Transmutations of Egyptian SF in the Work of Hosam El-Zembely'. *Foundation: The International Review of Science Fiction* 47, no. 3 (2018): 6–14.

Aysha, Emad El-Din. 'Egypt as a Test Case for Gender in Arabic Science Fiction'. *SFRA Review* 51, no. 1 (2021): 28–37.

Aysha, Emad El-Din. 'Foucault's Iran and Islamic Identity Politics beyond Civilizational Clashes, External and Internal'. *International Studies Perspectives* 7, no. 4 (2006): 377–94.

Aysha, Emad El-Din. 'Science Fiction by, about, and *for* Arabs: Case Studies in De-Orientalising the Western Imagination'. *ReOrient* 6, no. 1 (2020): 4–19.

Aysha, Emad El-Din. 'Zoha Kazemi on the Cybernetic Ties that Bind Iranian and Arab Science Fiction'. *The Levant*, 18 September 2022. https://theliberum.com/zoha-kazemi-on-the-cybernetic-ties-that-bind-iranian-and-arab-science-fiction/

Bakhsheshi, Iraj Fazel. Personal email, dated 6 September 2021.

Barlow, Aaron. *How Much Does Chaos Scare You? Politics, Religion, and Philosophy in the Fiction of Philip K. Dick*. Lulu.com, 2005.

Bayrakdar, Mehmet. 'Al-Jahiz and the Rise of Biological Evolution'. *Ankara Üniversitesi İlahiyat Fakültesi Dergisi* 27, no. 1 (1986): 307–15.

Beswick, Norman. 'Glimpses of Ecclesiastical Space'. *Foundation: The International Review of Science Fiction* 53 (1991): 24–36.

Boonstra, John. 'Final Interview with Philip K. Dick (part 1)'. *Rod Serling's The Twilight Zone Magazine* 2, no. 3 (1982): 47–52.

Campbell, Ian. 'False Gods and Libertarians: Artificial Intelligence and Community in Aḥmad 'Abd al-Salām al-Baqqāli's *The Blue Flood* and Heinlein's *The Moon is a Harsh Mistress*'. *Science Fiction Studies* 44, no. 1 (2017): 43–64.

Campbell, Ian. 'Science Fiction and Social Criticism in Morocco of the 1970s: Muhammad Aziz Lahbabi's *The Elixir of Life*'. *Science Fiction Studies* 42, no. 1 (2015): 42–55.

Crone, Patricia. *From Kavād to al-Ghazālī: Religion, Law and Political Thought in the Near East, c.600-c.1100*. Aldershot: Ashgate Variorum, 2005.

Defilippo, Joseph G. 'Aristotle's Identification of the Prime Mover as God'. *The Classical Quarterly* 44, no. 2 (1994): 393–409.

Determann, Jörg Matthias. *Islam, Science Fiction and Extraterrestrial Life: The Culture of Astrobiology in the Muslim World*. London: I.B. Tauris, 2021.

El-Daly, Okasha. 'Cairo Lecture: Medieval Arabic Scholars and Ancient Egyptian Hieroglyphs'. American Research Center in Egypt, Garden City, Cairo, 12 October 2022.

El-Daly, Okasha. *Egyptology: The Missing Millennium, Ancient Egypt in Medieval Arabic Writings*. London: UCL Press, 2005.

El-Zein, Amira. *Islam, Arabs, and the Intelligent World of the Jinn*. New York: Syracuse University Press, 2017.

Ellison, Harlan. '*Hadj*'. In *Microcosmic Tales: 100 Wondrous Science Fiction Short-Short Stories*, edited by Isaac Asimov, Martin H. Greenberg and Joseph D. Olander, 111–16. New York: Taplinger, 1980.

Elyta, Riawani. 'Raising the Elements of Locality and the Moral Story in SF: An Attempt to Make SF a Classy Genre in Indonesia'. In *Arab and Muslim Science Fiction: Critical Essays*, edited by Hosam A. Ibrahim Elzembely and Emad El-Din Aysha, 325–30. Jefferson: McFarland, 2022.

Ferré, Frederick and R. Ferré. 'In Praise of Anthropomorphism'. *International Journal for Philosophy of Religion* 16, no. 3 (1984): 203–12.

Goldberg, Ellis. 'Smashing Idols and the State: The Protestant Ethic and Egyptian Sunnī Radicalism'. *Comparative Studies in Society and History* 33, no. 1 (1991): 3–35.

Hoogvelt, Ankie. *Globalisation and the Postcolonial World: The New Political Economy of Development*. Basingstoke: Macmillan, 1997.

Hoskin, Michael. 'Astronomy in Antiquity'. In *The Cambridge Illustrated History of Astronomy*, edited by Michael Hoskin, 18–49. Cambridge: Cambridge University Press, 1997.

Hrotic, Steven. *Religion in Science Fiction: The Evolution of an Idea and the Extinction of a Genre*. London: Bloomsbury, 2014.

Ismailov, Hamid. 'Hamid Ismailov on the Remnants of Central Asian Fantasy and Science Fiction'. In *Arab and Muslim Science Fiction: Critical Essays*, edited by Hosam A. Ibrahim Elzembely and Emad El-Din Aysha, 217–29. Jefferson: McFarland, 2022.

Jacob, James R. and Margaret C. Jacob. 'The Anglican Origins of Modern Science: The Metaphysical Foundations of the Whig Constitution'. *Isis* 71, no. 2 (1980): 251–67.

Jannessari-Ladani, Zahra. 'An Eye on the Past, an Eye on the Future: Charting an Independent Course for Iranian SF'. In *Arab and Muslim Science Fiction: Critical Essays*, edited by Hosam A. Ibrahim Elzembely and Emad El-Din Aysha, 124–40. Jefferson: McFarland, 2022.

Kéchichian, Joseph A. 'The Father of the Theory of Evolution'. *Gulf News*, 27 September 2012. https://gulfnews.com/general/the-father-of-the-theory-of-evolution-1.1079209

Khafājī, Muḥammad ʿAbd al-Munʿim. *Al-Adab fī al-Turāth al-Ṣūfī*. Al-Qāhirah: Maktabat Gharīb, 1980.

Khan, Sami Ahmad. 'The Indian Recipe for Good Science Fiction: Technology, Politics, and Religion'. In *Arab and Muslim Science Fiction: Critical Essays*, edited by Hosam A. Ibrahim Elzembely and Emad El-Din Aysha, 259–67. Jefferson: McFarland, 2022.

Kinney, Jay. 'The Political Gnosis of Philip K. Dick'. *New Dawn Magazine*, 2002. https://www.newdawnmagazine.com/articles/the-political-gnosis-of-philip-k-dick

Linford, Peter. 'Deeds of Power – Respect for Religion *in Star Trek: Deep Space 9*'. In *Star Trek and Sacred Ground: Explorations of Star Trek, Religion, and American Culture*, edited by Jennifer E. Porter and Darcee L. McLaren, 77–100. Albany: State University of New York Press, 1999.

Matthew, Robert. *Japanese Science Fiction: A View of a Changing Society*. London: Routledge and Nissan Institute of Japanese Studies, University of Oxford, 1989.

McClymont, John D. 'Reading between the Lines: Aristotle's Views on Religion'. *Acta Classica* 53 (2010): 33–48.

Melchert, Christopher. 'Aḥmad Ibn Ḥanbal and the Qurʾān'. *Journal of Qurʾānic Studies* 6, no. 2 (2004): 22–34.

Mottahedeh, Roy. *The Mantle of the Prophet: Religion and Politics in Iran*. New York: Simon and Schuster, 1985.

Rāghib, Nabīl. *Zawāj al-ʿIlm wa-l-Adab*. Al-Qāhira: Maktabat al-Usra, 1998.

Robinson, John Mansley. *An Introduction to Early Greek Philosophy: The Chief Fragments and Ancient Testimony, with Connecting Commentary*. Boston: Houghton Mifflin, 1968.

Rose, Steve. 'The Pope has said that he would Baptise a Martian – But would they Want Our Religions?' *The Guardian*, 14 May 2014. https://www.theguardian.com/science/shortcuts/2014/may/14/pope-francis-baptise-martian-would-they-want-our-religions

Ṣalāḥ, Ḥusām. *Cultural Salon for the Egyptian Society for Science Fiction*, Nasr City, Egypt, 24 June 2022.

Sedgwick, Mark. *Against the Modern World: Traditionalism and the Secret Intellectual History of the Twentieth Century*. Oxford: Oxford University Press, 2004.

Shapin, Steven. *The Scientific Revolution*. Chicago: University of Chicago Press, 1996.

Shariati, Ali. *Marxism and Other Western Fallacies: An Islamic Critique*. Translated by R. Campbell. Preface by Hamid Algar. Berkeley: Mizan Press, 1980.

Simkins, Ronald A. 'The Bible and Anthropocentrism: Putting Humans in their Place'. *Dialectical Anthropology* 38, no. 4 (2014): 397–413.

Sturgeon, Theodore. 'Science Fiction, Morals, and Religion'. In *Science Fiction Today and Tomorrow: A Discursive Symposium*, edited by Reginald Bretnor, 98–115. New York: Harper, 1974.

Ward, Blaze. Facebook message, dated 5 September 2021.

WION Web Team. 'NASA is Hiring Priests to Prepare Humans for Contact with Aliens'. *WION*, 27 December 2021. https://www.wionews.com/science/nasa-is-hiring-priests-to-prepare-humans-for-contact-with-aliens-440433

Yalcinkaya, M. Alper. 'Science as an Ally of Religion: A Muslim Appropriation of "The Conflict Thesis"'. *British Journal for the History of Science* 44, no. 2 (2011): 161–81.

# Index

Page numbers followed with "n" refer to endnotes.


Ibn ʿAbbās 31–2, 32 n.20, 52, 69 n.47, 72, 73 n.63, 76, 88 n.6, 103 n.67, 119, 121, 122, 122 n.41, 122 n.42, 123–5, 132 n.89, 183
ʿAbbās, Ibrāhīm 208
ʿAbd al-Raḥīm, Maḥmūd 208
Ibn Abī al-ʿIzz, ʿAlī 99, 106, 109
Ibn Abī Rabāḥ, Aṭāʾ 123, 126
Ibn Abī Ṭālib, ʿAlī 60, 71
Ibn Abī Ṭālib, Makkī 118 n.18
Abū al-Ḍuḥā 31–2, 73 n.63
Abū al-Suʿūd, Muḥammad ibn Muḥammad 34, 38, 48 n.18, 51, 52, 63, 65, 183, 199
Adam 15, 18, 31, 35, 44, 53, 72, 73, 101, 179–82, 214
  Children of 88 n.6, 103, 117 n.13, 128, 185, 196, 225
  creation of 53, 69, 97–9, 181, 183–5, 188, 207–8
    angels' question 183–5
  descendants 97, 98, 103, 104, 106, 107, 121, 123, 144, 181, 184–6, 188
  and Eve 69, 70, 75
  physical appearance 183–4
  succession 97–9
  uniqueness of 181
Adamic exceptionalism 144
Adamski, George 182, 183
*Akwān* 210
Alam, Munazza 2–5, 8
*ʿālamīn* 117, 117 n.10, 119, 123
alchemy 211, 220, 222, 224
Alien Folklore 186
aliens 159–60
  creatures 69–70, 81–3
  intelligent 167–9, 172
  race 207, 209, 210
  religious beliefs 207
  *vs.* jinn 196
Allah 35, 37, 38, 49, 51, 53, 65, 75, 163, 216. See also God
  creation of seven heavens 72
Al-Ālūsī, Maḥmūd ibn ʿAbd Allāh 33, 63
Amin, Ma'ruf 176
Al-Andalusī, Abū Ḥayyān Athīr al-Dīn 62, 122 n.42
angels 10 n.46, 15–17, 28, 33, 36, 37, 51–3, 55, 61, 64, 74, 98–100, 117 n.13, 118, 119, 121, 126, 126 n.59, 127–31, 141, 144, 161–2, 179–80, 182–5, 188, 208
  in Christianity 162, 164
  God's creation of 75
  in heavens 121
  jinn and 161–2, 164, 165
  in Judaism 162
  Qurʾānic verses (Q. 16:8) 51–3
  superiority 147–8, 153
animals 117 n.13
  earthly 62
  of Hell 64
  and insects of Earthly sky 62–3
  of Paradise 63–4
anthropocentrism 214–16
anthropology 12, 18, 139, 153
anthropomorphism 214–16
Ibn ʿArabī 35, 163, 165
archangels 74–5
*al-arḍ* (Earth) 185, 187, 189
Aristotle 213–14
Asad, Muḥammad 189
Al-Ashʿarī, Abū al-Ḥasan 89
Ashʿarī doctrine 89–93, 103, 104, 106, 108–11, 142, 143, 152, 181, 197
  about God 150–1
  problem of evil 150–1
Ibn ʿĀshūr, Ṭāhir 194, 199

'Assassin' (Ward) 215, 216
Al-Asqalānī, Ibn Ḥajar 128 n.69, 129 n.73, 130 n.74
astrobiological evil 150, 151
Astrobiology 4
defined 6
exotheology and 10–13
and extraterrestrials 6–10
Atonement 145, 146, 153
Bakhsheshi, Iraj Fazel 222–4
Banī Adam hypothesis (BAH) 184–9
Al-Bāqir, Muḥammad ibn ʿAlī 69, 70
Al-Bārizī, Sharaf al-Dīn 129
*baththa* (*spread*) 67
Al-Baydāwī, ʿAbd Allāh 48 n.18, 49–51, 97–8, 100, 104, 108, 183
Al-Bayhaqī, Abū Bakr Aḥmad ibn al-Ḥusayn 31–2, 31 n.15, 32 n.20, 73 n.63, 122 n.42
Al-Bazdawī, Abū al-Yusr 105

Bible 145, 186, 212, 214
Bigelow, Robert 177
biological living creatures 64–5
*The Black Angel* (Al-Miṣrī) 208, 221
Blonds 182

Christianity 5, 18, 171, 205, 207, 216–19, 224
angels in 162, 164
conflicts in ETI (*see* extraterrestrial intelligent (ETI) life (ETI): conflicts in Christianity)
and extra-terrestrial intelligence 11
folk 171
and Islam 12, 17, 19, 218
Jesus Christ in 11
and Judaism, jinn as model for 170–1
theological doctrines 145–7, 153
cities, extrasolar 71, 82
civilization 73, 82, 186–8
Islamic 217, 218
Clarke, Arthur C. 207
class of beings 128, 130, 131
intelligent beings 90
moral accountability 87 n.1, 88, 90–4, 99, 108, 111
rational beings 91, 92, 109, 111
contingency 27–8
contingent things
of existence 28–30
of non-existence 29, 30
in revelation 29–30
creation
of Adam 53, 69, 97–9, 181, 183–5, 188, 207–8
angels 51–3, 55
of Earth 55, 62, 69
God 46, 48–50, 48 n.18, 53, 69–75, 82, 117–20, 123, 179, 181
of heavens 62, 73
and Earth 55
in Hellfire 51
living creatures on Earth 50
name and description of 54
in Paradise 51
sentient creatures 53–4
*The Creed of Tahawi* (*al-ʿAqīda al-Ṭaḥāwiyya*, Al-Tahawī) 104, 106, 107, 109, 145
Cremo, Michael 185–6
Crick, Francis 143

*dābba* 62–7, 82, 189–90, 195, 199
communication with humans 192
defined 193
hypothesis 189–94, 197
as intelligent being 190–1, 194, 198
meaning of 190, 194
race of 192
as species 193
story of Prophet Solomon's death 191–2, 194
translated as '*hewan melata*' 190
*dābbat al-arḍ* 192, 195
El-Daly, Okasha 220, 222
Al-Dārimī, Abū Saʿīd 123
Darwaza, Muḥammad ʿIzzat 67
Darwin, Charles 223, 224
Davies, Paul 11
Dawkins, Richard 142
Day of Judgement (*yawm al-qiyāma*) 16, 60, 61, 63, 67, 74, 75, 77, 78, 83, 98, 104, 147, 192, 221
place and oneness of 79–81
Day of Resurrection 103, 106
del Rey, Lester 207, 213

demons 162
Determann, Jörg Matthias 12–13, 210, 211
Al-Dhahabī, Shams al-Dīn 122 n.42
Ibn Di'āma, Qatāda 50, 121
discretion 16, 111
Drake equation 8–10

Earth
 classical views on 116–23
 creation of 55, 62, 69
  God' s 117, 123
 *khalīfa* on 179, 181, 182, 184, 185, 188, 189
 life on 50, 143
 Prophet's message 125–6
 seven/several 72–3, 120–2, 122 n.43, 124–5, 144
 successor (*khalīfa*) on, Q 2.30 97–9
 walking creatures 33–4
end of the world 74–6
eschatology 5, 15, 60, 61, 147
 extraterrestrials and 74–83
eternal life 146
Eternal Maidens 130
Eternal Paradise 130, 130 n.81
ethics 217
ETI life. *See* extraterrestrial intelligent (ETI) life
evidential problem of evil 148–9
evil
 existence of 149
 problem of 148–51
evolution 6, 18, 142, 143, 150, 222–5
 Islam and 144
 theory 139, 142, 185–6, 200, 224
exegetical register 96
existence
 of contingent things 28–30
 of evil 149
 of extraterrestrial intelligent (ETI) life 6, 10–12, 15, 26–30, 33–5, 37 39, 43–6, 50, 55–6, 59–61, 65, 67, 68, 72, 79–81, 83, 139–40, 144, 159, 167, 172, 176, 194
 God 91, 103, 142–3, 149, 159, 212, 217
 of a necessary being 27–8
 of several Earths 120–2
 of walking creatures 33–4
exoplanet (extrasolar planet) 1–2, 4, 6, 8, 43, 45–6, 82, 143
exotheology 140, 205–6, 213, 220
 and Astrobiology 10–13
 Islamic 12–13
 Muslim contributions to 221–5
 Western and Arab science fiction 18, 206–12
extrasolar cities 71, 82
extraterrestrial intelligence
 and jinn 166–8
 living creatures 70, 71
extraterrestrial intelligent (ETI) life 10–15, 25–6
 conflicts in Christianity 17, 140–1, 153
  Islamic doctrine 145–7
  Islamic scripture 143–5
  Islamic tradition 147–8
  Muslim narrative 151–2
  problem of evil 148–51
  theism 142–3
 defined 28
 eschatological salvation of 147
 existence of 6, 10–12, 15, 26–30, 33–5, 37, 39, 43–6, 50, 55–6, 59–61, 65, 67, 68, 72, 79–81, 83, 139–40, 144, 159, 167, 172, 176, 194
 Islamic 11, 13, 39
 mass-energy 26
 metaphysical reasoning 26–9, 33, 39
 publications 12–13
 Qur'ānic verses on 30, 33–4, 44
 Al-Rāzī, Fakhr al-Dīn 54–5
 revelatory reasoning 26, 29–39
 scientific information on 26, 34, 39
 scientific reasoning 27, 39–40
 Sunnī scholarly tradition 35–8
 theological information on 25, 26, 29, 31, 34–6, 39
extraterrestrial life
 defined 6
 discovery of 11–12
extraterrestrials 6–10, 54
 civilizations 9–10
 eschatology 74–82
 identity of 199

intelligent 65–6, 159–60, 170–1
in narrations (ḥadīth) 68–74, 82
in Qurʾān 61–8, 81–2

faith 217, 218
Abrahamic 161, 162, 171
Fall 145, 146, 153, 214. *See also* Atonement; Incarnation
fallen angel 162, 162 n.12
Al-Farrāʾ, Yaḥyā ibn Ziyād 62
Fermi's Paradox 9–10
*fīhimā* 55
first human 181, 183, 184, 186
forbidden 110
tree of knowledge 145
*For I am a Jealous People!* (del Rey) 207, 213
free will 162, 166–8, 195, 215
free-willed beings 191, 195, 196
The Frequented House (*al-bayt al-maʿmūr*) 118
Ibn Fūrak, Muḥammad 100

Al-Ghazālī, Abū Ḥāmid 45, 90–1, 94, 150, 197
Al-Ghaznawī, Abū Ḥafṣ Sirāj al-Dīn 105, 109
gigantic goats 63
God
Ashʿarī theology about 150–1
creation 30, 33–5, 37–8, 46, 48–50, 48 n.18, 53, 69–75, 82, 117–20, 123, 181
of Adam 181, 183–5, 207–8
heavens and Earth 117, 123
*khalīfa* 179
living creatures on Earth 50
non-human/non-jinn being 119
sentient creatures 53–4
universality of Islam 124
creative ability 117, 119
destruction of this universe 70–1, 74
domains of existence of 117, 119
existence 91, 103, 142–3, 149, 159, 212, 217
honouring of human beings by 37–9, 39 n.41
morally accountable to believe in 90–1
omni- 148–9, 151
replacing the humans 117, 119
revealed inspiration 126
revelation 88, 90–2, 94, 126
spread of creatures 117, 118 n.18
unseen matters 89, 93–5, 97, 111
wisdom 91, 111, 151–2, 184

ḥadīth 15, 44, 45, 47, 51–4, 56, 76, 77, 79, 82, 96, 118, 120, 127, 127 n.68, 130, 132, 132 n.88, 133, 143–5, 151, 161, 163, 192, 197, 220
anomalous 31, 33
chain of transmission 32, 54
critics 31, 32
extraterrestrials in 68–74, 82
inauthentic 32
narration 68–74
seven Earths 30–3, 144
*Hadj* (Ellison) 225–6
Haider, Shahbaz 12
*The Half-Humans* (Al-Zambīlī) 209, 217
Ibn Ḥammūsh, Makkī 64–5, 81
extraterrestrials in 68–74
Ḥanafī school 16, 89
Ibn Ḥanbal, Aḥmad 89
Ḥanbalī school 16, 89
Ḥaqqī, Ismāʿīl 122, 122 n.41, 122 n.43, 199
Harvey, Ramon 104
Ḥawwā, Saʿīd 67, 198
Al-Haytamī, Aḥmad ibn Ḥajar 32
*Ḥayy ibn Yaqẓān* 222
Ibn Ḥazm, Abū Muḥammad 117 n.13, 130 n.80
heavens 33, 130. *See also* Earth: angels; jinn
angels in 121
classical views on 116–23
creation of 55, 62, 73, 117, 123
living things in 34
sacred space 118–19
seven 33, 63, 72–3, 75, 117, 119, 120
walking creatures in 33–4
Heinlein, Robert 207
heliocentrism 214
Hell 60, 61, 75, 80, 82, 83. *See also* Paradise
animals of 64

coexistence with extraterrestrials in 78–9, 83
intactness of 76–8
oneness or multiplicity of 77–8, 83
Hellfire 15, 30, 44
creations in 51
Qurʾānic verses (Q. 16:8) 51
hermeneutical strategy 200
Jinn hypothesis (JH) 197
man hypothesis 193
smart *dābba* hypothesis (SDH) 191–2
hermeneutics 109, 152, 197
legal 95–6
Qurʾānic 177
honouring of human beings 37–9, 39 n.41
Hoogvelt, Ankie 216
*Houston, Do We Have a Problem? Extraterrestrial Intelligent Life and Christian Belief* (McIntosh and McNabb) 17, 140
human beings 65–6, 161–2, 167
Aristotle's definition of 168 n.36
jinn and 107–8, 161–2, 164, 192, 195, 197
specialness 168
superiority 147–8, 153
uniqueness 88, 181

Iblīs (Satan) 15, 44, 53, 78 n.72, 102, 121, 162, 162 n.12, 182, 193, 208, 213
Iblīs trickery hypothesis (ITH) 196–7
Ignorance 101, 102
*ijtihād* 218
Incarnation 145–6, 153
Indonesian Ulema Council (MUI) 176
injustice 101–2
innate disposition 92, 105, 106
insects, in the sky 63
intelligence 4, 10 n.46, 108, 111, 124, 126–30, 142, 148, 159, 161, 166, 167, 167 n.33, 171, 180, 192, 215, 216, 223, 225
of *dābba* 192
higher 127, 129
intelligent aliens 167–9, 172
intelligent beings 31, 37, 131, 182, 185, 191–5, 198
class 90, 115, 135
non-human 16, 28, 33, 115, 132
moral responsibility 126–9
intelligent extraterrestrial life (IEL). *See* extraterrestrial intelligent (ETI) life
invisible realm *versus* different planets 168–70
Iqbal, Muzaffar 12, 147, 148, 153
Iran 223–4
and Shīʿism 224
Al-Iṣfahānī, Abū Nuʿaym 54
Al-Iṣfahānī, al-Rāghib 189
Islam 5, 10 n.46, 13, 18, 44, 160, 161, 169, 170, 172, 205, 215–17, 223
Christianity and 12, 17, 19, 218
and evolution 144
narrative tradition 73
Prophet's message of 116, 124–5
Sunnī 15, 44
and ufology 200
universality in God's creation 124
Islamic
civilization 217, 218
doctrine 145–7
law, for moral personhood 109–10
moral responsibility 126–9
scripture 143–5, 147, 151, 152
Islamic UFO 17–18, 176–8, 199–200
Banī Adam hypothesis (BAH) 184–9
hermeneutical strategy 178
*Iblīs* trickery hypothesis (ITH) 196–7
Jinn hypothesis (JH) 195–8
man hypothesis 192–5
permanent *ghayb* hypothesis (PGH) 198–9
pre-Adamic hypothesis (PAH) 179–84
smart *dābba* hypothesis (SDH) 189–94
*Isrāfīl*, blow of 74–6
*Isrāʾīlīyāt* 53

Ibn Jabr, Mujāhid 194
Al-Jāḥiẓ, Abū ʿUthman ʿAmr ibn Baḥr 224
James Webb Space Telescope (JWST) 8, 45, 59, 160
Jesus Christ 11

salvation 145, 146
JH. *See* Jinn hypothesis (JH)
Al-Jīlānī, ʿAbd al-Qādir 162
jinn 10 n.46, 16–18, 28, 36, 61, 70, 78, 79, 81, 90, 97, 98, 110, 117 n.13, 119, 126, 126 n.59, 127–9, 131–3, 133 n.92, 134, 134 n.93, 141, 144, 162 n.12, 169, 182–4, 193, 208–11, 221
- aliens *vs.* 196
- and angels 161–2, 164, 165
- conception and reproduction of 163
- consuming food 163
- extraterrestrial intelligence and 166–8
- and human beings 107–8, 161–2, 164, 192, 195, 197
- killing of 163–4
- materiality 165
- as a model for Christians and Jews 170–1
- moral personhood, Qurʾānic verses 106–8
- Muslim concept of 161–6
- share with angels 165, 166
- share with humans 162, 164, 166
- tribes 163

Jinn hypothesis (JH) 195–8
Judaism 171, 224
- angels in 162

Judgement Day 117, 120
jurisprudence 16, 96, 131, 144, 152
Al-Juwaynī, ʿAbd al-Malik ibn Yūsuf 125
Ibn Juzayy, Muḥammad ibn Aḥmad 65
JWST. *See* James Webb Space Telescope (JWST)

Kaʿba 118, 119, 122
*kalām* 14, 26
Kant, Immanuel 214
Ibn Kathīr, Abū al-Fiḍāʾ 32, 122 n.41, 183, 197
Al-Kawāshī, Muwaffaq al-Dīn Abū al-ʿAbbās 121–3, 126
Kazemi, Zoha 224
*khalīfa*, on Earth 179, 181, 182, 184, 185, 188, 189
Khan, Sami Ahmad 219
Al-Khudrī, Abū Saʿīd 119
Al-Kisāʾī, Muḥammad ibn ʿAlī 162

legal hermeneutics 95–6
life on Earth 143
living creatures 50, 62–7
- biological 64–5
- extraterrestrial intelligent 70–3

logical problem of evil 149

Al-Maḥallī, Jalāl al-Dīn 183
McIntosh, C. A. 17, 140, 150–3
McNabb, Tyler Dalton 17, 140, 150–3
Mahmoud, Mustafa 219
Makārim, Nāṣir 66
Malik, Shoaib Ahmed 13
Mālikī school 16, 89
man hypothesis (MH) 192–5
Manṣūr, Anīs 211
Ibn Manẓūr, Abū al-Fatḥ Muḥammad 198
Al-Marāghī, Aḥmad Muṣṭafā 66
Mårtensson, Ulrika 193
Al-Masʿūd, al-Ḥusayn ibn ʿAlī 163
Al-Māturīdī, Abū Manṣūr 89, 98, 100, 104–6, 127 n.68
Māturīdī school 89–93, 111
Al-Māwardī, Abū al-Ḥasan ʿAlī ibn Muḥammad 16, 48 n.18, 52–4, 115, 120, 121, 124–7, 125 n.55, 127 n.68, 129, 135
- Prophet's message to earthly domain 124–6

Ibn Maymūn, ʿAmr 127–8
means of transportation 198, 199
*A Message Older Than Time* (Bakhsheshi) 222–3
metaphysical reasoning 26–9, 33, 39
MH. *See* man hypothesis (MH)
Al-Miṣrī, ʿAmmār 208–10, 221–2
modernity 66
monkeys 128, 128 n.69
monotheism 212–16
Montaigne, Michel de 214
moral
- evil 149, 150
- realism 90
- responsibility 166
  - for non-human intelligent beings 126–9

moral accountability 126–9, 127 n.68, 166, 168
 of personhood 87 n.1
  Ashʿarī school 89–93, 103–4, 106, 108–11
  class of beings 87 n.1, 88, 90–4, 99, 108, 111
  empirical determination of 90–3
  legal determination of 109–11
  Māturīdī school 89–93, 111
  reason 90–5, 106
  Salafī school 89, 92–3, 96, 106, 111
  scriptural determination of 93–7, 108
  succession (*khilāfa*) on Earth (Q. 2:30) 97–9, 107
  trust (Q. 33:72) 99–103, 107
  witnessing (Q. 7:172) 103–7
morality 217
Al-Mughniyya, Muḥammad Jawād 66
Muḥammad, Prophet 15–16, 29, 31–3, 39 n.41, 44, 45, 52–4, 60, 63, 68, 72, 76, 77, 83, 110, 115, 116, 120–2, 134 n.93, 169, 208
 message to earthly domain, Al-Māwardī 124–6
 *Sharīʿa* of 126 n.59, 129–31, 133, 134
 universality of message 126 n.59, 129–31, 133, 134
  Al-Subkī, Taqī al-Dīn 129–35
  Al-Suyūṭī, Jalāl al-Dīn 129–31, 135
*mukallaf* (morally accountable beings) 16, 60, 126, 126 n.59, 127–9, 132–4
Ibn Munabbih, Wahb 119
Al-Munāwī, Muḥammad ʿAbd al-Raʾūf 35
Al-Musayyib, Saʿīd ibn 119
Muslim narrative 151–2
Mutlu-Pakdil, Burçin 2–3, 19

Nagasawa, Yujin 149–50
narrations
 end of the world 74–6
 extraterrestrials in ḥadīth 68–74, 82
 Muslim 151–2
Al-Nasafī, Abū Barakāt ʿAbd Allāh ibn Aḥmad 48 n.18, 49, 64, 101, 118
Al-Nasafī, Abū al-Ḥafṣ 98, 101, 108
natural evil 149, 150
Noah 185–6
non-existence
 of contingent things 29, 30
 of impossible things 28
non-human rational beings, class of 91–2
non-intelligent extraterrestrial life (NIEL) 10
Nordics 182, 183
Nour Skaf 1–3, 6, 8

obedience 101
obligations 150
omni-God 148–9, 151

PAH. *See* pre-Adamic hypothesis (PAH)
Paradise 15, 30, 37, 44, 51, 60, 61, 75, 78 n.72, 80, 82, 83, 130. *See also* Hell
 animals of 63–4
 coexistence with extraterrestrials in 78–9, 83
 creations in 51
 intactness of 76–8
 oneness or multiplicity of 77–8, 83
 Qurʾānic verses (Q. 16:8) 51
permanent *ghayb* hypothesis (PGH) 198–9
PGH. *See* permanent *ghayb* hypothesis (PGH)
pillar of light 16, 72, 72 n.60, 82
*Planet of the Viruses* (Al-Zambīlī) 217, 221
Plato 214
pre-Adamic hypothesis (PAH) 179–84
primordial covenant 103–6
primordial witnessing 106
problem of evil 148–51
prophetic revelation 52
Protagoras 215, 216
Ptolemy's geocentric model 214

Al-Qāsimī, Jamāl al-Dīn 66, 194
Ibn al-Qayyim al-Jawziyya, Muḥammad ibn Abī Bakr 95, 98–9, 102, 105, 106
Qurʾān 28, 29, 31, 45, 56, 133, 143, 151, 169. *See also* Bible

exegesis 45, 96
extraterrestrials in 61–8, 81–2
on human specialness 36–9
jinn in 165
Qur'ānic verses 15, 45, 132
Day of Judgement (*yawm al-qiyāma*) 16, 60, 61, 79–81
exegetical tradition 45
on existence of extraterrestrial life 30, 33–4, 45–6
The Frequented House (*al-bayt al-ma'mūr*) 118
on heavens 116–18
moral accountability of personhood
jinn 106–8
succession (*khilāfa*) on Earth (Q. 2:30) 97–9
trust (Q. 33:72) 99–103
witnessing (Q. 7:172) 103–6
Q. 2:30 179–85, 188, 189
Q. 2:31 185, 188
Q. 2:32 179–80
Q. 2:33 185, 188
Q. 4:69 78
Q. 6:38 127
Q. 6:130 107
Q. 7:44 78
Q. 7:172 127 n.62
Q. 7:179 107
Q. 8:22 191
Q. 8:55 191
Q. 11:6 192
Q. 11:49 185
Q. 11:56 192
Q. 13:15 190, 192, 193, 195
Q. 14:22 78 n.72
Q. 16:4-8 144
Q.16:4-8 144
Q. 16:5 198
Q. 16:8 33, 44, 46–7, 54, 55, 198, 199
angels 51–3
Hellfire 51
interpretation of 48–54
life on Earth 50
open statement without qualification 48–50
Paradise 51
sentient creatures 53–4
Q. 16:49 190, 191
Q. 17:44 66
Q. 17:70 88 n.7, 117 n.13
Q. 22:18 191
Q. 24:45 191
Q. 27:21 127 n.66
Q. 27.82 192
Q. 29: 60 192
Q. 31:10 192
Q. 34:14 191
Q. 35:15-17 119
Q. 35:24 127
Q. 35:28 191
Q. 37:50 78
Q. 37:55-60 78
Q. 39:68 74–5
Q. 42:29 33, 39, 66–8, 81, 88 n.7, 118, 190, 193, 194, 198, 199
Q. 46:29-32 106
Q. 51:56 107
Q. 55:29 66
Q. 55:31 107, 195, 197
Q. 56:15-16 78
Q. 65:12 72–3, 73 n.63
Q. 72:14 78 n.72
Q. 72:15-16 106
Q. 74:40-42 78
Q. 95:4-6 181
Qurashī, Ayatollah 67
Al-Qurṭubī, Abū 'Abd Allāh Muḥammad ibn Aḥmad 48, 48 n.18, 50–4, 120, 121, 124

Rafsanjānī, Hāshimī 67
Rā'if, Aḥmad 209
rational beings, class of 91–2, 108, 111
Al-Rāzī, Fakhr al-Dīn 33–4, 44, 48 n.18, 52, 54–5, 64, 66, 95, 100, 103, 103 n.64, 104, 107–8, 118, 119, 129, 129 n.73, 184, 194, 197
reason 90–5, 106
reasoning
metaphysical 26–9, 33, 39
revelatory 26, 29–39
scientific 27, 39–40
religion 212, 216–18, 223–4
science and 219
religious pluralism 212, 223, 224
repentance 102, 146
revelation 88, 90–2, 94, 123

revelatory reasoning 26, 29–30, 39
Qur'ān
on human specialness 36–9
verses on extraterrestrial life 33–4
seven-Earths ḥadīth 30–3
Sunnī scholarly tradition 35–6
rhetorical force 38
Al-Rustughfānī, Abū al-Ḥasan 104, 106

Al-Ṣābūnī, Nūr al-Dīn 94
Al-Ṣādiq, Jaʿfar ibn Muḥammad 69–70
Al-Ṣādiqī, Muḥammad 67
Al-Sakhāwī, Shams al-Dīn 122 n.41
Salafī school 89, 92, 93, 96, 106, 111
Ṣalāḥ, Ḥusām 220
Salatun, Raden Jacob 175, 176
Saleh, Walid 200
salvation 11, 116, 145–7, 171, 171 n.37, 223
*samā'* 63
Al-Samarqandī, Naṣr ibn Muḥammad 65, 81
*al-samāwāt* (heavens) 189
Satan 15, 44, 53, 78 n.72, 102, 121, 162, 162 n.12, 182, 193, 208, 213
science fiction (SF) 206
Arab 18, 208, 210–11, 219, 221
Egyptian 211, 219–20, 225
Hindus 219
Muslim 18, 208, 210–11, 221
Western 207–8, 212–14, 216, 217
scientific reasoning 27, 39–40
scriptural silence 144
scripture 45, 108
and moral personhood 93–7, 108
theology and 14–16
SDH. *See* smart *dābba* hypothesis (SDH)
search for extraterrestrial intelligence (SETI) 6–8
secularism 206, 212, 213
sense of humour 167, 167 n.34
sentient creatures 53–4
SETI. *See* search for extraterrestrial intelligence (SETI)
seven Earths 72–3, 120–2, 122 n.43, 124–5, 144
ḥadīth 30–3
seven heavens 33, 63, 72–3, 75, 117, 119–20
SF. *See* science fiction (SF)
Shāfiʿī school 16, 89, 128, 131
Shapin, Steven 214
Al-Shaʿrāwī, Muḥammad Mutawallī 198
*Sharīʿa* 126 n.59, 129–31, 133, 134, 147
Shariati, Ali 223
Sharīf, Nihād 211
Al-Shiblī, Badr al-Dīn 126 n.60
Shihab, Quraisy 179, 200
Shīʿī 12, 15, 60, 68, 79, 82, 83, 123, 123 n.49, 161, 161 n.6
Shīʿism 16, 60, 221, 224
Al-Shirbīnī, al-Khaṭīb 35
Al-Shirbīnī, Muḥammad ibn Aḥmad 63
*shūrā* 209, 217
sin 145, 146
Skaf, Nour 1–4
smart *dābba* hypothesis (SDH) 189–94
Solomon, Prophet 127, 127 n.66, 191, 208
death 191–2, 194
souls 4, 11, 35, 52, 76, 78, 78 n.72, 88, 94, 105, 146 n.41, 195, 221
of believers and disbelievers 76, 78, 82
human 78, 83
immortal 88
intelligent aliens 159, 168, 172
jinn 168
Paradise and Hell 76, 78, 83
spiritualism 219, 222
spirituality 11
Sturgeon, Theodore 206–7, 213
Al-Subkī, Taqī al-Dīn 16, 115, 116, 129, 132 n.88
universality of Prophet's message 129–35
succession (*khilāfa*), on Earth (Q. 2:30) 97–9
Sufism 161, 212, 215, 221–2
Sulaymān, Muqātil ibn 182, 188
Sunnī 16, 25, 26, 60, 82, 83, 161, 161 n.6
ḥadīth tradition 15
Islam 14–15, 44, 89, 105
ten classic exegetical works in 47–54
*kalām* 14, 26
scholarly tradition 26, 29, 31, 32, 34, 37–8
on human specialness 35–6

*Sūrat al-Naḥl* (Q. 16:8) 54, 56
*Sūrat al-Shūrā* (Q. 42:29) 55
Al-Suyūṭī, Jalāl al-Dīn 16, 31–2, 31 n.16, 115, 126 n.59, 129–31, 129 n.73, 135, 183
  universality of Prophet's message 129–31, 135
systemic problem of evil 149–50

Al-Ṭabarānī, Sulaymān ibn Aḥmad 64, 81
Al-Ṭabarī, Abū Jaʿfar ibn Jarīr 183, 194
Al-Ṭabarsī, Faḍl ibn Ḥasan 64, 65, 81
*tafsīr* 62–3, 177, 178, 182–4, 188, 189, 194, 197, 200
Al-Ṭaḥāwī, Abū Jaʿfar Aḥmad 104, 106, 107, 109, 145
Ṭanṭāwī, Muḥammad Sayyid 199
*tawaqquf* 50, 68, 95, 105
Ibn Taymiyya, Taqī ad-Dīn Aḥmad 89, 92, 94, 95, 97–9, 101, 102, 105, 110, 164
Al-Thaʿālibī, ʿAbd al-Raḥmān ibn Muḥammad 65
*thaqalān* 195–7
theism 142–3
theological hermeneutics 95–6
theology, and scripture 14–16
theory of evolution 139, 142, 185, 186, 200, 224
Al-Ṭībī, al-Ḥusayn ibn ʿAbd Allāh 48 n.18, 51
trust (Q. 33:72) 99–103
Al-Turkistānī, Shujāʿ al-Dīn 105, 107, 109

ufology 177, 192, 193, 197
  Islam and 200
ufonauts, identity of 199, 200
unidentified flying objects (UFOs) 17, 175–6
  Islamic (*see* Islamic UFO)
universe 1, 37, 69 n.51, 70, 70 n.55, 75, 88 n.7, 185
  contingency of
  destruction of 70–1, 74
  end of the 74–6
  God's creation of 75, 82
  metaphysical 27
  Ptolemy's geocentric model of 214
universe as contingent 27
unseen (*ghayb*) matters 89, 93–5, 97, 111, 198–9

Vallée, Jacques 197
visible realm 169
volition 16, 90, 101, 111

Ward, Blaze 211, 216, 225
Winter, Tim 151
witnessing (Q. 7:172) 103–6

Al-Yāsīn, Muḥammad 206

Al-Zajjāj, Ibrāhīm ibn al-Sarī 62
Al-Zamakhsharī, Abū al-Qāsim 118, 118 n.18, 119, 123, 194, 197, 199
Al-Zambīlī, Ḥusām ʿAbd al-Ḥamīd 209, 219, 225
El-Zein, Amira 161

www.ingramcontent.com/pod-product-compliance
Lightning Source LLC
Chambersburg PA
CBHW071824300426
44116CB00009B/1433